Accelerator Keys

Key	Function
F1	Help
F2	Edit
F4	Select All
F6	Import Data (from Graph Data & Titles window)
F7	Page New
F8	Move priority back one object
F9	Redraw page
F1	Menu
Delete	Clear
Alt+F1	Compose sequence, for producing alternate characters
Alt+F4	Close application
Alt+F7	Page duplicate
Alt+F9	Show output colors for current device
Alt+F10	View/Screen show
Alt+Backspace	Edit/Undo
Ctrl+F1	File Save
Ctrl+F2	Spell Check
Ctrl+F3	Replicate selected object
Ctrl+F4	Close window (close current presentation)
Ctrl+F6	Next window (move to next presentation)
Ctrl+F7	Print
Ctrl+Z	Edit/Undo
Ctrl+X	Cut
Ctrl+C	Copy
Ctrl+V	Paste
Ctrl+Esc	Switch to... (Summon Windows Task List)
Ctrl+Insert	Copy
Shift+Delete	Cut
Shift+Insert	Paste
Shift+F4	Cursor size toggle, from big cross hair to small cross hair
Shift+F6	Arrange/Points Mode on/off
Shift+F7	Snap to Grid on/off
Shift+F8	Move priority forward one object
Shift+F9	View SmartMaster/Presentation Pages toggle

The First Book of

Freelance® Graphics for Windows™

The First Book of

Freelance® Graphics for Windows™

James G. Meade

toExcel
San Jose New York Lincoln Shanghai

The First Book of Freelance® Graphics for Windows™

This edition republished by arrangement with toExcel,
a strategic unit of Kaleidoscope Software, Inc.

For information address:
toExcel
165 West 95th Street, Suite B-N
New York, NY 10025
www.toExcel.com

ISBN: 1-58348-033-1

Library of Congress Catalog Card Number: 98-88984

Printed in the United States of America

0 9 8 7 6 5 4 3 2 1

To my sisters, Barbara, Janet, and Vicki, who know how much my successes are Dad's, even after 30 years.

Contents

Quick Guide to Quick Steps

Look for this symbol for a quick guide to these common tasks.

Introduction

"I would like to be a free artist and nothing else, and I regret God has not given me the strength to be one."

Anton Chekhov
Letter, September 11, 1888

Most of us just don't think of ourselves as business artists. We usually think we can write; we'll tackle our income tax or spreadsheet functions. We'll take photographs. We'll even fix our own PCs. But be business *artists*? Few would be so bold.

In Freelance Graphics for Windows, however, Lotus has automated many of the business artist's tasks—not just charting, graphing, and drawing (DOS programs have done that much for several years). Lotus has made Freelance Graphics to be more, however, than just a DOS graphics program that runs under Windows. Freelance Graphics has automated something never automated in the same way before: being a graphic artist.

To be an artist, you just "push a button"—or, in this case, click the mouse. You can create printed reports, overheads, and on-screen slide shows that are better than those you used to commission from the graphics department or a service bureau. You still do not have to think of yourself as an artist. But you can perform like one.

Who This Book Is For

If you were shaking your head as you read the preceding section, thinking, "Not *me*. Nothing could automate being an artist for me," this book is for *you*. This First Book is for you, regardless of whether it is your first time creating graphic art, your first time using a computerized graphics program, your first time using any PC program, or just your first time using Freelance Graphics for Windows.

It is also for you if you are accomplished at using a PC, at creating graphics, or even at using Freelance Graphics for Windows—but have not done all at once before. Perhaps you would like to become familiar with the overall product and have information at your fingertips to use right away when you have to have it, even if you don't use it every day.

A First Book is an introduction in two senses of the word. First, it goes only so far and no further in explaining any given Freelance capability. When you find out about a feature, you do not necessarily find out everything about it at once; reference manuals attend to that. You find out enough to get started and—just as important—enough to get comfortable.

A First Book is also an introduction in that it helps set priorities for you. Which features should you get to know, and in what order, to become proficient as quickly as possible? When should you find out about SmartMasters? Printing in color? Links with spreadsheets? In the course of this book, you do get to see most Freelance features—and all the most important ones. You do not meet them until you are ready, however— not until you have the background you need.

If you are new to something about this program, then—whether it be graphics, Windows, software in general, or the right business uses of the software—this book is for you. If you are a business user, and if you want to devote your time to doing business rather than doing graphics or software, this book is your solution.

Features of the Book

If the content of the book itself aims to make Freelance Graphics for Windows easy to use, certain features of the book aim to make it even more so.

Quick Steps

If you really want to spend your time doing your business—and not learning software—you might try just referring to the *Quick Steps* and doing nothing else. Quick Steps summarize the most important procedures in Freelance Graphics for Windows—the ones you use over and over again, the ones you often cannot get too far without. Look for the special Quick Steps icon.

Q Quick Steps

1. Designed for frequently-used procedures, Quick Steps list the steps to follow in colored type in the left column.	The right column tells you what you can expect to see as the result of each action.

☐

FYIdea

As much as Freelance Graphics for Windows may have automated artistry for you, it has not covered all the possible uses of its various features; many of the more unusual alternatives may or may not have been spelled out by Freelance's designers. The *FYIdea* sections of this book suggest creative (sometimes unconventional) uses for Freelance's features, in hopes of inspiring additional ideas of your own.

> **FYIdea:** You may understand the conventional uses of a product feature. Turn to the FYIdea section to learn innovative uses—not necessarily the ones the product's designers had in mind.

Tips, Notes, and Cautions

Certain explanations in the text stand out from the others. At times, though you can accomplish something perfectly well using conventional procedures, you can accomplish it faster or better using certain other procedures. *Tips* suggest such alternatives for you.

Sometimes, too, there is information that you do not have to know to perform an activity but that might be useful as background. You find such information in *Notes*. At other times, too, there are hazards, the pitfalls you're not supposed to fall into, but just might anyway. *Cautions* warn you of such hazards.

Tip: Possible alternatives and helpful suggestions appear as tips in boxed text throughout this book.

Caution: Warnings of possible hazards, also in boxes, can prevent you from costly miscues.

As you keep this book around as a reference—even after you feel comfortable with the program—you may want to skim these Tips, Notes, and Cautions as a way to enrich your own use of Freelance Graphics.

Typeface Conventions

Italics in this book designate a new term when first introduced and occasionally add emphasis. Screen messages appear in `computer typeface`. Text for you to type in is shown in **`color computer typeface`**. Color is used to emphasize the names of the keys you press and the selections you click on with the mouse. When you are supposed to press two keys simultaneously, the keys appear as in this example: Alt+F4. Names of menus (for example, the File menu) are capitalized.

Acknowledgments

For providing the concept of the First Book, for tirelessly helping me learn the requirements for creating one, and above all for giving me the opportunity to write one, I want to thank Marie Butler-Knight at Sams. I also want to thank C. Herbert Feltner for thorough, excellent technical review, as well as Production Editor Chuck Hutchinson and Copy Editor Barry Childs-Helton for careful attention that transformed a mere manuscript into a final, published work.

I want to thank Lloyd Short of Que Corporation for permission to work on this book, even though I have published a book on the DOS version of Freelance Plus with his company.

At Lotus Development Corporation, I remain indebted to Allison Parker—who, among numerous other things, communicated to me her enthusiasm and her insights into the breakthrough approach used in Freelance Graphics for Windows. Also (again), I would like to thank Vici Kins, who introduced me to Freelance several years ago and started me on the journey from graphics novice to graphics expert.

I thank Fairfield writers Joyce Matozzi, LaDawn Smith, Kirk Neff, and Lewis Billingsley for their participation in early drafts of the manuscript.

Above all, I am indebted to my family—Nina, Molly, Ben, and Josh.

Trademark Acknowledgments

Chapter 1

A Brief Overview of Freelance Graphics

In This Chapter

- ► *What Freelance Graphics for Windows is*
- ► *What kinds of graphics you can create*
- ► *How you use a "process" to create them*
- ► *Special features you will see, such as SmartMasters*

What Freelance Graphics for Windows Is

Freelance Graphics for Windows is the communications graphics software that you (almost) do not have to know anything about to use. You have to know only what you already know—your business. It creates high-quality artwork for you, without asking you to know about art yourself.

Freelance Graphics for Windows is literally point-and-click all-purpose graphics software that runs under Windows and uses predesigned formats (called *SmartMasters*) to create its graphics. Examine these aspects of Freelance one at a time.

Point-and-Click Software...

Take, first, the idea of *point-and-click*; it means you can make selections by pointing and clicking with the mouse, rather than always wrestling with the keyboard. A difference in the *interface* (the arrangement of the screen that allows you to give directions to the software) makes this possible. Freelance Graphics for Windows uses a *graphical user interface* (or *GUI*, often affectionately referred to as "gooey"); it shows your choices as pictures. Point-and-click software, then, is software that has a graphical user interface.

Before the GUI, the interface was often a problem. It could be a single, cold *prompt* (such as the word COMMAND:); you had to know what to type in before you could continue. Or the interface could have been a *menu*—a list of possible commands. You would select what you wanted from a menu, then something else from a *submenu* within the menu, and so on. (Of course, you would have to know how to make the menus work.)

Menus were a giant leap beyond simple prompts, but they too could be difficult to use. Although a graphical user interface still shows menus on the screen, it also gives you more, as Figure 1.1 illustrates.

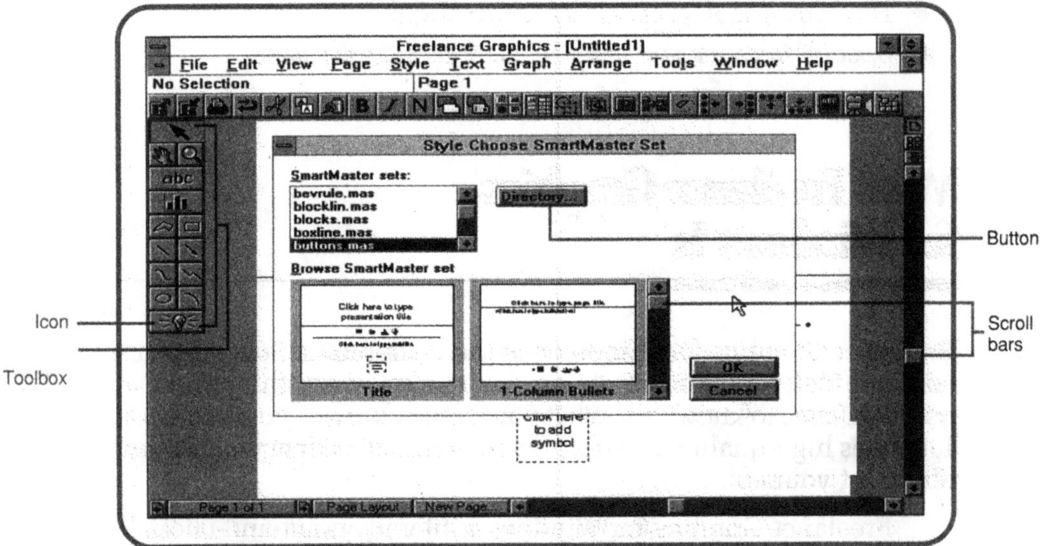

Figure 1.1 Freelance Graphics for Windows offers a graphical user interface.

You have *graphics*; these include small pictures called *icons*, which you click on with the mouse in order to accomplish certain tasks, and *buttons*, which you activate by clicking on them. You also have *scroll bars* with arrows on both ends, which you can click on to move up and down the page. You have, in short, handy little pictures on the screen. All you have to do to accomplish your tasks is click on them. You do not have to know complex keystrokes to move the pointer. Just push the mouse back and forth, and watch where the pointer goes. In Chapter 2, "Getting Started with Freelance Graphics," you will find out the details about the interface. For now, the point to remember is that the interface is there and that it is easy.

You do, however, have to learn what the icons stand for. (If they seem like hieroglyphics at first, don't worry. They *are* like hieroglyphics—but only at first.) You will have to get used to clicking and double-clicking if you have not done that before, and learn how to "drag" an item with the mouse if that is new to you. You will also need to learn where things are on the menus and on the screen. You will learn all that and more in the coming chapters.

Much of what you learn, though, will become unconscious—almost second nature. With the "gooey" interface, you do not have to spend time learning and relearning how to use the software itself; before long, you will just think about what you want to say, and use the software smoothly to say it.

Every Windows package has a graphical user interface. Lotus is particularly proud of its own GUI; *SmartIcons*, for instance, are a Lotus original. SmartIcons mean that you can accomplish, with a single click, a task that might otherwise require several commands. (To perform the same task from a menu, you might have to choose options from two or three menus.) The *Toolbox* at the left side of the screen in Figure 1.1 enables you to implement many drawing commands (such as the command to draw a rectangle) with a single click. You can even choose a picture to place on your page by clicking, looking through miniatures of the available pictures, and clicking again.

That Runs Under Windows . . .

Freelance Graphics for Windows has the advantage of running under Windows. This lets you have all the pages of your presentation in memory at the same time, which means you can readily outline your whole presentation. If you decide that Slide Three should become Slide Eight, you just click on it and drag it over to position number eight. You do not have to think about how to rearrange all your files (sometimes a tricky process under DOS). You need only think about what you want to say. Arranging and rearranging becomes almost automatic.

The second major advantage to working under Windows is that you use all Windows applications in basically the same way. You change the size of windows the same way for any of them. You choose from menus the same way for any of them. You move through the pages of the document (or go to the top of the document) the same way for any of them. If you know one Windows application, then you know the basics of any application.

... And Uses Predesigned SmartMaster Formats

Software that runs under Windows and uses point-and-click already has powerful capabilities, but there is more. Freelance Graphics for Windows uses predesigned formats called SmartMasters, shown in Figure 1.2.

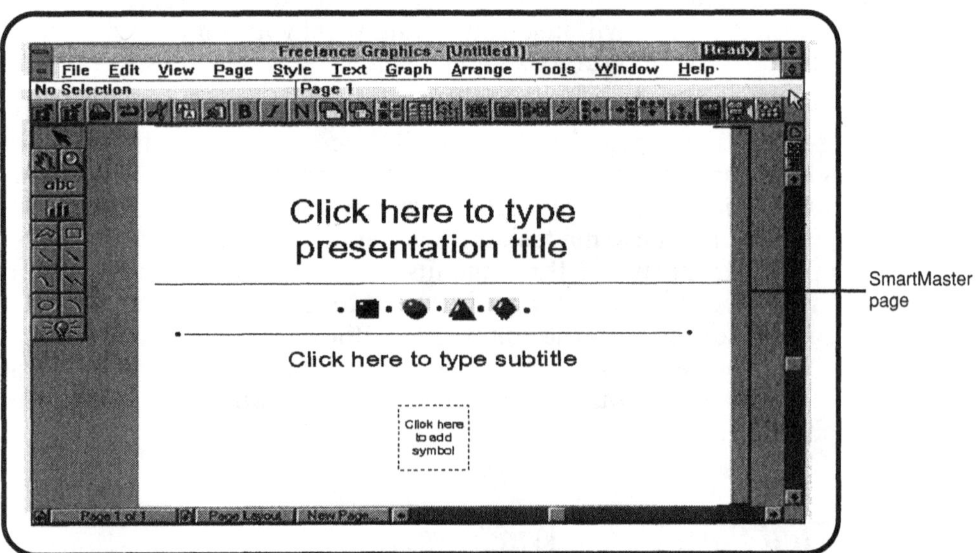

Figure 1.2 SmartMasters provide artistically designed, ready-to-use formats for your presentation.

GUI under Windows means you don't have to spend your time learning and relearning the software whenever you want to produce an overhead, a handout of a bar graph, or a nice-looking title page for your monthly report. The SmartMasters also mean that you need not know anything about art to create your graphic.

Before Windows, computer graphics was an activity for pioneers. You had to be willing to learn something about art or design to go ahead with your presentation. Using fonts and typefaces, for instance, can get complicated. Which ones look best for scientific presentations? Which for art? Which for newspapers? Which for reports? Which ones can you mix with each other? Which sizes do you use? Is it all right to use bold in headlines? Or is it all right to use bold anywhere except in headlines? What about italics? Caps? What is the difference between caps and small caps, and when do you use which? Is it good to mix small caps and regular caps, or is it a mortal sin (like wearing white socks with a tux)?

Just deciding on fonts could get you completely flummoxed back in the days when you had to do that—and fonts are just one small aspect of design. Another aspect, with just as many questions, is how to lay out a page. Is it good or bad to indent bullet points? How many levels of bullets are effective? How many lines should there be at the top of a page before the title? Should the title be centered? If design is not your main business, such questions can be worrisome.

SmartMasters take care of the artistic considerations for you; just choose the SmartMaster you want to use. You add the words to the title, but the SmartMaster decides whether the title should be, for example, 18-point Helvetica bold centered or something else entirely. The SmartMaster decides such matters as what size body text goes with what size title text, what shape bullets to use, which colors to use in the background and foreground, and where to place a graphic. You need only concentrate on what you want to say; you don't have to think about art.

If you are to believe this introduction, then Freelance Graphics for Windows is (almost) software you can use without learning about software, which helps you create art without learning about art. This "artist in a bottle" presents your ideas powerfully and artistically, and all you have to think about is your ideas.

All of this, of course, sounds too good to be true—and it is. (That is the reason for inserting "almost" in the midst of the previous claims in this section.) Even with all its ease of use as software, Freelance is not foolproof. You can find yourself asking, "How do I get a legend on this chart?" or "What happened to the page I was just on?" You can get just as confused in Freelance Graphics for Windows as you can in any other software.

Once you start experimenting with the artistic side of things, you can get stuck there, too. Suppose you have a picture of a cat on the screen and all you want is a cat's tail. How do you get rid of the cat's body? How do you change its color? You cannot always do such things intuitively.

To minimize these potential sources of confusion, you will initially need to get acquainted with the product a little. As you want to do more with it, you can learn more. The learning, in fact, can go on for quite some time; although Freelance has features that make it relatively simple to use, it is not a simple-minded program. It is rich in capabilities.

6 What You Can Do with Freelance Graphics

What can you do with Freelance Graphics for Windows? Almost anything that has to do with graphics for business (and even a few things beyond that).

If you want to think in terms of the output you might create, there is quite a range of possibilities. You can output in color or black-and-white, to a printer or a plotter. You can create slides, either by using your own slide-making device or by sending your Freelance files to a slide service. Particularly handy is that you can use your own monitor as an output device. You can create a screen show right on your own desktop. If your conference room is equipped with a large screen that shows computer files, you can display large-screen slide shows using Freelance Graphics for Windows.

What kinds of graphics can you create? Unlike some packages designed almost exclusively for slides, Freelance is not just for "presentation" graphics. Certainly, you can create presentation materials—finished slides for your company's annual meeting in Las Vegas, for example, or for the annual meeting of whatever professional group you belong to. People also use Freelance Graphics for Windows to make CAD/CAM-like drawings of floor plans or computer networking systems. (Freelance is much easier to use than the CAD/CAM systems, requires only a PC, and produces drawings that are perfectly suitable for the purpose in many cases.)

Freelance Graphics for Windows has a versatility, however, that goes beyond presentations. You can create handouts for an informal meeting with two or three people, for example, as shown in Figure 1.3—simple text charts with one or two bullets on them and perhaps a picture of an airplane or a telephone on the page just to add pizazz. Or you can create a one-page poster for your company's bowling party, a cover page for your ninth-grader's science fair paper, award certificates to hand out at a departmental meeting, or joke award certificates to hand out to your family while watching "The Simpsons."

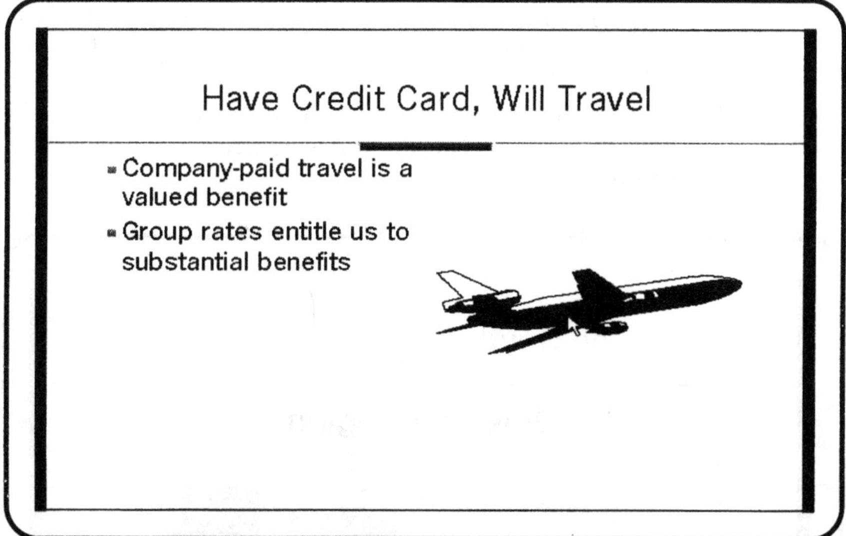

Figure 1.3 A simple handout created with Freelance Graphics.

You can create any of these types of graphics or all of them. For example, one marketing specialist for a major company prepares all of them. He uses Freelance to equip sales people with "multimedia" presentations. That means making slides, black-and-white handouts, and booklets, as well as transparencies in color or black-and-white. The only part of the multimedia presentation he does not create on Freelance is the videotape.

Freelance, then, is for whatever you want to use it. As a number of users have noted, the only limit is your own imagination.

The range of possible output devices is one way to think of what Freelance can do. Another way is to consider the types of graphics that are possible—high-end presentations, low-end handouts, and everything in the middle range. A third way is to look at the program's own internal capabilities of comprehensive charting, drawing, symbols, and text—as well as the ability to edit all of these.

- When *charting* with Freelance, most people are more likely to create *text charts* (words on the page, perhaps with graphics) than *data charts* (any of the numerous chart forms for presenting numerical information). For text charts, you simply choose the type of page you want from the SmartMaster—one-column bullet, two-column bullet, or perhaps basic layout—and type in the text you want. If you prefer data charts, you can create 17 different types of them, from bar charts (shown in Figure 1.4) to multiple pie charts and XY scatter charts. For each, you can make numerous choices about colors and about such features as legends and axis labelling.

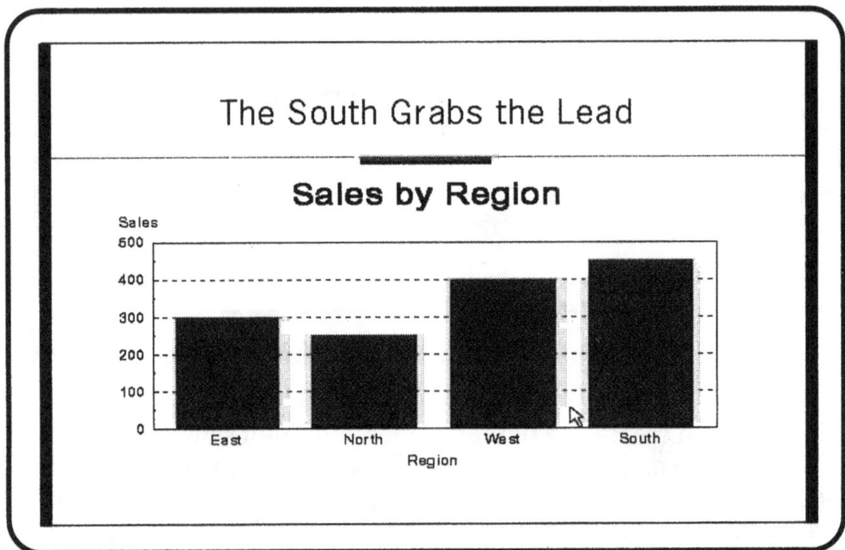

Figure 1.4 With Freelance Graphics, you can create 17 different kinds of data charts. Bar charts (shown) are one example.

- *Drawing* is a particular Freelance strength and has been throughout the history of the product. Freelance has always offered superb drawing capabilities. If you want to do your own lines, circles, squares, polygons, freehand drawings, Bezier curves, or combinations of all of the above, Freelance can help you do so as well as any PC graphics package on the market.
- *Symbols* in Freelance are predrawn pictures, often called clip art elsewhere. You do not have to be able to draw to create finished illustrations with Freelance. Just click on the "light bulb" icon in the Toolbox, browse through the symbols until you see one you like, and click it into your page, as shown in Figure 1.5. You can add simple or complex pictures—anything from an umbrella or a key to a motorcycle or a map of Canada—and you do not have to draw a single line of your own. There are more than 500 symbols to choose from.

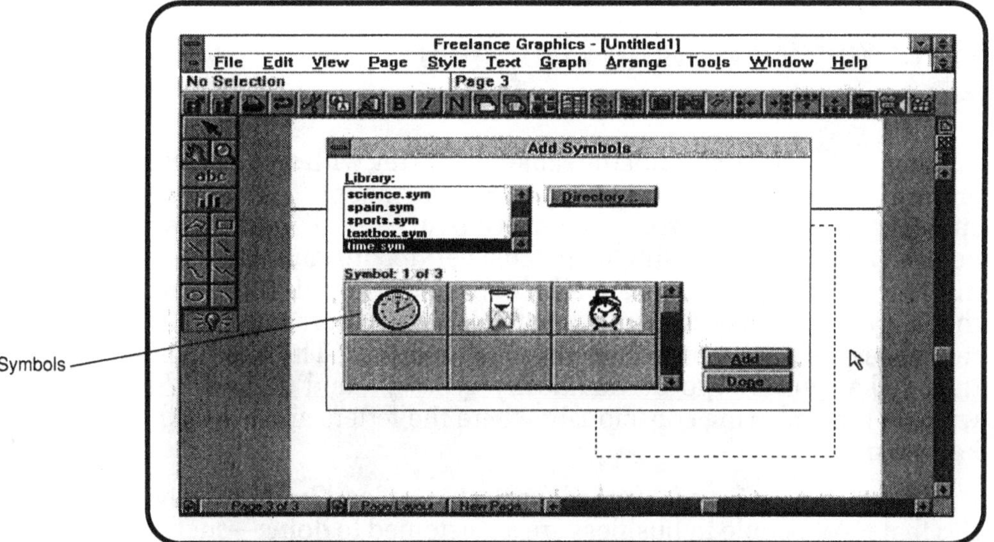

Figure 1.5 You can browse through over 500 predrawn symbols to illustrate a presentation.

- As for *editing*, you can use familiar text-editing tools like "cut and paste." You can also use tools for aligning, moving, shaping, sizing—even rotating or flipping—selected text or objects. Once you have a symbol on the page, for instance, you can apply editing tools to it. You can add a label if you want or change it into something else—perhaps take the handle off a magnifying glass and turn it into a pen (or a hammer). You can crop scanned images (that is, change their size) or rotate them.

You no longer have to worry about one of the most embarrassing oversights for any presenter—spelling errors on your overheads or slides. (You could spend days perfecting a single chart, getting the colors just so, the meaning just as you want it, and the placement of all the parts just so. Spell one word wrong, and that is all anybody will notice on the chart.) The Freelance Graphics for Windows spell checker works just like a spell checker in a word processor. (You still can't say "their" when you mean "there." The spell checker will not detect the wrong choice of word, but it will find the error if you type "ther" by mistake.)

10 How You Work with Graphics

Working with graphics is not the same as working with spreadsheets or word processors for one simple reason: people tend to use spreadsheets or word processors every day. Even difficult things become automatic. In using a spreadsheet, for instance, a person might say, "Oh, I just automatically hit the slash key, the F key, and the R key to get back a file that I want." Everyday users often hardly remember the names of the keys they are pressing. They just press them, like typists who automatically type "p" and "z" and "d" without remembering consciously where the letters appear on the keyboard.

Word processing and spreadsheets, too, at least involve activities that most people in business are accustomed to doing—such as writing an essay or working with columns of figures. Most people in business, though, did not create their own presentations before. They might have created the content of the presentations, but the "artwork" was somebody else's responsibility.

The designers of Freelance Graphics for Windows, then, faced a difficult hurdle. No matter how well they designed the program, people would forget the steps for doing things. Second, even if people did know the steps for doing things, they would be reluctant to do one major thing—namely, create graphic art. The activity itself was unfamiliar.

To overcome the dual problem, Lotus designers have conceived of Freelance Graphics for Windows as a *process* you perform, rather than as a *product* you master. You simply begin and become familiar with a certain range of possibilities within a broader "universe."

Point-and-click, as already mentioned, is a common-sense way to work. You do not have to memorize much of anything to be able to use it. It works well as a process; the longer you use the Windows interface, the more you can do with it.

SmartMasters, in turn, provide a process that enables you to produce the look of accomplished art, without having to develop expert artistic technique first. Thanks to SmartMasters, you are as good an artist as the best artists Lotus can hire to design your presentations for you.

A SmartMaster, as mentioned, is a predesigned presentation consisting of predesigned individual pages. The SmartMaster already has a color scheme, and all the pages in the presentation conform to it. It has taken care of the layout. Words on the page tell you where to put text, a graph, a diagram, or a symbol. It may have a border for the page. If so, it uses the border consistently for all pages. It has the proper page layout for each type of page in the presentation—title page, bullet chart, two-column bullet chart, graph, combined graph and bullets, basic layout (blank except for certain design features and reminders of where to type text). There are 50 SmartMasters, each with the same nine types of page layout shown in Figure 1.6.

When you feel comfortable with Freelance Graphics for Windows, you can change the elements on any one page—or, if you want, for an entire SmartMaster. You can leave the original SmartMaster intact and create a new one of your own based on the original. You can change the color scheme, the fonts, the size of objects, and the placement of objects on the page. As you go through the process of creating presentations time after time, you can continue to grow in what you do as an artist.

What is the process? It is, mainly, thinking about what you want to say. The process might go more or less like this, though you can work in whatever sequence you like:

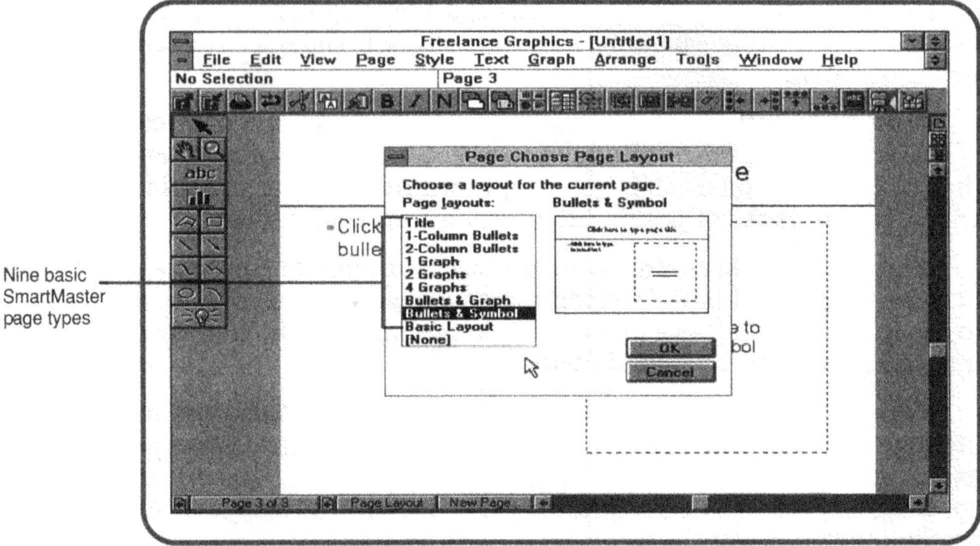

Figure 1.6 Each SmartMaster includes the same nine basic page types.

1. First (and continuously as you go along), think about what you want to say. What point do you want to make? If you know your point, you can readily choose the right type of chart to make the point.
2. Choose a SmartMaster that is suitable for your overall presentation.
3. Choose a page type. Your first page type may well be a title page. After that, you may use a series of one-column bullets or any combination of the pages available.
4. Type what you want on the page. Perhaps add charts, drawing, or text.
5. Print the result or show it on the screen.

And that, in five simple steps, is the process. You can grow with it, but you can do it successfully almost right away.

Almost any way you look at it, Freelance Graphics for Windows is powerful. It has many special features that allow you to know almost everything you need to know right away, while allowing you room to continue learning about the program for almost as long as you want.

Special Features of the Program

Perhaps most important, Freelance Graphics for Windows is a *What You See Is What You Get (WYSIWYG)* program. When you work on the screen, you see the very page you will get when you print the page or send it to a slide-maker. Colors are the same as in the final output. Fonts are the same. Sizes of fonts are the same. When you put in numbers for a chart, you see a chart based on those numbers. You don't have to work in a form and see your output later. You don't have to work with screen fonts that change to quite different print fonts in the final product. You may use your imagination about how you want to use the page—but you don't have to imagine what it will "really" look like. It will look like what you see.

The next few sections describe some of the most outstanding special features, many of which help to create the WYSIWYG environment.

Preselected Color Palettes

Color is one of the most difficult presentation tools to master. It is difficult to know which colors look good as backgrounds, which as typefaces. More than one presenter, for instance, has shown a yellow typeface on a white background and had people complain that they just could not see it. It is difficult to know which colors look good together. Even if you know the rules for using colors (such as the rule that colors near one another on the color wheel look good together), you may run into difficulties when applying the rules. Freelance Graphics for Windows has color palettes already set up for you to use. The colors look good together automatically; you won't need to study them in order to use them.

Windows Features

Windows itself offers a number of features that make Freelance Graphics for Windows powerful. As mentioned previously, under Windows you can often point and click with the mouse to accomplish what you want. One feature you can point at and click is the *Toolbox* in the upper left part of the screen. Just point and click at one of the tools (the circle, for instance), and you can begin using it. Point and click at the *SmartIcons* along the top, and you can implement complete commands without choosing from the menu.

The SmartIcons, in fact, are astonishingly powerful. You can display them on the screen whenever you want. You can have them as a "floating" group of icons and simply "push them around" as you work, keeping them close enough to be handy and far enough away to be out of the way. You can also "customize" the palette and have it display the icons you use most, in the order you are most likely to use them.

If you have used Windows at all, then *dialog boxes* are familiar already. After you choose a command, you often encounter these boxes, which allow you to enter additional information. When you choose Print, for instance, you see a dialog box for specifying how many copies you want, whether you are printing a normal page or a handout page, and so on. Dialog boxes are an easy way to choose additional options for the command you are using.

Freelance Graphics for Windows takes its dialog boxes one step beyond those used in many previous Windows programs. In a box on the dialog box itself, you can see a graphical representation of what you are going to get for the option you choose. Click on bar graph, for instance, and in the dialog box you see what the bar graph is going to look like, as shown in Figure 1.7. Some designers refer to the feature as *What You See Before You Get It (WYSBYGI)*.

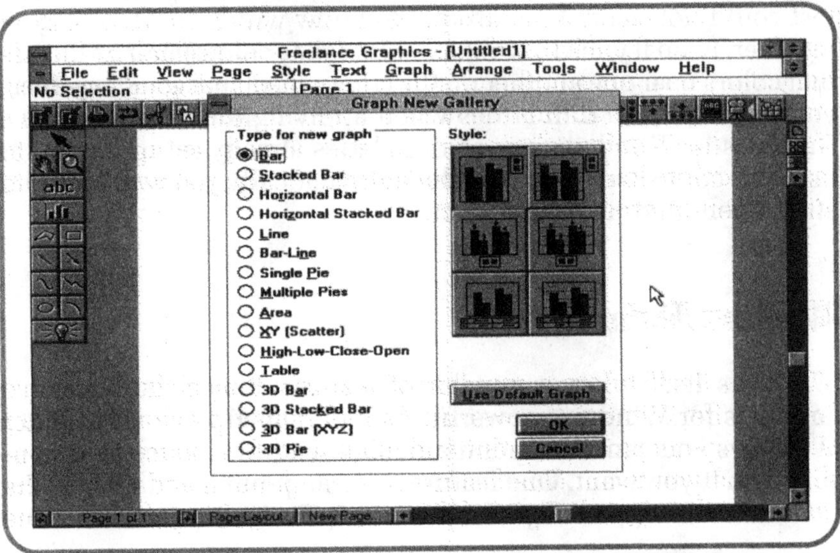

Figure 1.7 Many dialog boxes let you preview your options before you select them.

When you click on the "light bulb" in the Toolbox, you can see pictures of the symbols you want to use before you bring them onto the page. With the WYSBYGI dialog box, you can just browse through the actual pictures. Click on the one you want, and you have it on the page.

Microsoft Windows also offers additional power in features such as the *Windows Clipboard*. If you cut or copy something in any Windows application, it goes into the Clipboard. If you want, for instance, you might copy clip art from PowerPoint (or some other clip art library) into the Clipboard. Then you could copy it into Freelance Graphics for Windows.

Working Views: Current Page, Outliner, and Screen Show

Thanks to the power of Windows, you can call up *working views* of your presentation that give you control of its parts. You can work with the whole presentation at once; if you want to work on just the current page, the *Current Page* working view (chosen from the View menu or by clicking on the Current Page icon) lets you watch "what you see" become "what you get." If you want, though, you can also work with just the words alone.

With the Freelance Graphics for Windows *Outliner* working view, you see a yellow notepad on the screen, as shown in Figure 1.8. You can enter the titles for your pages and the words to appear on the pages. You can change the order of the pages and do about everything you would do with a yellow pad. (You can't crumble up a page in disgust, but you can delete it if you want.)

You can work with the entire presentation at once in a text format or in the form of miniature slides (*thumbnails*). While you might want to work with the Outliner when you are planning the words for individual pages, you can use the Page Sorter view (shown in Figure 1.9) when changing the order of pages and when deciding what to leave in and what to delete. You get this view by clicking on the Page Sorter icon or by choosing View and then Page Sorter.

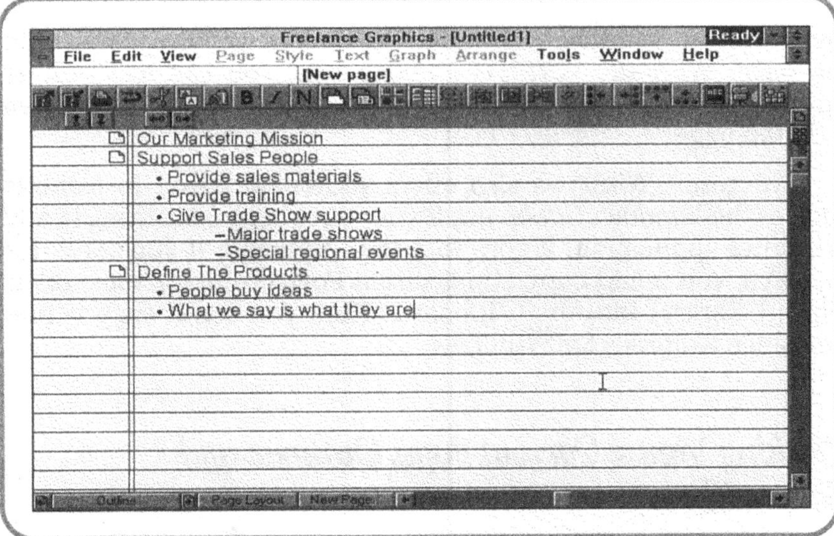

Figure 1.8 The Outliner lets you enter and change text on a screen "note pad."

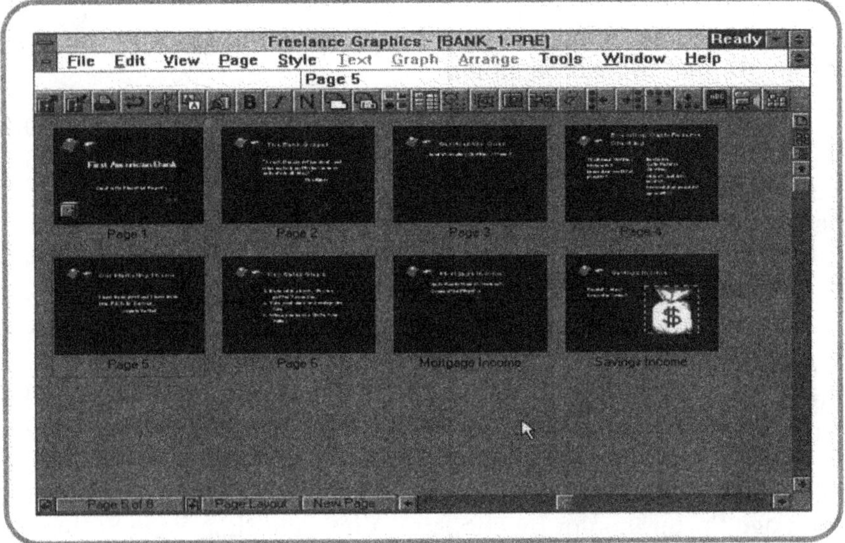

Figure 1.9 The Page Sorter view lets you preview, arrange, and rearrange the pages in a presentation.

You can work with all your slides at once in a third way—by running a *Screen Show*, which is a simple menu choice under Windows. Choose Screen Show from the View menu, and your pages will project on your computer screen as a slide show.

Windows-style Help is also available. You do not have to take long to learn how to use the Help files. Just point and click; Help is in a separate window. If you want, you can have this window on one side of your screen and Freelance on the other side; then you can work on the application in one window while reading the instructions in the other. Freelance goes one better, in this respect, than previous Windows packages you may have seen; the Help files are customizable. If you want to put in reminders or explanations just for yourself, you can.

Heritage from Previous Versions of Lotus Freelance

If Windows helps make Freelance Graphics for Windows powerful, so does its long heritage as a member of the Lotus family of products. Freelance, for one thing, uses Lotus-style menus. If you have used 1-2-3, you are familiar with the menus for Freelance Graphics for Windows. Another advantage to these menus is that whenever you highlight a command on a menu, you see a line of Help that explains it.

As mentioned in the previous section, Freelance Graphics for Windows also has a number of powerful drawing tools. For instance, you can create a polygon and, if you do not like its shape, turn it into points. Then you can drag the points to change it to any shape you want. You can select objects in a number of useful ways—such as selecting all the objects that are "like" the first object you select (all straight lines, for instance, or all matching text).

In addition to powerful drawing and editing tools inherited from previous versions, Freelance Graphics for Windows offers a spell checker, which first appeared in Freelance Plus version 4.0. As you create a presentation, you do not have to stop to look up the spelling of words or scrutinize each page for typographical errors. You can have the spell checker do it for you.

Though the Undo command is nothing new, Lotus has taken it to new heights in this Windows product by offering *20-level Undo*. This means that each time you select Undo, you undo one previous command. As you choose the Undo command consecutively, you can undo up to 20 previous commands. You may not often get that far along before realizing you want to go back to the way things were before. If you do have the need, however, the capability is there.

The *Graph Gallery* has evolved over time, too. Lotus has found out which graphs most people are likely to use most of the time. (After text charts, people use bar graphs the most. Based on its experience, Lotus has made Bar the first choice in the dialog box when you create a new graph.) Lotus has also determined which graph features people are most likely to need. These include some fairly specialized features, such as whether to have tick marks on the grid in the bar chart. (You will learn about tick marks, grids, and other options in later chapters.) Altogether, Freelance Graphics for Windows offers you 96 chart styles to choose from.

The *symbol library*, too, is a Freelance feature that has evolved over time. Not only is it easy to choose the symbols (as explained previously in this section), but the symbols, such as a dollar sign and a picture of a dollar bill, are those which experience has shown to be most useful to business people. Altogether there are more than 500 clip art symbols, which allow you to "draw" without having to take the time to do the drawing.

Freelance Graphics for Windows allows you to achieve so much by doing so little, it may very well live up to a claim that you hardly need to know anything about it in order to use it. A program has to be very powerful in itself to attain such ease of use. (By analogy, driving a Mercedes may not be difficult, but it took a lot of engineering to make it that way.) Freelance is probably as feature-rich and capable as you are ever likely to want. You may feel that you know it right from the start, but you can continue to learn more about it for as long as you use it.

What You Have Learned

- When you work with Freelance Graphics for Windows, you can think more about what you want to say and less about how to use graphics to say it.
- Freelance Graphics for Windows is point-and-click, all-purpose graphics software; it runs under Windows and uses predesigned formats (called SmartMasters) to create its graphics.

- The graphical user interface (GUI) helps you use the program almost automatically.
- The predesigned SmartMaster templates help you create professional art without having to think about art.
- You can use Freelance Graphics for Windows to create anything from professional presentations to informal announcements.
- You can output to a printer, a plotter, a slide-maker, or your computer screen.
- Working with Freelance Graphics for Windows is a process in which you can feel at home almost right away, but which you can continue to learn and refine indefinitely.
- Freelance Graphics for Windows has outstanding special features, including SmartMasters, SmartIcons, a library of more than 500 predrawn symbols, and an environment where "what you see is what you get."

Chapter 2

Getting Started with Freelance Graphics

In This Chapter

- *Starting the program*
- *Using the keyboard and the mouse*
- *Working in dialog boxes*
- *Getting Help*
- *Exiting the program*

The point of the "Windows revolution" is that you should not have to struggle to use software any more. To perform tasks, you point and click. That should be that.

To get started using Windows, you have to find out how to point and click, and how to use the keyboard instead if you prefer. You have to learn a few basics about the screen display, menus, and the powerful tools available (such as SmartIcons). In this chapter, you learn these basics.

Starting the Program from Windows

If you have not already installed Freelance Graphics for Windows, see Appendix B, "Installing Freelance Graphics for Windows," for instructions. Once you have the program installed, start it the same way you start any Windows program.

From the Windows Program Manager, double-click on the Lotus Applications group icon. The icon will open into a group window containing the Freelance icon and icons for any other Lotus Windows products you have installed. Double-click on the Freelance Graphics icon to load the program.

The Main Screen

As Freelance is loading, you see a title screen, which shows the same picture as the one on the icon and also shows copyright and licensing information. After a few moments, you see the Welcome to Freelance Graphics screen, where you can see the SmartMaster look that is selected for your presentation. This default SmartMaster shows as the highlighted name in the list of SmartMasters and also in the boxes at the bottom of the dialog box. (If you have opened Freelance before, the default SmartMaster is the one you used in your previous session.)

If you are familiar with using list boxes from other Windows programs, you can choose a different SmartMaster before you even begin. Just move the highlight to the SmartMaster you want to use. You can also wait until later to learn about choosing a SmartMaster. Just click on OK in the dialog box, and you go on to the main Freelance screen, shown in Figure 2.1.

Many parts of the screen, such as the *title bar*, behave in Freelance the same way they behave in Windows itself. Their names alone suggest what they do. For instance, you use the *vertical scroll bar* to move up and down through a document. The following sections of the chapter talk about key items on the screen.

On the main screen in Figure 2.1 there are also three sets of *icons*. The *SmartIcons* are located on the fourth line down from the top. The *Toolbox icons* are arranged down the left side of the screen and are also discussed later in this chapter. There are also the *View icons* (discussed in Chapter 6), and you can have an optional set of icons ranged along the bottom of the screen (the *Function Key icons*, which are discussed in the last chapter). Take note of these icons; you'll return to them later.

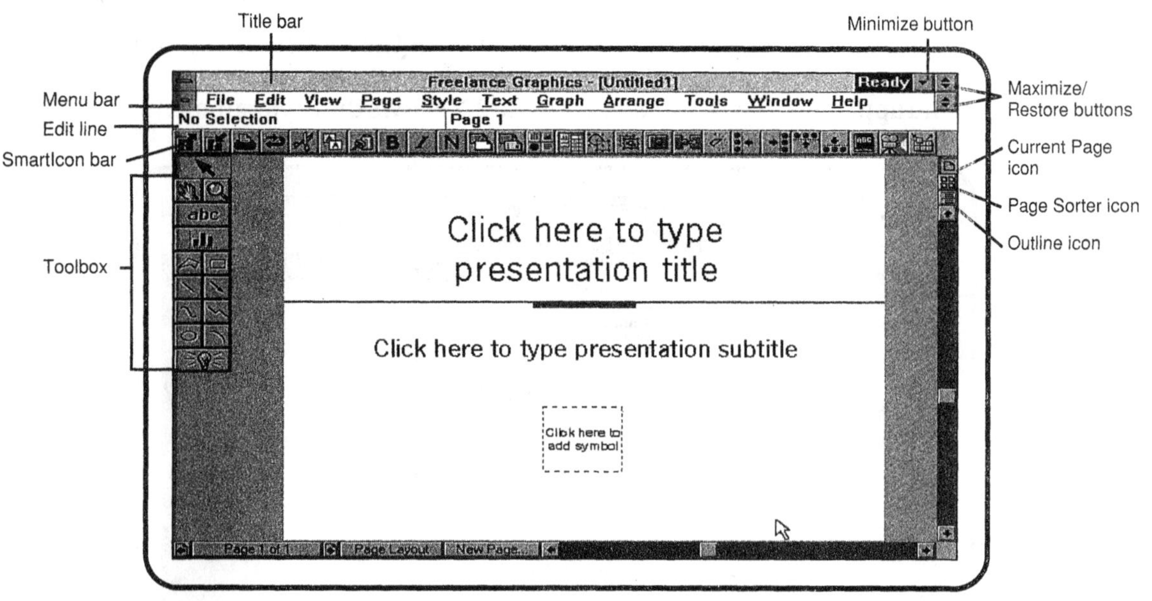

Figure 2.1 The main Freelance screen.

Using the Menus

The second line of the screen, right below the title bar, is the Main menu. The Main menu is a list of menus arranged logically by topics. Activities related to opening, closing, and printing files appear under the File menu, for instance.

You can choose from the menus with either the mouse or the keyboard. If you want to use the mouse, just point at the menu item you want and click once. (Using the keyboard is not very difficult either, as explained later in this section.)

Suppose, for example, that you want to change a SmartMaster set for a presentation. A SmartMaster, as explained in Chapter 1, "A Brief Overview of Freelance Graphics," sets the tone for an entire presentation. Once you have the SmartMaster in place, you have taken care of the artistic side of the presentation—you've set the colors and patterns for the background and other elements, as well as the typefaces for the text.

To choose a different SmartMaster with the mouse, first point to the word Style in the Main menu and then click once. A second menu appears, called a *submenu*. Figure 2.2 shows the Style submenu.

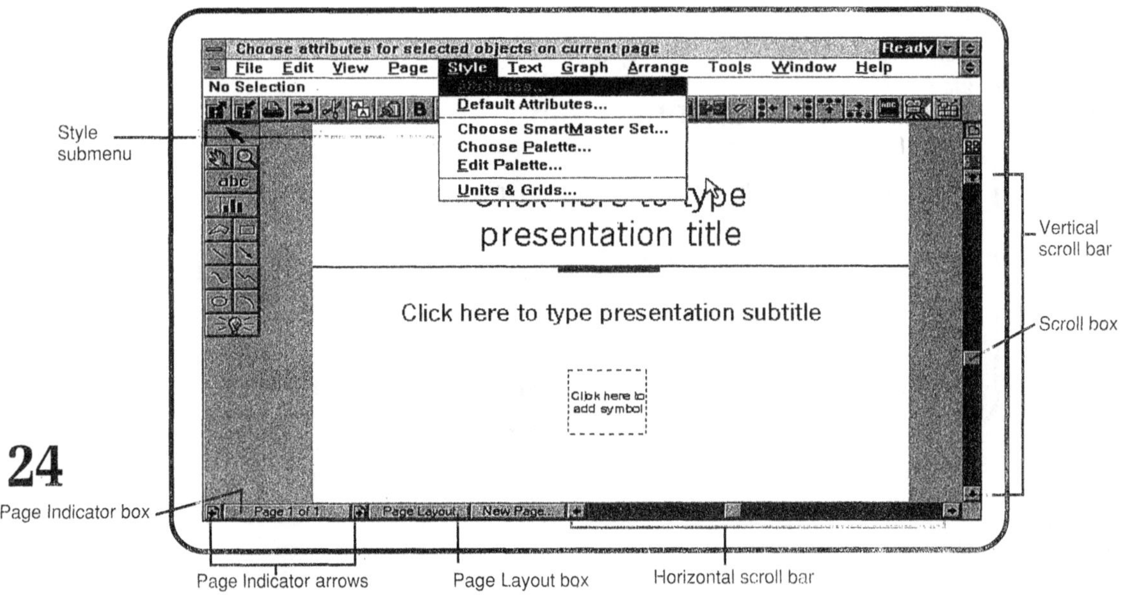

Figure 2.2 The Style submenu.

> **Tip:** When you point to a menu item, an explanation of the item appears in the title bar, the very top line of the screen. If you get into the habit of referring to the explanation in the title bar, you get continuous help as you work, without having to use the Help files.

With the mouse, you choose from the submenu the same way you choose from the Main menu: you move the mouse pointer to what you want and then click once. To choose a SmartMaster set, for example, point to the menu item that says Choose SmartMaster Set... and click once. A dialog box opens. Later in the chapter you'll learn how to enter information in a dialog box to complete the command.

> **Tip:** Ellipsis or three dots (...) after any item on the menu (for example, `Choose SmartMaster Set...`) mean the item has a dialog box. The three dots are useful to you as you explore the menus and "just play around." You can always click on any item with three dots and know that you will not accidentally implement the command. A dialog box always follows.

Using Menus with the Keyboard

Knowing how to navigate Freelance with the keyboard is also useful, and sometimes you might work with a computer that has no mouse. Here is how to choose commands with the keyboard. If you look at the menus in Figures 2.1 or 2.2, you notice that one letter is underlined in each command on the menus. The underlined letters allow you to work with the keyboard instead of the mouse if you prefer.

> **Tip:** Using the keyboard is slightly more complicated than using the mouse, but it's faster. It takes a moment or two to slide the mouse pointer to what you want. The keyboard is instantaneous. The saved time adds up if you are choosing several commands in a row.

To choose a command from the Main menu, hold down the Alt key (on the bottom row of most keyboards) and press the underlined letter. To open the Style menu, for instance, press Alt+S.

To choose a command from the submenu, just press the underlined letter itself, without the Alt key. (You use the keyboard with menus in this way in all Microsoft Windows applications.) Press M for Choose SmartMaster Set... on the Style menu.

Instead of pressing the underlined letter on the submenu, you can use the arrow keys (up, down, left, right, Home, and End) to move to and highlight the item you want. Then press Enter.

Tip: Using the arrow keys in the menus is a good way to browse through them because you can see a description of the highlighted item in the title bar.

If you have highlighted a command but not yet implemented it, you can cancel it if you want. With the mouse, just click outside the menu. With the keyboard, press Esc to move back one command at a time. When you cannot back up any further, the title bar on the right side says READY.

Entering Information in Dialog Boxes

As you have seen in the case of the Choose a SmartMaster Set command, sometimes you see a dialog box after choosing an item from a submenu. In general, you can accomplish much of what you want to do in a dialog box by pointing at what you want with the mouse and clicking. You may forget (or never learn) the specific names of all the parts of a dialog box. Understanding how each works can save you time, however, and there are several distinct types of items in a dialog box.

Figure 2.3, for instance, shows the dialog box you see after you select Choose SmartMaster Set... from the Style menu.

Tip: The dialog box behaves like many other windows. You can drag it around on the screen. If it is in your way as you try to see something beneath it, click on the title bar of the dialog box and drag it to another location.

The box labelled SmartMaster sets is a *list box*. As its name implies, a list box gives you a list of items from which you can choose. Click on the up and down scroll arrows on the side of the box to see additional items in the list. In this example, the list consists of all the SmartMasters currently available—angles.mas, asia.mas, and so on right down to world2.mas. To choose an item from the list box, point to it with the mouse and click.

A second list box, below the SmartMaster sets list box, contains a very special kind of list. It shows pictures of the items in the SmartMaster sets box. Figure 2.4, for instance, shows the dialog box after you choose `shadowb1.mas` from the first list box. You see a miniature picture of the actual SmartMaster.

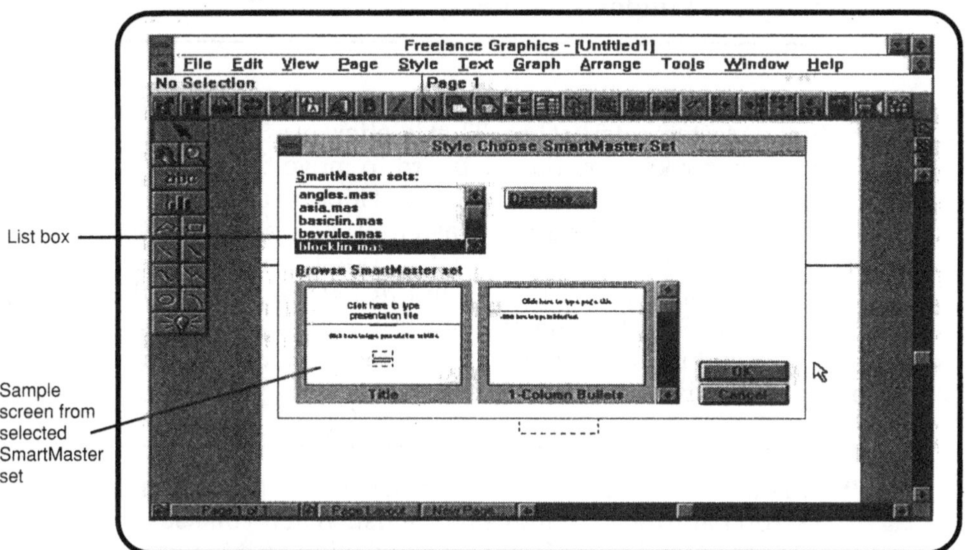

Figure 2.3 The Choose SmartMaster Set dialog box, selected from the Style menu.

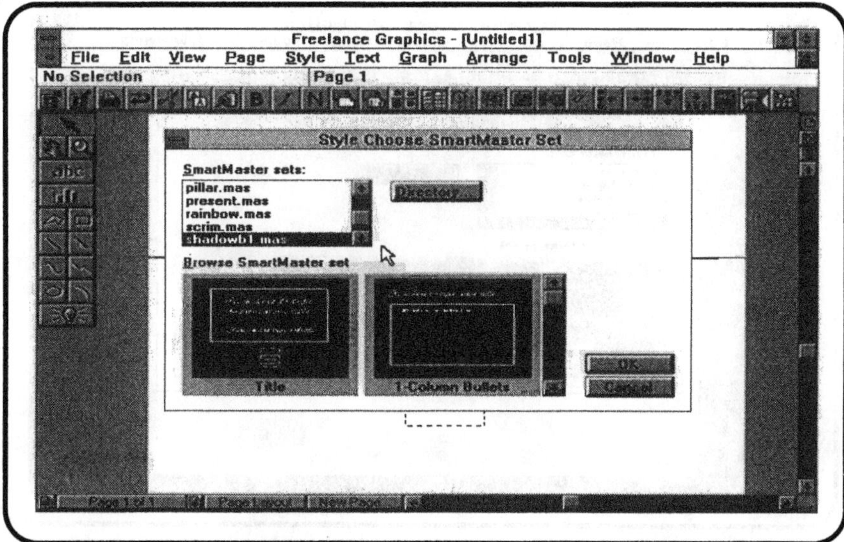

Figure 2.4 The dialog box after you choose shadowb1.mas from the first list box.

Tip: If you see the SmartMaster you want in the list box, you can use a shortcut to select it and return to the main screen. Double-click on the item in the list box to put it into action (a technique you can use in list boxes found in dialog boxes throughout Windows).

You use the Browse SmartMaster set list box almost the same way as the SmartMasters sets: list box. That is, click on a SmartMaster page or use the arrow keys on the keyboard to move the highlight over the miniatures of the SmartMaster pages. Click on the scroll bar arrows to see more pages in the SmartMaster set. As you do, you see actual pictures of what you will see (that is, What You See Before You Get It, as mentioned in Chapter 1). In this list box, you see the various pages in the SmartMaster sets—`Title`, `1-Column Bullets`, `1 Graph`, and so on. In Figure 2.5 you see a `2-Column Bullets` page and a `1-Graph` page in this particular list box.

Tip: You can click on the scroll arrow or drag the box in the scroll bar to see the items in the list. When you see a name you want in the SmartMaster sets box, click on it to view it in the Browse SmartMaster set box.

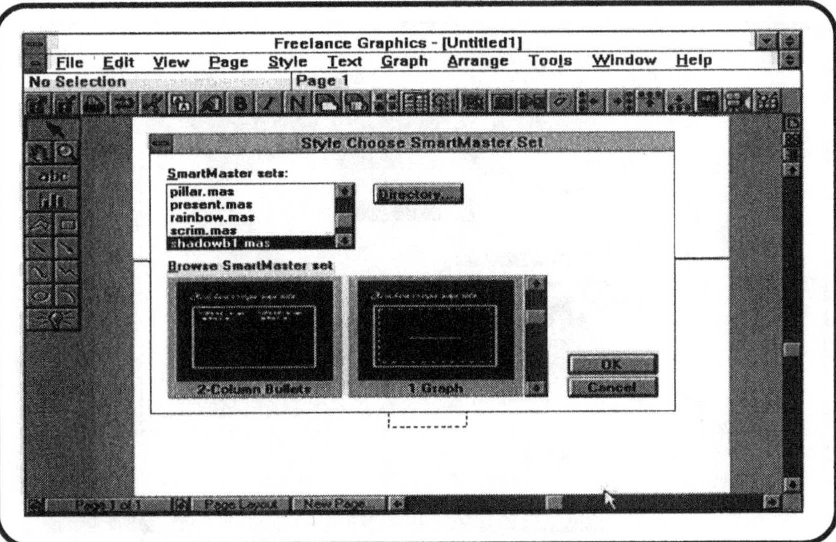

Figure 2.5 The Browse SmartMaster set list box, showing a 2-Column Bullets page and a 1-Graph page.

The small box to the right of the SmartMaster sets list box, with the word `Directory...` on it (note the three dots), is a *command button*. To use a command button with the mouse, point to it and click. If you point to this particular command button, you will see a second dialog box, this time containing additional text boxes and other Windows options. If a command button appears dimmed on the screen, it is not available at that time.

At the bottom right of the Style Choose SmartMaster Set dialog box are two important command buttons, labelled `OK` and `Cancel`. Click on OK to implement your choices in the dialog box and close the dialog box. Click on Cancel to exit without implementing or changing any of the dialog box options. After you choose the SmartMaster set you want, for instance, choose OK. Choose Cancel if you want to go back to the menus without using the dialog box at all.

In the Choose SmartMaster Set dialog box, you see only list boxes and buttons. In other dialog boxes, you will occasionally encounter other kinds of boxes and buttons as well. You use them in almost exactly the same way you use command buttons and list boxes. Figure 2.6 shows the different elements of dialog boxes.

- In *check boxes*, you'll see an item with a small box for an "X" next to it. Point to the box and click. If an `X` appears in the box, you have selected the option. With option buttons, which are round, the choices are mutually exclusive. You can select only one option from the list.
- *Drop-down list boxes* work almost the same as the list boxes you have seen, except you see only the first choice and no others. When you click on the arrow next to the box, other choices appear.
- *Text boxes* are like the list boxes you have seen, but they allow you to type in a choice of your own.
- In *combo boxes*, you have a choice of either selecting from a list or typing in a choice of your own.
- In a *scoped dialog box*, you make a first selection, such as to work with the X-axis. When you do, the dialog box changes and presents you with choices that apply to what you have selected, such as what kind of labels to apply to the X-axis.

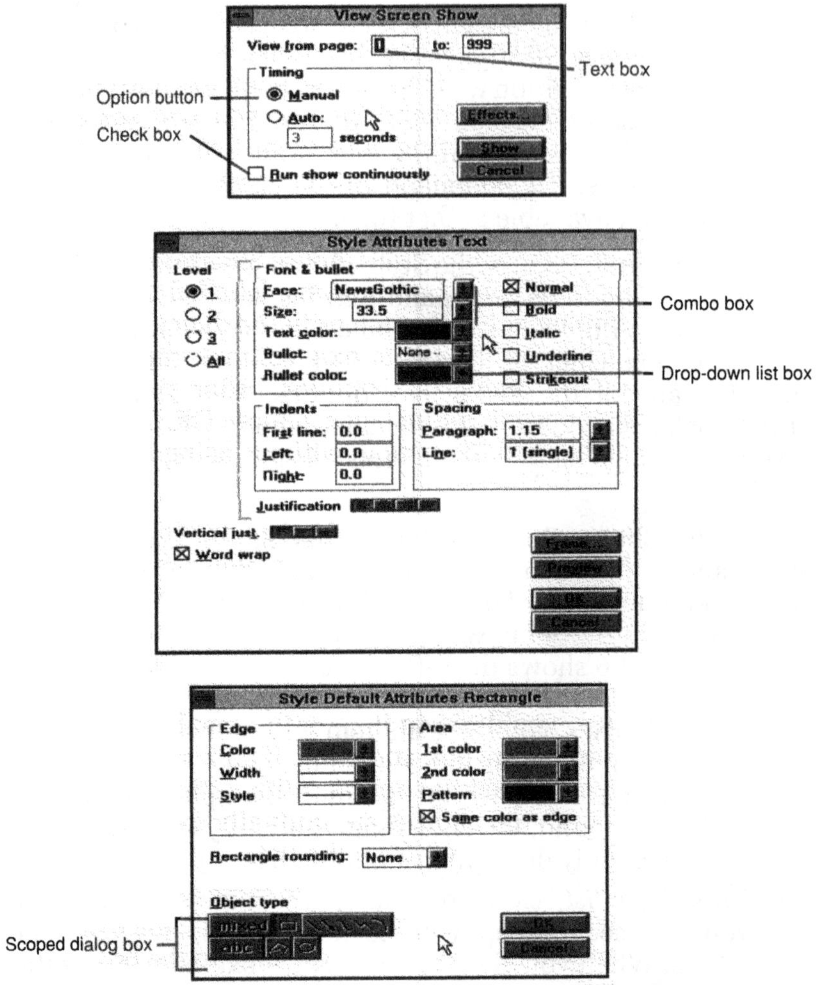

Figure 2.6 Dialog boxes may contain one or more of these elements.

Each type of button or box has a name. If you know how to use the text boxes and command buttons in the sample dialog box, you should be able to work effectively in any Freelance dialog box.

Using the Keyboard with Dialog Boxes

The mouse is an easy way to use dialog boxes, but the keyboard works as well (and can sometimes be faster). You do not have to decide to use either the mouse or the keyboard. Many people use a combination of both, as suits them at the moment. Following are the basic keystrokes you will use with dialog boxes:

- Use the Tab key to move forward from one button or box to another. Use Shift+Tab to move backward.
- In a list box, use the direction keys on the keypad to move up and down.
- If you want to select an option (place an X in a box), press the space bar.
- Press Enter to implement your choices in the dialog box and close the dialog box. This is the same as clicking on OK with the mouse.

In this example, once you choose a SmartMaster set you want, select OK (or press Enter) to implement the choice and close the dialog box. When you return to the main Freelance screen, you then see the SmartMaster set you chose in the dialog box, as shown in Figure 2.7.

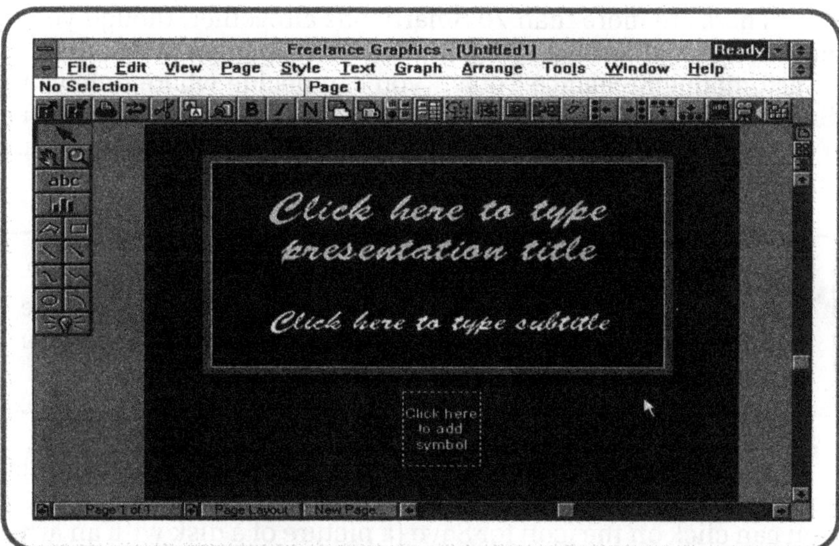

Figure 2.7 The main Freelance screen, showing the SmartMaster set chosen in the dialog box.

Using SmartIcons

The keyboard may serve you well with many activities in Freelance Graphics for Windows, but it will not work with icons on the main screen. To work with icons, you always have to point and click with the mouse.

The *SmartIcons* are a shortcut to performing menu commands. How do you use a SmartIcon? You point at it and click. Suppose you want to cut and paste some text from one part of the page to another. If you are not using a SmartIcon, you must first select the text, then choose Edit, choose Cut, move the cursor, choose the Edit menu again, and then choose Paste. It takes some time for the Edit menu to pop down each time. It also takes time to read the menu and move the cursor to your choice.

Cutting and pasting is easier with the SmartIcon. After you select the text, just move the pointer to the SmartIcon for Cut (a picture of a pair of scissors) and click once. To paste the text, click on the SmartIcon for Paste (a picture of a glue pot).

There are more than 70 SmartIcons altogether, though you do not see them all on the screen at first. As explained in Chapter 15, "Customizing Freelance Tools," you can decide where to have the SmartIcons display—top, bottom, left, right, "floating," or not at all. You can also decide which SmartIcons to display on the screen and in what order.

> **Tip:** The meanings of some SmartIcons may not seem self-evident. To see an explanation of the SmartIcon in the title bar, point to the SmartIcon and press the right mouse button.

At first, you may find it useful to use SmartIcons as a shortcut for things you do frequently. When you save your file, for example, you can click on the icon for Save (a picture of a disk with an arrow pointing in) instead of choosing Save from the menu. Use the SmartIcons to cut, paste, print, or change the typestyle (for example, to bold or italic) of the text you have selected. Get into the routine of using them; as the process becomes familiar, you can set them up so that the SmartIcons available are the ones you use the most, in the order you use them.

Using the Toolbox

The *Toolbox icons* (on the left of the main Freelance screen, with an arrow at the top and a light bulb at the bottom) are slightly different from the SmartIcons (refer to Figure 2.1). With these, you do not just point and click. After you point and click, you return to your page and perform an additional action. The tools in the Toolbox are primarily drawing tools. For instance, if you click on the circle, you then move the pointer back to the page and draw a circle. These tools are given detailed discussion in Chapter 11, "Simple Drawing Techniques."

You may want to become familiar with some of the drawing tools right away, such as the arrow. You can use an arrow to point at what is important in a chart you created. For the most part, though, you may want to wait until you feel comfortable with Freelance before experimenting with the drawing tools.

You do not have to take the time to draw objects on your own if you do not want to. One of the tools in the Toolbox—the light bulb—provides you access to more than 500 drawings, known in Freelance as *Symbols* (and in many other places as *clip art*).

Try clicking on the light bulb. You will see a dialog box like the one for choosing a SmartMaster (discussed earlier in this chapter). This one is the Add Symbols dialog box, shown in Figure 2.8.

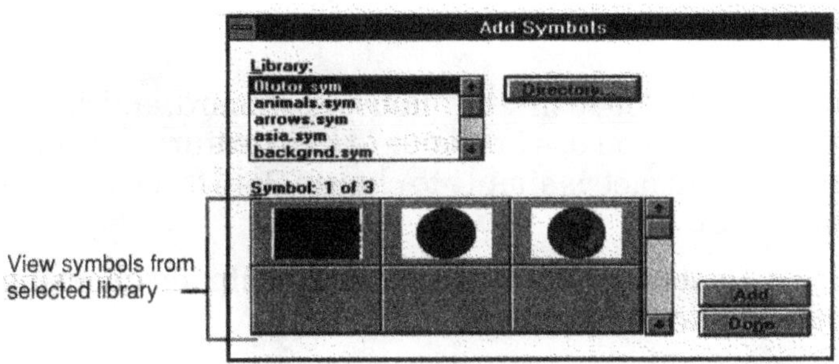

Figure 2.8 The Add Symbols dialog box, with Otutor.sym symbol library shown.

In this box, you can browse through symbols to your heart's content, looking for one to use in your presentation. Click on the names of the symbols and look at the pictures. Figure 2.8, for instance, shows the dialog box after you highlight Otutor.sym in the Library text box.

As you will see in Chapter 3, "Creating a Simple SmartMaster Presentation," you just click on a symbol to add it to your presentation.

Accelerator Keys

As mentioned previously, the keyboard is slightly faster than the mouse for many commands. For certain commands, there are *accelerator keys* whose purpose is to allow you to work almost instantaneously from the keyboard.

As you look over the submenus, you see such keys listed. The accelerator key for Cut on the Edit menu, for instance, is Shift+Delete. The accelerator for Paste is Shift+Insert. As you use the menus, you may want to make mental note of such shortcuts; use them for things you do often. A list of these shortcut keys is provided on the inside front cover of this book.

Getting Help When You Need It

What you have learned about using the mouse, keyboard, and menus should serve you well as you use Freelance's *Help* feature. The most basic way to use Help, in fact, is simply to choose Help from the Main menu (see Figure 2.9).

Suppose, for instance, you want to see Help on choosing SmartMaster sets. Follow these steps.

1. Click on Help in the Main menu. Freelance displays the Help menu, as shown in Figure 2.9.
2. Click on Index. You see the first page of the Help index, called Freelance Graphics for Windows Index (see Figure 2.10).
3. Point to the topic Style (underlined and showing on a color monitor in green). The mouse pointer changes to a hand, indicating that you can click and receive additional information.

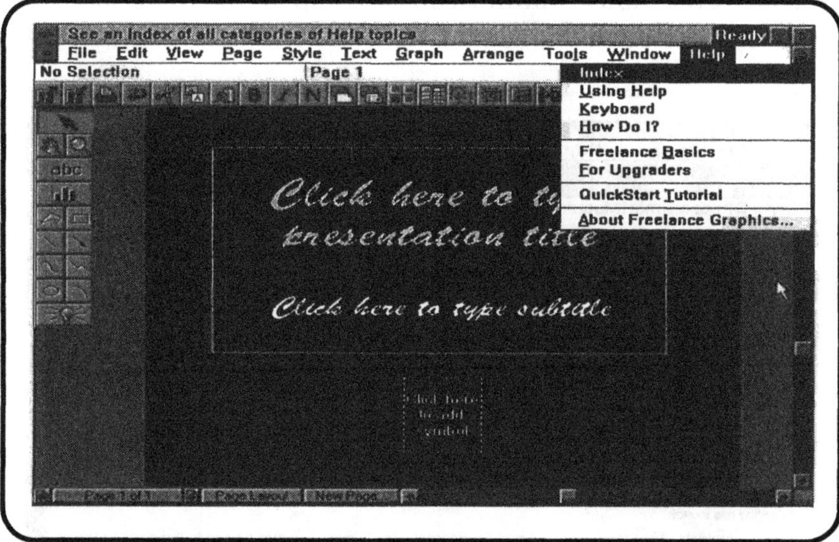

Figure 2.9 The Help menu.

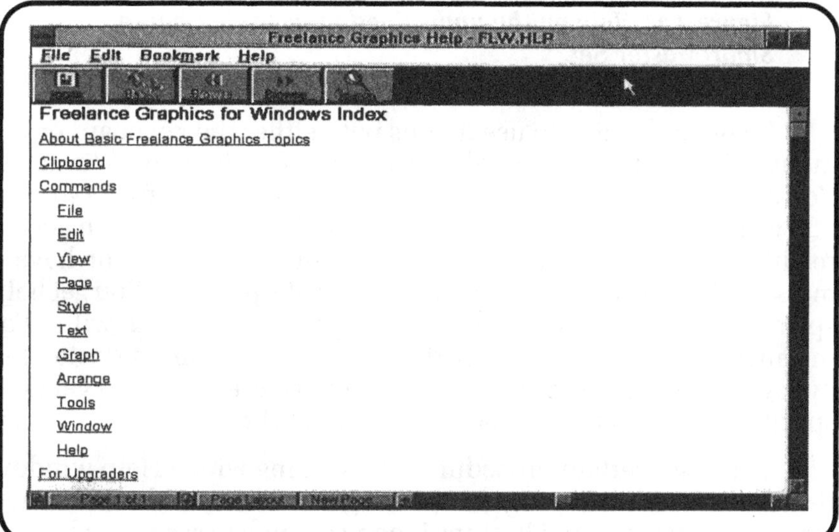

Figure 2.10 The first page of the Help index.

4. Click once. You see a new Help page called Style Commands.
5. Move the pointer to the words Choose SmartMaster Set. When the pointer is on the green, underlined words, it changes to a hand.

6. Click the mouse button. You see Help on the underlined topic, as shown in Figure 2.11.

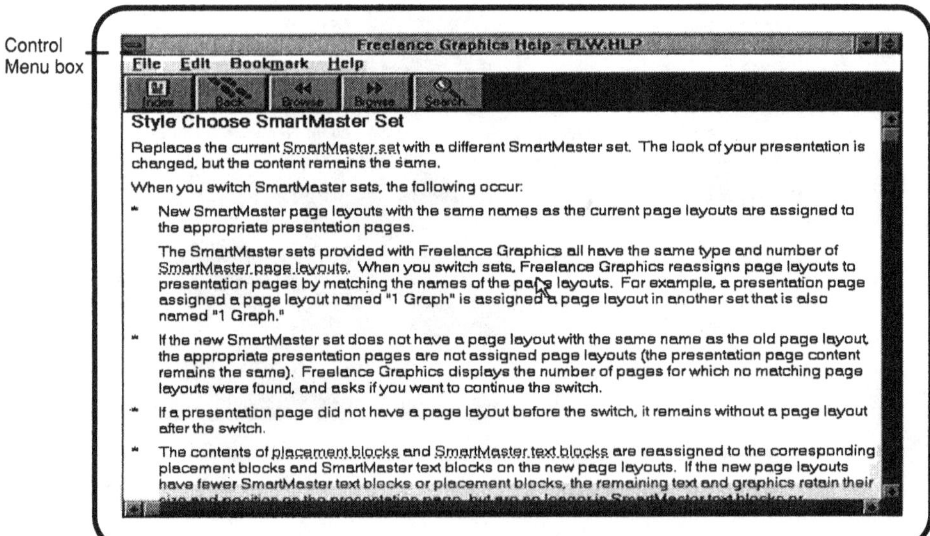

Figure 2.11 Help on the underlined topic Style Choose SmartMaster Set.

If you know how to use menus with either the keyboard or the mouse, then you know enough to get help in Freelance for Windows. You do not have to work your way through the Index to find a subject you want; you can use *context-sensitive* help, which you can access readily from where you are. If you are in a dialog box or have a message displayed on the screen, for example, press F1. You get help specifically on the immediate topic you are dealing with. For instance, suppose you are in the Style Choose SmartMaster Set dialog box (discussed earlier in the chapter). Press F1. You get help specifically on that dialog box (see Figure 2.12).

There are certain procedures for working with a Help window like the one shown in Figure 2.10. Again, what you have learned already about icons and buttons is good enough to serve you here. It is useful to understand each of the buttons in the Help icon bar. Table 2.1 shows the use of each Help icon.

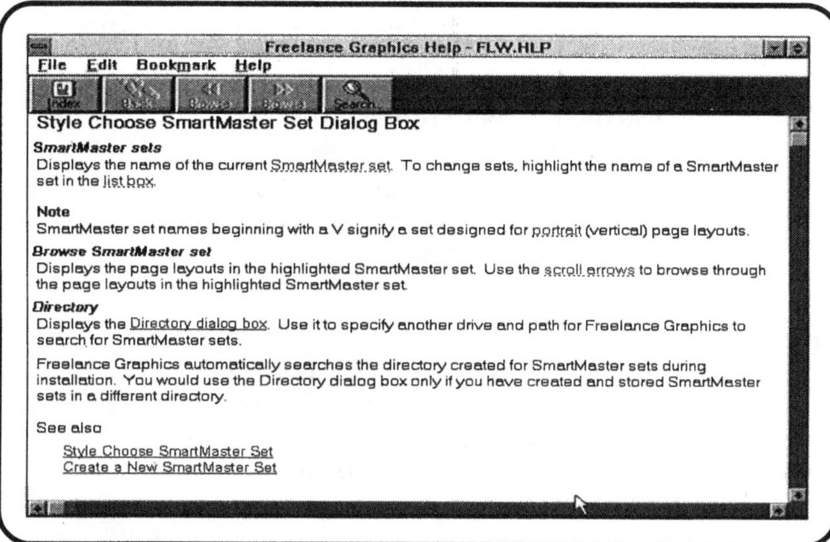

Figure 2.12 Help with the Style Choose SmartMaster Set dialog box.

Table 2.1 The buttons in the Help icon bar.

Help Button	What It Does
Index	Displays the first page of the index.
Back	Takes you to the previous topic you read.
Browse (with left arrows)	Takes you back one topic in the index.
Browse (with right arrows)	Takes you forward one topic in the index.
Search	Opens the Search dialog box, where you can search for a topic by name.

When you have Help displayed, it's a window; you do not have to close it to return to your work. You can leave it open, change its size, or drag it to one part of the screen as you work in another window. You can treat Help just like an open manual. Put the Help window on one side of the screen and what you are working with on another side; read the instructions from Help in one window and implement them in another.

When you finish with Help, there are three ways to exit the Help system:

- You can use the keyboard or the mouse to choose Exit from the Help File menu.
- You can open the Control menu and choose Close.
- You can double-click on the Control menu box in the Help window (in the top left of the Help screen).

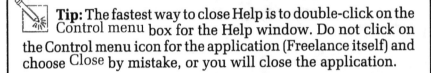

Tip: The fastest way to close Help is to double-click on the Control menu box for the Help window. Do not click on the Control menu icon for the application (Freelance itself) and choose Close by mistake, or you will close the application.

Exiting Freelance

In the preceding section you saw how to exit from Help. Exiting from Freelance itself is almost identical. Before you exit, be sure you save your presentation and any other presentations you opened. If you have not saved your work, you get a message on the screen asking if you want to save it. (Saving your work is explained in more detail in Chapter 3.) Use the following Quick Steps to exit Freelance.

Q Exiting Freelance Graphics

1. With either the mouse or the keyboard, choose File from the Main menu.	You see the File menu.
2. Choose Exit.	If you saved your changes, Freelance is closed. If you have not saved your changes, you see a message saying, `Do you want to save modified windows before closing?`
3. Choose OK, No, or Cancel.	You exit Freelance and return to the Windows Program Manager. □

Tip: You can also close the application by choosing Close from the Control menu for Freelance. (A shortcut for choosing from the menu is pressing Alt+F4.) Or you can double-click on the application's Control menu box (in the uppermost left corner of the screen).

What You Have Learned

- To start the program, double-click on the Freelance for Windows icon in the Windows Program Manager.
- Choosing from menus with the mouse is a matter of pointing and clicking, but choosing with the keyboard is sometimes faster.
- In dialog boxes, you can browse through your options for a particular command and then make your choices.
- The SmartIcons are shortcuts for menu commands and require a mouse. With the Toolbox, you point, click, and then return to the page to perform an action. Accelerator keys, listed on the menu, are even faster than the mouse for some operations.
- You can get Help from the menu, but you can also get it for your present situation by pressing F1 when you are in a dialog box.
- The fastest way to exit Freelance is with a standard Windows procedure: double-clicking on the Control menu icon for the application.

Chapter 3

Starting a Simple SmartMaster Presentation

In This Chapter

- *Creating a presentation using a SmartMaster*
- *Moving to a title page in the SmartMaster*
- *Adding text to the predesigned page*
- *Adding a picture to the page*
- *Working in Outliner mode*
- *Saving and closing the presentation*

"Well begun is half done" goes an old saying. The beginning of any presentation is the title page. By using SmartMasters to create a good title page, you create a good impression and communicate your message right at the outset. In this chapter you learn how to create a good-looking title page simply by typing in the words of your message. You learn how to add symbols to give flair and a professional look to your page, as well as how to use the Outliner to see the presentation all on one page. Finally, you see how to save and close your presentation. The example used in this chapter is a quarterly financial report for First American Bank.

Presentation Planning

For most people, organization is the hardest part of giving a presentation. You should know clearly the point you want to make. When putting together your presentation, keep in mind the motto of the world's great speakers: "Tell 'em what you're gonna tell 'em. Tell 'em. Then tell 'em what you told 'em." Essentially, you introduce your subject, expand upon it with details and examples, and then conclude with a summary.

Before you begin writing, define your purpose. Ask yourself what point you want to make and try to crystallize it into a single sentence. Then, consider your audience. Will you be addressing other experts in your industry or introducing a product to customers? Think about the audience's age, profession, income level, sex, and education.

When you know who you'll be talking to, it's time to research your topic. With the audience clearly in mind, you can gauge the most useful information for your presentation more accurately.

The final step is to write, design, and revise. Remember that great presentations are not written, but *rewritten*. Give a copy of your first draft to every good writer and presenter you can, and incorporate all their suggestions that work toward your goal.

Once you have these matters in hand, SmartMaster sets let you quickly give your presentation a polished look. Your presentations are going to be more professional and effective than ever before.

You can create a presentation either from the SmartMaster pages directly or from the Outliner. If you create from the SmartMaster page, what you see as you create is what you get when you print the page. The SmartMaster lets you see text where it will appear on the page, and the graphics as well. If you create from the Outliner, you see only the text itself (this can help you focus on the ideas of your presentation). Once you switch to the SmartMaster pages, all the text appears in the proper places. In the Outliner, you can work with all your SmartMaster pages at once. Chapter 6 tells you more about the Outliner, describing how you can use it to arrange and rearrange your presentation.

Starting a Presentation from SmartMaster Pages

To set up your first presentation, you select a SmartMaster set that matches your style. Like your company stationery, the SmartMaster makes a statement about you and sets the tone for your presentation. Unlike your stationery, SmartMasters adapt to your needs with flexible formats.

To find the SmartMaster set that is the best match for your presentation, choose File from the Main menu and then choose New. The dialog box shown in Figure 3.1 appears.

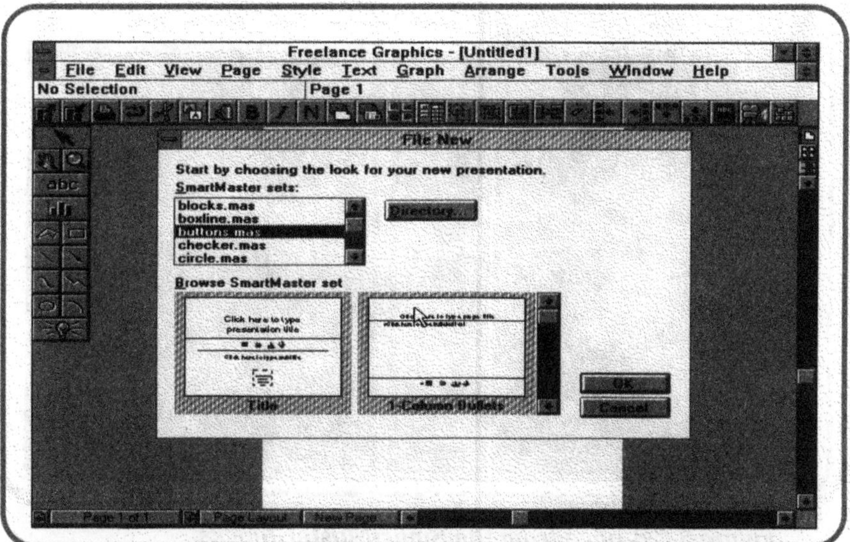

Figure 3.1 The File New dialog box.

> **Note:** To change the SmartMaster for an existing presentation, choose Style from the Main menu and then select Choose SmartMaster Set.

As explained in the previous chapter, the SmartMasters are listed by name in a list box in the upper left corner. You can browse through the SmartMaster sets just as you would the pages of a catalog. Select a name that looks interesting and click the mouse on it. The sample design appears at the bottom of the box.

To see the different types of presentation pages each SmartMaster has, highlight the SmartMaster's name (click on the name or use the arrow keys to move the highlight bar over the name) and then click on the scroll arrows or use the arrow keys in the Browse SmartMaster set list box. When you find a SmartMaster you like, click on OK. For the example, choose Blocks. The Blocks SmartMaster page appears, as shown in Figure 3.2.

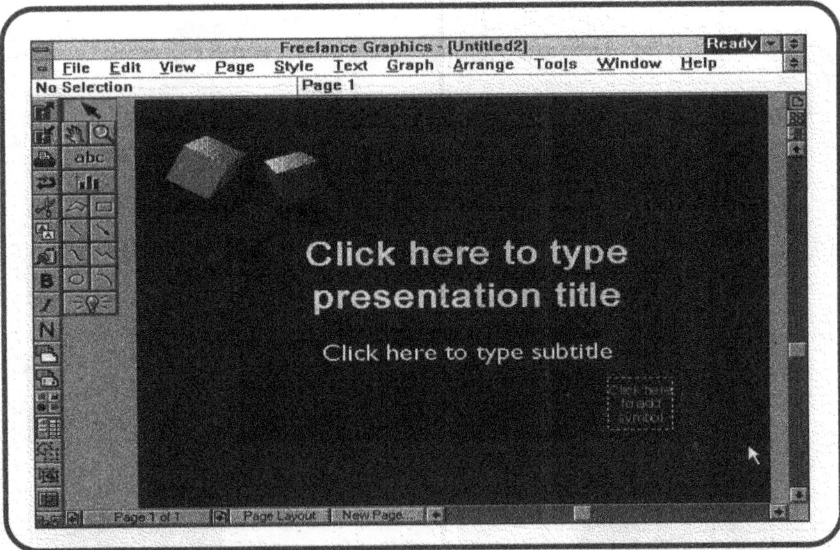

Figure 3.2 A page from the SmartMaster Blocks.

Once you return to the main screen, you are ready to create your title page. The following Quick Steps summarize selecting a SmartMaster set.

Selecting a SmartMaster Set for a New Presentation

1. From the Main menu, select File. — The File menu appears.

2. From the File menu, select New.	The File New dialog box appears.
3. On the File New dialog box, highlight the name of the SmartMaster you want to use.	The highlight SmartMaster appears in a sample box.
4. Click on OK or press Enter.	

□

Creating a Title Page

Your complete presentation may be a series of slides, a group of overheads, an on-screen slide show, or even a printed report you have prepared separately. The *title page* states the topic of your presentation, much as the cover of a book does.

A title page is brief—in general, the briefer the better, as long as you describe your topic effectively—and it should be visually striking (a first impression is often a lasting impression). A title page generally has only a few lines; the typeface is usually large, bold, italic, or some combination of these. If you use the SmartMaster, of course, you do not have to concern yourself with typeface, layout, or the striking impression. All you need do is choose your words. (Be careful not to use too many; the SmartMaster does not limit your words. You have to do that yourself.)

After you choose your SmartMaster, the first page you see on the screen is a page type called `Title`. You are ready to create a title page. Notice that the title page gives you two prompts:

```
Click here to type presentation title
```

and

```
Click here to type subtitle
```

Typing the title in the top text block serves two purposes—one for the presentation itself, and one for storage. For the presentation, the title states the main subject; for storage purposes, the title labels the presentation so you can find it easily later. If you want to choose this particular page from the Page Sorter or the Outliner later on, you use the name you type here. (You will learn about the Page Sorter in Chapter 6.)

To type in the title, follow these steps:

1. Point to the prompt: `Click here to type presentation title.`
2. Click once and then type your title. For the example, type **`First American Bank`**.

Notice the I-beam inside the text area (called the text block). This tells you where the next character you type will appear. You may also want a *subtitle* to expand upon and explain your title. To type in the subtitle text block, follow these steps:

1. Point to the prompt: `Click here to type subtitle.`
2. Click once and type your subtitle. For the example, type **`Quarterly Financial Report`**.
3. Click outside the text block. Figure 3.3 shows the completed title page.

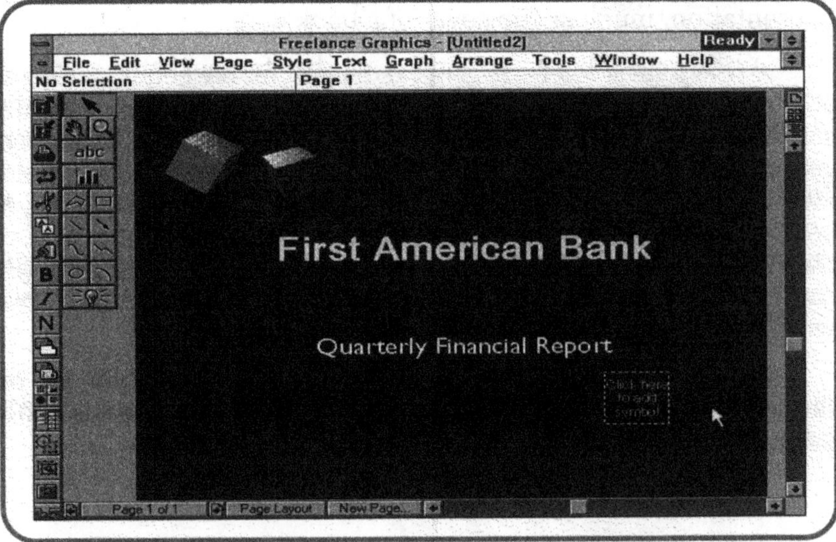

Figure 3.3 Sample title page using a SmartMaster.

Correcting Mistakes in Title Page Text

If you make an error while typing text on your title page, fixing it is not hard. Simply move the I-beam to the mistake. From within the text block, you can reposition this I-beam by moving the pointer with the mouse and clicking at the desired location.

Using the keyboard, you can use the arrow keys to move the I-beam; the left- and right-arrow keys will move you character by character, and the up- or down-arrow keys will move you line by line. You can get around much faster in the text block if you use the Ctrl key with the arrow keys. Ctrl with the right arrow skips to the end of the next word; Ctrl with the up or down arrows will move the I-beam to the beginning or end of a line.

Once you reach the mistake, use the Delete key to remove it. Then type your correction. (More complete text editing instructions are provided in Chapter 4, "Adding Text Charts to Your Presentation.")

Tip: To begin editing without using the mouse, press F2 (Edit). The I-beam appears in the first text block. When you finish editing, you can leave the text block by pressing the Escape key (Esc).

Adding a Text Block

Now your title page has all the text it needs to announce your presentation. You may want to add additional information, however, that you don't want centered (such as a list of authors). For this you will need to add another text block to your SmartMaster page, which you can do by using the tools in the Toolbox as follows:

1. Click once on the text block tool (abc). Your mouse pointer turns into a plus sign, like the cross hairs on a periscope.
2. Place the pointer where you want your text block to begin and then click.
3. Drag the mouse until the text block is the size and shape you want and then release the mouse button.
4. When the cursor is inside the box, start typing.

For more information on this process, see Chapter 4.

Adding a Graphic Symbol

Graphic symbols add interest to a page that would otherwise be dominated by text. A symbol can often contain the theme of the talk or at least make the audience visually aware of the topic you are presenting. The SmartMaster encourages you to add a symbol by placing a box on the title page, which displays the `Click here to add symbol` prompt. To add a graphic symbol, click in the box. The Add Symbols dialog box appears, as shown in Figure 3.4.

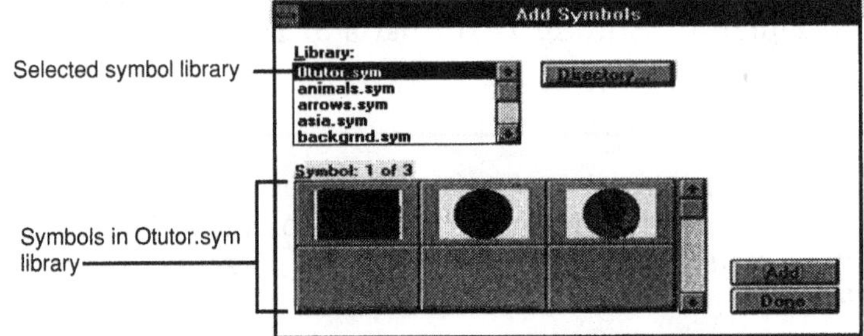

Figure 3.4 The Add Symbols dialog box.

As in the File New dialog box, you can scroll through a list of names (in this case, the names in the Library box). As you move the highlight from one name to another, the Symbol box shows you symbols from the highlighted library.

In Figure 3.4, the selected symbol and the total number of symbols in the highlighted library are indicated by `Symbol 1 of 3` in the display. This means the highlighted symbol (the one without the gray box around it) is the first of three in that library.

For this example, use a dollar bill. Select finance.sym from the library. All the financial symbols appear below; the dollar bill is the first of four. Choose it by clicking twice on it (or click once, choose Add, and then choose Done to close the dialog box). The dialog box disappears. Your symbol appears in the title page, as shown in Figure 3.5. The following Quick Steps summarize the process.

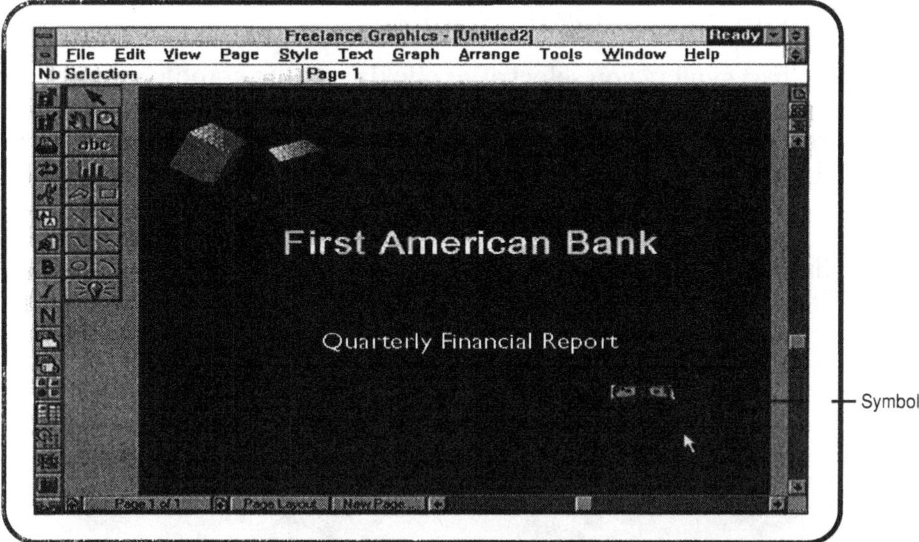

Figure 3.5 The symbol is now pasted on your title page.

Adding a Symbol to a Page

1. Click on the graphic symbol box on the page (or on the Symbols SmartIcon). — The Add Symbols dialog box appears.
2. Click on the name of the symbol library you want to view. — The symbols in that library appears in the preview boxes below.
3. Scroll through the preview boxes until you see the symbol you want.
4. Double-click on the symbol you want to add. — The dialog box disappears, and the symbol appears on the page.
5. To add more than one symbol, click once on a symbol and then click on Add. Repeat for other symbols you want to add. Then click on Done to leave the dialog box and return to the page. — All the symbols you selected appear on the page.

□

Moving and Sizing the Symbol

The first symbol you select after clicking on the graphic symbol box is placed inside the box automatically. You may also select additional symbols, as indicated in the preceding Quick Steps. These additional symbols appear on the page outside the graphic symbol box. You have to size and position them yourself. Suppose, for instance, that you add the symbol of the safe to the title page, in addition to the dollar bill. It would appear in the position shown in Figure 3.6. Notice that eight small squares (called *handles*) appear around the symbol. These indicate that the symbol is selected and that it is ready to size or move.

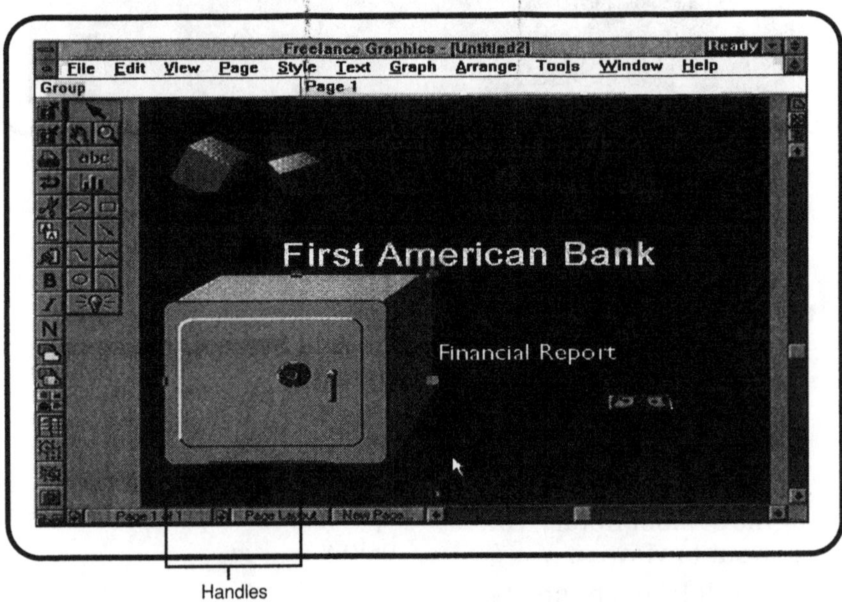

Figure 3.6 Handles indicate that the symbol is selected.

You can easily manipulate a symbol on your title page with your mouse. To move the safe symbol, for example, you would follow these steps:

1. Click anywhere on the symbol inside the handles and hold the mouse button down.
2. Drag the symbol to the location you want it to occupy. For example, drag the safe symbol to the bottom left corner of the page.

3. Release the mouse button.

You may want to change the size of a symbol, so that it fits in the location you choose. Unless you want to change the look of the symbol, however (this is covered in Chapter 12), you probably want to keep the same proportions. To resize a symbol without changing its proportions, follow these steps:

1. Hold down the Shift key. Click on one of the corner handles and hold the mouse button down. For example, click on the handle in the top right corner of the safe symbol.
2. Drag the handle toward or away from the center of the symbol. A broken line box appears around the symbol as you drag the handle, showing the new size of the symbol. For this example, drag the top right handle of the safe toward the center of the symbol. The broken line box should show the symbol size growing smaller.
3. When the broken line box is the size you want, release the Shift key and the mouse button.

When you finish moving or resizing a symbol, click outside the symbol to deselect it. Figure 3.7 shows the resized safe in its new location at the bottom left corner of the page.

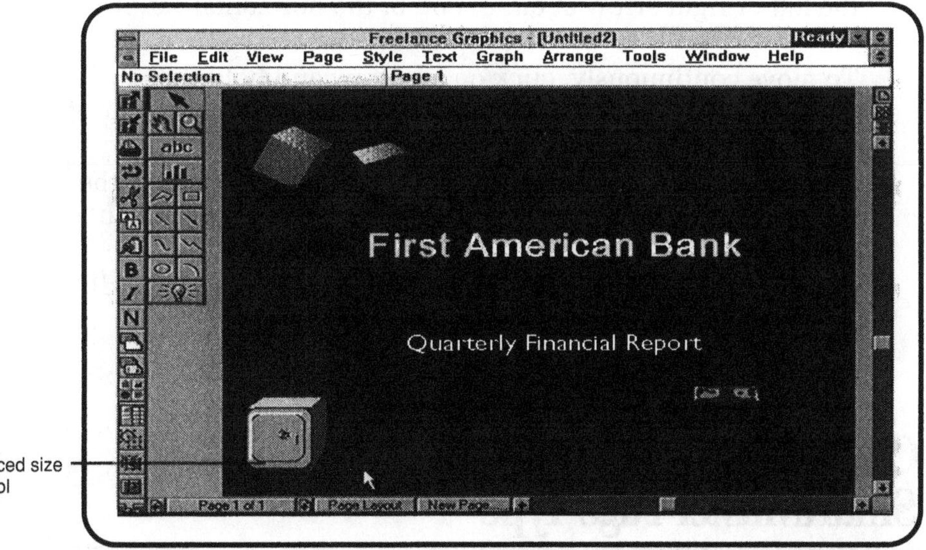

Figure 3.7 The resized symbol moved to a new location.

Moving Within a Page

There is more than one way to move the cursor around. You can point the mouse anywhere on the page, but if you click outside a text block, nothing happens. More than one person has looked at an initial SmartMaster page and said, "But how do I make something happen?"

One way is to click at the place where it says `Click here to type presentation title`. If you click there, a text block appears automatically. You do not have to know it is a text block, and you do not have to know how to create your own; you can always type over the `Click here to type presentation title` prompt. You don't need to delete it to type in your title or subtitle.

In the current example, you have been able to see on the computer screen everything that is on the drawing page, though the page is actually larger than what you see on the screen. To move to different parts of the page, use the vertical scroll bar on the right side of the screen or the horizontal scroll bar at the bottom of the screen.

- ► To move up or down a line at a time, click once on the up or down arrow at the top or bottom of the vertical scroll bar. To move to the left or right in small increments, click once on the left or right arrow at either end of the horizontal scroll bar.
- ► To move continuously, click on an arrow and hold the mouse button down. Release the mouse button to stop scrolling.
- ► To move several lines at a time, click just above or below the scroll box in the vertical scroll bar, or just to the left or right of the scroll box in the horizontal scroll bar.
- ► You can also scroll by clicking on the Scroll icon (the hand) in the Toolbox.

Changing to a Different SmartMaster Page Type

In the course of creating a presentation, you may decide that a particular page would work better in a different format. Perhaps you want to add a second column of information to a bulleted list. Do you have to start over? Not at all. You can keep the same information and change the page type. Then you can add or rearrange information on the new page type. To change to any other page type in a SmartMaster set, follow these Quick Steps.

Q Changing to a Different SmartMaster Page

1. From the Page menu, choose Choose Page Layout.	The Page Choose Page Layout dialog box appears.
2. Highlight the page type you want in the Smart-Masters box.	The SmartMaster page you select appears in the preview box.
3. Click on OK.	The page you selected appears. □

> **Tip:** You can also change page types by clicking on the Page Layout button in the status bar at the bottom of the screen and selecting the page type you want.

Starting a Presentation in Outliner Mode

Switching back and forth between SmartMaster pages can be time-consuming when you're still trying to get the words down. There is an alternative: you can use the Outliner to see the text of all the pages of your presentation together in one place on the screen. The Outliner displays the first two text blocks from every page of your presentation. Any changes you make in the Outliner are instantly updated in your presentation and vice versa. That is, if you switch from the Outliner to the Current Page view, you see the words from your outline on the actual page, placed in appropriate text boxes. With the Outliner you can quickly see how your presentation flows and make sure it's logically organized.

Conventional wisdom calls for planning the presentation before you create it; alternatively, you can use the Outliner to plan your presentation as you create it. The Outliner is so flexible that you can make changes to your text—and to the order of your pages—just as quickly as in your word processor. And it's much faster than using a paper notepad.

As you saw earlier in this chapter, you start a presentation by choosing File from the main menu and then choosing New. You have the opportunity to choose the SmartMaster right away. Once you have done so and are in a presentation page, you can switch to the Outliner at any time. To do so, follow the Quick Steps below.

Switching to Outliner View

1. From the main menu, select View. — The View menu appears.
2. From the View menu, select Outliner. — The presentation switches to the Outliner format, as shown in Figure 3.8. □

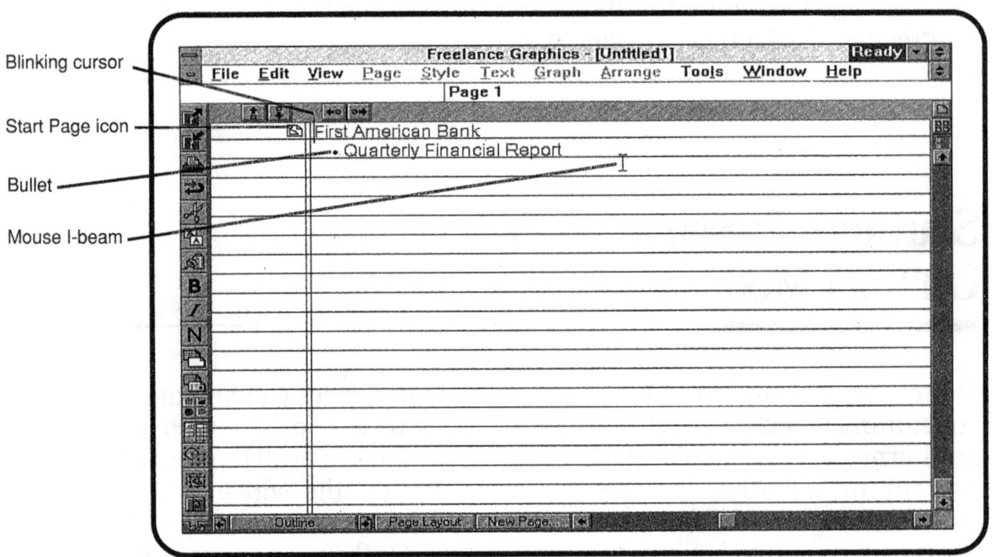

Figure 3.8 The Outliner makes it easy to enter the text for your presentation pages.

Another way to switch into Outliner mode is to click on the Outliner icon (shaped like a legal pad); it's at the right of your screen, third from the top.

Adding Text in the Outliner

The Outliner lets you ignore the layout of your presentation for a little while and focus on getting the words right. To begin adding text in the Outliner, follow these steps:

1. Click at the start of the first line. The cursor appears in that spot. The cursor is a vertical line that shows where the next character you type will appear.
2. Type the title for the presentation page. When you reach the end of the title, press Enter. Notice that a Start Page icon appears at the beginning of the line. (Figure 3.8 shows the Start Page icon. Notice the small triangle in the icon. This indicates that the page contains a graphic element, such as a symbol.)
3. To type the next level of text (a major bullet, for example), press Tab first and then type the text. When you finish typing the bullet, press Enter. Notice that the Start Page icon is replaced by a bullet and the text is indented one level (see Figure 3.8). When you press Enter, the cursor moves to the next line, at the same level as the line you just typed.
4. If you want to type a sub-bullet, indented one more level, press Tab again before you type the sub-bullet text. Press Enter when you are finished.
5. After you complete the text for a page and press Enter, press Shift+Tab until the cursor moves back to the left edge of the Outliner page and the Start Page icon appears at the beginning of the line.

Tip: If you reach the end of a line and continue typing, the text that doesn't fit on the first line will move automatically to the next line. This is called *wrapping*.

Just as a handwritten outline has roman numerals, capital letters, numbers, etc., your presentation can have up to four levels of text—the title, bullets, sub-bullets, and dashes. Later in this chapter, you will see how to change the level of text.

When you are ready to view your text in the SmartMaster pages you selected, select Current Page from the View menu or click on the Current Page icon (the top icon on the right side of the screen). Your presentation appears at the page where your cursor was in the Outliner. You can flip between presentation pages by using the Page Indicator arrows in the lower left corner of the screen. To return to the Outliner, click on the Outliner icon or select Outliner from the View menu.

Editing Text in the Outliner

As you create the text for your presentation in the Outliner, you are likely to think of points you forgot to include, change your mind about including other points, or decide to change the order or importance of your points. The ability to make text changes easily is one of the big advantages of working in the Outliner.

Before you can insert, delete, or move text, you must first know how to move around in the Outliner. The easiest way to move the cursor is with the mouse. Simply move the I-beam with the mouse to the location you want and then click once. The cursor will appear at that location. If you prefer to use the keyboard, press the arrow keys. As the cursor moves, it goes between the characters.

To insert text at the cursor location, simply start typing. All existing text to the right of the cursor moves to the right to make room for the new text you type.

To delete or move text, you must first select it. Selected text appears highlighted. To select text with the mouse, follow these steps:

1. Click on the first character of the text and hold the mouse button down. The character appears highlighted.
2. Drag the highlight across the text you want to select.
3. When all the text you want to select is highlighted, release the mouse button.

Selecting from the keyboard is especially useful if you have a hard time positioning the cursor exactly where you want it with the mouse. To select text using the keyboard, position the cursor on the first character of the text. Then use the key combinations shown in Table 3.1 to select the text. (Table 3.1 summarizes the commands and keystrokes you can use in the Outliner to select and edit text.) Figure 3.9 shows text selected prior to deleting.

Table 3.1 Editing commands in the Outliner.

Command	Function
Shift and left or right arrows	Selects a character.
Shift+Ctrl and left or right arrows	Selects a word.
Shift and up or down arrows	Selects a line.
Shift+Ctrl and up arrow	Selects to beginning of sentence.
Shift+Ctrl and down arrow	Selects to end of sentence.
Cut command (Edit menu)	Deletes selected text and places it on the Clipboard.
Clear command (Edit menu)	Deletes selected text permanently (does not place it on the Clipboard).
Copy command (Edit menu)	Copies selected text to the Clipboard and leaves original text intact.
Del key	Deletes selected text (does not place it in the Clipboard).
Paste command (Edit menu)	Inserts text from the Clipboard at the cursor location.

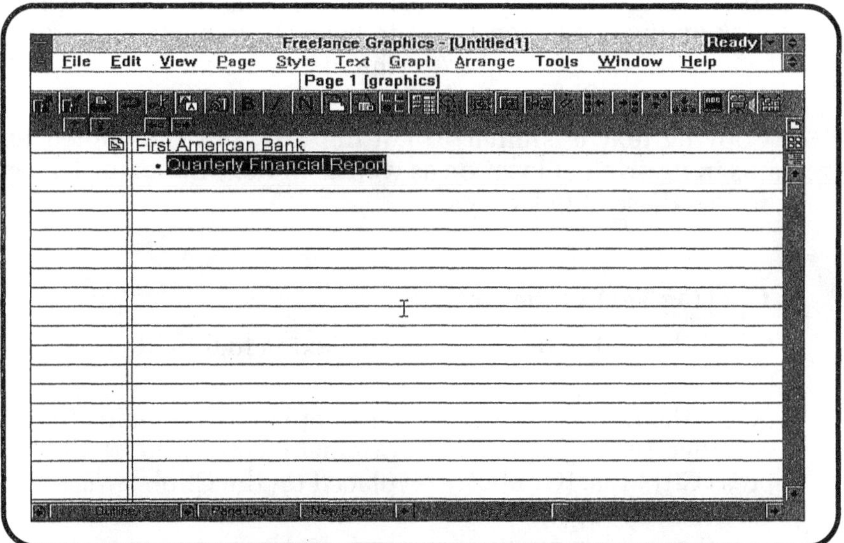

Figure 3.9 To delete text, select the text and press Del.

After you select text, you can delete it simply by pressing the Del key. If you think you may want to reinsert it somewhere else in the outline, select the Cut command from the Edit menu instead. This places the deleted text in the Windows Clipboard, where it remains until you cut or copy new text over it. Text in the Clipboard can be *pasted* into any other location in your outline.

To move text from one location in the outline to another, follow these Quick Steps.

Moving Text in the Outliner

1. Select the text to be moved. — The text is highlighted.
2. Select the Edit menu and then select Cut or press Shift+Del. (Or click on the Cut icon.) — The cut text is deleted from its original location and placed on the Clipboard.
3. Move the cursor to the location where you want to move the text.
4. Select the Edit menu and then select Paste or press Shift+Del. (Or click on the Paste icon.) — The text is inserted from the Clipboard into the new location. Existing text moves to the right to make room for the inserted text. □

Copying text is similar to cutting text, but the copied text remains in its original location as well as in the Clipboard. To copy text, follow these Quick Steps.

Copying Text in the Outliner

1. Select the text to be copied. — The text is highlighted.
2. Select the Edit menu and then select Copy or press Ctrl+Ins. (Or click on the Copy icon.) — The copied text remains in its original location and is also placed on the Clipboard.
3. Move the cursor to the location where you want to copy the text.

4. Select the Edit menu and then select Paste or press Ctrl+Ins. (Or click on the Paste icon.) — The text is inserted from the Clipboard into the new location. Existing text moves to the right to make room for the inserted text. □

Changing the Level of Text

The Outliner also saves you time by allowing you to change the *level* of the text in your presentation quickly. Decreasing the level of text (for example, changing a page title into a bulleted item) is called *demoting*. Increasing the level of text (for example, making a sub-bullet into a bullet) is called *promoting*. If you want bulleted text to be indented further as a sub-bullet, you would demote it, as shown in the following Quick Steps.

Q Demoting Text in the Outliner

1. Click at the beginning of the text line. — The cursor appears.
2. Press Tab. — The text is indented and rebulleted at the next level down.
3. To demote the text again, press Tab again. — The text is demoted to dash level. □

If you decide, on the other hand, that one of your presentation's subheads should really be a page heading, you can promote it to a page title. To promote any text in the Outliner, follow these Quick Steps.

Q Promoting Text in the Outliner

1. Click at the beginning of the text line. — The cursor appears.
2. Press Shift+Tab. — The text is rebulleted at the next higher level.
3. To promote the text again, press Shift+Tab again. — The text is promoted to the next higher level, as high as page title. □

Undoing an Action

Even if you do accidentally alter your symbol (or make other changes you decide later you do not want to make), you can fix it. To undo your last action at almost any place except in the Outliner, use the following Quick Steps.

Undoing Your Most Recent Action

Using the Undo icon:

1. Press Alt+Backspace. or Click on the Undo icon.	Freelance cancels your last action.

Using the Edit menu:

1. Choose Edit from the Main menu.	The Edit menu opens.
2. Choose Undo.	Freelance cancels your last action. □

Whichever method you choose, your most recent menu command will be erased. You can continue to choose Edit Undo to undo up to 20 actions, such as cutting, clearing, or pasting an object, changing the attributes of an object (such as a bold or italic typestyle), assigning SmartMaster pages, and a good deal more. The capability to undo so many commands is quite powerful. You may not see the need for it now, but when you do need it, you may be thankful it is there. You can easily ruin an entire page with one mistake; Undo enables you to get back to an earlier version without starting over.

Caution: You cannot use Undo in the Outliner, so be careful when using the Del or Backspace keys in this view.

Saving Your Presentation

Before you close your presentation, you need to save it, or all your work on it will be lost. When you save a presentation, the entire presentation is stored in a single file. The first time you save your presentation, you need to name the file. The following Quick Steps show how to save and name a presentation file.

Saving and Naming a Presentation

1. From the Main menu, choose File. — The File menu opens.
2. From the File menu, choose Save. — The File Save As dialog box appears (as in Figure 3.10). A default path for your file appears in the File name box.
3. Position the cursor in the File name box, at the start of the default name but after the drive and directory name.
4. Type a name for your presentation. — The name appears in the File name box.
5. Click on OK or press Enter. — Freelance saves your presentation to the drive and directory specified in the File name box. □

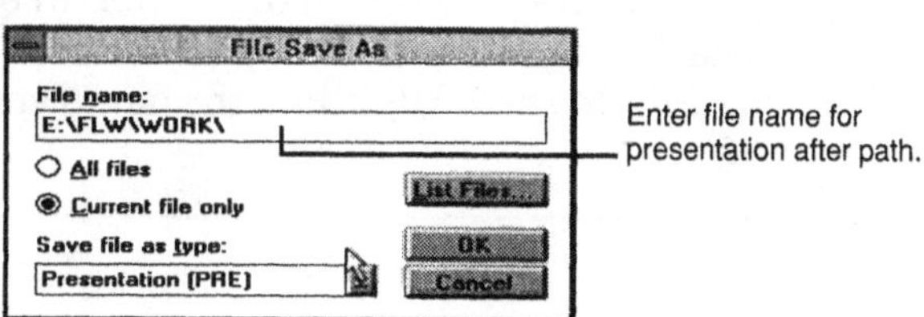

Figure 3.10 The File Save As dialog box.

Tip: You may be familiar with DOS file names. Freelance names follow the same conventions. They can be up to eight characters long. Freelance automatically assigns the file extension .PRE when it stores the file.

After you save your presentation, you can continue to work on it or choose File Close if you're done. Closing a file removes it from memory and clears the screen for the next task. When you close a file, Freelance asks you if you want to save any changes made since the last time you saved. If you choose Yes, it saves the changes. It then stores the file on the disk in the directory you specify. To use it again, select Open from the File menu.

After you save a file once, you can use the shortcut keys Ctrl+F1 to save the file. You no longer see the File Save As dialog box when you save the file. Freelance simply saves the file under the name you assigned when you saved it the first time.

Tip: You may want to save a modified presentation under a new name, while keeping the original presentation under the original name. For example, you may want to keep the original presentation but make a special version to show branch offices. To save under a new name, select Save As from the File menu. When the File Save As dialog box appears, type in a new name for the modified file.

Tip: If you want to save a file under an existing file name but can't remember it, click on the List Files button in the File Save As dialog box. Highlight the name you want to use and select OK.

What You Have Learned

- Plan your presentation by knowing your purpose and knowing your audience.
- You choose a title page from the Page menu. The predesigned title page allows you to pay attention strictly to your content, rather than to its packaging.
- Graphic symbols can express the theme of your presentation and add life to the page. To choose a symbol, click on the graphic symbol box with the `Click here to add symbol` prompt or click on the Symbols icon in the Toolbox. You can preview the symbols in the dialog box.
- To move a symbol, click inside the handles and then drag the symbol to the desired location.
- To change the size of a symbol, click on a handle and drag it toward or away from the center of the symbol. A broken line box shows the new size of the symbol.
- To move within the page, point and click at one of the text boxes (at the text or at the prompt). To work in other parts of the screen, you can add symbols or text boxes. To see other parts of the screen, use the scroll bars.
- With Outliner mode, you can work with multiple pages at once, concentrating on contents rather than appearance. Text appears automatically in the proper boxes in the presentation pages.
- You can undo up to 20 previous actions by choosing Edit Undo.
- To save your presentation, choose Save from the File menu and complete the dialog box.

Chapter 4

Adding Text Charts to Your Presentation

In This Chapter

- *Opening an existing presentation*
- *Creating a new page in a presentation*
- *Creating bullet charts with a SmartMaster Page*
- *Creating a text chart from a Basic Layout page*
- *How to perform basic editing on text charts*
- *Using and customizing the spell checker*
- *How to move from page to page in a presentation*

Text charts with simple, direct statements are the foundation of a powerful presentation. Flashy graphics might impress some people, but a simple message well-conveyed will convince the rest. Most presenters, most of the time, use *text charts* in their presentations.

Text Charts

A text chart is a single-page chart that carries text. When most effective, it carries a simple message (anything from a single quotation to emphasize a point, to many lines of text). You can use text charts to start a presentation, summarize main points, or present a series of ideas.

A well-thought-out text chart is an efficient way to condense complex information. You can combine text and data charts, which enables your audience to examine both the complex data (in the form of tables) and succinct accounts in the text. Brief text bullets can arouse their interest and summarize key information.

A text chart may or may not have graphics; if it does, its graphics and format should be easy to read, leaving out distracting elements such as ornate fonts or a complex layout. It should not look like the front page of a supermarket tabloid nor like the index of an encyclopedia.

Figure 4.1 shows an example of a text chart that consists of a single quotation used for introducing a presentation by First American Bank. In this chapter you will examine this company and its presentation in more detail. You will learn the basic mechanics that allow you to put all other matters aside and think about what you want to say in the text itself. You will find out how to open a presentation to work on, how to get a page to write on, how to choose a basic format for text if you want (bullet charts, for instance), and how to set up a page with no format.

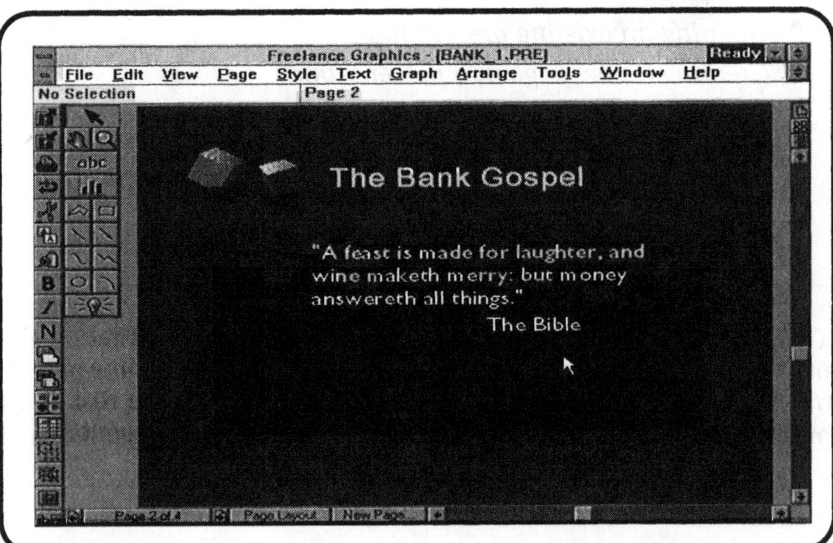

Figure 4.1 An example of a simple text chart.

Once you have text, you almost always have to edit it. You find out here how to edit it, how to check your spelling, and—finally—how to move from one page to another as you work on your text charts.

Opening an Existing Presentation

The first time you work on a presentation (as you saw in the last chapter), you create it using the File New command. Once you have created it, however, you are likely to close and open it many times as you continue to work on it. Some presenters keep their presentations for years and continue to open and update them (rather than having to create new ones each time). A quarterly report, for instance, may be the same basic report time after time. Only the numbers in the report change. The following Quick Steps summarize how to open an existing presentation.

Q Opening an Existing Presentation

1. Pull down the File menu.	The File menu drops down from the Main menu.
2. Choose Open.	The File Open dialog box appears.
3. Scroll through the listings on the left side of the dialog box and click on the presentation you want to open. (For this example, select bank1.pre, the presentation created in the preceding chapter.)	The presentation you select is highlighted.
4. Click on OK.	The presentation you select opens as a page on the screen. ☐

When you open a presentation, you start on the page you were on when you last closed the presentation. If you want a new page to work on, you have to open one (as explained in the next section).

Creating a New Page

To create a new page, you have two options. You can open a new page from the Current Page view in an existing presentation (simply select Page, New, or press F7), or you can use the Outliner, as was explained in Chapter 3. The following Quick Steps show how to create a new page from the Current Page view.

Q Creating a New Page

1. Choose Page from the Main menu. — You see the Page menu.
2. Choose New from the Page menu. — The Page New dialog box appears, as shown in Figure 4.2.
3. Choose the Page Layout you want. — The selected layout appears highlighted.
4. Choose OK. — The new page appears on the screen. The page indicator in the *status bar* at the bottom of the page indicates the new page number. □

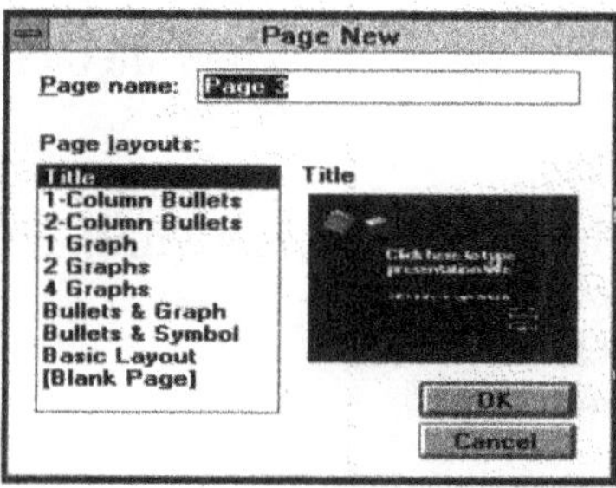

Figure 4.2 The Page New dialog box.

For example, you can create a new page for the bank presentation, using a SmartMaster Bullet Chart.

FYIdea: You may want to work on a blank page without a SmartMaster. Many people prefer to work that way. If you want to create your own format for the page, choose Blank Page in the Page New dialog box.

It is not hard to create your own formats. To get started (as you saw in the previous chapter), just click on the abc icon in the Toolbox, create a text box, and start typing. Later in this chapter you find out how to enhance such text with bold type or larger-sized type.

Adding a SmartMaster Bullet Chart

The *one-column bullet chart* is an old standby in business. It is hard to beat as a method for presenting a series of single points in a way that calls attention to each point one at a time. If you do not use SmartMasters, though, the task of creating bulleted lists is not always trivial. You have to answer such questions as "What style bullets shall I use?" "How far shall I indent each bullet?" "How much space do I leave between bullets?" Using the SmartMaster page, you just type your text and press Enter at the end of a bullet. The predesigned format takes care of the rest.

To create a one-column bullet chart, select New from the Page menu. The Page New dialog box appears (see Figure 4.2). Scroll down the list of page types in the box and click on 1-Column Bullets. Then click on OK. The new page appears, having the same design elements as the title page, but now formatted for one-column bullets, as shown in Figure 4.3.

Setting Up the Bullet Chart Title

You can start entering text in any area of the bullet chart, but it makes sense to start with the title. Click on the `Click here to type page title` text prompt. A text block appears with alignment icons, indent level icons, and a text ruler, as shown in Figure 4.4.

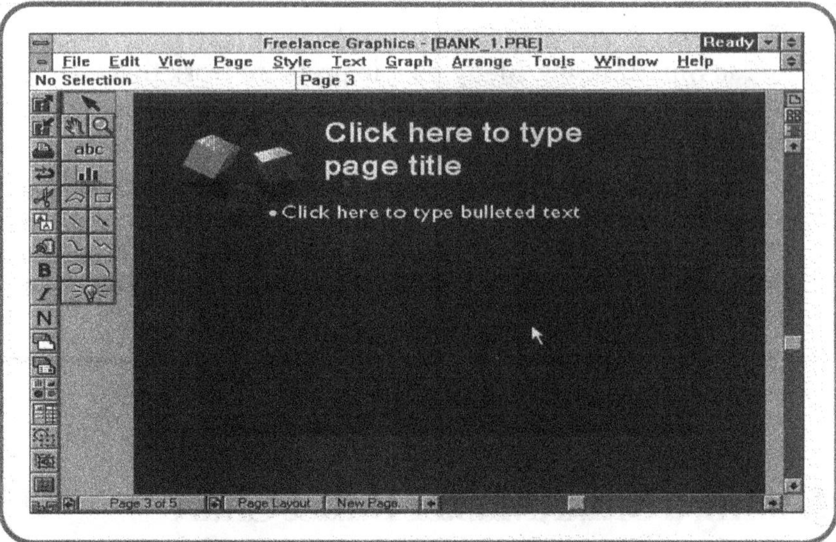

Figure 4.3 A new page, using the SmartMaster format of one-column bullets.

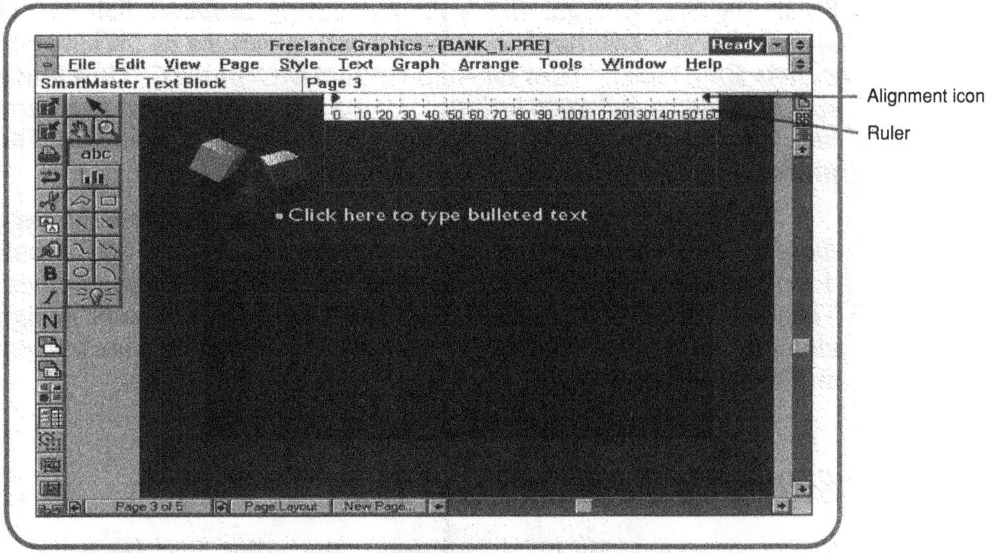

Figure 4.4 Text block icons and ruler.

Later in the chapter you will find out how to use the ruler and the icons. You can use them in any text block that you create yourself (as opposed to those in the SmartMaster itself). Here, you do not set the alignment or tabs or change the margins. The idea of the SmartMaster is that you just type. The SmartMaster takes care of formatting for you.

Tip: If you are an experienced layout person, you may want to set up formatting yourself and may even wonder why you cannot do it in the SmartMaster block. If you want to set up your own formatting, choose a different page type—either Basic Layout or Blank Page. Click on the abc in the Toolbox to add a text block and then set up formatting as you want.

To begin entering text, just type (for this example, `Services We Offer`). The resulting screen is shown in Figure 4.5.

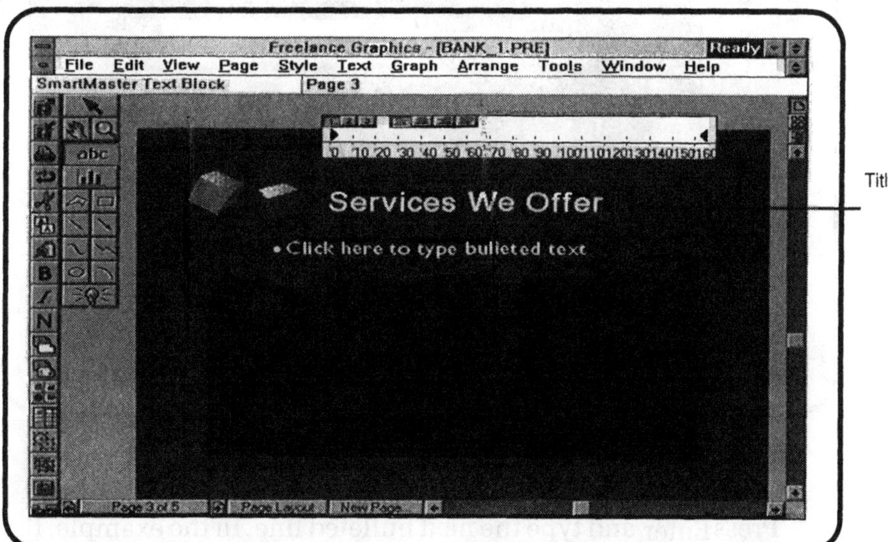

Figure 4.5 The sample bullet chart with title entered.

Tip: If you need to correct any text, highlight it by dragging the mouse over it. When you type over highlighted text, the previous text is replaced.

Adding Bullet Text

To switch to the body text area (where you will type your bullet text), simply click on the body text block where it says `Click here to type bulleted text`. Notice that when you click out of the title area, the ruler and icons disappear from the title area, and the title you typed appears as it will on the finished chart.

Type the text for your first bulleted line (**`Interest-bearing Checking Accounts`** for the example). The line appears with a bullet in the SmartMaster style you selected in the previous chapter (as shown in Figure 4.6).

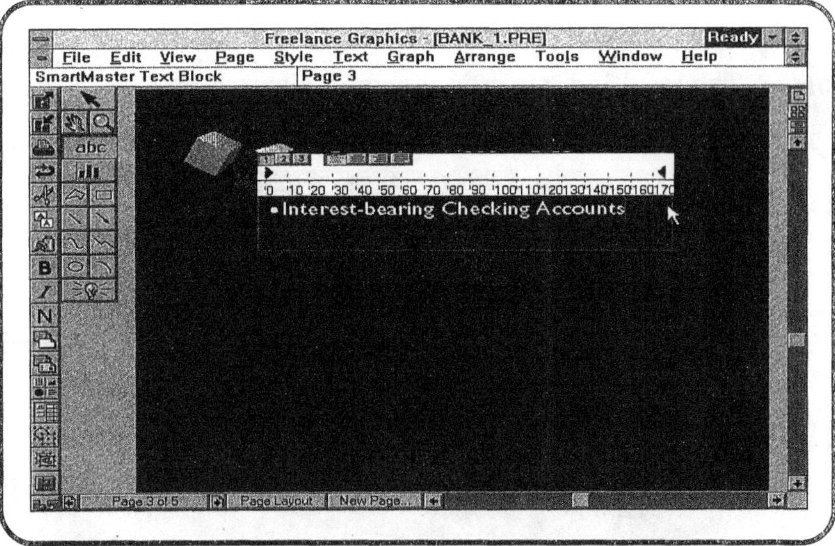

Figure 4.6 The first line of a sample bullet chart.

Press Enter and type the next bulleted line. In the example, this line is **`Reserve Account Checking Accounts`**. When you finish adding bulleted lines, click outside the text block (or press Esc) to exit the box.

FYIdea: One-column bullet charts are ideal for creating a *build chart*—a chart where you build a series of points one at a time for a cumulative effect. You can put one point on the first bulleted page, create a new page of the same type for the second page (adding your second point), and so on for as many points as you want. Viewers then can see the context while focusing on the point you are making at the time.

Two-column Bullet Charts

You will find `2-Column Bullets` as another choice on the list of SmartMaster pages. Choose it the same way you choose a one-column bullet chart.

1. Select New from the Page menu. The Page New dialog box appears.
2. Scroll down the list of layouts in the box and click on 2-Column Bullets.
3. Click on OK.

The new page appears with the same design elements as the title page, but it is now formatted for two-column bullets, as shown in Figure 4.7. Freelance creates the two-column format by setting up two separate but adjoining text blocks. To place text in the second column, you need to click on that text block.

The most common reason to use a *two-column bullet chart* is to make a point-by-point comparison. Each entry in the left column has a parallel entry in the right column. The left column, for instance, might present several features of the traditional checking account. The right column might present comparable features, point by point, in an "Executive, Cash-Reserve" checking account. Other examples might be to show (in medicine) a comparison between a healthy eye and a diseased eye or (in business) last year's sales results by district in one column, this year's in the other column.

Two-column bullets are not always easy to set up with a word processor. If you try to create them using the tab settings, for instance, you can run into nightmares. (If you are in Column Two and the text goes past the end of the line, it spills into Column One. Then you have to fix that.) In a SmartMaster text block, on the other hand, it is hard *not* to format two-column bullets properly. You just enter text.

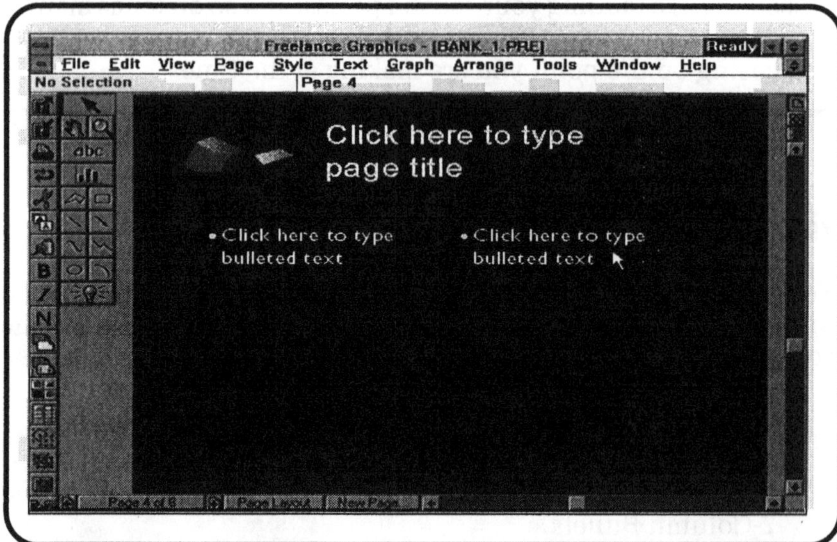

Figure 4.7 New page using the 2-Column Bullets SmartMaster format.

Follow these steps to create an example two-column bullet chart:

1. From the Page menu, choose New. You see the Page New dialog box.
2. In the Page layouts box, choose 2-Column Bullets and then choose OK. A blank page appears in the 2-Column Bullets SmartMaster format (see Figure 4.7).
3. Click in the title area and type a title for the chart—for the example, **`Executive, Cash-Reserve Checking`**
4. Click on Click here to type bulleted text in the first column. Type in the text for the first column— **`Traditional checking`**
5. Click on Click here to type bulleted text in the second column. Type **`Executive, Cash-reserve Checking`**
6. Click on abc in the Toolbox and then click on the first column.

7. Press Enter. A new bullet appears. Type in the second bullet for the column.
8. Click on the second column.
9. Press Enter. A new bullet appears. Type in the second bullet for the column.

Repeat steps 4 through 9 until you have typed in as many bullets as you want. Figure 4.8 shows a completed two-column bullet chart.

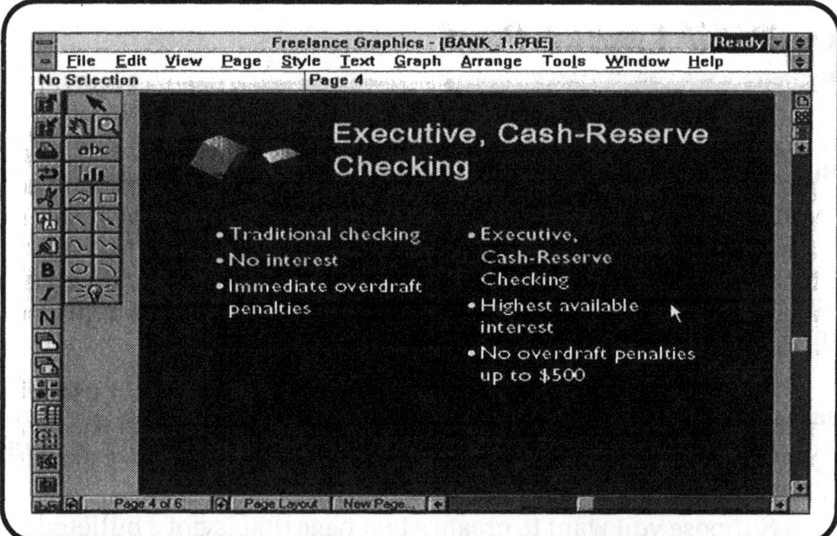

Figure 4.8 Sample completed 2-Column Bullets chart.

> **Caution:** After you exit the text block for the second bullet and want to enter text into the first again, you have to click on abc in the Toolbox before clicking on the first bullet. Otherwise, you cannot type in new text.

If you know all the bullets for a column, type all the bullets for that column and then all the bullets for the other column. That way, you do not have to click on abc in the Toolbox repeatedly as you return to the SmartMaster text block.

> **FYIdea:** Two-column bullet charts are great for showing cause and effect. Type the cause in the left column, the effect in the right. The Quick Steps in this book are two-column charts.

Creating Your Own Text Blocks Using the Basic Layout Page

If you want to create a page that is consistent with the other SmartMaster pages in a presentation but does not have a predefined layout (such as 2-Column Bullets), use the *Basic Layout page*; its main advantage is its simplicity. You can add your own text blocks wherever you want them and format them as you want. (The Basic Layout also has advantages for making global changes, as explained in Chapter 13, "Making Global Presentation Changes.")

The Basic Layout page has a block for the title, and it uses the same background and color scheme as other pages using the same SmartMaster. The rest of the page is blank; it does not have existing blocks for adding text, graphs, or symbols.

Suppose you want to create a text page that is not a bulleted list or title page. It could be, for instance, just a quotation. First, create the new page as you create other new pages. Either click on the New Page icon in the status bar at the bottom, or choose Page from the Main menu and then choose New. For the page layout, choose Basic Layout. You see a page like the one in Figure 4.9.

Such a page is ideal for typing a simple quotation, for instance. First, type in your title for the slide in the usual way. Click on the prompt and then type. For the example, type the title `Our Marketing Theme` and click outside the title text block. Then, to type text into a Basic Layout page (which, by definition, does not have an existing block for text), follow these Quick Steps.

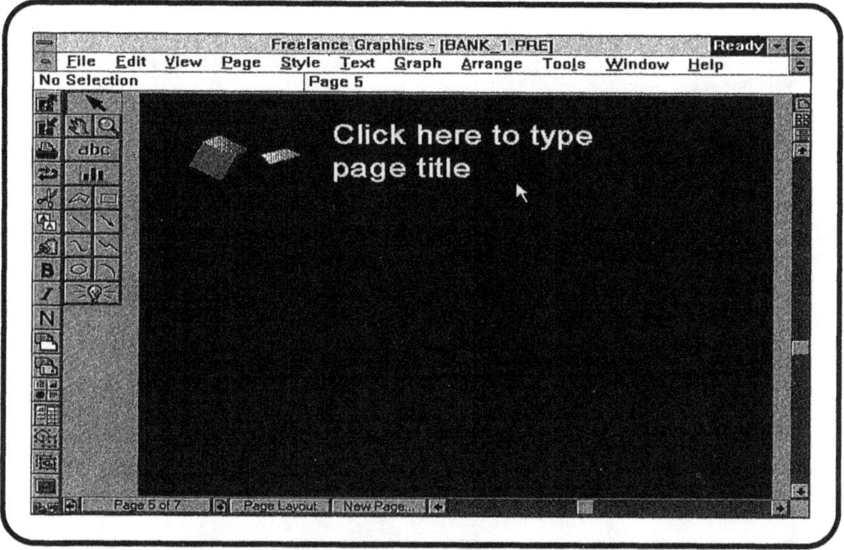

Figure 4.9 Blank page using the Basic Layout page type.

Q Adding Text to a Basic Layout Page

Step	Result
1. Click on abc in the toolbox.	The pointer changes from an arrow to cross hairs.
2. Move the pointer onto the page, click once, and drag the pointer to create a text block.	A broken line rectangle appears to show the shape of the text box.
3. Release the mouse button.	A text block appears, with a ruler at the top.
4. Type your text.	The text appears in the text block.
5. Click anywhere outside the text block.	The text block disappears, and the text remains on the page. □

You can create your own customized text blocks, and you can set your own tabs. If you want to create a bullet chart, you can define the type of bullets you want to use and how far you want to indent them. Figure 4.10 shows a sample text block containing the well-known quotation from Sophie Tucker: "I have been poor and I have been rich. Rich is better."

Figure 4.10 Text entered in a Basic Layout page.

Editing a Text Chart

With Freelance Graphics, you can easily add, delete, or revise text, or change type size, appearance, style, and color. You can edit with the *text ruler*, *menus*, or *attribute box*. The text ruler lets you edit in terms of simple text alignment, margins and indents, or basic formatting. The menus and attribute box let you change the appearance of your text. In this section, you will look first at editing with the text ruler.

Using the Text Ruler To Change a Format

To edit text, you must enter the *Text Edit mode*. There are four basic routes into Text Edit mode:

- Create a new text block by clicking on the Text icon and dragging the cross-hair cursor.

- Click on a text block to select it and then press the F2 (Edit) key.
- Click on the Text icon and then click inside the text block you want to edit.
- For a SmartMaster text block, click on the prompt that invites you to enter text.

To illustrate the ease with which you can do basic text formatting, use the text chart with the Sophie Tucker quote created in the previous section. You can align text before or after you type it. To align text that you have already typed, select it before you perform the following steps:

1. Align your text by clicking on the appropriate icon for left-aligned, centered, justified, or right-aligned. These icons are the four boxes in the upper left of the text ruler box. For this example, select left-aligned.
2. Set your margins by clicking on and dragging the left and right *margin icons* to the point on the ruler where you want the margins set.

Note: Click on the center apex of the triangle of these margin icons. Clicking on the bottom (and sometimes top) triangle of the left margin icon will split it into *sharkfins*, which you use for setting indent levels.

3. In the ruler in the text box, you see a triangle on the left side. The triangle is for controlling the margin and the indentation. The top part of the icon controls the indentation of the first line in each paragraph; the bottom part controls the margin as a whole. For instance, if you want to keep the margin at 0, but set the indentation for the first line to 20, use the mouse to drag the top part of the icon to 20. Point to the top part of the icon and click. Do not release the mouse button. Drag right to the position you want and release. Just the top part of the icon moves as you drag. Figure 4.11 shows the text block with the ruler set up to keep the margin at 0 but indent the first line to 20.

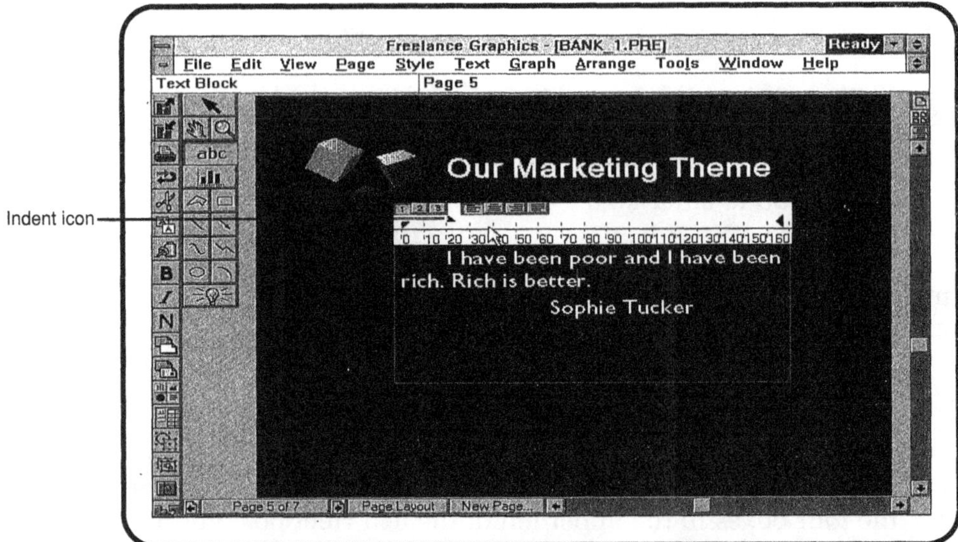

Figure 4.11 Text block with the ruler set up to indent the first line to 20.

4. Next, make a *hanging indent*. This means that the second line will be indented underneath the first line. Both first-line indents and hanging indents are effective techniques for emphasizing points in text charts.
5. Click on the bottom angle of the margin icon and drag it to where you want your hanging indent to begin. (You must drag it further right than the top shark fin.) Notice in Figure 4.12 how the second line in each item in the numbered list is automatically indented for a hanging indent.

When you finish editing, exit the Text Edit mode by clicking outside the text block or by pressing Esc.

FYIdea: You can use hanging indents in place of bullets. They are also particularly effective for numbered lists or numbered steps. The number "hangs" in the left column, and the text is automatically indented.

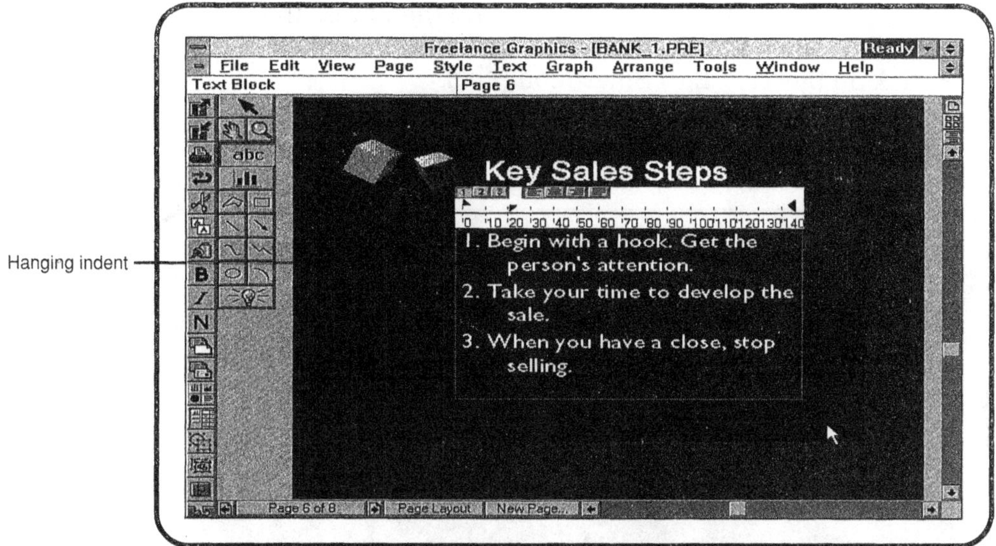

Figure 4.12 Text block chart with a hanging indent.

> **Caution:** You can change the indent and margin icons only in text blocks you create yourself. In SmartMaster text blocks, they simply display the existing settings. To change a SmartMaster text block to a regular text block (one where you can change the ruler), place the cursor in the SmartMaster text block and then choose Unlink Page Layout from the Page menu on the Main menu.

Next, you will learn how to change the appearance of text. As an example, you will change the size and color of part of the Sophie Tucker quotation.

Changing the Appearance of Text Using the Menus

As you have seen, the SmartMaster itself makes decisions for you about the appearance of your text. You can also change the appearance of text yourself. Suppose, for instance, you want to change the format of the most famous (and funniest) part of the Tucker quotation—the words "Rich is better."

1. Click on the text block to select it and then press the F2 (Edit) key; or click inside the text block and then click on the Text Edit SmartIcon (abc).
2. Select the text that will have its appearance changed. Figure 4.13 shows selected text in the example quotation.

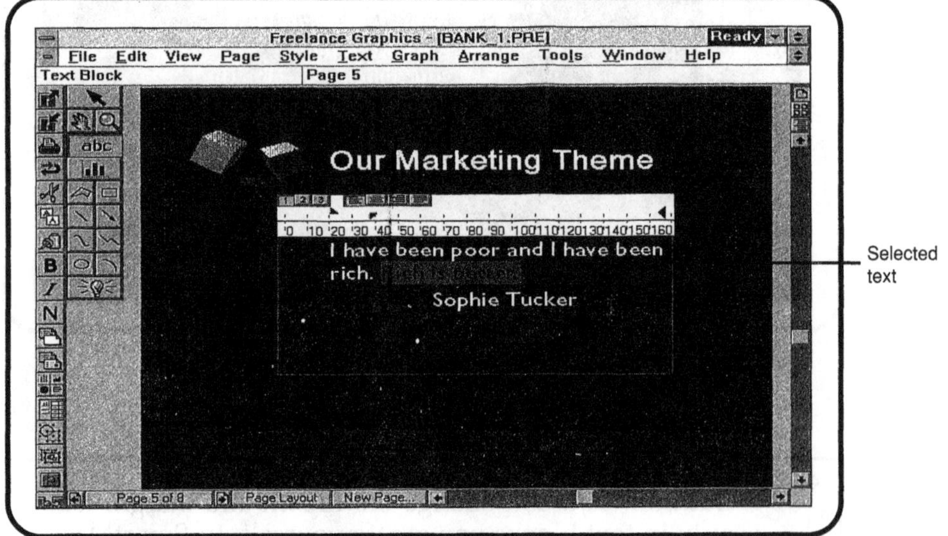

Figure 4.13 Selected text to be changed.

3. Pull down the Text menu and choose Size. A submenu opens to the right (see Figure 4.14), showing various size options in *points* (a point is approximately 1/72 of an inch).

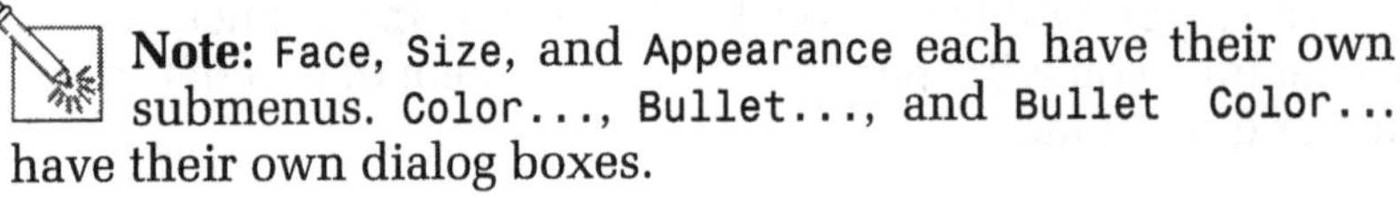

Note: `Face`, `Size`, and `Appearance` each have their own submenus. `Color...`, `Bullet...`, and `Bullet Color...` have their own dialog boxes.

4. For this example, make the type size 40 points. Because that size is not on the submenu, select the Other item.
5. In the dialog box that appears, type **40** for the size of the text and then click on OK to close the dialog box.
6. While the text is still highlighted, select Color from the Text menu.

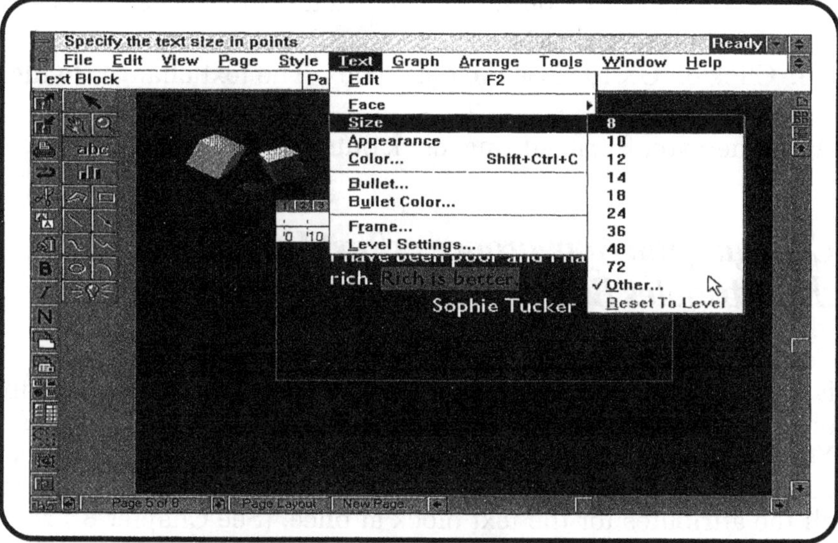

Figure 4.14 The Size menu with point size options.

7. In the Text Color dialog box, click on the arrow on the right of the color box. A *color palette box* opens on the right, as shown in Figure 4.15.

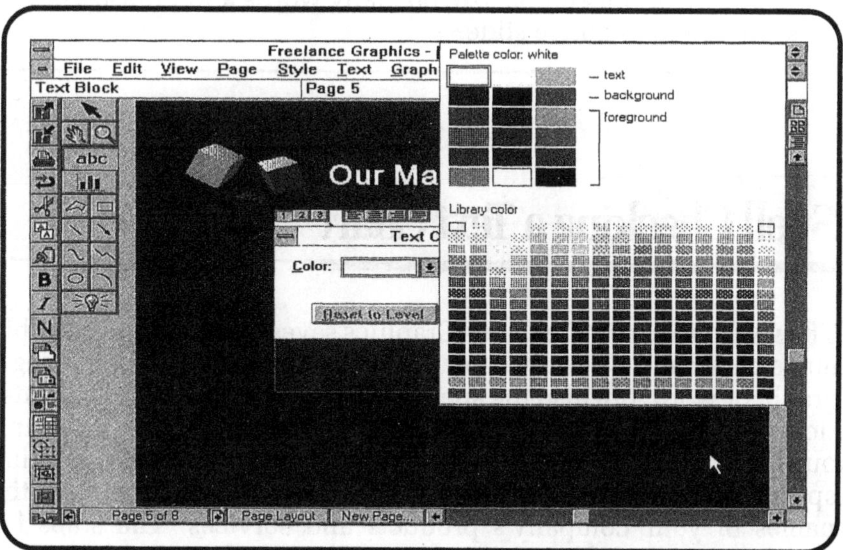

Figure 4.15 The color palette, partially obscuring the Text Color dialog box.

8. Select the color you want. The palette closes. The text is now the color you chose.
9. Click on OK to close the dialog box. The text changes to the new color.
10. When you finish editing, click outside your text block.

Changing the Appearance of Text Using the Attributes Box

You have learned how to edit a text chart through the menus. This is often done when you need to "override" the general text attribute of a block to change the look of a single word, line, etc. for emphasis. You can also edit a text chart through the *attributes box*. The attribute box is the way to change more than one attribute at a time or to set all the attributes for the text block at once. (See Chapter 8, "More About Text," for details.)

FYIdea: Changing attributes is one of the oldest ways to call attention to certain text; with the power of modern graphics, you can do it in new ways. To emphasize a word, make it a larger point size and put it into a color that stands out. However, do not emphasize too many words and phrases; one is enough for a single slide.

Spell Checking a Text Chart

The *spell checker* in Freelance Graphics saves you time and possible embarrassment. Not only can it check the spelling of a single page, graph, or word, but also the spelling throughout an entire presentation. The spell checker can also examine SmartMaster pages and outlines. The spell checker has a custom dictionary for entering specialized foreign words, business or technical terms, and the names of your company's products and services. The steps for creating a custom dictionary come at the end of this section.

To start the spell checker, follow these steps:

1. Pull down the Tools menu and choose Spell Check.
2. You can also click on the Spell Check SmartIcon, which is the ABC on the upper right of the screen (*not the same* as the lowercase abc icon in the Toolbox) or press the Ctrl+F2 (Spell) accelerator key combination. A submenu opens to the left of the Spell Check menu, as shown in Figure 4.16.
3. Set the scope of the spell check to be performed by selecting one of the options labelled Word, Current Page, or Presentation on this submenu.

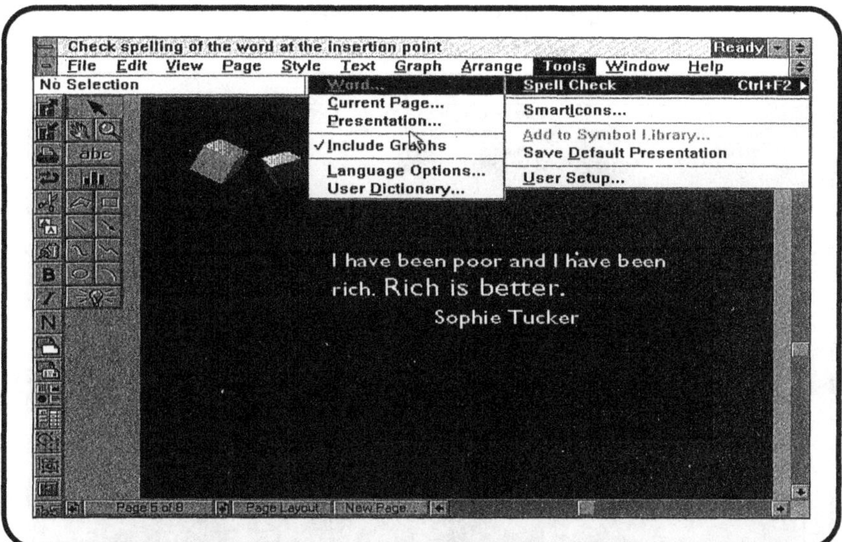

Figure 4.16 The scope of spell-checking, selected on the Spell Check submenu.

For this example, choose Presentation, which will spell check the entire presentation. To determine your spell-checking needs, remember the options described in Table 4.1.

Table 4.1 Spell-checking options.

Option	What It Covers
Word	The word on which the insertion point rests. You can use the spell checker in Text Edit mode, unless you are using the Outliner view.
Current Page	Current page and its SmartMaster Page.
Presentation	The entire presentation.

When the spell checker finds a word that is not contained in its dictionary, the Tools Spell Check dialog box appears, showing the word underlined at the top of the box (see Figure 4.17).

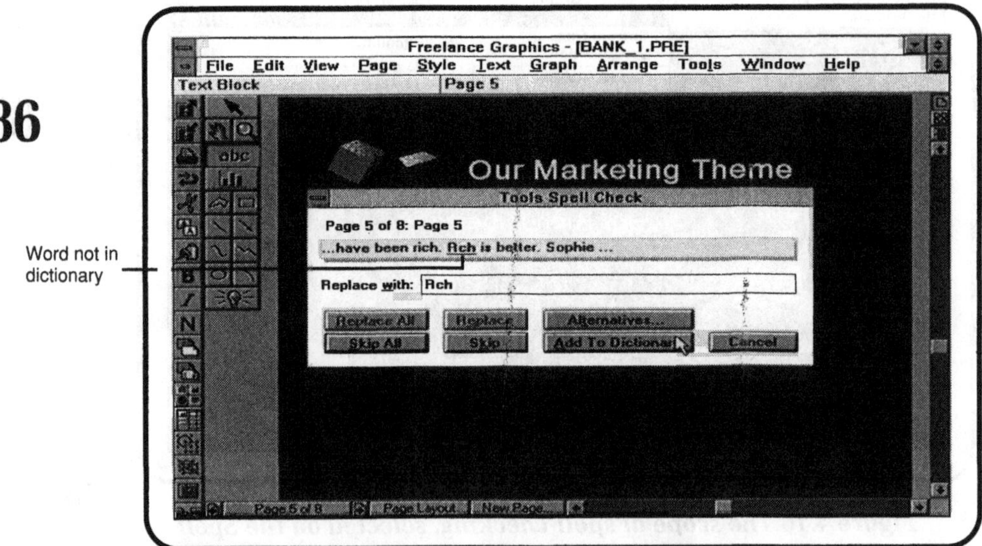

Figure 4.17 Word not contained in the dictionary.

At this point you have several options. Start with the most basic option, one which may be familiar to you if you have used other spell checkers:

1. Click on Alternatives to search the spell-checking dictionary for words with similar spellings or phonetic structure.
2. Click on the correct word from the Alternatives list. (A sample Alternatives list is shown in Figure 4.18.)

3. Click on Replace or Replace All in the Alternatives dialog box, after selecting the correct word. Replace corrects only the selected word; Replace All replaces all occurrences of the misspelled word.

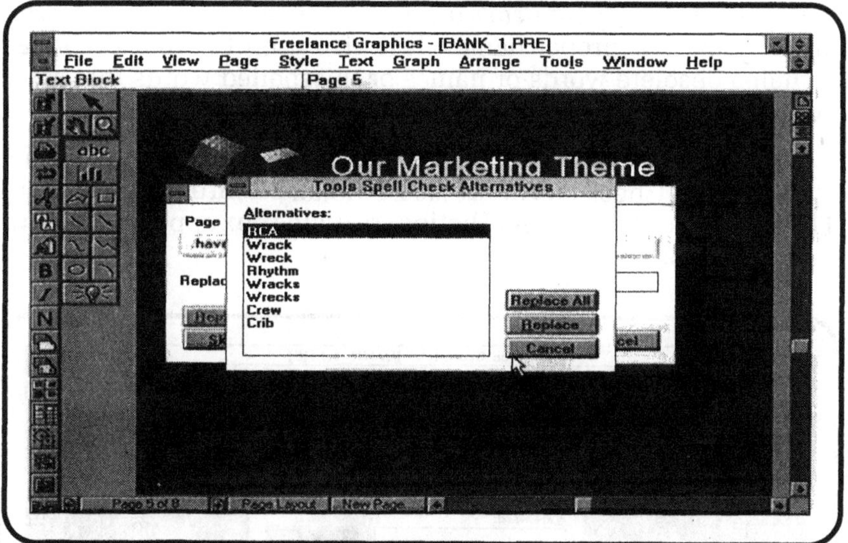

Figure 4.18 A sample Alternatives word list.

Once a word appears in the Replace with text box, you can simply retype it if you want. Press Backspace to delete the incorrect characters and then type in the correct spelling.

Once the correct spelling is in the Replace with box, you have two choices. You can replace the current instance of the misspelling or all instances. Click on either Replace or Replace all.

Often the spell checker may flag a word that is in fact correct but is just not in its own list. Proper nouns, for instance, often are not in the dictionary. Many technical computer terms also do not appear. If the term is correct but the spell checker flags it anyway, choose Skip (to have the spell checker ignore the word) or Skip all (to ignore all instances of the word in the current spell-checking session).

You may want to ignore all instances of the word in every spell-checking session. To do so, add the word to the dictionary. The Add To Dictionary option adds the unknown word to the spell-checking dictionary. Use this option to add the brand name of a product or service, a proper name, or a specialized technical or foreign word. Make sure, however, that the word is spelled exactly the way you want it spelled.

Select Cancel if you want to stop the spell-checking operation and close the box. A dialog box informs you when your spell checking is complete.

You may also add words to or delete words from your "customized" dictionary without starting up the spell checker. This is very handy for entering your firm's unique technical or specialized terms, brand names, or proper names. It is also useful if your dictionary contains obsolete words or names or misspelled words that somehow managed to enter the dictionary.

To "customize" your dictionary, pull down the Tools menu and open the Spell Check and then User Dictionary item on the submenus. The Tools Spell Check User Dictionary dialog box appears, as shown in Figure 4.19.

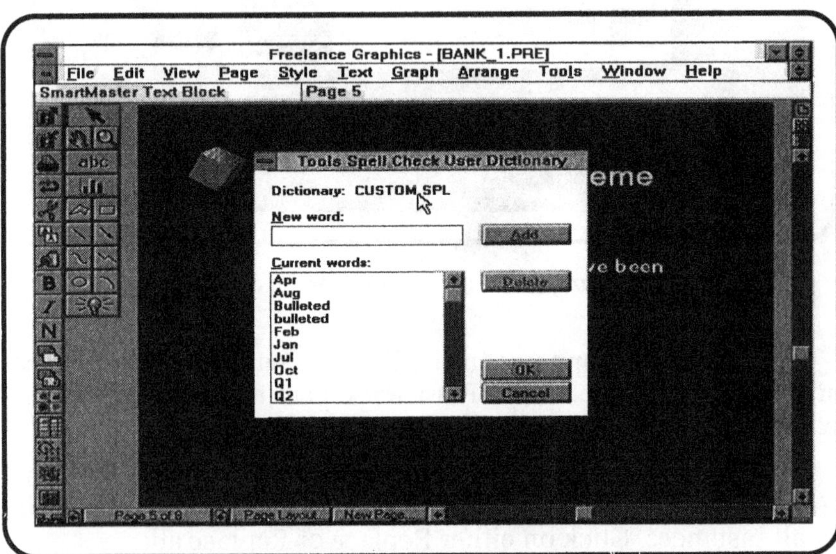

Figure 4.19 The Tools Spell Check User Dictionary dialog box.

If you want to add a word:

1. Type the word in the New word: edit box at the top of the dialog box.
2. Click on Add or press Enter. The word will be added exactly as you typed it, both with and without initial capitalization.

If you want to delete a word:

1. Click on the word in the Current words: list box in the lower left corner of the dialog box.
2. Click on Delete.

When you finish adding words to (and deleting words from) the dictionary, click on OK to save your changes or click on Cancel to undo any changes (which will, instead of saving your changes, discard all added words and cancel all deletions). The Cancel feature is very useful if you have made errors or want to undo the changes for other reasons.

Moving from Page to Page

Now that you have created several pages, it's useful to know how to flip back and forth between them. There are several ways to move around. You can use the Outliner, as explained in the previous chapter; you simply click with the mouse on the page you want. If you want an overview of all pages as you decide which page you want to view, use the Page Sorter; click on the Page Sorter icon (second from the top on the right side, beneath the Current Page icon), or follow these Quick Steps.

 **Moving Between Pages of a Presentation**

1. Pull down the View menu.	The View menu unrolls.
2. Select Page Sorter.	Your presentation appears, laid out like a deck of cards in miniature.
3. Double-click on the page to which you want to move.	The page you click on appears as a regular screen. □

> **Tip:** You can move forward or backward within your presentation by clicking on the *page indicator arrows* in the lower left corner of your screen or clicking on the button between the arrows (the one saying `Page x of x`) and then clicking on the page you want.

Saving Again

To prevent loss during power surges, power losses, or other glitches that might arise, you will want to save your presentation frequently. A general guideline is to save your data every 15 to 30 minutes, and whenever you take a break or quit for the day.

To save your presentation at regular intervals:

1. Pull down the File menu and choose Save or use the Ctrl+F1 accelerator key combination. The hourglass appears, and your disk drive starts "grinding" as your presentation is stored in its present form.
2. When the hourglass changes its shape into a pointer again, the program has switched out of Save mode. Resume work on your presentation.

What You Have Learned

- To create a new page in a presentation, choose New from the Page menu.
- To create a one-column chart, choose the page type 1-Column Bullets from the Page New dialog box.
- To create a two-column chart, choose the page type 2-Column Bullets from the Page New dialog box.

- To change the indentation and alignment of chart text, as well as the color, appearance, and size of text, use the Text menu.
- To start the spell checker, choose Spell Check from the Tools menu.
- To add your own text blocks and format them as you want, use the Basic Layout page.
- There are several ways to move between pages. To have a view of all the pages in the presentation as you select a page to view, use the Page Sorter.

Chapter 5

Adding Graphs to Your Presentation

In This Chapter

- ► *Choosing the best style for your graph*
- ► *Labelling the graph axes*
- ► *Entering data into your graph*
- ► *Adding titles and comments*
- ► *Editing graph data*
- ► *Previewing your graph*
- ► *Changing graph type or appearance*

The Graph Gallery

There's nothing like a graph to make numerical data easy to understand at a glance. Freelance Graphics offers a wide selection of graph styles for you to choose from—it's called the *Graph Gallery*.

The type of graph you choose depends on what you're trying to show. If you want to compare two or more things, a *bar graph* is usually a good choice. If you want to show change over time, a *line graph* may be best. To compare parts with the whole, a *pie graph* does nicely.

Consider a few examples. You want to compare the sales volume of three salespeople who work for you. You decide to use a bar graph. The salesperson who has the highest bar is obviously the top performer. This chart might look like Figure 5.1.

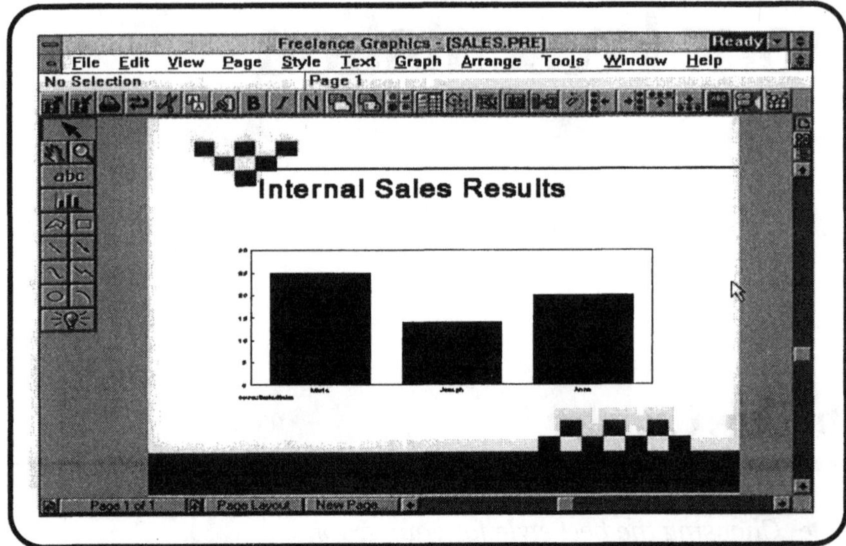

Figure 5.1 A bar graph helps you compare two or more items.

In another case, you want to show how the price of raw materials used in your business has fluctuated over the past year. You also want to show how this fluctuation is tied to the stock market. You decide to use a line graph with one line showing the cost of materials and the other line showing the stock market index. This chart might look like Figure 5.2.

What if you want to know the portion of your revenue that comes from sales and the portion that comes from service? In this case, a pie graph would be best. As illustrated in Figure 5.3, a pie graph makes it easy to see that sales revenue is about one third of your total income.

With bar, line, and pie charts, you can take care of most of your charting needs. Freelance Graphics does have other options for special applications, as well as variations on these "big three." You will discover these other options later in this chapter.

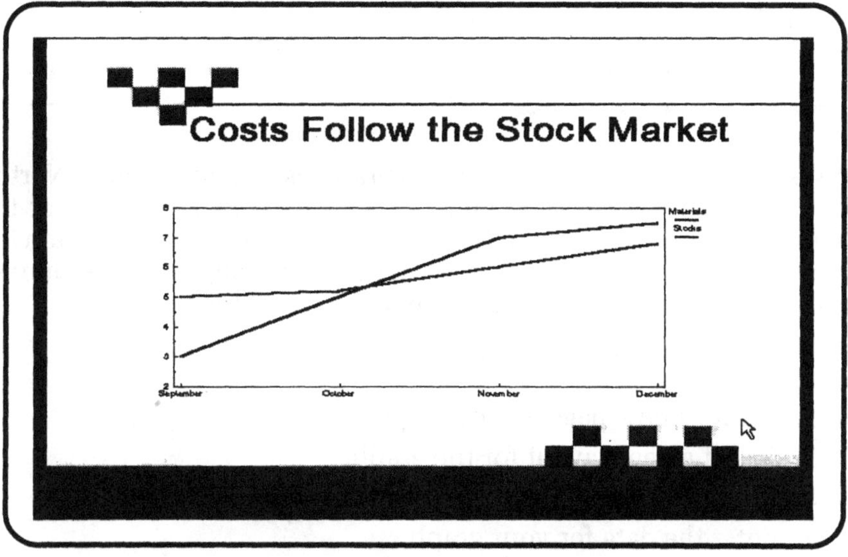

Figure 5.2 A line chart shows change over time or against another variable.

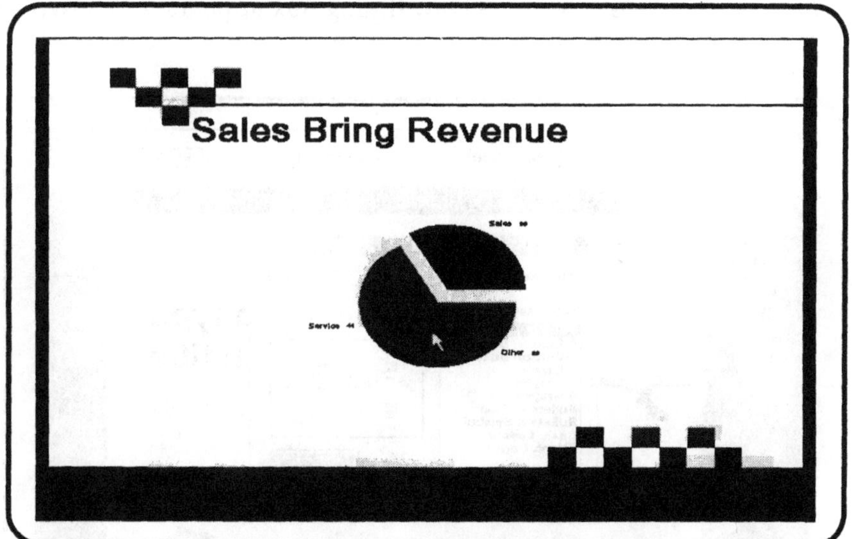

Figure 5.3 A pie chart compares parts to a whole.

Creating a Bar Graph for Your Presentation

Suppose you are the owner of three pizza restaurants—Metro North Pizza, Metro South Pizza, and Central Metro Pizza. You want to contrast the revenues from the three restaurants in a presentation to your partners. You decide to use a bar chart to compare the revenues from the restaurants during the first quarter of the year.

To do this, you will follow these steps:

1. Create a new page for the graph.
2. Select a page layout for the graph.
3. Select a graph type from the Graph Gallery.
4. Enter the data for your graph.

You have created the Title Page for your presentation and want to put your first graph on the second page of the presentation. From the Title Page, click on the New Page button in the status bar at the bottom of the page. The Page New dialog box appears, as shown in Figure 5.4.

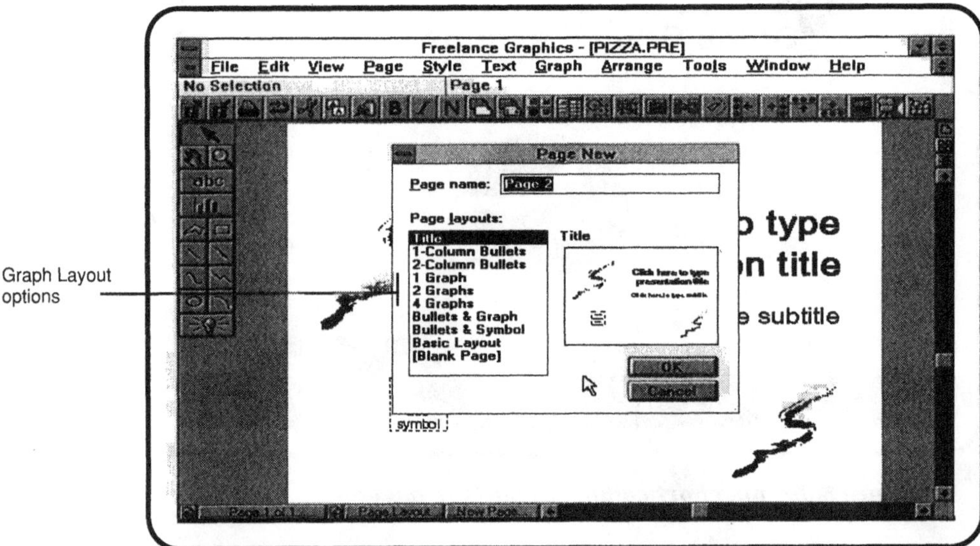

Figure 5.4 The Page New dialog box displays three options for graph layout.

You will find three layout choices in the Page layouts selection box, visible in the Page New dialog box.

- A page with one graph.
- A page with two graphs.
- A page with four graphs.

For this example, choose a one-graph page layout and then choose OK. The following Quick Steps summarize this procedure.

Q Choosing a Graph Layout Page

1. Click on Page in the menu.	The Page menu opens.
2. Click on the New Page button.	The Page New dialog box displays three layout choices for graphs.
3. Click on 1 Graph, 2 Graphs, or 4 Graphs.	Your page is set up with a graph box (or boxes) as you have specified.
4. Click on OK.	The dialog box closes, and the page you selected appears. □

Setting the Page Title

Because you selected a one-graph layout for the example, Freelance Graphics displays the second page of your presentation with space for the title at the top and a box for the graph at the bottom. You enter the title for your graph by placing the insertion point at the beginning of the title prompt and typing your title (for this example, type the title `Metro Pizza Revenues`). For information on typing text into a text box, review Chapters 3 and 4.

Creating a New Graph

Now it's time to create your graph. Click on the page at the `Click here to create graph` prompt. The Graph New Gallery dialog box appears, as shown in Figure 5.5.

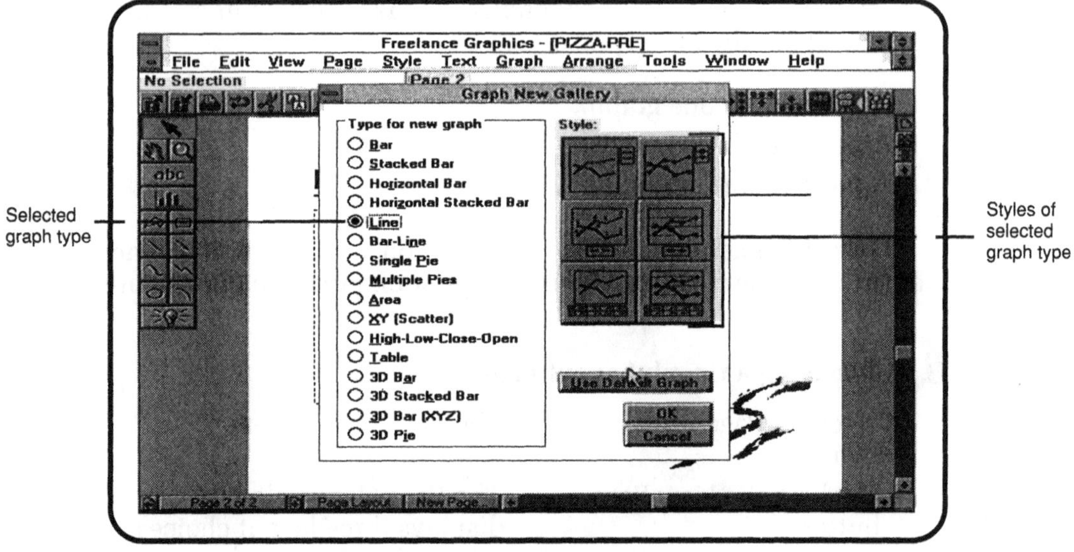

Figure 5.5 The Graph New Gallery dialog box.

Clicking on the page is the easiest way to enter the Graph New Gallery dialog box. Doing so also allows you to use the predesigned format; this sizes the finished graph correctly and places it attractively on the page. You can also open the dialog box directly from the Main menu. The following Quick Steps summarize the use of the Graph New Gallery dialog box.

Q Creating a New Graph

1. Click on Graph in the menu bar.	You see the Graph menu.
2. Choose New.	You see the Graph New Gallery dialog box.
3. Click on the option button next to the graph type you want.	Style choices for that graph type appear in boxes to the right.
4. Click on the style choice you want.	The box around your style choice is highlighted.
5. Click on OK.	You go to the Graph Data & Titles window. □

> **Tip:** You can also open the Graph New Gallery dialog box by clicking on the Graph icon in the Toolbox at the left. The Graph icon looks like a bar graph and is near the middle of the Toolbox.

The Graph New Gallery dialog box is where you pick the type of graph and the style you want. On the left side, choose Bar for your graph type; point to the circle next to the Bar option and click.

The Style box at the right works like the boxes in the Style Choose SmartMaster Set dialog box you have seen in earlier chapters. As you make choices in the box at the left (labelled `Type for new graph`), you see samples of these types on the right. In the Style box at right, you see six style choices displayed for a bar graph. You can choose a plain bar graph, one with the number values printed above the bars, or one with number data printed in a table at the bottom. Also, for each of these, you can either have dotted lines to compare bar height or no lines at all.

For this example, choose a plain bar graph with lines. Click on the box in the second column of the first row and then click on OK. You see the Graph Data & Titles window in its Edit Data view, as shown in Figure 5.6.

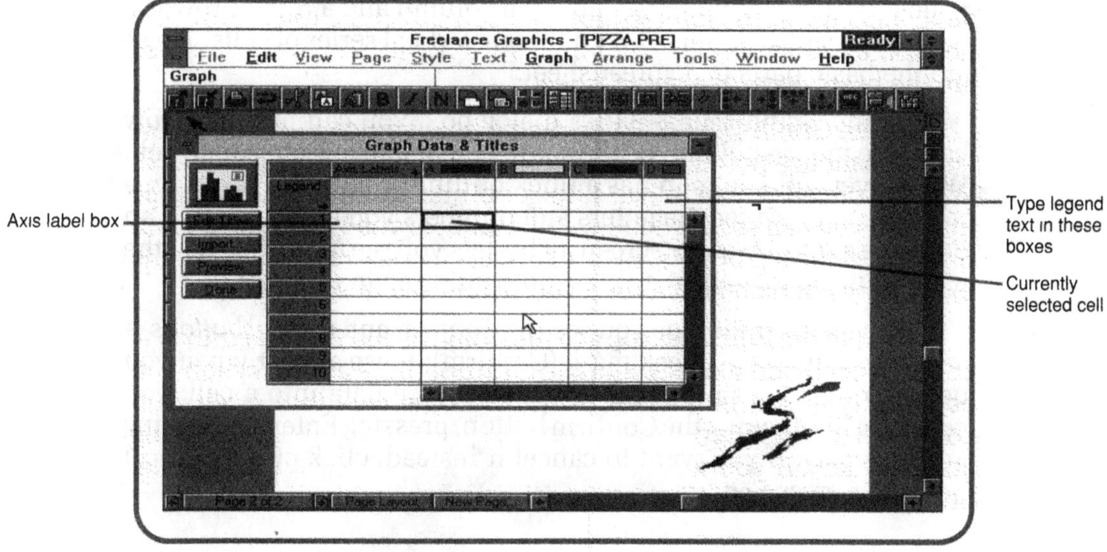

Figure 5.6 The Graph Data & Titles window in the Edit Data view.

You are ready to add titles and data to your bar graph, as explained next.

Adding Titles and Data

In the Graph Data & Titles box, you put in the actual information that the graph is to represent. If each bar in a graph represents a number, such as the income from one pizzeria in one quarter, you have to enter that number somewhere. You do so in the Graph Data & Titles box. You also put in other information, such as the label for the X (horizontal) axis, the label for the Y (vertical) axis, and text for headings and notes.

The Graph Data & Titles box is not really one box—it is two. You use one to enter data (numbers and labels for the numbers), the other to enter text such as notes and headings. When you enter data in the Edit Data box, the Edit Titles button is displayed (so you can move to that box). When you enter text in the Edit Titles box, the Edit Data button is displayed.

Typing data into the dialog box when you are in the Edit Data view is like using a spreadsheet (as you might expect from Lotus, the makers of Lotus 1-2-3 spreadsheets). If you have not used spreadsheets before, it doesn't matter. You will need to be familiar with three terms: *cell*, *column*, and *row*. A cell is a single box for entering data; it occurs at the intersection of a column and a row. A row is a horizontal series of cells. A column is a vertical series of cells. These are the basic parts of a spreadsheet.

In the Graph Data & Titles dialog box, you can use the arrow keys, the mouse pointer, or the scroll bars to move from cell to cell. Whichever cell you're in has a thick outline around it. As you type in a cell, you can see the letters and numbers you type appear in an *Edit Line* at the top of the screen. (This lets you see more than just the usual nine characters at a time you would see in each cell.)

Next to the Edit Line you see the *Confirm* and *Cancel buttons*— an X (Cancel) and a check mark (Confirm); these appear when you begin to type text into a cell. After you type data into a cell, you confirm it by clicking the Confirm button, pressing Enter, or pressing an arrow key. If you want to cancel it instead, click on the Cancel button or press Esc.

Adding Legends and Axis Labels

Notice the letters `A`, `B`, `C`, and so on across the top of the Graph Data & Titles dialog box. On the screen, each is next to a different colored bar. These colored bars will represent the three restaurants in the example. The boxes under `A` and the other letters are where you type your *legend* for each colored bar.

When you display the graph, the *legend labels* appear in the upper right corner of the graph to tell what the bar, line, or whatever represents. In this graph, for example, each column represents sales results for a particular restaurant. Put the insertion point in the first box under `A` and type **`Metro North`**. Repeat this for `B` and `C`, typing **`Metro South`** and **`Central Metro`**.

Then you need to put in *axis labels*. Axis labels are not labels for the axis itself. They are labels that display along the axes to identify the values represented by different points along the axes. In the example, for instance, the labels `January`, `February`, and `March` will appear on the X axis, showing that you are tracking revenue from the first quarter of the year, month by month. (The placement of the axis labels will change depending on the type of chart you use.)

To create these labels, put the insertion point in the first axis label box and type **`January`**. Go to the second box and type **`February`**. In the third box, type **`March`**.

Tip: You can move the legend—or not display it at all—if you want. You can also adjust the font type and size used in the legend, and much more. To do so, choose Graph from the Main menu and then choose Legend. The Graph Legend dialog box appears, as shown in Figure 5.7. (These options are described in more detail in Chapter 9, "More About Graphs.")

To change the font type or size for the axis labels (or to make other changes to them), choose Graph from the Main menu and then choose Axis Titles & Labels. Then choose either Titles or Labels. Figure 5.8 shows the dialog box that appears if you choose Labels. The options on this dialog box are explained in more detail in Chapter 9, "More About Graphs."

You have put in the labels for the chart. Of course, above all, you need numbers. The numbers—sales results in the example—tell

Freelance where to draw the lines in a line chart, or how tall to make the bars in a bar chart. Next, you see how to put these in.

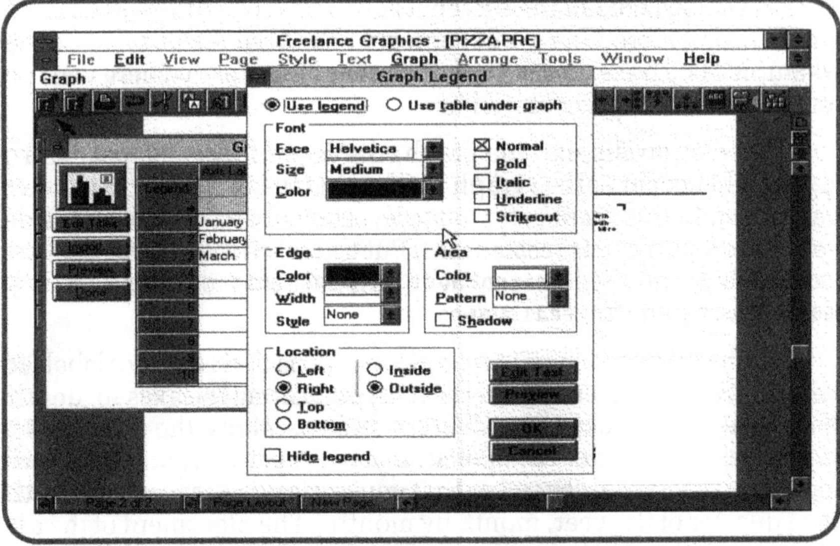

Figure 5.7 Click on any option you want to change in the Graph Legend dialog box.

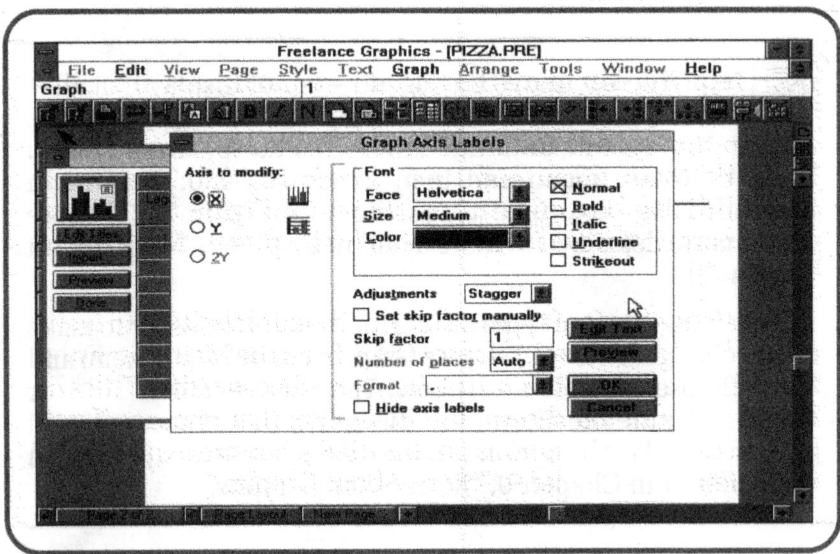

Figure 5.8 The Graph Axis Labels dialog box.

Entering Data

You are ready to type in your data. In the January row under letter A, type in the January revenue from the Metro North restaurant, **8000**. The February and March figures for this restaurant go in the cells below. Type **7050** for February and **9500** for March. In the next column, type the January, February, and March revenue figures for the Metro South restaurant: **12050**, **10000**, and **14500**. Metro Central figures go in the third column: **16000** for January, **14005** for February, and **18450** for March. When you finish, your screen should look like Figure 5.9.

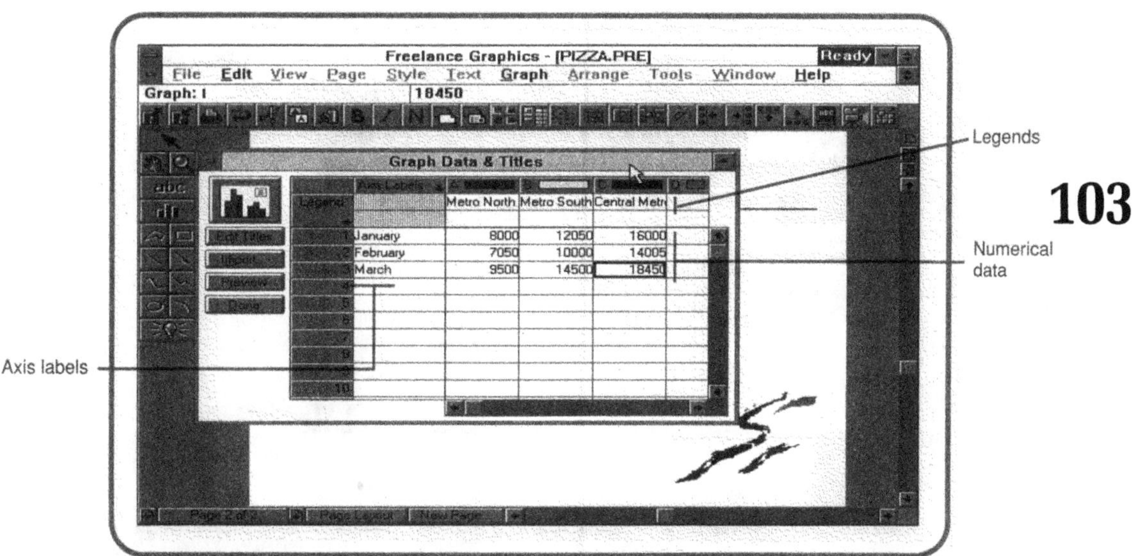

Figure 5.9 Sample graph data entered in the Graph Data & Titles window.

Entering Graph Titles

Finally, you can put the finishing touches on the graph by giving it titles. You have already typed in a title for the page. The headings and titles you enter now are less for show than the main title, and more for information. While the title you typed for the page does, in fact, describe the whole page, the heading and titles you type for the graph describe the graph itself.

The headings appear above the graph. Notes appear below it and to the left, and they are just what the name implies—special notes you want to make about the graph. You can cite your sources, put in disclaimers, or simply put in additional information you did not include in the graph. *Axis titles* (unlike the axis labels discussed earlier) *do* describe the axis itself. What does the X axis represent? The Y axis?

Click on the Edit Titles button on the left; you will see the Graph Data & Titles window in its Edit Titles view (shown in Figure 5.10). (Note that the button you just clicked now says **`Edit Data`**. Clicking on it takes you back to the Data screen you just left.)

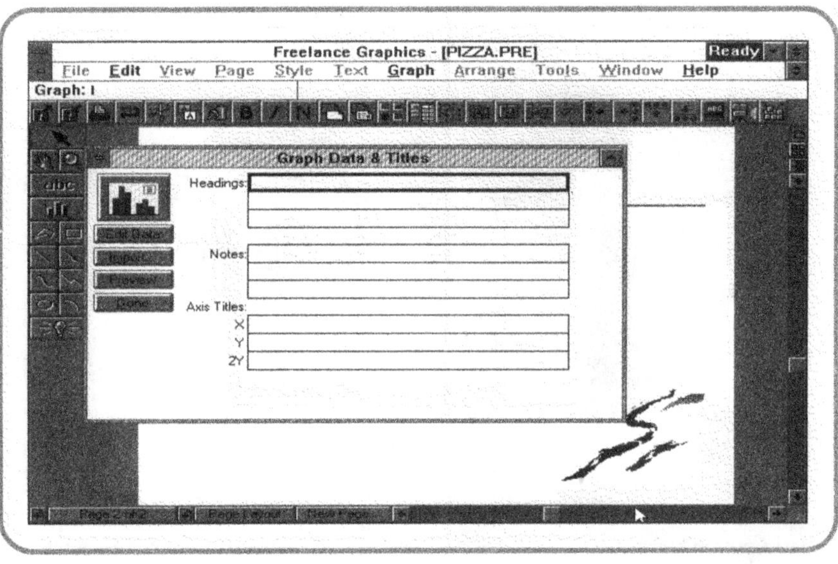

Figure 5.10 The Graph Data & Titles window in Edit Titles view.

Probably the easiest way to understand these titles is to see them in an example. Under Headings, type **`First Quarter Revenues Compared`** on the first line and **`Metro North, South, and Central`** on the second line. In the Notes section, type **`Preliminary`** and **`Confidential`**. Last is the Axis Titles section. The X field will appear across the bottom of your graph. Type **Revenues by Month** in the X-axis field. The Y field will appear on the left side of the graph. Type **Total Dollar Income** in the Y-axis field.

When you finish, click on Done, and Freelance creates your graph on the presentation page, as shown in Figure 5.11.

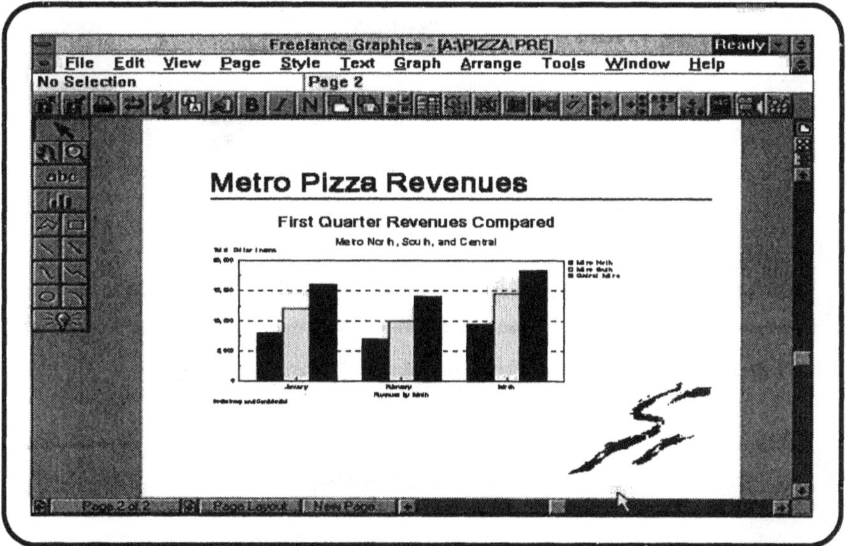

Figure 5.11 The new example graph on the presentation page.

As with legend titles and axis titles, you can change the font, alignment, and certain other characteristics for these titles. From the Graph menu, choose Headings & Notes. Figure 5.12 shows the Graph Headings & Notes dialog box.

FYIdea: Shadow boxes dress up a heading or notes and give a finished look. To place a shadow box around the heading, for instance, choose Graph and then Headings & Notes. Click on the Frame button. Select the box next to Shadow. Choose a solid line style for the Frame edge. (Do not leave the Frame edge at None, or you will not see the shadow box.) Figure 5.13 shows the heading and notes with shadow boxes around them.

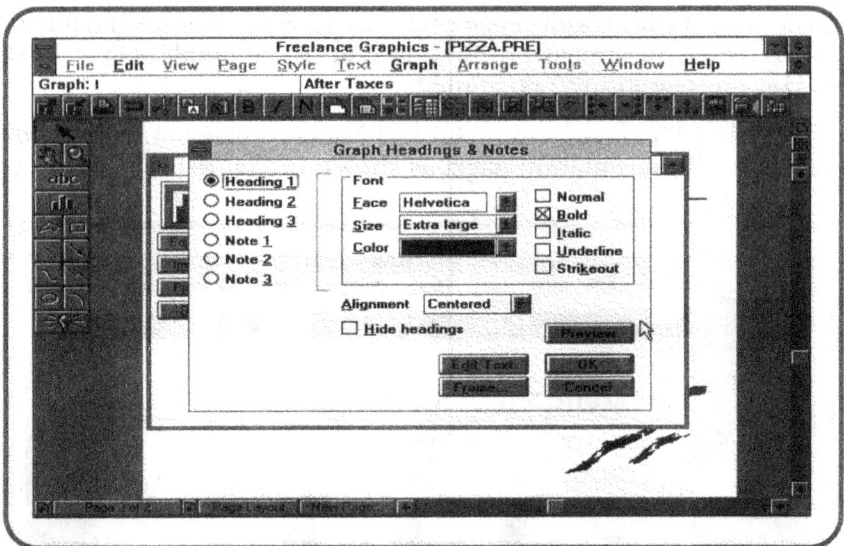

Figure 5.12 The Graph Headings & Notes dialog box.

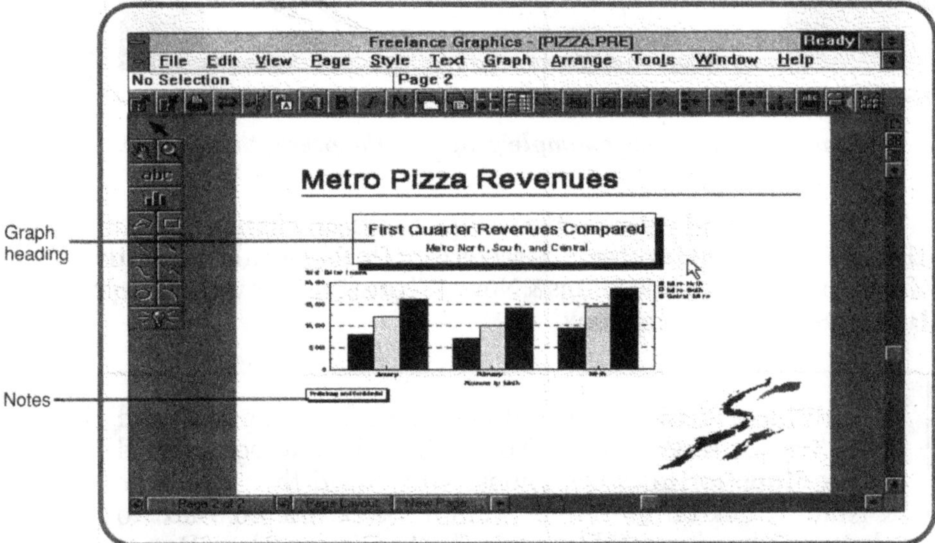

Figure 5.13 The sample graph with shadow boxes around the heading and notes.

Previewing the Graph Before It's Done

If you want, you can preview the graph before accepting it and positioning it on the page. Notice that in the Graph Data & Titles window you see a Preview button on the left (see Figure 5.6). Click on that button, and your graph appears behind the Graph Data & Titles window, as shown in Figure 5.14. To get a look at your graph, reduce the size of the Data and Titles window (move the pointer over to one of the borders of the window; when the pointer becomes a two-headed arrow, drag the border inward) or drag the window out of the way (point to the title bar; then click and drag).

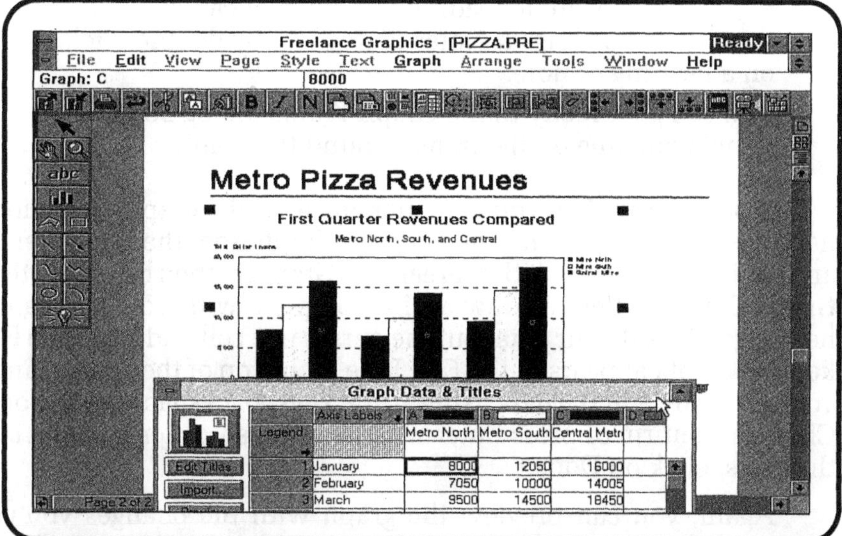

Figure 5.14 The preview graph appears behind the Graph Data & Titles window. Move or size the window to see the graph.

After viewing the graph, drag or resize the Data & Titles window back to its original position. Make any changes you want and then click on Done.

Tip: Until you get quite practiced creating graphs—and perhaps even then—you are likely to want to preview a graph several times before you get it "just right." Preview is faster than reviewing the final graph because you do not have to keep exiting and re-entering the Data & Titles window.

Editing Data

If you need to go back to your graph to edit your data, there are several ways to do it by clicking or double-clicking with the mouse. You can edit the graph or one of its elements.

- To edit the graph, double-click inside the frame where the graph is located. Be careful—make sure the pointer is inside the frame for the graph but not *on* a component of the graph, or you'll end up editing one of the graph components instead. If you accidentally click on one of the components, just choose Cancel from the dialog box that appears.
- If you want to edit a heading or note, you can go directly to the Graph Headings & Notes dialog box by double-clicking on a heading or note.
- You can go directly to the Graph Frame dialog box by double-clicking on the frame around the graph.

As an alternative, you can click once on the graph. Selection handles appear around it. Then choose Graph from the Main menu and choose Edit Data & Titles. Freelance Graphics then brings up the Graph Data & Titles window again, complete with your data and headings. To edit your data, put the cursor in a cell and press the F2 key. Your data appears in the Edit Line at the top of the screen, and you can easily edit the data using arrow keys, Backspace, and so on. Click on Confirm or press Enter when you finish. After you edit all the titles, click on Done.

Again, you can preview the graph with the changes you've made (while keeping the Graph Data & Titles window open) by clicking on Preview.

Changing Graph Type

You might find you have chosen the wrong type of graph for your needs—or you might want to use the same type of graph but go to a different style. You can easily change the graph type or style. First, double-click on your graph to bring up the Graph Data & Titles window. At the top left of the window, you see a button depicting the graph type you are using. Click on this button, and you see the Graph Gallery dialog box. Finally, select the new graph type or style you want and then choose OK. You can also select the graph by clicking on it and then selecting Edit Data & Titles from the Graph menu. The following Quick Steps summarize the procedure.

Changing Graph Type

1. Double-click on your graph.	You see the Graph Data & Titles window.
2. Click on the graph type button in the upper left corner of the Graph Data & Titles window.	You see the Graph Gallery.
3. Select the type and style of graph you want to change to. Click on OK.	Your graph is changed to the new type.

FYIdea: You can readily use the same data to emphasize different information by using it to create different graph types. For instance, you might create a table out of the information (to show, for example, sales for a number of regions). Then you could create a pie chart to show how each region contributes to overall sales—and, if you want, put the table and the pie on the same page by choosing the 2 Graphs layout.

Changing Graph Settings

You do not have to make decisions about such matters as the font type and size for the headings or the type of frame around the graph. Freelance has default settings for all such matters. You can use them if you want, and you can be confident that the standard settings conform to rules of good artistic usage. However, Freelance also gives you the flexibility to change design settings.

Perhaps you want to emphasize one element or another, such as the heading for a graph. You may want to move one component to make room for a symbol you want to add. Or perhaps the graph just does not look quite right to you when you are done. To change the appearance of one or more elements in your graph, select the graph you want to modify by clicking on it and then chooseGraph on the menu bar. You see the Graph menu, shown in Figure 5.15. (You can also double-click on the graph or on one of the components, as explained earlier in the chapter for a different menu.)

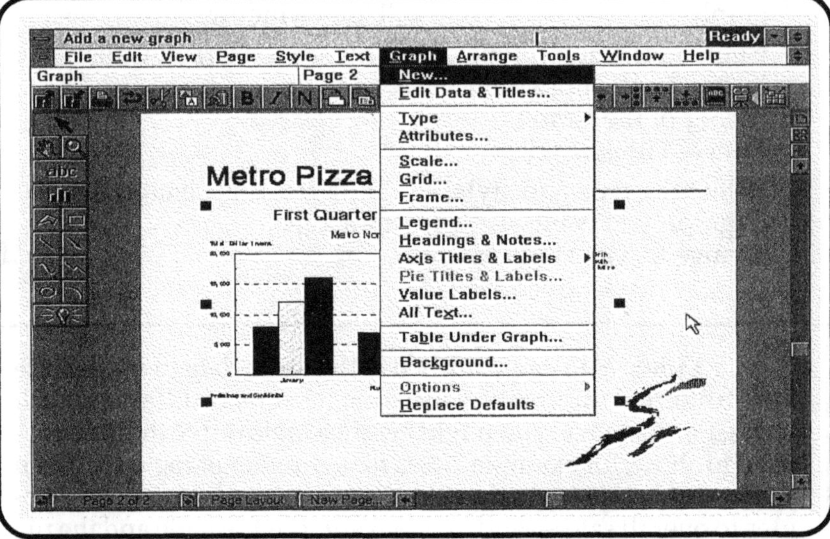

Figure 5.15 The Graph menu.

> **Caution:** If you do not select the graph you want to work on as a first step, all but the first option in the Graph menu will appear dimmed (even though you are working on only a single graph). This happens because you may know which graph you want to modify, but Freelance does not know which one until you select it.

Try clicking on some of the menu choices. Freelance gives you great flexibility in modifying the appearance of your graph once you create it. To try out one of the capabilities, chooseAttributes . You will see the Graph Attributes Bar dialog box—which, in the case of a bar graph, looks like Figure 5.16.

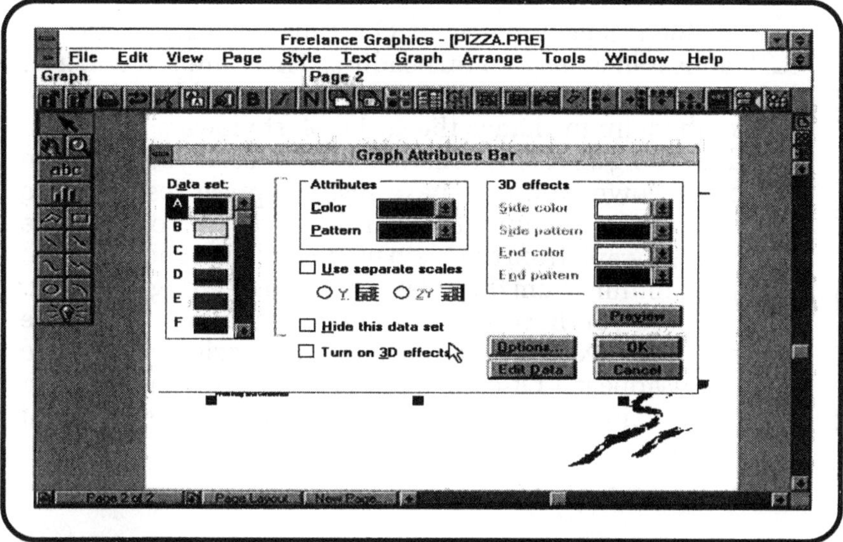

Figure 5.16 Graph Attributes Bar dialog box.

If you want to change the way the bars look, select a bar in the Data set box at the left. Next click on Color or Pattern to change the color or pattern of that bar. You have many possibilities to choose from. When the first bar looks the way you want it to, select another, and make changes to it.

> **Tip:** A *data set* is another term for the information that makes up a graph component such as a bar. In the Edit Data & Titles screen, you list data for a bar or a slice of a pie. On the graph, the data set appears as a bar or pie slice.

At the right of the Graph Attributes Bar dialog box are choices to modify the 3-D effects; a check box at the center of the dialog box lets you turn off 3-D altogether. Another check box lets you hide the data set that's selected. The data still exists but does not display on your graph. Freelance Graphics recomposes the graph without the data.

FYIdea: Sometimes your chart may be correct, but its appearance may be misleading. There are a number of things you can do to change the emphasis. One of these is to use the Graph menu to change the scale. Most viewers are accustomed to seeing an X-axis of zero, for instance. If you move the axis up or down, you can make results appear less or more dramatic, depending on what you want to say. To move the axis, choose Graph from the Main menu and then choose Scale. Change Minimum from the default of 0 to the setting you want.

Suppose you have negative results of minus ten in one column. Set the X-axis to minus ten. Like magic, the negative results "disappear." Of course, don't use such techniques to mislead but simply to highlight information in the way that works best.

What You Have Learned

- You choose New on the Graph menu (or click on Graph in the Toolbox) to enter the Graph Gallery to choose your graph.
- You can double-click on an existing graph to enter the Graph Data & Titles window and make changes to a graph.
- From the Graph Data & Titles window, you can click on the graph type button to choose a new graph type.
- In the Graph Data & Titles window, you choose Edit Data or Edit Titles to move from one window to the other.
- Use arrow keys or click the mouse to highlight a cell you want to select. Press F2 to edit a cell you have selected.
- Use Preview to view a graph without closing the Graph Data & Titles window.
- Choose Attributes on the Graph menu to change the appearance of your graph.

Chapter 6

Arranging and Rearranging Your Presentation

In This Chapter

- *Viewing your presentation in the Page Sorter view*
- *Changing page order using Page Sorter view or Outliner view*
- *Adding and deleting pages using the Outliner*
- *Copying pages in a presentation*
- *Running a Screen Show*

Windows programs like Freelance Graphics have a big advantage in the capability of working with multiple pages (or even multiple programs) at the same time. In Freelance Graphics, you can use either the *Page Sorter view* or the *Outliner view* to view and sort the pages in your presentation easily.

The sample for this chapter is a presentation called "Making Your Employees Feel at Home." You can compare the example with any presentation that has more than one page. The presentation is from a committee of employees to company management (committees often have to rearrange their presentations). Its purpose is to present research results and to persuade the company to institute company-sponsored child care.

Viewing Pages in the Page Sorter View

The Page Sorter lets you change the order of the pages in your presentation as easily as you would rearrange a stack of index cards. When you work with your presentation, you use either the *Current Page view*, the *Page Sorter view*, or the *Outliner view*.

The views are all different ways of looking at the same presentation. Most of the time you work in the Current Page view, on an individual page. Sometimes, however, you will want to work with the content of the overall presentation. If you are thinking about changing the wording, for example, the Outliner is an excellent way to work with your overall presentation. If you are thinking about the appearance of the presentation and want to think exclusively about the sequence of pages (rather than their meaning), the Page Sorter view is the best way to go. In the Page Sorter you can see your graphics in miniature. If you want to reconsider the symbols and other graphic effects you used in the overall presentation, the Page Sorter view is the way to do so.

To use the Page Sorter, select Page Sorter from the View menu. Your presentation appears on the screen as a series of *thumbnail* sketches, as shown in Figure 6.1. Each of the pages appears as a miniature on the page. The actual text, symbols, and graphics on the page appear on the thumbnail version. The pages are in order, left to right. Beneath the page is its title, if you typed in a title. If you didn't, the page number appears.

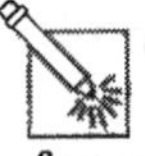

Tip: You can also get into the Page Sorter view by clicking on the Page Sorter icon at the right of your screen, second from the top.

Arranging Pages Using the Page Sorter

After viewing your presentation, you may decide that a particular page would be more effective in a different location. In the example, you might want to show the benefits of a plan before the results of the employee survey. To rearrange pages using Page Sorter, perform the following Quick Steps.

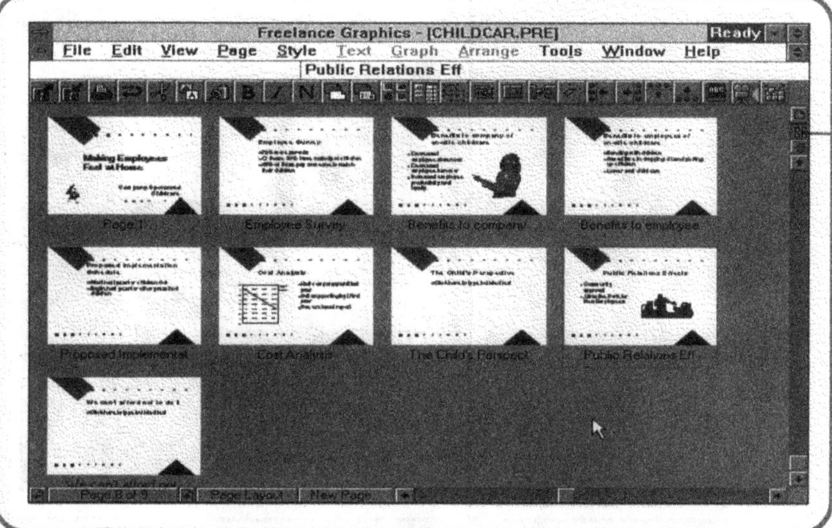

Figure 6.1 The Page Sorter view lets you easily rearrange your pages.

Rearranging Pages from the Page Sorter View

1. Click on the page you want to move. — A broken box around the page shows it is selected.
2. Drag the page to its new location. — As you drag the selected page over the other page, a broken box shows you where the page would be if you released the mouse button (see Figure 6.2).
3. Release the mouse button. — The page appears at its new position within the presentation. □

Tip: You can select and move multiple pages at a time. To select multiple pages, press the right mouse button as you point to each page. To move the multiple pages, drag them in the same way you drag a single page.

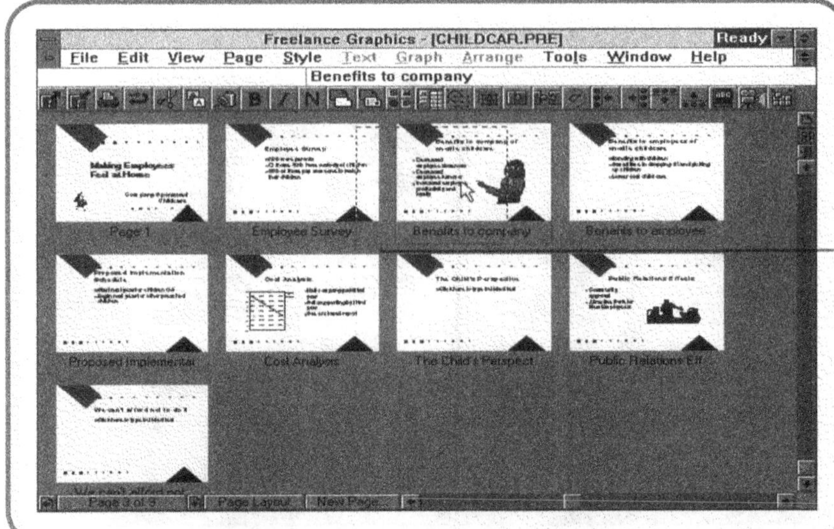

Figure 6.2 Moving a page to a different location.

Arranging Pages in the Outliner View

In Chapter 3 you learned how to switch to the Outliner by choosing Outliner from the View menu (or by clicking on the SmartIcon). You also learned to start a presentation from the Outliner, promote and demote text, and edit text. You can also change the order of a presentation from the Outliner, if you are currently working in the Outliner (or prefer working from the Outliner view).

With the Outliner, rearranging the order of your pages is as simple as pointing. Suppose you want to move your final page to the beginning of your presentation, right after the title page. The following Quick Steps show how to move any page while working in the Outliner.

Q Arranging Pages in the Outliner

1. Click on the Start Page icon to select the page.
   A box appears around the page. The cursor turns into a replica of the Start Page icon with an arrow on the side, as shown in Figure 6.3.
2. Drag the icon to the line where you want the page to begin.
   You see the page icon move along the page.
3. Release the mouse button.
   The page reappears in its new position. □

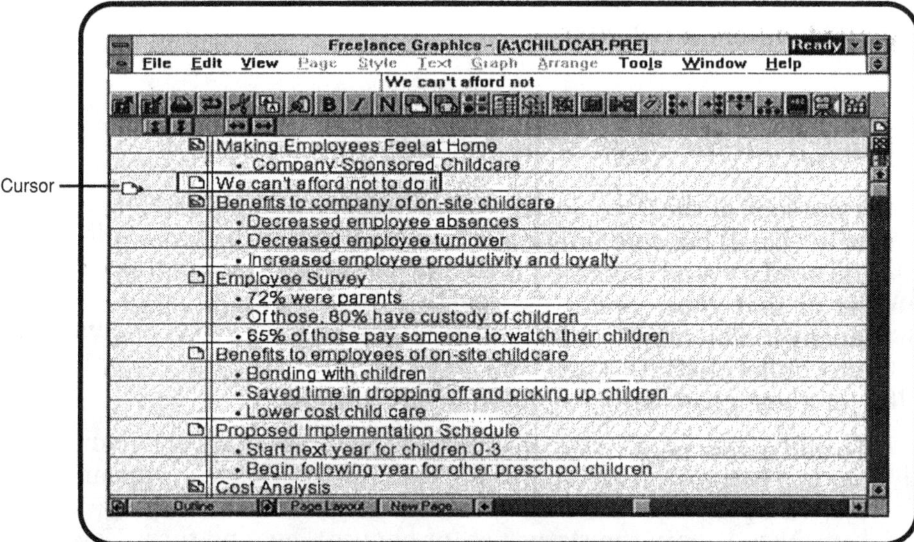

Figure 6.3 Moving a page in the Outliner.

> **Tip:** You can also change page order by selecting the page and then using the Cut and Paste commands from the Edit menu, as you would in any word processing program. Click on the page you want to move. The selection box appears around it. From the menu, choose Edit and then Cut. Move the cursor to the position where you want the page to appear. From the menu, choose Edit and then Paste. SmartIcons are a fast way to do a cut and paste.

Adding a Page to a Presentation

Sometimes, of course, you want to do more than move an existing page. Sometimes you want to add a new page altogether. You have seen that you can create a new page in the Current Page view by clicking on New Page(or choosing Pageand then Newfrom the Main menu).

When you read your presentation in the Outliner, you might decide you need a new page or even several pages. You might want to break up an existing page into more than one page, add a fresh conclusion, support your presentation with additional data, or add a fresh graph. Perhaps an existing graph is fine for what it does, but you feel an additional graph of the same data would bring out an important, different emphasis.

Adding from the Page Sorter View

When you look at the Page Sorter view, other considerations (often primarily visual) become important. You may notice, for example, that you need a visual transition from one part of the presentation to another or that your conclusion needs a more dramatic chart to accompany it. You may decide to add one or more pages; if you have too many bullet charts in a row, you may decide to interpose a graph chart (or a text chart with a symbol) to add variety.

To add a new page when you are in Page Sorter view, click on the page just before the one where you want the new page to appear. For the example, click on the page that says Benefits to Employee Click on New Pagein the status bar (or choose Pageand then New from the Main menu.)

You see a dialog box asking you to name the page and assign a SmartMaster page layout. Type in a name—`Survey Methods`—and choose a page layout just as you would if you were working in Current Page view. When you choose OK in the dialog box, Freelance adds the new page. To add text or other elements to it, switch to the Outliner or the Current Page view.

Tip: To change to Current Page view from the Page Sorter, double-click on the page you want to work with.

For the example, change to Current Page view. Click where it says `Click here to type page title`. Type in the title **`Survey Methods`**.

Adding from the Outliner View

To add a page in the Outliner, use Outliner procedures; place the cursor at the end of an existing page, just before the place where you want the new page to appear, and press Enter. If you see a bullet instead of a Start Page icon where you want the page to begin, press Shift+Tab as many times as it takes to change the bullet into a Start Page icon.

To add a new page, follow these Quick Steps.

Q Adding a New Page from the Outliner

1. Click at the end of the text line that will precede the new page.	The cursor appears in that location.
2. Press Enter.	The cursor moves to a new line at the same indent level as the previous line.
3. Press Shift+Tab as needed to move the cursor to the left edge of the page and display the Start Page icon.	The Start Page icon indicates you are ready to start a new page.

□

Suppose, for instance, you want to add two additional pages after the title page in the Outliner. Click after the words "Company-Sponsored Childcare," press Enter, and then press Shift+Tab once. Figure 6.4 shows the result.

Type in the text for the first new page. The first line is the title for the page: **`The Need is Immediate`**. After you press Enter, you move to a new line with another Start Page icon.

To type bullets for the current page instead of creating another new page, press Tab. The Start Page icon disappears and a bullet replaces it. Type the bulleted text: **`More Mothers Working than Ever`**. Press Enter and type a second bullet: **`Fathers, too, Demand Childcare`**. Press Enter and then Shift+Tab to begin the second new page. Figure 6.5 shows the example, with sample text added for the new page.

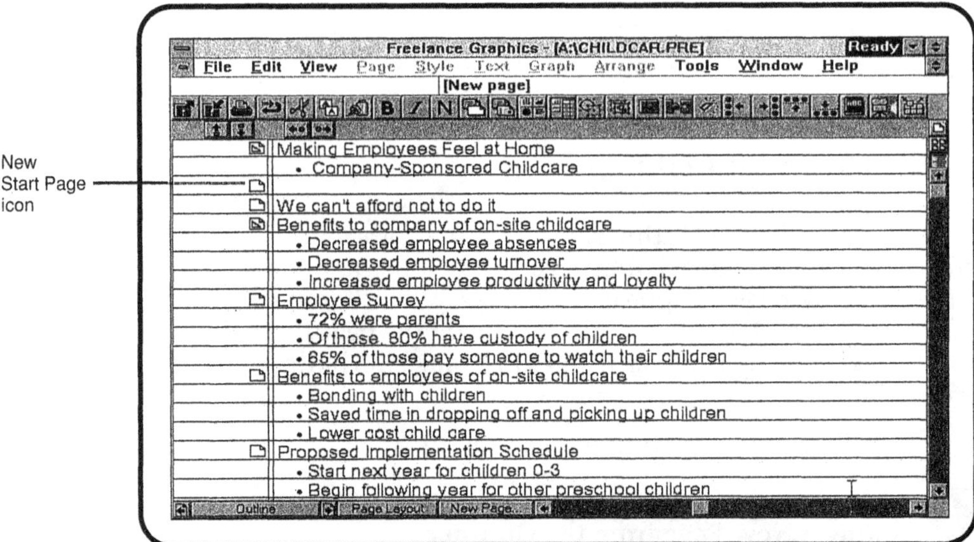

Figure 6.4 The Start Page icon indicates the beginning of a new page. The new Start Page icon does not include the triangle that indicates a graphic element on the page.

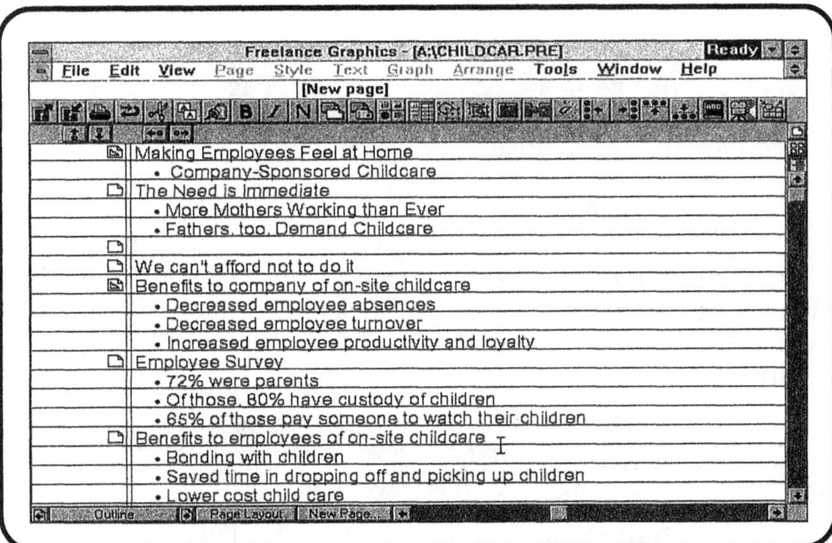

Figure 6.5 Sample Outliner with pages.

Each page in the Outliner (text following a Start Page icon) is a page in the presentation. To see any page as a full page, place the cursor on that page and click on the Current Page icon or select Current Page from the View menu. Figure 6.6 shows what happens if you click on the Current Page icon with the cursor in page 2 of the example presentation.

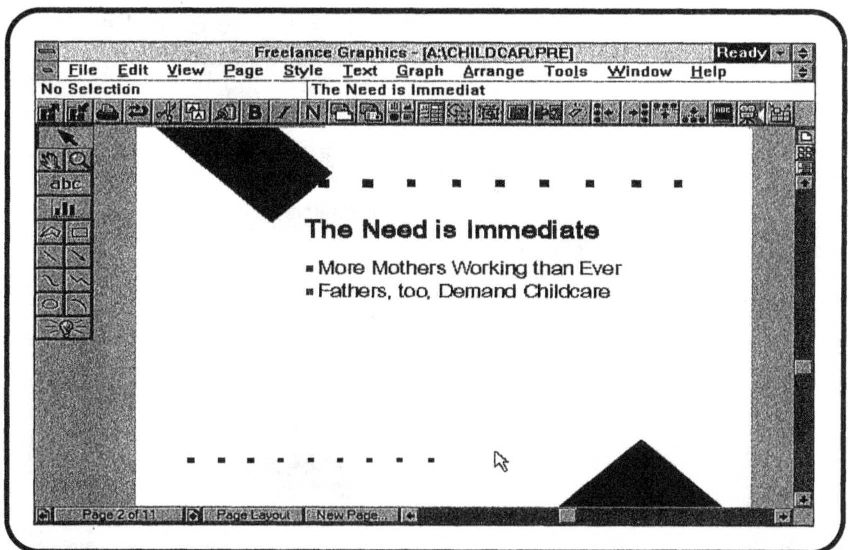

Figure 6.6 Current Page view of page 2 from the Outliner.

You cannot assign page types in the Outliner. To assign page types, you have to click on the Current Page view. Suppose you want to add a symbol to page 2 and use a SmartMaster page to do it. From the Outliner, you would click on the Current Page icon. To assign a page type, follow these Quick Steps.

Q Assigning a Page Type to Pages Created in the Outliner

1. With the current page displayed, click on the Page menu. — The Page menu appears.
2. Select Choose Page Layout. — The Page Choose Page Layout dialog box appears, as shown in Figure 6.7.

3. Highlight the page layout you want. For the example, choose Bullets & Symbol. — The selected page layout appears highlighted.
4. Select OK. — The page displays in the selected page type. □

Figure 6.8 shows the Current Page with the new page layout selected for the example page and a symbol added.

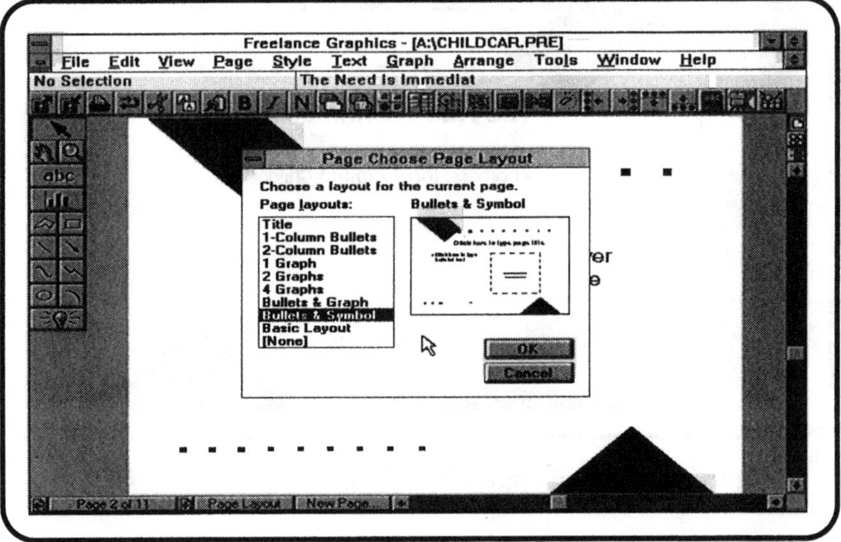

Figure 6.7 The Page Choose Page Layout dialog box with Bullets & Symbol selected.

Tip: A faster way to choose a page layout is to click on the Page Layout button in the status bar at the bottom of the page and then click on the Page Layout you want.

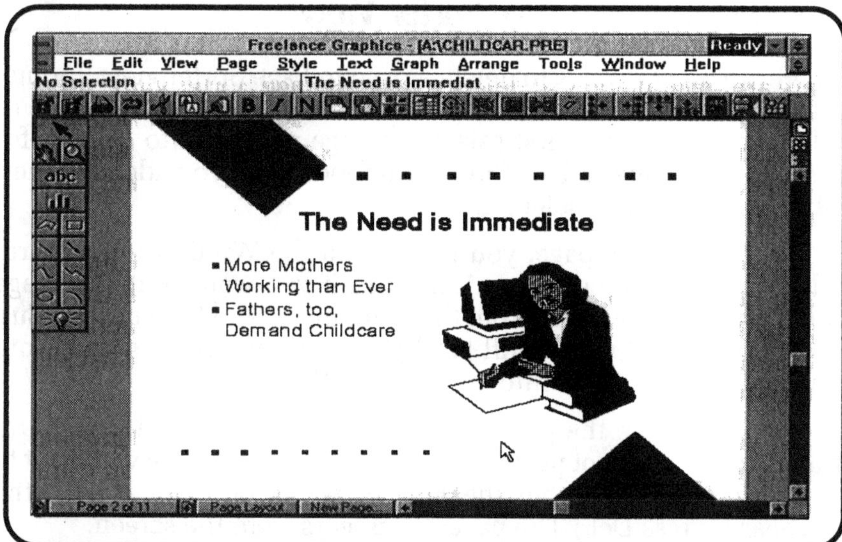

Figure 6.8 The new page layout (Bullets & Symbol) with a symbol added.

Deleting Pages

Deleting pages is as much a part of preparing a presentation as adding them or rearranging them. For a presentation to be effective, it should be concise. When you review your complete presentation in the Page Sorter or Outliner, you get a fresh perspective on individual slides. Something that is quite good in itself may not be good in the flow of the whole presentation, so you may decide to replace or delete it.

You can delete a page from any of the main views—Current Page, Page Sorter, or Outliner. To delete the page in Current Page view, choose the Pagemenu and then choose Remove Next, you'll learn how to delete a page in the Page Sorter or Outliner views.

Deleting from the Page Sorter View

There are several ways to delete a page in Page Sorter view, though all the ways are just variations on two methods: Cut and Delete. For all the methods, you first select the page you want to delete—for instance, the page called "Survey Methods" that you added earlier. Click on the page to select it.

If you cut the page, you place it on the Windows Clipboard, which means you can paste it back in if you want. With the page highlighted, choose Edit from the Main menu and then choose Cut. (On the keyboard, press Shift+Del.) You can paste the page back into its original position or into another position.

If you delete the page, you do not place it on the Clipboard; therefore, you cannot paste it back in. Click on the page you want to delete to select it. From the Edit menu, choose Clear. (On the keyboard, press Del.) The page disappears from the screen.

> **Tip:** If you change your mind after you use Delete to remove a page in Page Sorter view—and want to restore it—choose Edit from the Main menu and then choose Undo. Freelance restores the page to the position where you deleted it.

Deleting from the Outliner

If you are working in the Outliner (or prefer working in the Outliner view), you can easily delete a page from your presentation, as follows:

1. Click on the Start Page icon. All the text on that page is selected.
2. Press the Del key. After you select OK in the warning box, the page disappears and the other pages move up in the Outliner.

You can also get rid of a selected page (or any amount of selected text) from the Outliner by selecting Cut from the Edit menu or clicking on the Cut SmartIcon (scissors). The Cut command has one advantage over the Delete key. If you cut the wrong text, you can easily paste it back in. (In the Outliner, once you delete a page, you cannot use Undo to get it back, as you can in the Page Sorter and Current Page views.) When you select a page and choose Delete, you see a message saying `Delete this page permanently?` If you choose OK, you cannot get the page back unless you re-create it from scratch.

Copying Pages

At times you'll want the same page to appear twice in your presentation. Suppose you want three copies of the page named "Employee Survey." That way, you would have one page for each bullet in the three-bullet list. You could later highlight one point at a time, one page at a time, to create a *build chart* (more about build charts later in the chapter). You can save yourself some time in this process by copying a page. As with adding and deleting pages, you can copy a page from either the Page Sorter view or the Outliner. You can copy pages to other Freelance for Windows presentations (or to other Windows applications), as well as copying them from one part of a presentation to another. When you choose Copy, you leave the original page in position and place a copy of it in the Windows Clipboard. From there, you can paste the copy into any Windows program.

For instance, you might have a page showing sales results that you use for a meeting with management. Later, you might prepare a presentation to investors where you also need the page on sales results. You can copy the page from the presentation for management into a presentation for investors. You might even want to take the text from a page—perhaps a summary of main points—and use it in your Windows word processing program. Copy the text to the Windows Clipboard, open the word processing program, and use the word processor's "cut and paste" program.

Caution: You cannot copy from a Windows program into a non-Windows program. The Windows Clipboard is for Windows programs only.

Copying Pages from the Page Sorter View

To copy pages in Page Sorter view, first click on the page you want to copy to select it. Then, from the Edit menu, choose Copy. (You can also use the SmartIcon with two capital A's on it or, on the keyboard, press Ctrl+Ins) The page remains in its original location on the Page Sorter, but you have now placed a copy of it in the Clipboard.

Next, select the page that you want to appear just before the new copy. In the example, keep the Employee Survey page selected. From the Edit menu, choose Paste(Shift+Inson the keyboard). A copy of the page appears after the selected copy. For the example, choose Pasteagain to add a second copy. Figure 6.9 shows the Page Sorter view after you create two copies of the "Employee Survey" page.

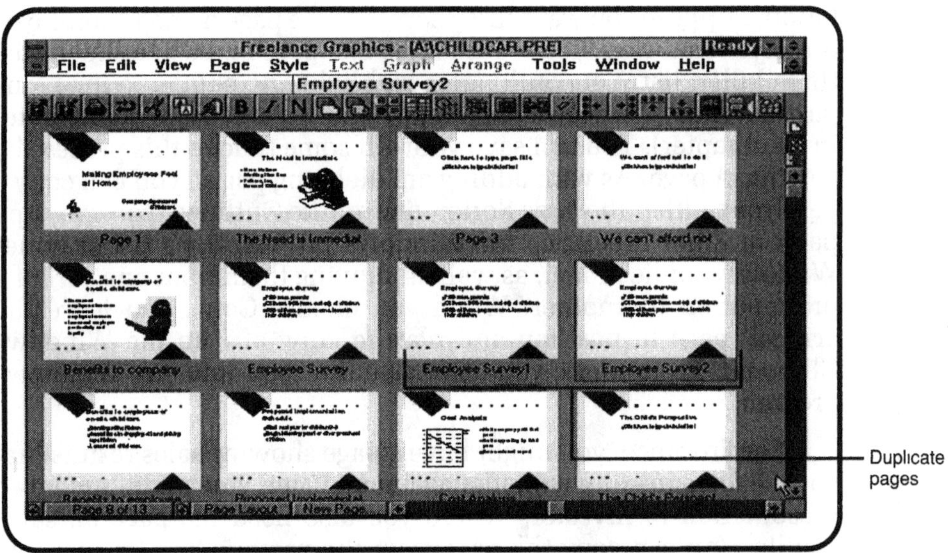

Figure 6.9 Use the Edit Copy and Paste commands to copy pages in the Page Sorter view.

Moving pages from existing presentations into new ones is often a useful way of "recycling" earlier work. Thanks to Windows, you can run an existing presentation simultaneously with a new one. This allows you to copy the page in one presentation, move to the other, and paste in the page.

Tip: When you paste a page from one presentation into another that uses a different SmartMaster, the page uses the SmartMaster in the presentation that is receiving the slide. Freelance automatically keeps your presentation uniform.

Copying Pages from the Outliner

Copying a page in the Outliner is a familiar process, much like copying text in a word processor. You select the text, copy it to the Clipboard, and then paste the copy into the new location. To copy a page in the Outliner, follow these steps:

1. Click on the Start Page icon. The entire page is selected.
2. Choose Copy from the Edit menu. Freelance places a copy of the page in the Windows Clipboard.
3. Choose Paste from the Edit menu. The copied page appears immediately after the original.

A fast way to copy a page is with the SmartIcon for Duplicate (two squares containing the letter A). After you copy the page, click on the Paste SmartIcon to insert the duplicated page.

FYIdea: Use the Duplicate capability to create a build chart. Perhaps you want to build to five points in your final page of the chart. Create the last page first. Duplicate it four times. Then, start with the first page and delete all but the first point. On the second page, delete all but the first two points, and so on.

FYIdea: Use Duplicate to create a primitive "animation." For instance, start with a page showing a picture of a truck near the left margin and duplicate it. On the duplicated page, select the truck and drag it 1/2 inch to the right. Then duplicate that page and drag the truck further, and so on with each page. When you run the presentation as a slide show (explained later in this chapter), the slides will give the appearance of motion.

Previewing Your Presentation/Running a Screen Show

When you finish creating your presentation, it's a good idea to make sure you have what you think you have. An easy way to do that is by running a *Screen Show*—a full-screen display of each page in the presentation. Before you can have a Screen Show, you will want to have your presentation pages *optimized*, that is, "translated" into a full-screen display. To optimize pages for a Screen Show, follow these steps:

1. Pull down the File menu and choose Printer Setup. The File Printer Setup dialog box appears, as shown in Figure 6.10.
2. Click on Optimize for screen show.
3. Choose OK.

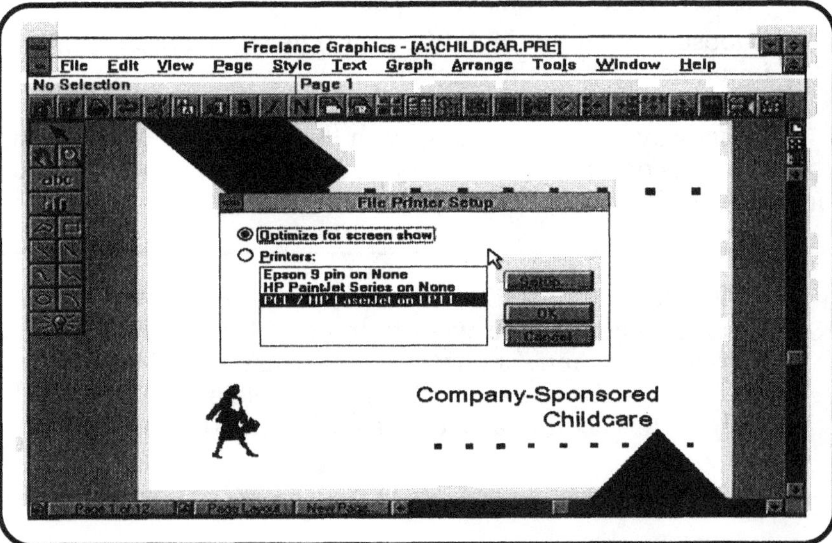

Figure 6.10 File Printer Setup dialog box for Optimizing a Screen Show.

Start the Screen Show by following these steps:

1. Pull down the View menu and select Screen Show (the accelerator key combination is Alt+F10) or click on the

SmartIcon (movie projector). The View Screen Show dialog box appears, as shown in Figure 6.11. This box gives you two basic options: `View from page: to:` (from a certain page to a certain page) or `Run show continuously`.

2. View from page: to: is the default—if you don't change anything, that's what it does. Running the show continuously might be an appropriate way to give your presentation at a trade show, but right now you want to view your show from beginning to end. Click on the Show button.
3. Enjoy the show.

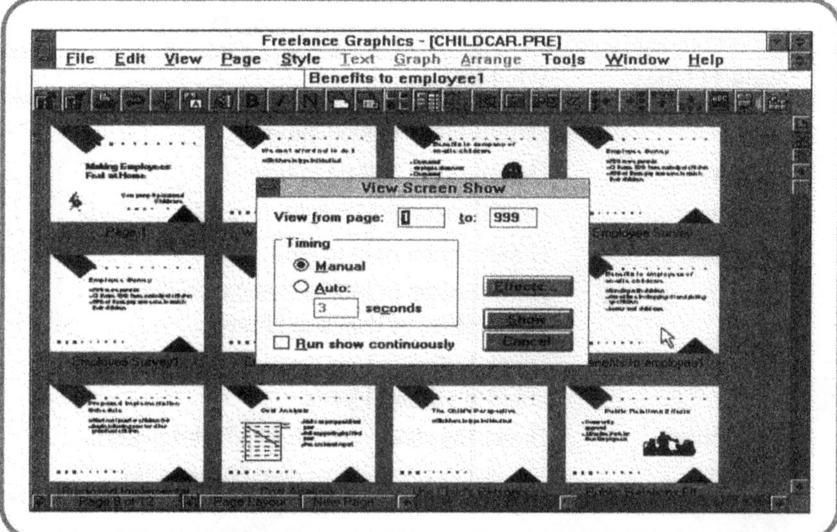

Figure 6.11 The View Screen Show dialog box.

Tip: You can start the Screen Show at any time by pressing Alt+F10.

FYIdea: A continuously running Screen Show is a great way to put out announcements. If you have a PC in the lobby of your building, for instance, you can use Screen Show to present the announcements in an attractive way.

Using Special Effects in Screen Shows

Movie special effects used to be for the Steven Spielbergs of the world. Not any more. You can add special effects to your screen shows; use them to add excitement to the viewing and to emphasize certain points.

A Screen Show's special effects are applied to the way the slide comes onto the screen. Unless you specify otherwise, a new slide replaces the previous slide, using the effect called *Replace*. There are, however, other effects you can use, as listed in Table 6.1.

Table 6.1 Special effects for Screen Shows.

Name of Effect	What it Does
Top	Draws screen top to bottom.
Bottom	Draws screen bottom to top.
Leftside	Draws screen left to right.
Rightside	Draws screen right to left.
Blinds	Draws screen in four horizontal sections, giving effect of Venetian blinds.
Louvers	Draws screen in four vertical sections, giving effect of vertical blinds.
Checkboard	Draws the screen in a checkerboard pattern.
Center	Draws the screen in a spiral out from the center.
Box	Draws the screen starting as a rectangle in the center.
Zigzag	Draws the screen in a zigzag pattern, starting in the upper left and right corners.
Hsplit	Draws the screen from both the top and bottom.
Vsplit	Draws the screen from both the left and right.
Replace	Redraws the screen from top to bottom very quickly (not really a special effect, but rather, the basic way to move to another screen).

Experiment with the special effects yourself. They are easy to use. To assign a special effect to a slide, follow these steps:

1. Choose View from the Main menu and then choose Screen Show.
2. Click the Effects button, which is the first button on the right side of the dialog box. The View Screen Show Effects dialog box appears, as shown in Figure 6.12.
3. In the box on the left side, click on a page where you want the special effect to begin.
4. In the box on the right side, click on the arrow to show a library of effects. Choose an effect.
5. Click on OK to return to the View Screen Show dialog box.

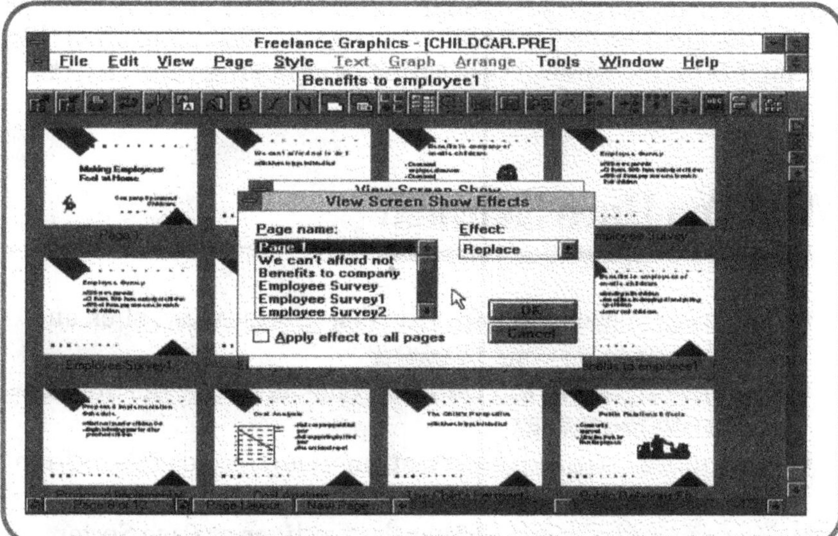

Figure 6.12 The View Screen Show Effects dialog box.

> **Tip:** If you want to have an effect apply to all the slides in a show, select Apply effect to all pages in the View Screen Show Effects dialog box.

In the View Screen Show dialog box, select either Manual or Auto. If you select Auto, each slide replaces the previous one in the interval specified in the seconds box (the default interval is three seconds). If you choose Manual, you click once on each slide to replace it with the next one.

> **FYIdea:** Most of the time you will want the slides in your Screen Show to replace one another quickly. To create suspense before a climactic slide, you might want to increase the time, perhaps up to 10 seconds. But don't vary the times often—only when you want to heighten the effect.

Have fun with special effects. That is their main purpose. Use them to surprise and delight your audience. To have them be a surprise, of course, you should use them at "just the right moment"—to call the viewer's attention back to the screen—rather than all the time. You'll be surprised, though, at how often you can use the effects; they look so professional, you can use them more often than you might think—without distracting or annoying your viewers.

What You Have Learned

- To change page order with the Page Sorter view, click and drag the page you want to move.
- To move a page in the Outliner, click and drag the Start Page icon with the mouse.
- To duplicate a page using Outliner view, choose Copy from the Edit menu (or use the SmartIcon.)
- You can add a page in either the Outliner or Page Sorter views. In the Page Sorter, select Page and then New from the Main menu. In the Outliner, move to a new line and (if necessary) press Shift Tab to get to the Start Page symbol.
- You can delete a page in the Outliner or the Page Sorter. If you delete it, however, you cannot paste it back in later (as you can if you cut it instead of deleting it).
- Running a Screen Show shows you how your presentation looks.
- You can add special effects to your Screen Show to create drama and arouse interest. Use the View Screen Show Effects dialog box.

Chapter 7

Printing Your Presentation Pages

In This Chapter

- *Adding headers and footers to your pages*
- *Setting the print options*
- *Printing your presentation as full pages, handouts, or disk files*
- *Printing in color or black-and-white patterns*

When you prepare a presentation, you may be thinking of preparing slides or of playing back a Screen Show for your audience—often, however, you have reason to print your presentation. If you are presenting overhead transparencies, you print them on your own printer. If you are giving out handout pages along with your presentation, you print them. Even for slides, you may want to print them so you can proofread them (and review them with others) before you prepare the actual slides.

In this chapter you find out how to add headers and footers—elements that show up only when you print the page. You will also see how to set up the printer for printing, print a single page or multiple pages, and print in color if you want.

Adding Headers and Footers

Headers and *footers* are text you add at the top (header) and bottom (footer) of a page. The header is located just below the top margin, and the footer is located just above the bottom margin. Use the headers or footers to identify your presentation and to provide other pertinent information.

You may want to include a title or description in the header or footer, as well as page numbers or dates. Freelance prints the headers and footers automatically and prints the page numbers sequentially. However, the headers and footers and their contents do not appear on the screen; they appear only when you print your page. The following Quick Steps summarize how to add a header and footer. The sections that follow the Quick Steps provide more details.

Adding a Header or Footer

Step	Result
1. Choose Page Setup from the File menu.	The File Page Setup dialog box appears (see Figure 7.1).
2. Type your header in the upper box and your footer in the lower box. Use the vertical bar character (¦) for aligning, the number sign (#) for page numbering, and the "at" sign (@) for dates or systems dates.	You see the header or footer typed in the box with appropriate codes.
3. Click on OK.	The header and footer are in place. They print when you print the page. □

You may include up to 45 characters in your header or footer. If you want the text of your header or footer to have more than one line, separate the text for each line with a tilde (~). For example, in the Header field you might type`Quarterly Report~Draft` to have the words appear on two lines. To place the page number in the footer, type`#` in the Footer field.

Freelance prints the text of your header or footer in 10-point Ariel MT type. You cannot change this typeface or size.

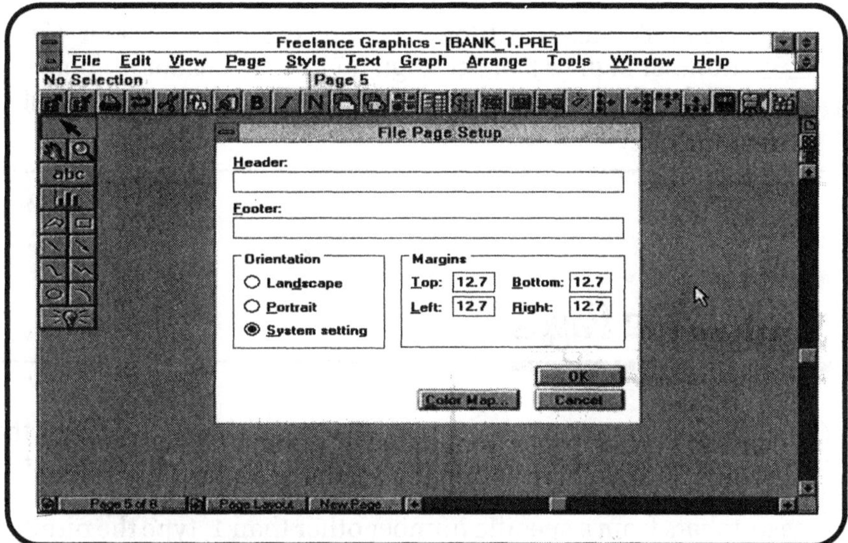

Figure 7.1 The File Page Setup dialog box.

Aligning Text Within Headers and Footers

You can set the text within your headers and footers in three positions: left-aligned, right-aligned, or centered. Unless you insert the vertical bar character (¦) before it, the text will be left-aligned automatically. Inserting one vertical bar character will center the text; inserting two vertical bar characters will align it to the right.

If you want your text to have more than one part and want these parts to be separately aligned, precede each part with the appropriate number of vertical bar character strikes. For example, in the Header field you might want to type the name of the report aligned with the left margin, the date centered, and the company name aligned with the right margin. To do so, type the information like this:

```
Quarterly Report¦@¦¦First American Bank
```

Note: To insert a tilde (~), vertical bar character (¦), number sign (#), or "at" sign (@) in the header or footer, precede the character with a backslash (\) to tell Freelance not to treat the character as a code.

Numbering Pages

You can have your pages sequentially numbered by typing the number sign (#) anywhere within the header or footer. If you type the symbol by itself, the page numbering starts at 1. To print sequential page numbers from a specific number other than 1, type the number sign twice (##), followed by the page number with which you want to start. For example, in the Footer field type **##2**. In this case, page numbering will begin on page 2.

Adding the Date

To print the *system date* (the date your computer's clock shows as the current date) in the header or footer, type the "at" sign (@) anywhere in the header or footer. The system date will appear in the format MDY (month-day-year) unless you specified a different format in the Tools\User Setup\International dialog box.

Setting the Margins

As you can see in Figure 7.1, you can also use the File Page Setup dialog box to set the margins and orientation for printing. (These are the margins for the printed page, as opposed to the margins for text within a text block.) The margin you set tells Freelance where to place headers and footers in printing.

To set margins in the File Page Setup dialog box, click in the text box next to Top, Bottom, Left, or Right or press the Tab key. Then type in the number of *inches* for that margin (the default setting is 0.50, which is 1/2 inch).

Orientation refers to whether the page is printed vertically (Portrait) or horizontally (Landscape.) The orientation you set applies to all the pages in a presentation. Vertical works well for most handouts because people are accustomed to looking at a page in this configuration. Horizontal orientation also works well for handouts—particularly if you have long lines of text or wide charts. For overheads, you can choose whichever you prefer.

To set orientation in the File Page Setup dialog box, simply click on the option button next to the orientation you want. If you click on System Setting, Freelance uses the orientation set up in Windows under Control Panel Printers.

Printer Setup

With headers or footers in place and margins set, you are almost ready to print the pages of your presentation. Freelance Graphics lets you print in many different ways, but first you need to make sure your printer is set up properly. This includes several considerations, such as:

- The brand and type of printer you are using.
- The degree of resolution you want (which affects the quality of the printout, and the speed with which it prints).
- The size of the paper you are using.

If you are uncertain about the type of printer you are using, consult your printer manual. The following Quick Steps summarize the setup procedure. You can also set orientation in the Printer Setup dialog box. If you set it in both places, Freelance uses the more recent setting.

Q Setting Up Your Printer

1. Pull down the File menu and select the Printer Setup option.	The File Printer Setup dialog box appears, as shown in Figure 7.2.

2. Click on the second option, Printers, and select the appropriate printer; make sure the selection matches your printer.	Your printer appears highlighted.
3. Click on the Setup button.	The setup box for your printer opens.
4. Check the default settings to make sure they are the resolution you want, orientation, paper size, etc. Make any necessary changes by clicking on settings options.	Changes you make will affect printing.
5. Click on OK.	The box closes with any new settings.
6. Click on OK to close the File Printer Setup box.	The box closes, and you return to the presentation. □

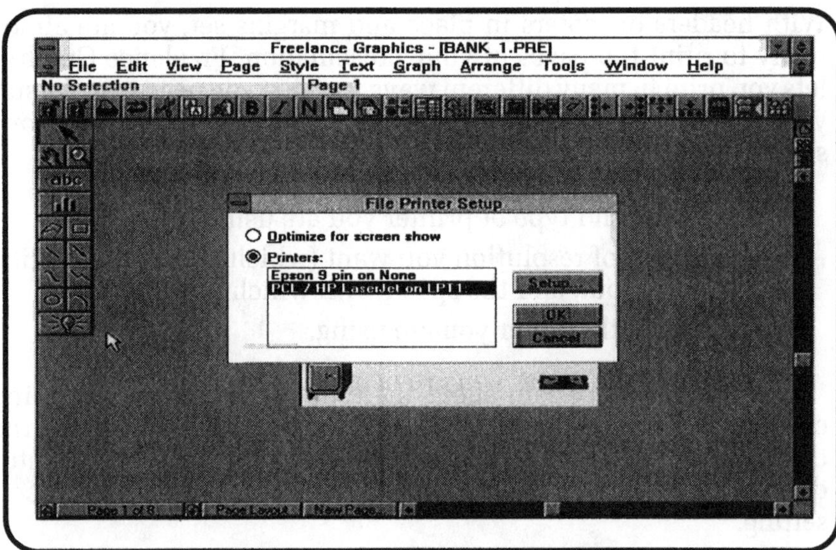

Figure 7.2 The File Printer Setup dialog box.

Note: If you switch printers during a session, Freelance Graphics will revert to the default printer settings (brand of printer, graphics resolution, etc.) the next time you open the program.

Seeing Your Presentation in Print

When you print, you have the option of printing only the page on which you are working, a section of the presentation, or the entire presentation. In addition, you have the option of printing either full pages or *handout pages* (special "overview" pages that contain two, four, or six pages from your presentation).

If you want to print from within the Outliner, you can print all or part of the presentation, but you cannot print the Outliner itself. To print from within the Outliner, choose File from the Main menu and then choose Print. You see the File Print dialog box, just as you would if you were in Current Page view.

Tip: If you want to print a SmartMaster set, you must turn its pages into presentation pages first (because choosing File and then Print will not print blank SmartMaster pages). To make this change, follow these steps:

1. Apply each SmartMaster page in a SmartMaster set to a blank presentation page.
2. Print the entire presentation.

Placement blocks and prompt text in SmartMaster text blocks will not be printed if you print with this method, but you will be able to print a SmartMaster set for reference.

Printing Only the Current Page

Printing the current page only lets you check the text or graphics in "hard copy" form, show the page to a colleague, or excerpt a particular page from a presentation for distribution. To print the current page, use the following Quick Steps.

Printing the Current Page Only

1. Display the page you want to print in the Current Page view or click on the page in the Page Sorter view.	If more than one page is selected in the Page Sorter view, the program prints the page whose title is displayed in the Edit Line.
2. Pull down the File menu and select Print.	The File Print dialog box appears, as shown in Figure 7.3. In the top section of the box, three options are displayed: `Number of copies`, `From page: to:`, and `Current presentation page only`.
3. Click on the Current presentation page only box.	An `X` appears in the selection box.
4. Move the mouse pointer to the bottom of the dialog box and click on Print.	After you print, `Current presentation page only` will be automatically deselected. □

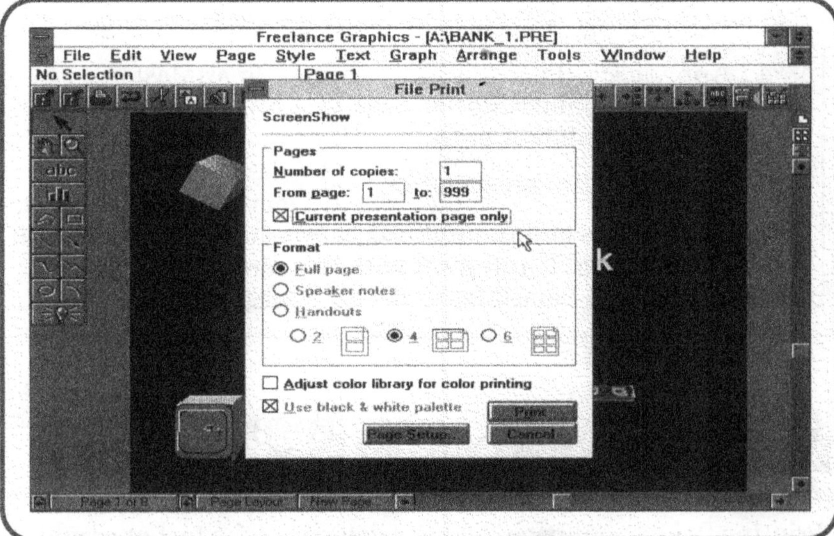

Figure 7.3 The File Print dialog box, with the Current presentation page only option selected.

Printing a Section or All of Your Presentation

Often you do not want to print an entire presentation. Perhaps you want to print just a series of graphs or a single graph to allow viewers to look at the information up close. Perhaps you want to print a single page so that you can proofread it. To print a section (page range) of your presentation, follow these steps:

1. Pull down the File menu and select Print.
2. In the File Print dialog box, click on the From page: box and set the starting number; then click on the to: box and set the ending page number of the section (page range) you want to print. For example, if you want to print from page 5 to page 8, enter **5** in the From page: box and **8** in the to: box, as shown in Figure 7.4.
3. Click on the Print button.

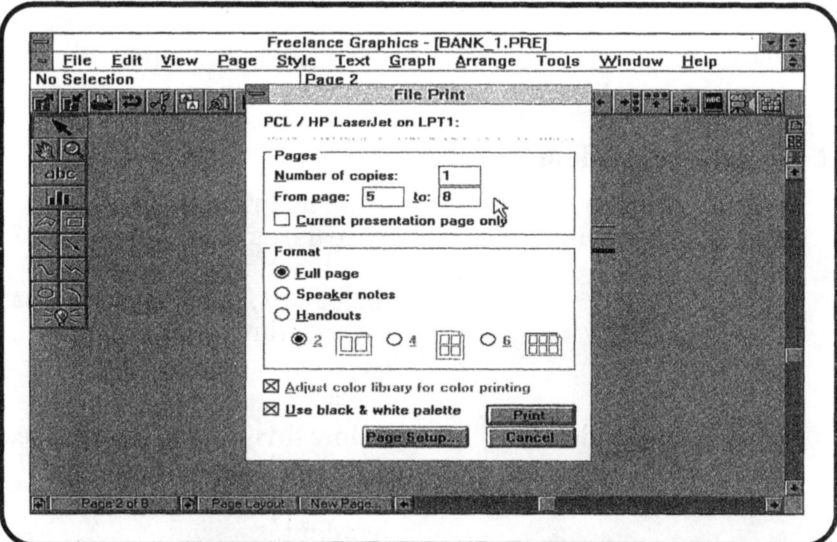

Figure 7.4 Choosing a starting and ending page number.

To print your entire presentation, set the starting page number at **0** and leave the ending page number at **999**. Freelance Graphics will start printing at page 1 and print until the end of your presentation.

Printing Handouts

You may want to distribute *handouts* to your audience before, during, or after the presentation; handouts allow them to get an overview of your presentation, follow its main points, or review its contents later. Each handout sheet can hold two, four, or six pages from your presentation. You will have to determine how many presentation pages per handout sheet will be most effective and appropriate. If your presentation has complex graphics and detailed text, probably no more than two pages printed on each handout sheet would be best. If your presentation has simple graphics and short text, you may be able to print six pages of presentation text on each handout sheet without bewildering your audience.

Note: Freelance prints only the header and footer at the top or bottom of the printed page that corresponds to each handout sheet. The multiple pages represented on your handouts will not have their own headers and footers.

To print handouts, use the following Quick Steps.

Printing Handout Sheets

Step	Result
1. Pull down the File menu and choose Print.	The File Print dialog box appears, as shown in Figure 7.5. In the bottom section of this dialog box, listed under `Format`, you see three options: `Full page`, `Speaker notes`, and `Handouts`.
2. Click on Handouts.	Below this option you will see three grids, which represent two, four, or six pages per handout.
3. Click on the grid most appropriate for your handouts.	Your handouts are set to show the selected number of presentation pages.
4. Click on the Print button.	Your handouts are printed. □

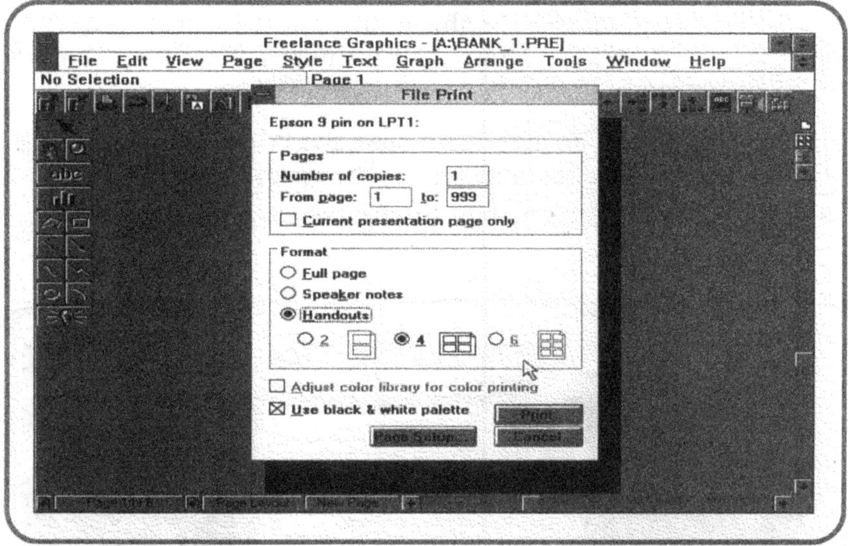

Figure 7.5 Printing handouts from the File Print dialog box.

Use handouts liberally. They are a separate medium from your slides, overheads, or screen show. They reinforce your message. Even for a brief presentation to a small group (even to one person), create a handout with two pages per handout. Encourage your listeners to make notes on the handouts as you present.

> **FYIdea:** The name "handout" suggests that the printed pages accompany a main presentation. For some situations (such as an intimate presentation to close associates), however, you can use the handouts in place of the presentation. They convey your main ideas quickly and informally.

Printing in Color

Freelance Graphics can print your presentation in color or black and white. For color, you have a number of *palettes* that allow you to use up to 256 colors in a single presentation. This range of colors is called the *color library*. Each palette contains 18 colors that go well together.

Although Freelance Graphics allows you to use up to 256 colors in a single presentation, your color printer may not print the exact color displayed on the screen. If this is the case:

1. Pull down the File menu and open the Print item. The Tools File Print dialog box appears, as shown in Figure 7.6.
2. Make sure the Adjust color library for color printing box is selected.

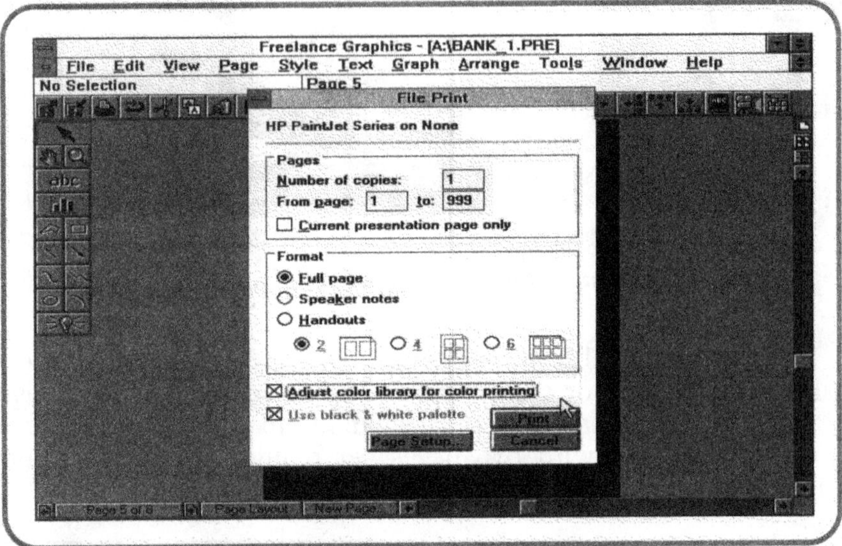

Figure 7.6 The Adjust color library for color printing box is selected.

When `Adjust color library for color printing` is set to `on`, Freelance Graphics attempts to compensate for any discrepancies between the colors displayed on the screen and the colors your output device (printer) prints. This is accomplished through an alternate version of the color library. Try printing with this option in both the `on` setting and the `off` setting to see which setting produces the most satisfactory results.

Freelance Graphics lets you edit palettes to your specifications or create your own custom palettes. You may also edit any library color to any other color to meet your specifications. Editing colors and color palettes is described in Chapter 10, "Using Color Effectively."

Changing Colors to Patterns

If you print a color presentation on a black-and-white printer, Freelance translates the library colors to black, white, and shades of gray when you print. You can also use a *color map* to translate colors into black-and-white patterns so that several different colors are not represented as subtle shades of gray.

Note: Using a black-and-white color palette enables you to print these contrasting patterns in place of colors without having to edit colors. Open the Style menu and click on Choose Palette. (See Chapter 10, "Using Color Effectively.") Freelance Graphics automatically changes colors to patterns according to their location on the new palette.

Tip: You can use the Alt+F9 accelerator key combination to view printer colors or patterns on the screen. This key combination allows you to toggle back and forth between colors and contrasting black-and-white patterns.

To change the settings for translating colors to contrasting black-and-white patterns:

1. From the File menu, select Page Setup. The File Page Setup dialog box appears.
2. Click on the Color Map button in the bottom center of the dialog box. The File Page Setup Color Map appears, as shown in Figure 7.7.
3. If you want to set up your own patterns, click on the Use customized color map button. In most cases, though, the Windows settings are satisfactory.
4. Click on the patterns to the right of each color bar or on the arrows at the right of each pattern.

A box offering fifteen contrasting black-and-white patterns and None appears each time you click on the patterns or the arrows on the far right of the color bar. Figure 7.8 shows this box.

5. Click on one of these patterns to "translate" the color into a contrasting black-and-white pattern.
6. Click on the OK button to close the File Page Setup Color Map. The File Page Setup dialog box reappears.
7. Click on the OK button to close this box and return to the Main menu or to your presentation.

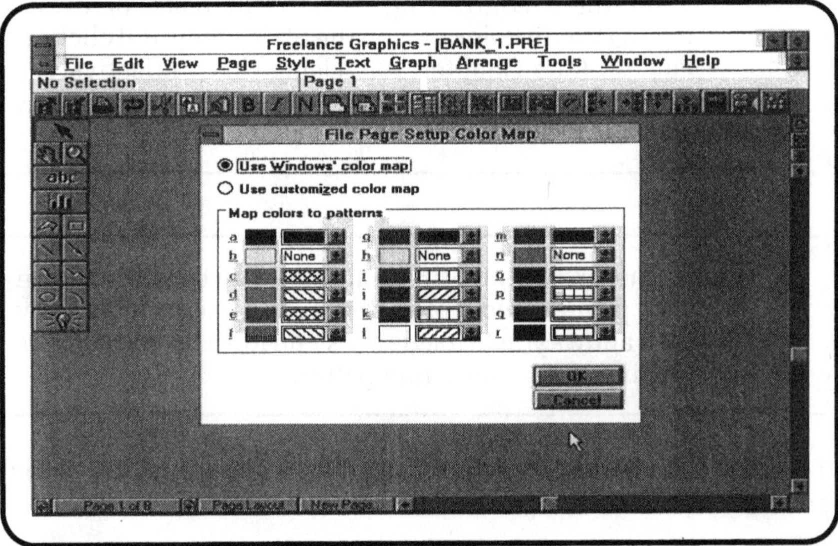

Figure 7.7 The File Page Setup Color Map.

You can also reach the Color Map through an alternate route:

1. Pull down the File menu and select Print.
2. Click on the Page Setup button in the File Print dialog box.
3. Click on the Color Map button in the File Page Setup box.

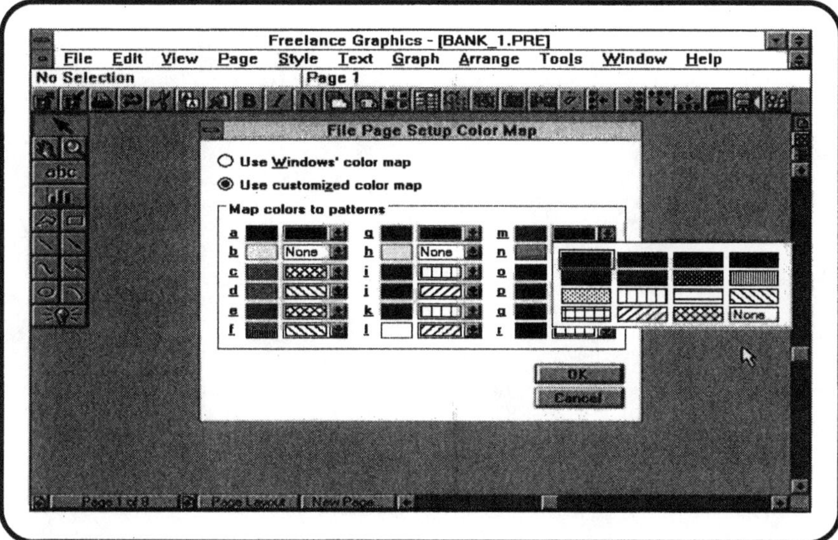

Figure 7.8 Color patterns.

What You Have Learned

- To type in a header or footer, type the text into the box in the Page Setup dialog box.
- Before printing the first time, check Printer Setup from the File menu to be sure you have the correct printer selected.
- You can print a single page, a selection of pages, or an entire presentation.
- To print handouts, choose Handouts from the Print option on the File menu.
- When you print in color, first select Adjust color library for color printing in the File Print dialog box.
- You can use a color map to print a color presentation so that it looks good in black and white.

Chapter 8

More About Text

In This Chapter

- *Creating stand-alone text charts*
- *Making quick, attractive changes to all the text in a text box*
- *Using multiple text blocks together on the page*
- *Placing text on top of predrawn symbols for a professional look*

In Chapter 4 you learned how to create a text chart using a SmartMaster page—and how to format the text by making it bold, changing its color, or changing its size. Once you become familiar with the basics in working with text charts, you are ready to think creatively about using text charts to get your message across in numerous ways.

Creating a Stand-alone Text Chart

At times you may create text charts as part of a series of text charts in a presentation. Often, though, you may want to create a *stand-alone text chart* (a single text chart for a single purpose). If you create a printed report, for instance, you may want to use Freelance to create a single title page for the report. You may want to use Freelance to create simple signs—"Company Picnic Changed to Tuesday, 3 PM" or "Librarians' Conference Here." If you speak about a number of main points during a presentation, you can use a single stand-alone text chart to make these points.

To create the stand-alone text chart, use a single SmartMaster page. Follow these Quick Steps.

Q Creating a Stand-alone Text Chart

Step	Result
1. From the File menu, choose New.	You see the File New dialog box, with the cursor in the SmartMaster sets text box.
2. Choose a SmartMaster set. For the example, accept the default, which will be the last one you used. (Because of the page type you choose in the next step, the SmartMaster does not show up in this case.) Choose OK.	You see the presentation on the screen with a Title Page SmartMaster displayed.
3. From the Main menu, choose Page and then Choose Page Layout. Choose None.	You see a blank page with no text boxes or prompts.
4. Click on abc in the Toolbox and drag the mouse on the page to create a text block.	You see a blank text block on the page with a ruler at the top. The cursor is in the block, and you are ready to type. See Figure 8.1.
5. Type your text. For the example, type **`Meeting Cancelled`**.	The text appears on the page.

After you have the text block on the page, you are free to use it just as you would use a word processor. If you want to use bullets, graphics, two-column bullets, or other choices available on a SmartMaster page, you should choose that page type at Step 3. (If you want, you can create the bullets and position the graphics yourself, but you save time and assure a professional look by using the SmartMaster.)

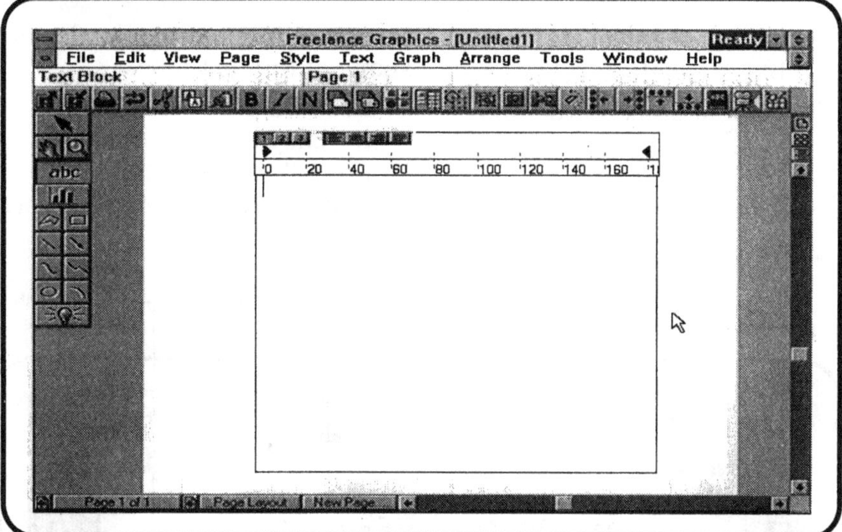

Figure 8.1 A text block before you add text.

Choosing the blank page, as you did in this example, shows you that you can have the versatility to do what you want with text charts—even if what you want is to create a very simple sign.

Formatting Text

After you have your text block in place (as in the example from the preceding section), you can work with it in many ways. You can have a SmartMaster do your formatting for you (often a good idea), or you might have some ideas of your own (for instance, big and bold text in a simple box) that require formatting.

You can format the text by selecting it and using the Text menu, much as you would in any word processor. If you want, you can format it in a quicker way. Follow these Quick Steps to use the Style Attributes Text dialog box.

Q Formatting Text in a Text Box

1. Click once outside the initial text block. — The box with the ruler at the top disappears.

2. Click once near the text block to select it.

   Selection markers appear in the shape of the text block.

3. Double-click on the text block.

   You see the Style Attributes Text dialog box, as shown in Figure 8.2. You can make all the changes there. □

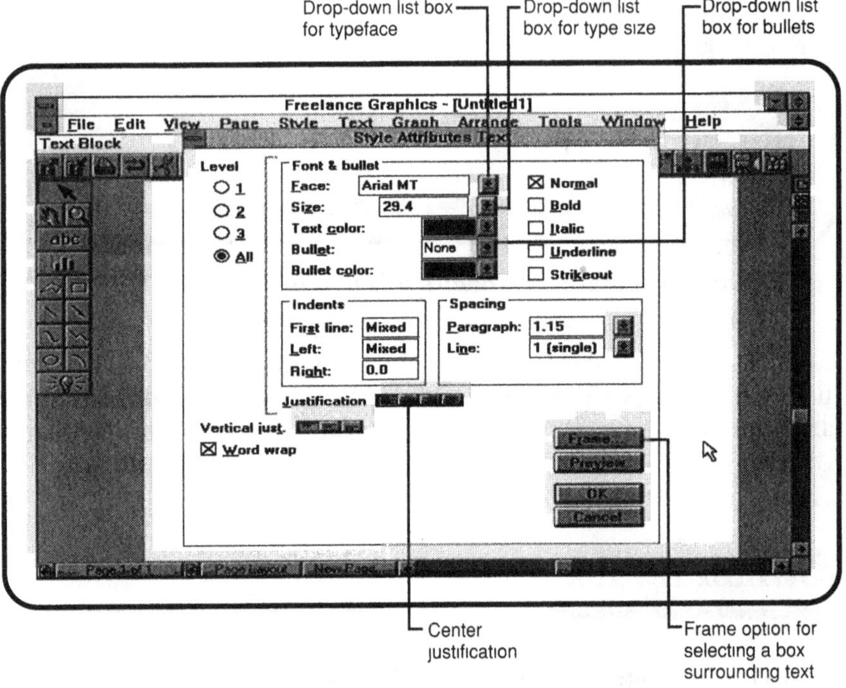

Figure 8.2 The Style Attributes Text dialog box.

Use your imagination to enhance the text in your chart. When you have artistic power at your fingertips, use it. For instance, you might choose Utopia Bold for the face. For size, you could choose 48. Why not add a bullet? From the Bullet category, choose the arrow (sixth down from the top). For justification, click on the button for Center (second button from the left, with centered lines pictured on it). Choose OK. Figure 8.3 shows the result.

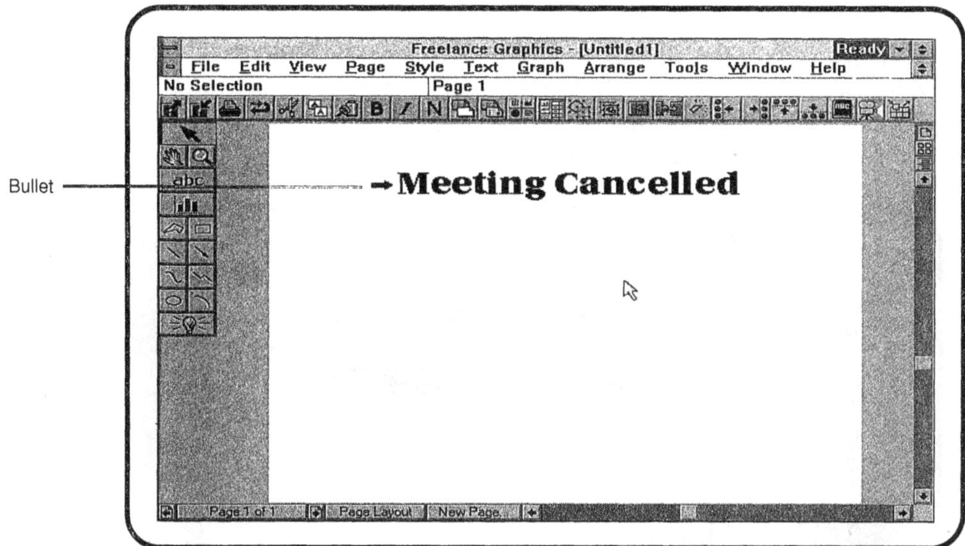

Figure 8.3 Sample text chart modified with the Style Attributes Text dialog box.

You can add a box around your text chart, too. If the text box is not selected already, click on it once to select it. Double-click to see the Style Attributes Text dialog box. Click on the Frame button at the lower right of the dialog box. You see the Style Attributes Text Frame dialog box, as shown in Figure 8.4.

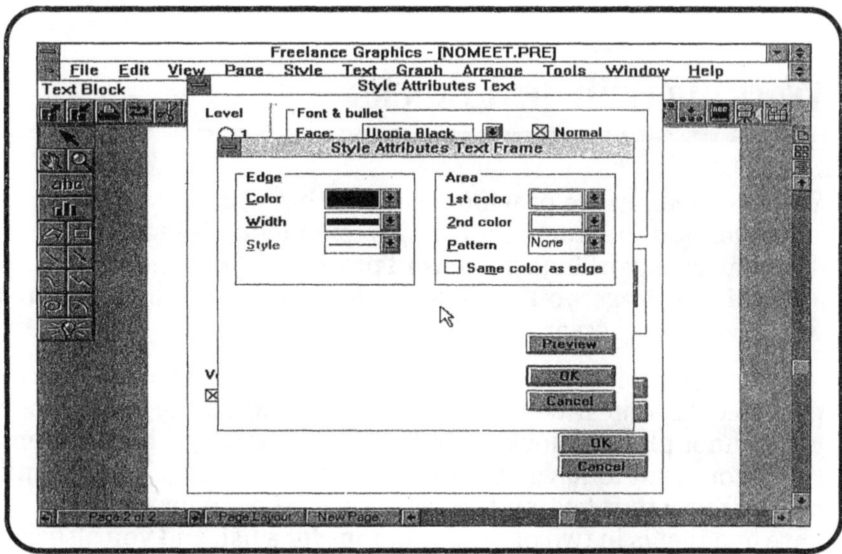

Figure 8.4 The Style Attributes Text Frame dialog box.

Choose a style, such as a solid line. Choose a width for the line, such as a moderately thick line. Choose OK to exit the second dialog box and then OK again to return to the page. Figure 8.5 shows the sample text chart with a box around it.

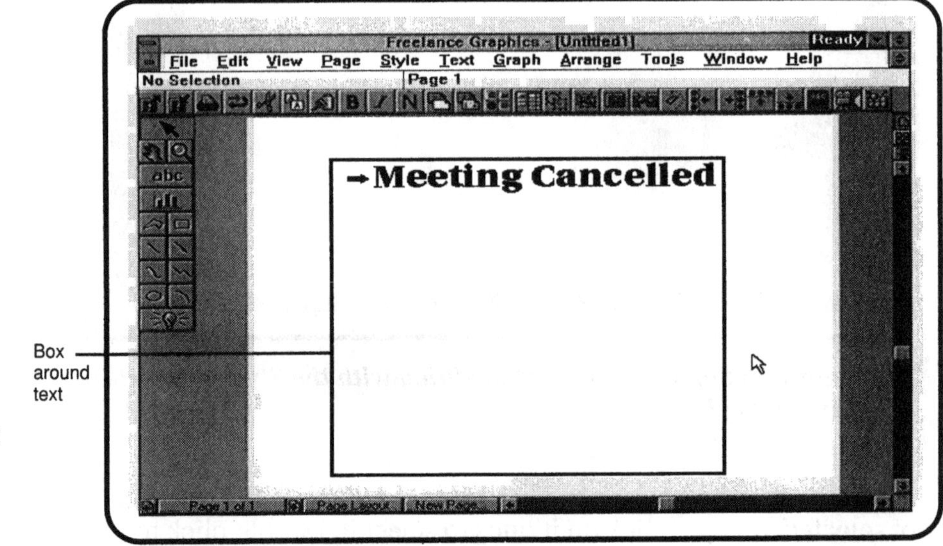

Figure 8.5 Sample text chart with a box around it.

Working with Text Blocks

You have seen in the previous sections that you can work with the attributes and the frame for a single text block. Doing so is not too different from working with a word processor. Freelance, after all, is a graphics package; you ought to be able to surpass what you can do with a word processor.

And you can. You are not limited to a single text block. You can place blocks almost wherever you want them on the page (though you cannot place a block entirely inside a previous block). Sometimes you want to have text on one part of your page differ significantly from other text on the same page. Maybe, for example, you have text that is in two or three columns for a list, and you also want to have a block of text that spans all the columns. You can put a text block at the top and assign it characteristics of its own (for instance, make it into a single wide, shallow column).

Any presentation is your opportunity to present your own commentary; it can appear on charts, maps, bulleted items in a list, or whatever you include within the presentation. You do not have to limit the commentary to spoken words as you present. Use text blocks to put your ideas on the page—and to remind you of important points you want to bring out during the meeting.

Suppose, for instance, you want to change the simple "Meeting Cancelled" notice from the previous sections into a reminder that a new meeting is to take place. You want the text in the reminder box to appear different from the main text. You can place it in a smaller box set to the side (as if you are whispering an aside to the viewer) and choose a typeface that looks like handwriting.

To create the new text box, follow the same steps you used for creating the original. Click on abc and then click somewhere outside the text box you already have. (If you click inside the text box, you once again see the ruler at the top and can add further text to the original text box.) For instance, you can add a text box with the words:

```
Don't worry, though. We've rescheduled it.
Adobe Room
11 AM
Tuesday, May 9
```

Figure 8.6 shows the result. (See Chapter 4, "Adding Text Charts to Your Presentation," for information about adding bullets to your message.)

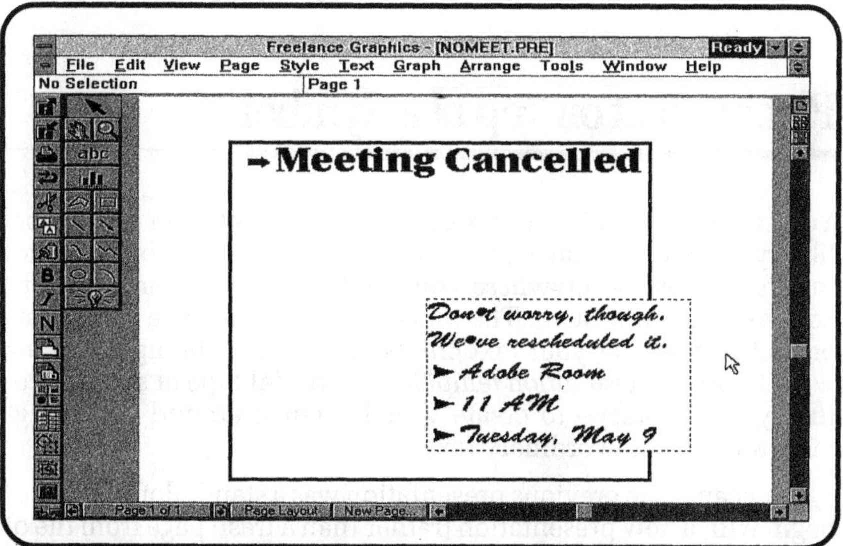

Figure 8.6 Text chart using two text boxes.

FYIdea: Separate text blocks can be a visually attractive alternative to bullets. Instead of placing your text items in bullets, try placing them in separate text blocks. Figure 8.7 is an example.

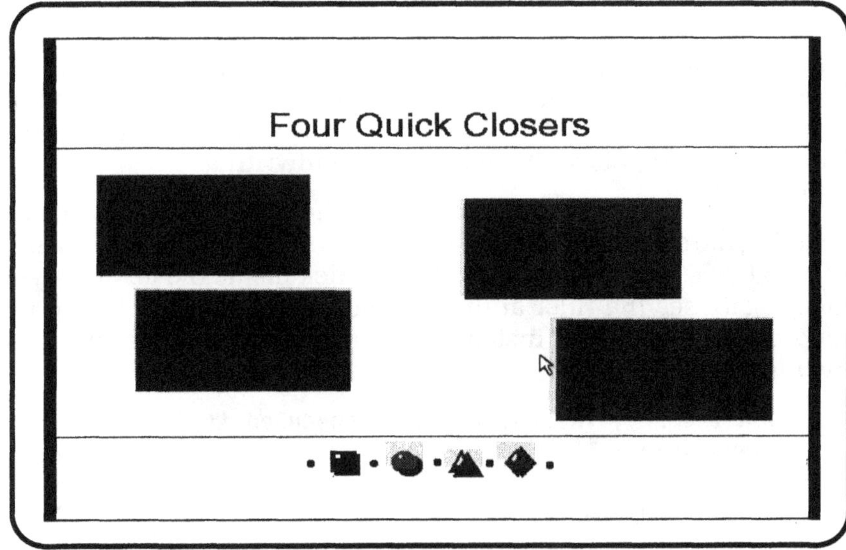

Figure 8.7 Text chart using text blocks instead of bullets.

Placing Text on Top of a Symbol

You can also add a text block on top of a symbol from the symbols library (or, for that matter, on top of a graph, next to a bulleted item in a text chart, or anywhere you want to provide some "editorial comment" of your own). The SmartMasters give you a broad range of backgrounds for your text charts. Sometimes, though, you may want to use a *presentation template*—a special type of symbol from the symbol library—to create visual interest around what might otherwise be quite ordinary text.

Because the previous presentation was a stand-alone text chart, begin with a new presentation (rather than a fresh page from the old one) for the next example. Choose New from the File menu and choose a SmartMaster (Buttons.mas works fine for the example). For Page Layout, choose Basic Layout. (You can use a symbol on any page type, but Basic Layout gives you room to put in a large symbol without cluttering the page.) Type in a title for the page (for the example, **`In Sales, Appearances Matter`**).

Once you are on the page where you want to use a presentation template, click on the light bulb symbol in the Toolbox. (You are familiar with adding symbols from Chapter 3 and elsewhere.) Follow these Quick Steps to add text to a symbol.

Q Adding Text to a Symbol

Step	Result
1. Click on the light bulb symbol in the Toolbox.	You see the Add Symbols dialog box.
2. Browse through the library of symbols.	In the Symbol text box, you see the actual symbols in each library you highlight.
3. Double-click on the symbol you want. For the example, choose hands.sym from the library and choose symbol 1 of 4.	The symbol appears on the drawing page.
4. Click on the handles of the symbol and stretch it to fill the screen (see Chapter 12 for details).	The symbol becomes the right size and proportion to be a backdrop for your text.
5. Click on abc in the Toolbox.	The cursor turns into crosshairs.
6. Click on the symbol at the position where you want the text box to start and then drag to create the text box.	The text box appears on the symbol.
7. Type the text.	The text appears on the symbol.
8. If necessary, adjust the size of the symbol (or the text box) to get the right look.	You see a symbol with text that satisfies you.

□

Figure 8.8 shows an example of a symbol with the text added to it.

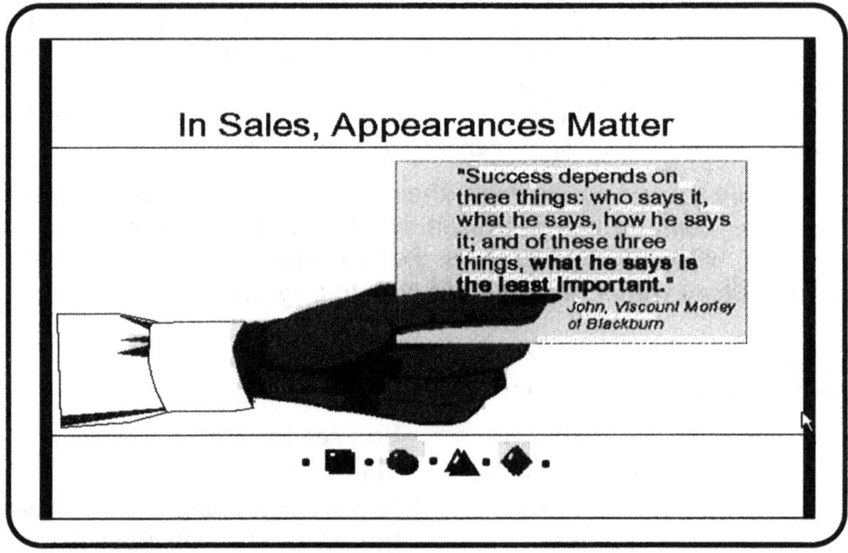

Figure 8.8 A symbol with text added to it.

You may have to drag the symbol handles several different ways until the symbol looks right to you. You will probably have to do the same with the text box. Placing the text box on the symbol is not an exact science, but it is no more difficult than dragging checkers back and forth on a checker board. You have more leeway than you might think. The tools you are working with are so professional, your results are likely to look that way—even if you're anything but a professional artist.

Use the technique of placing text onto symbols liberally. Some of the symbol libraries you can choose (and which work particularly well as presentation templates or backgrounds for text) are backgrnd.sym, diagram.sym, hands.sym, offobjct.sym, presentn.sym, puzzle.sym, and textbox.sym.

For instance, you can place your words on a picture of an easel and put in a human figure pointing to the words. You can put the words on the side of a manila folder, on a sheet of paper tacked to a wall, across a map, on pieces of a puzzle, on a computer screen, or on anything else you can find a symbol for.

Combine a SmartMaster background with this technique of placing text on top of symbols, and you will create page after page of images that look just like the kind available from the expensive slide services. Yours will look the same because they *are* the same.

FYIdea: Placing text on top of symbols is a great way to show the flow of information or present other concepts. For instance, choose one of the diagrams from the diagram.sym library and add words to create a *concept chart*. Figure 8.9 shows one of many possible examples.

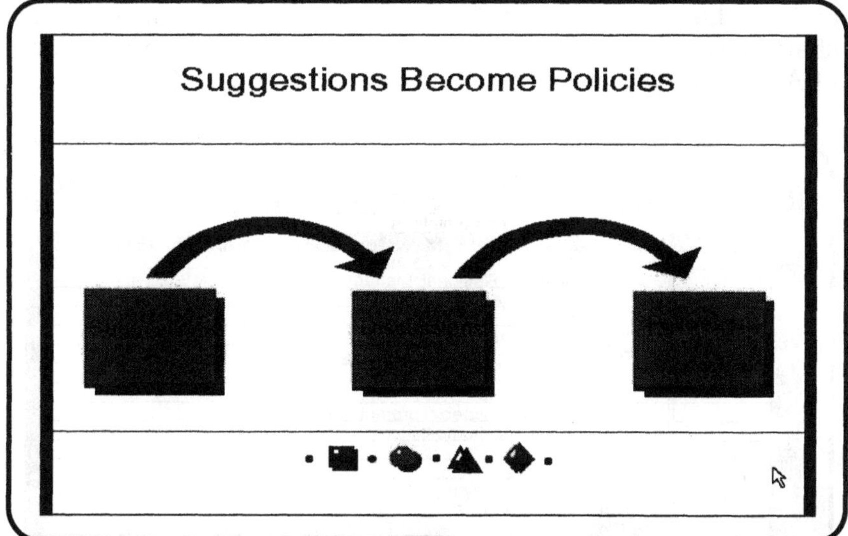

Figure 8.9 Sample concept chart taken in Screen Show view.

Creating Text Charts with the Outliner

Earlier in this chapter, you saw how to work with your text charts as visual objects. That is, you saw how to work with text blocks on the page and with symbols. When you work with text, however, you work, for the most part, with the *meaning* of words. If you use the Outliner to create your text charts, you can concentrate on meaning just as completely as you would if you were working on a yellow legal pad. The words you place on the Outliner automatically appear on the presentation page.

In Chapter 3 you saw how to add and edit text in the Outliner, how to move the cursor there, how to add and delete pages, and how to promote and demote text. Put these and additional skills to use to make the Outliner your primary way to create text charts.

Suppose, for instance, you want to create a presentation called "How to Increase Franchise Sales" with the subtitle "Suggestions for Regional Managers." Click on the Outliner icon (the third one down from the right on the right side of the screen). You see a blank yellow pad on the screen. Figure 8.10 shows a presentation using text charts based on the Outliner. (The name of the presentation is FRANCHIS.PRE, and it uses the blocks.mas SmartMaster.)

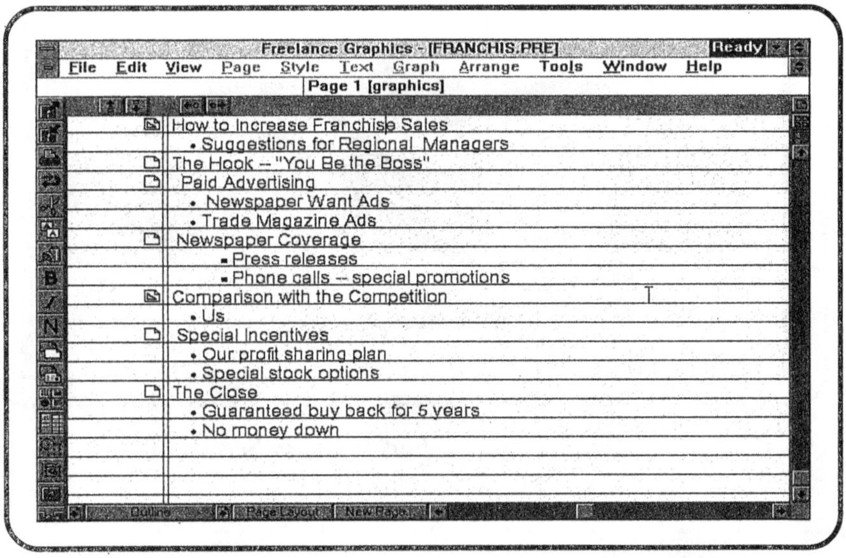

Figure 8.10 Sample text charts in Outliner view.

To create comparable presentations of your own, just type in the text. You can move slides around, add and delete text, and—above all—concentrate on your ideas themselves.

Although the Outliner is a powerful tool for developing your text, there are advantages to being able to go back and forth quickly between the Outliner and the Current Page view.

- ► In the Outliner mode, you cannot assign text attributes, such as bold or italic type. You have to switch back to the Current Page view to do that.

- In the Outliner, you can work with only three levels of text for each page. If you want more levels, you have to use the Current Page view.
- If you use bullets, the Outliner automatically limits you to using a one-column bullet chart. You cannot set up a two-column bullet chart in the Outliner. Nor can you assign a two-column SmartMaster page layout (or any SmartMaster page layout, other than Title Page or 1-Column Bullets) in Outliner mode.
- In the Outliner, you cannot see symbols you have added to the page.
- You cannot print the outline itself. You can choose Print from the File menu. Freelance then prints all the pages, not the Outline itself.

The fastest way to see an Outliner page in the Current Page view is to double-click on the Start Page icon. Figure 8.11 shows the page titled "Paid Advertising" in the Current Page view.

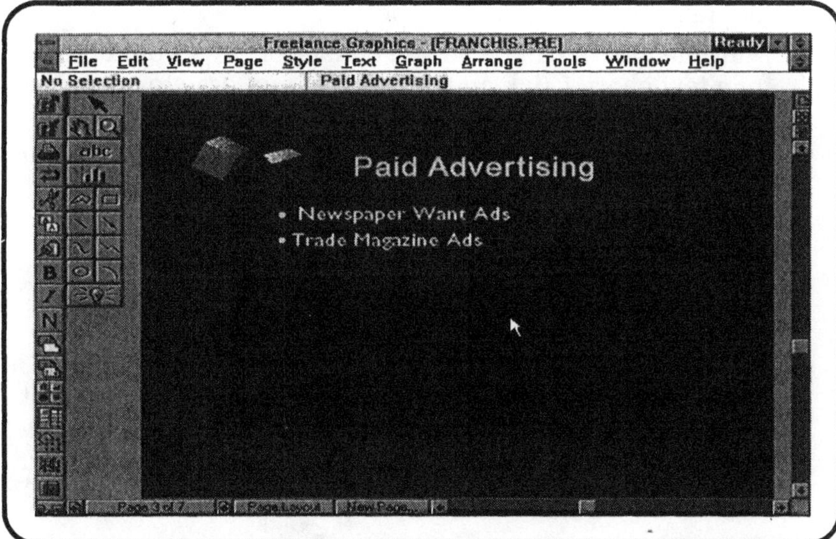

Figure 8.11 A page from the Outliner, shown in Current Page view.

Many of the restrictions you face in the Outliner, however, are virtues in disguise. When you are in the Outliner, you should think strictly about what you want to say and not think much about symbols or attributes; probably you shouldn't go beyond three levels of text because you will lose the view of the whole (and perhaps lose the thread of the presentation). After you put together the content of your presentation, you can switch to Current Page view and make as many visual enhancements there as you like.

What You Have Learned

- Stand-alone charts are great for everyday uses such as signs. Use a single SmartMaster page.
- To make wholesale changes to the text in the block, double-click on a text block and use the Style Attributes Text dialog box.
- Use multiple text blocks on the page to provide editorial comment on existing elements on the page. Click on the text tool (abc), drag a box, and type.
- Multiple blocks can be a good change of pace from bullets for a text chart. Click on the text tool and drag to create each text block. Then type the text.
- Typing text on top of symbols enables you to create finished-looking artwork, without having to do the "finishing" yourself. Add a symbol from the symbol library. Click, drag, and then type to add the text.
- Certain predrawn symbols are excellent for creating concept charts. Add the symbols and then put text on top of them.
- The Outliner is, in many ways, the ideal way to create multiple text charts. You can see the entire presentation at once, and develop it just as if you were working on a scratch pad. Click on the Outliner icon to switch to Outliner view.

Chapter 9

More About Graphs

In This Chapter

- *Creating stand-alone graphs*
- *Creating a Table Graph*
- *Placing multiple graphs on one page*
- *Combining graphs and text*
- *Creating an organization chart*

In Chapter 5 you learned how to create a basic graph in Freelance: choose your SmartMaster, enter your data, and let Freelance do the rest. Sometimes, however, you may not want your graph to be part of a presentation. Here you learn how to create a *stand-alone graph*. It is also powerful to combine graphs with other elements, such as other graphs or text; here you see how to do that. Finally, in this chapter you see how to prepare a particular, widely used form of graph—the *organization chart*.

Creating Stand-alone Graphs

In Chapter 5 you learned how to create a graph as part of your presentation. Instead of a presentation, what if you want to create just a single graph to accompany a report?

To create a stand-alone graph, first choose File New, then choose a SmartMaster set for your stand-alone graph. After you make a selection, start from the first page of a new presentation. On the menu bar, choose Page and then select Choose Page Layout. Then you can select 1 Graph or any other graph layout that suits your needs. When you choose OK, Freelance Graphics places the box for your graph on your page. Then you can continue to create your graph just as you did in Chapter 5. Follow these Quick Steps to review the procedure.

Q Creating a Stand-alone Graph

1. From the first page of a presentation, choose Page on the menu bar.	You see the Page menu.
2. Select Choose Page Layout.	You see the Page Choose Page Layout dialog box.
3. Specify the graph format you prefer and then choose OK.	A box to hold your graph is created on your page.
4. Click where it says `Click here to create graph.`	You see the Graph New Gallery dialog box.
5. Choose the type of graph you want and then choose OK.	You see the Graph Data & Titles window for your graph.
6. Enter your graph data and then choose Done.	Your graph and data are placed on your page. □

Suppose, for instance, you want to create a stand-alone pie chart to show how the budget for a company is divided among its departments. First, choose a SmartMaster and a Page Layout. (The example uses the finance.mas SmartMaster and the 1-Graph page layout.) Click in the box that says `Click here to create graph.`

In the Graph New Gallery dialog box, choose Single Pie. For Style in that same dialog box, choose the pie chart in the top left of the Style box. Then choose OK.

Now you enter the data in the Graph Data & Titles window, as you did in Chapter 5, "Adding Graphs to Your Presentation" (see Figure 9.1).

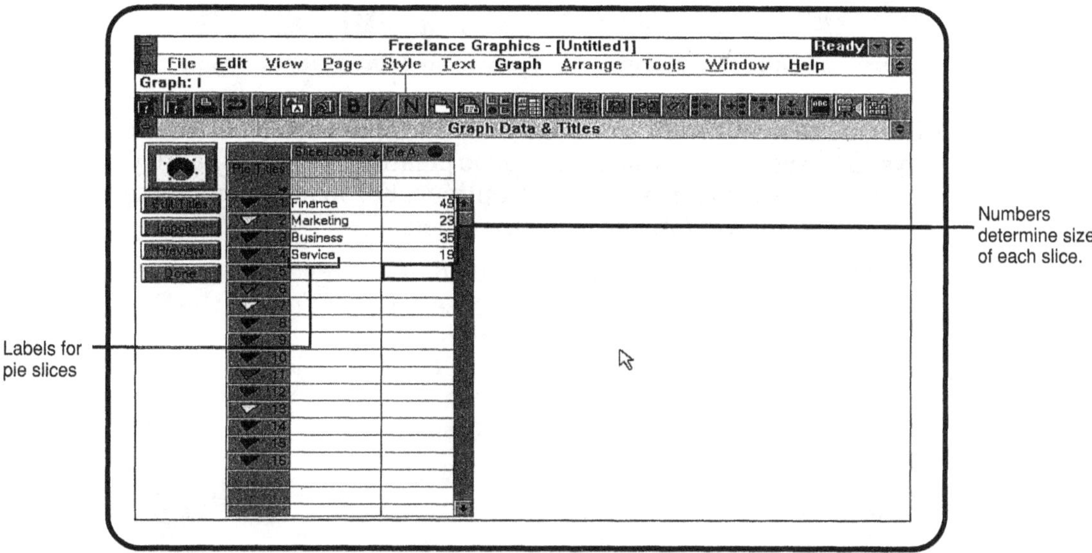

Figure 9.1 Sample Graph Data & Titles window for a pie chart.

Choose Done to display the graph. You see a basic pie chart. Click where it says `Click here to type page title` and add the title: **`Budget by Department`**. Click outside the box. Figure 9.2 shows the sample pie chart.

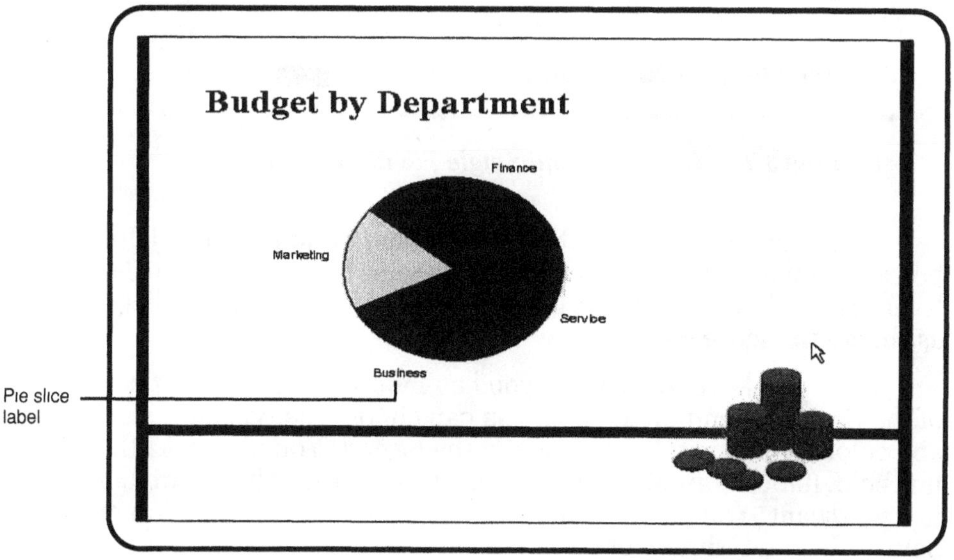

Figure 9.2 Basic pie chart created from sample data.

Enhancing a Graph with Legend Options

After you see your graph, you may want to "play with it" in certain ways. Once you become accustomed to creating the basic graph, you are likely to want to exercise your options. For instance, you might want to use a *legend* instead of slice labels.

Be sure that the pie chart is selected. If it is not, click on it once to select it. From the Graph menu, choose Legend. You see the Graph Legend Single Pie dialog box, as shown in Figure 9.3.

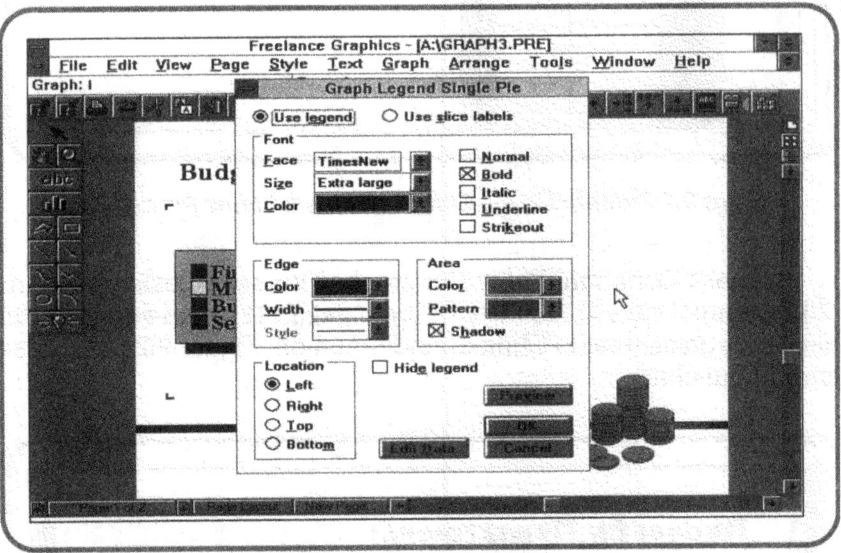

Figure 9.3 The Graph Legend Single Pie dialog box.

If Use slice labels is selected, all the other options in the dialog box are dimmed; that is, you cannot use them. If you click on Use legend, though, the pie uses a legend instead of labels for the slices, as shown in Figure 9.4.

Once you have the legend, you can modify it. In the Font box of the Graph Legend dialog box, you can choose the typeface, size, and color for the text that appears in the legend. You can make the text bold, italic, or underlined. You can have strikeout lines through it if you want. You can also have it appear in any combination of bold, italic, underlined, or strikeout.

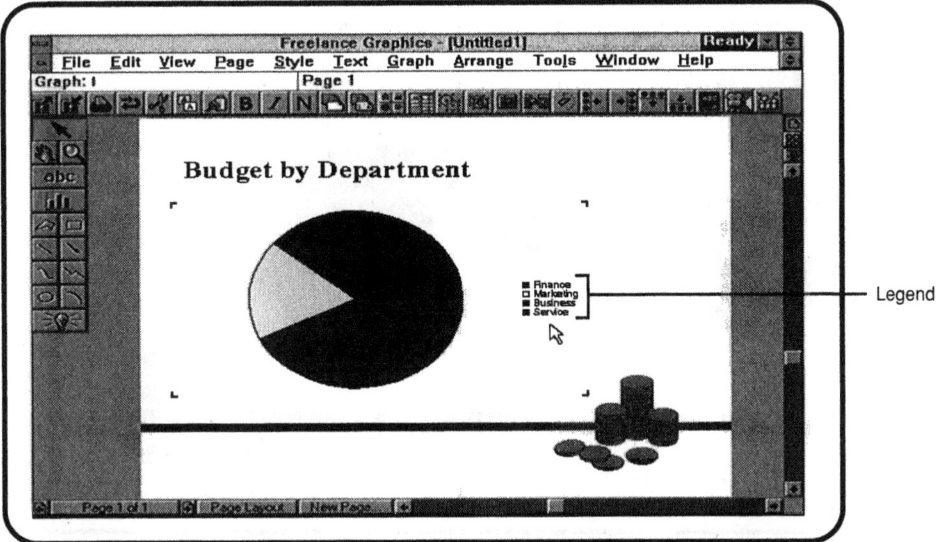

Figure 9.4 Pie chart with a legend instead of slice labels.

Besides changing the text for the legend, you can change the characteristics of the lines that outline the legend. In the Edge box, you can choose a color for the lines, a width, and a style (including a style of no line).

In the Area box, you can choose the color and background pattern of the legend area, and you can even have the legend box appear with a shadow behind it. With the Location box, you can have the legend appear on the left, right, top, or bottom of the page. If you add symbols or text to the page, you may want to move the legend to make room for them.

You also can hide the legend if you want. You may wonder why you would create it just to hide it. The chances are you would not hide it on your stand-alone chart, but you might hide it if you used the same graph on a second or third page.

Experiment with the options yourself and see what they do. Figure 9.5 shows the sample graph with Times New Roman typeface, extra large and bold. The line around the edge is a solid line, medium width, in red. The Area is a solid pattern in gray. There is a shadow around the legend, and it appears on the left side.

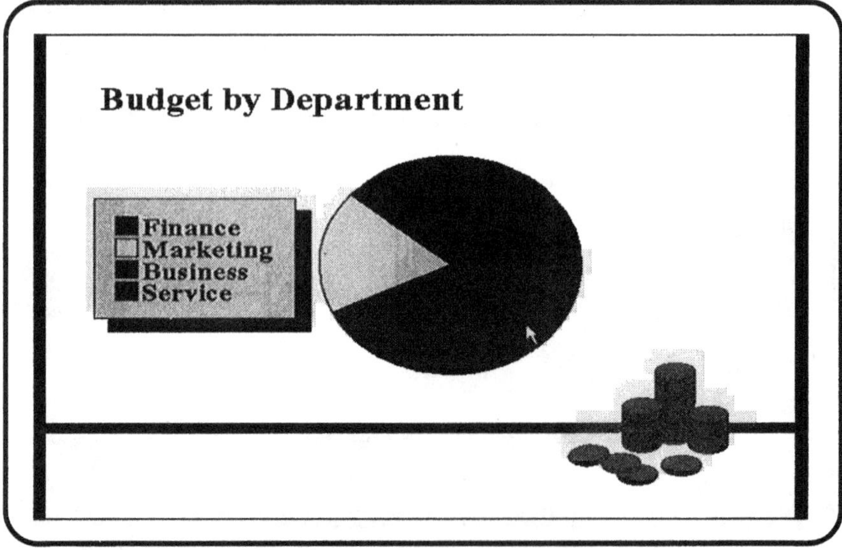

Figure 9.5 The legend with several options from the Graph Legend dialog box applied to it.

The point is that you can make such adjustments yourself—just for the fun of it, if you want. You may also make changes for practical reasons, such as to call attention to the legend (or away from it).

Enhancing a Graph's Axis Labels and Titles

On a pie chart like the one in the previous section, you cannot work with axis labels; a pie chart does not have X and Y axes. In bar charts and many other charts, however, you can enhance the axis labels just as you enhanced the legend in the preceding section. Again, you may not want to do so at first. It is enough to learn how to create the bar chart so that it reflects the data the way you want it. Once you know how to create the basic chart, you can experiment with enhancing it.

Suppose, for instance, you want to create a *stacked bar chart* showing costs for publicity over several years. Figures 9.6 and 9.7 show the Graph Data & Titles window and a basic graph created from sample data.

Freelance Graphics - [GRAPH3.PRE]

File Edit View Page Style Text Graph Arrange Tools Window Help

Graph: C | 16

Graph Data & Titles

	Newspaper	Television	Trade shows
1988	27	18	35
1989	29	14	37
1990	31	21	33
1991	33	24	40

X-axis labels

Legend titles

Figure 9.6 The Graph Data & Titles window with data for a stacked bar chart.

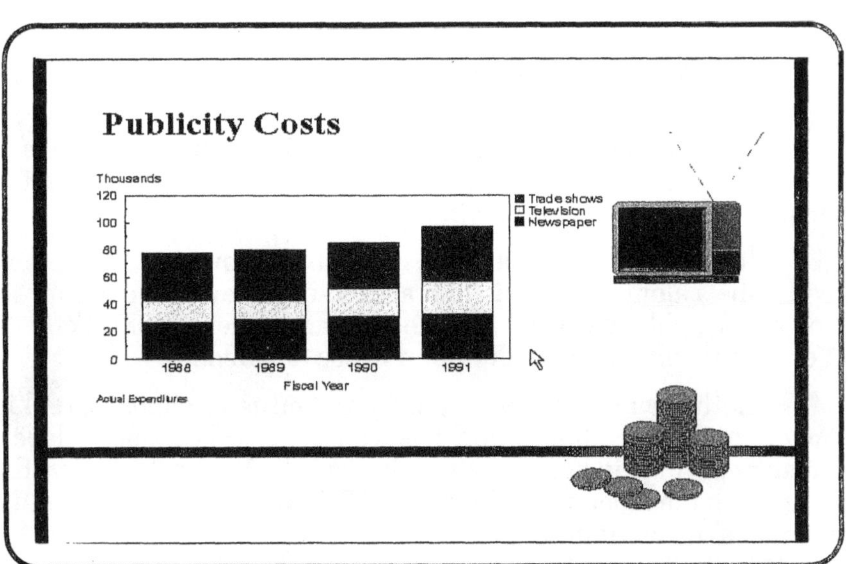

Figure 9.7 The stacked bar chart showing costs for publicity.

Just as you can enhance the legend, you can embellish other ingredients in the chart, such as the axis titles and labels. To modify axis titles and labels, first be sure the chart is selected. Then click on the Graph menu and choose Axis Titles & Labels. Then choose Labels. You see the Graph Axis Labels dialog box, as shown in Figure 9.8.

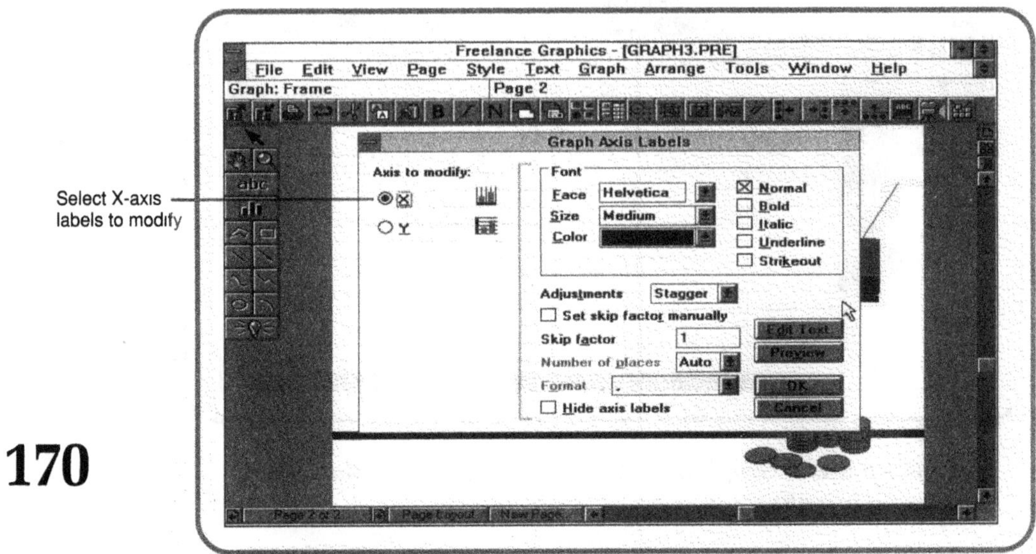

Figure 9.8 Graph Axis Labels dialog box.

You can choose to modify either the X-axis or Y-axis labels at one time. The choices for font are the same as those you saw in the preceding section for enhancing a legend.

The Adjustments area of the dialog box allows you to contend with labels along the X axis that are too big; they may overlap. To solve this problem, you can slant them, stagger them, or shrink them. You might want to try each option to see its effect.

Another way to solve a space problem is to choose Set skip factor manually. This option lets you specify how many labels Freelance will skip between those it displays. Figure 9.9 shows the chart with the label using the Ariel MT Bold Extra Large font and a manual skip factor of 2.

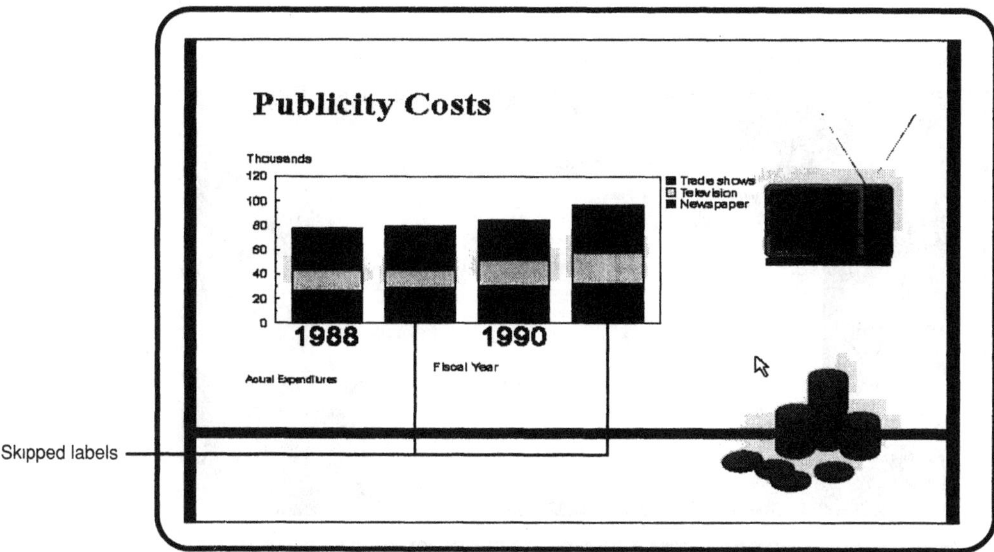

Figure 9.9 The sample chart using Ariel MT Bold Extra Large and a manual skip factor of 2 for the labels.

You also can modify Titles. Figure 9.10 shows the Graph Axis Titles dialog box. As with labels, you modify X-axis titles or Y-axis titles at one time; you cannot do both at the same time. The choices for fonts are the same as in the dialog boxes for legends or for labels. The one choice that may not be familiar is Rotation. It applies only to the Y-axis titles; if you want, you can have the Y-axis title be vertical instead of horizontal on the page. (Remember, however, that a horizontal title is easier to read than a vertical one.)

Modifying Graph Headings and Notes

If you have gone through the previous sections on legends and titles, you should have no trouble understanding how to modify headings and notes as well. Unless you have a reason for wanting one set of labels to stand out more than others—titles to stand out more than notes, for instance—you may want to modify all the kinds of text that appear on the page to make them consistent with one another.

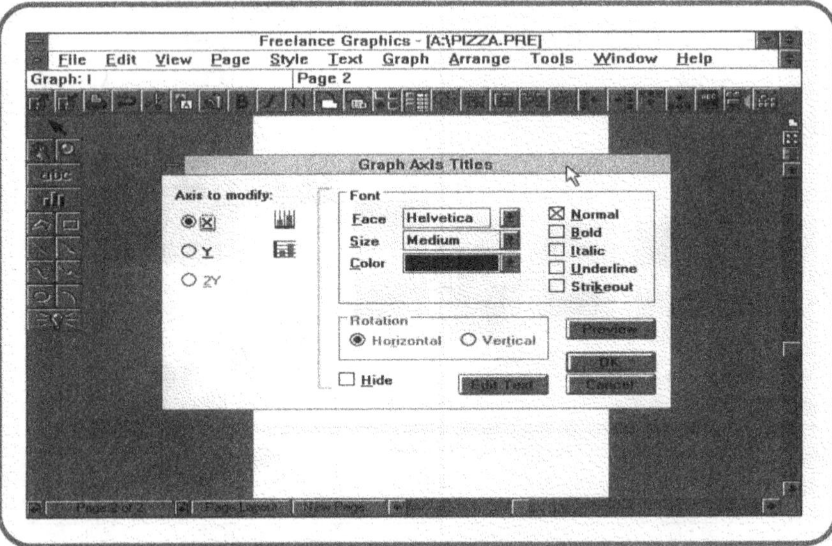

Figure 9.10 Graph Axis Titles dialog box.

Figure 9.11 shows the Graph Headings & Notes dialog box from the Graph menu. You use it to modify the headings and notes. The settings deal with fonts and with alignment (centered, left, or right). You can also hide the headings, which you might want to do in a series of charts after you have shown the headings and notes in the first chart of the series.

Creating Table Graphs

Freelance has a special type of graph called a *table graph*, which presents your data in a row-and-column format that is easy to read. To illustrate how you use table graphs, suppose you own an insurance agency, and you have enrolled your salespeople in a sales training program. You want to compare their sales performance before, during, and after the training. You decide to use a table graph to present the data. On the page in your presentation where you want the graph, click on `Click here to create graph`. You'll see the Graph New Gallery dialog box, as shown in Figure 9.12.

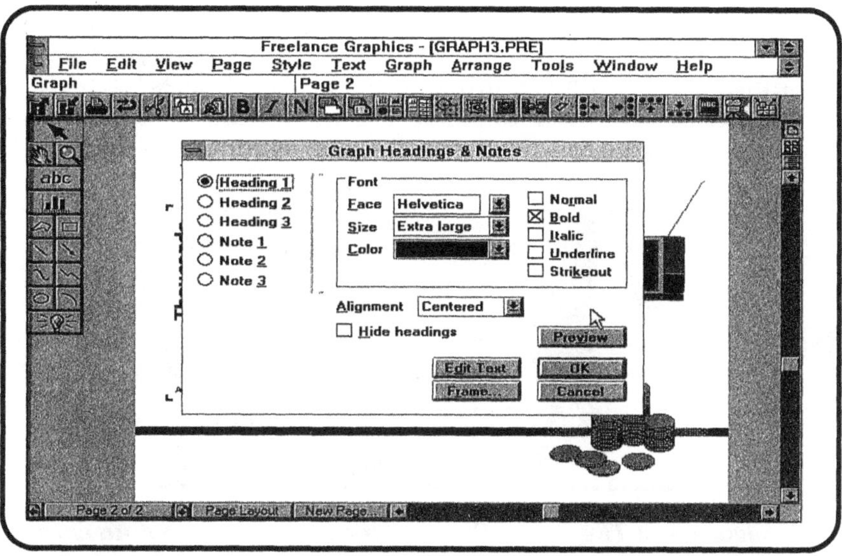

Figure 9.11 Graph Headings & Notes dialog box.

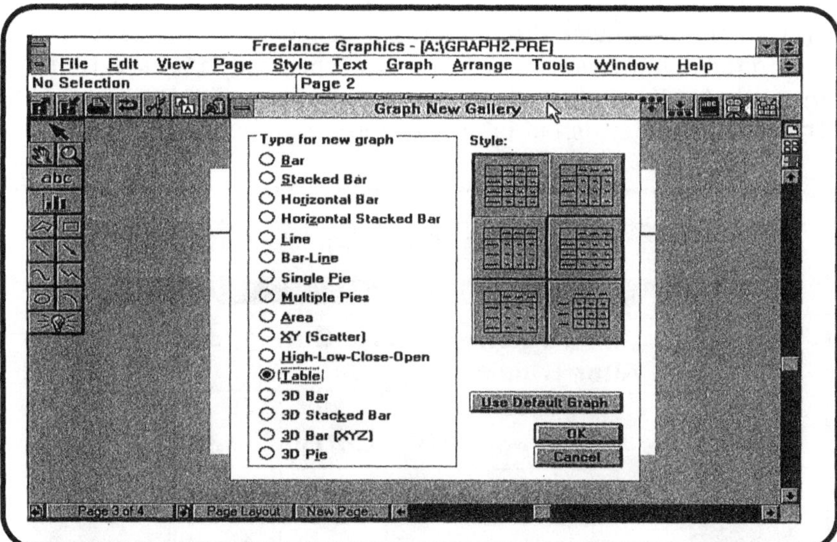

Figure 9.12 The Graph New Gallery dialog box.

Next, choose Table as the graph type. There are six table styles on the right for you to choose from; for this example, click on the one in the upper left and then choose OK. Then you see the Graph

Data & Titles window, where you fill in your data. This works just like the window you used in Chapter 5. You type in your column headings and your data, putting the name of each salesperson in the first column, followed by their before, during, and after sales volumes across the row next to each name, as shown in Figure 9.13.

Graph Data & Titles

	Tom	Larry	Dawn
Before	8000	8500	9900
During	9400	9500	12000
After	10000	9900	13000

Figure 9.13 The Graph Data & Titles window with data entered for an insurance agency's table graph.

After you finish entering the data in each row, click on Done, and Freelance places the table on your page. On the SmartMaster page, click where it says `Click here to type page title` and then type in a title for the graph: **`Sales Volume Before, During, and After Training`**. Your finished table will look like the one in Figure 9.14.

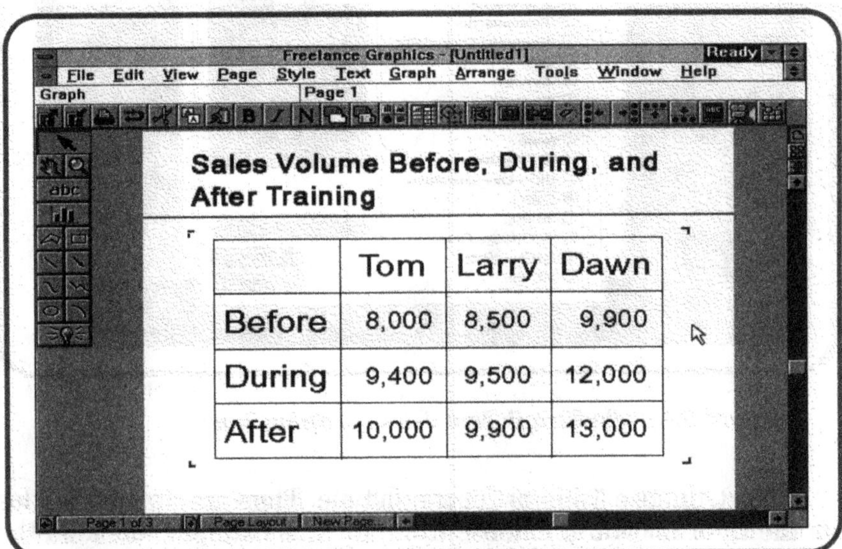

Figure 9.14 The completed table graph.

The following Quick Steps summarize the process of setting up table graphs.

Creating a Table Graph

1. Click on the page where it says `Click here to create graph.`	You see the Graph New Gallery dialog box.
2. Choose Table as the Graph type. Choose a table style and then click on OK.	You see the Graph Data & Titles window.
3. Type in your data and headings. Click on Done.	Your table is placed on your page.
4. Click where it says `Click here to type page title` and then type the title.	The title appears, completing the page.

Multiple Graphs

There are situations where displaying more than one graph per page may be very effective. In the example, suppose you want to compare the performance of the three candidates before, during, and after training. You could display the table so that you have the raw statistics. But you could also display the data in a *line chart* at the same time. That way you could refer to the table for the numbers and to the graph to see overall trends. To demonstrate all this data at a glance, you may decide to put two graphs on one page.

First, choose Page and then New to bring up the presentation page that will hold the graphs. In the Page New dialog box, choose 2 Graphs (See Figure 9.15).

Freelance Graphics makes a page with two graph boxes for you to use, as shown in Figure 9.16.

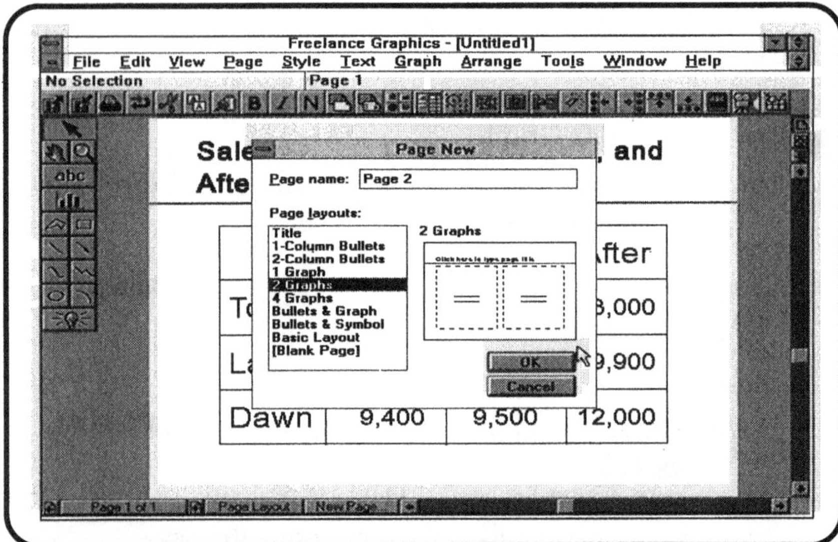

Figure 9.15 Choose 2 Graphs from the Page layouts box.

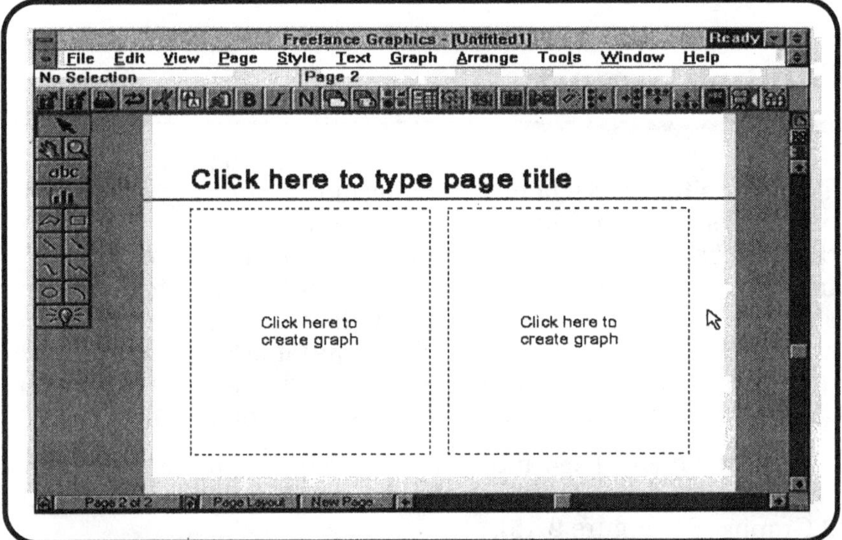

Figure 9.16 A blank two-graph SmartMaster page.

Click at the top where it says `Click here to type page title` and type a title—**`Comparative Sales of Trainees`**. To make your first graph, you follow the usual graphing procedure:

1. Click on the page at the prompt `Click here to create graph`. In this case, click on one of the two prompts—the left box. The Graph New Gallery dialog box appears.
2. Specify the type and style of your graph.
3. Click on OK.

You want to use the table graph format to display the data on the salespeople. Create this table as you did in the preceding section. When you click on Done, your graph is displayed on the page. It is sized automatically to fit, as shown in Figure 9.17.

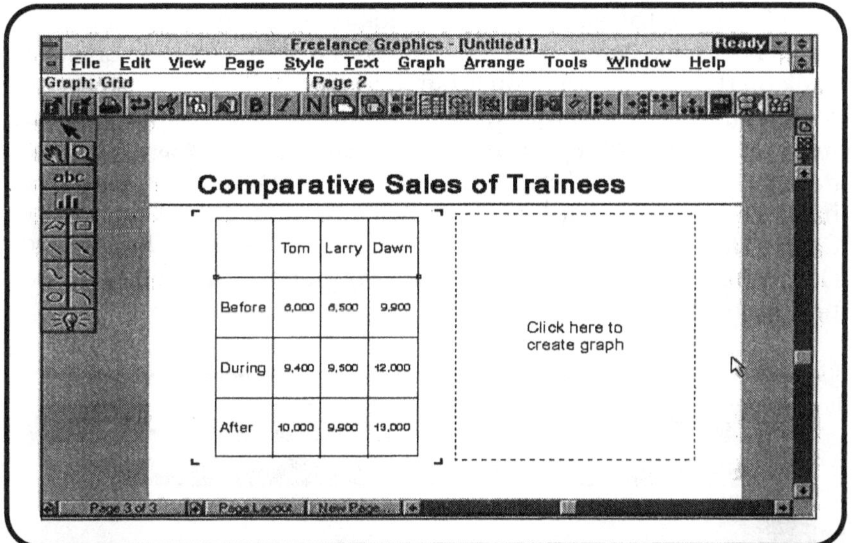

Figure 9.17 The first graph on a two-graph page.

For the example, you can copy the data from the previous graph. Use the Page indicator arrow to return to the preceding page. Click on the graph to select it and then choose Graph. Choose Edit Data & Titles. You see the Graph Data & Titles window you used before.

Click on one of the shaded cells in the top left, hold down the mouse button, and drag the highlight to the bottom right of the data. All your data should now be highlighted. From the Edit menu, choose Copy (or click on the Copy SmartIcon). You have now placed all the data in the Windows Clipboard. Choose Done to close the Graph Data & Titles window. Click on the Page indicator arrow to return to the page with two graph boxes on it.

Click on the box where you want to copy the data—the one on the left. Choose Table for your graph type, then choose the Style in the top left (as you did for the previous example), and click on OK. In the Graph Data & Titles window, place the cursor in the same box where you placed it to begin your copying in the previous page. Choose Paste. Your date appears in the new Graph Data & Titles window. Then choose Done. Now you have copied the data without having to retype it.

If a graph is not in the box that says `Click here to create graph`, you can select and copy the completed graph from one page to another.

To create the second graph, click on the page in the other box that says `Click here to create graph`. For type, choose Line, then click on the Style in the upper left, and then click on OK. When you see the Graph Data & Titles window, place the cursor in the same cell in the upper left that you used before and again press Paste. If you have not placed anything else into the Clipboard since you pasted into the previous graph, Freelance copies the same data into the Graph Data & Titles window for the second graph. Then choose Done. When you finish, you have two graphs side-by-side on one page, as shown in Figure 9.18.

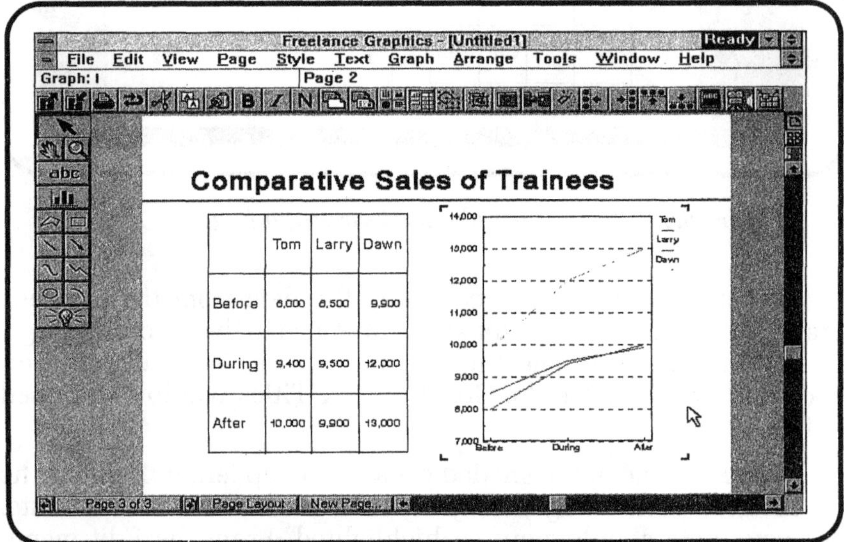

Figure 9.18 Page with two graphs.

The following Quick Steps summarize the procedure of creating and placing more than one graph on the same page.

Creating Multiple Graphs on One Page

1. On the Page menu, choose Page Layout. In the Page Layout dialog box, choose 2 Graphs or 4 Graphs for the layout and then choose OK.	You get a Freelance Graphics page with two or four graph boxes.
2. Click on the page where it says `Click here to create graph.`	You see the Graph New Gallery dialog box.
3. Choose the type and style for your graph and then click on OK.	You see the Graph Data & Titles window.
4. Enter the data and titles for your first graph. Click on Done.	Your first graph is displayed on the page.
5. Repeat steps 2-4 for each additional graph.	Your page holds multiple graphs. □

FYIdea: A table graph combines well with almost any other kind of graph. Tables in themselves take some time to decipher. Any time you have to present a table graph, ask yourself, "What other kind of graph can I combine with this one to best summarize the data it contains?"

Combining Graphs and Text

Graphs represent data pictorially. They tell you more than the raw data itself. In the graph in the preceding section, for instance, the numbers in the table were just numbers. The line chart interpreted them in a certain way by showing certain trends. Often, however, you want to make specific points about the data. You have to tell the viewer what is important about information in a table or in another graph. To do so, you can combine text and graphics.

There are two ways to combine text and graphs on one page. You can either select a page layout that has a bullet list alongside a graph, or you can use one of the other graph formats and then add text labels. For the next example, try the bullet list method first.

The data in the preceding example shows that sales performance improved after employees completed sales training. You might want to include, along with the graph, a series of bulleted points that describe the benefits of the training program. Follow these steps:

1. From the Page menu, choose New.
2. For page layout, choose Bullets & Graph.
3. Click on OK.

Your page is then set up with a bullet list on the left and a graph box on the right, as shown in Figure 9.19.

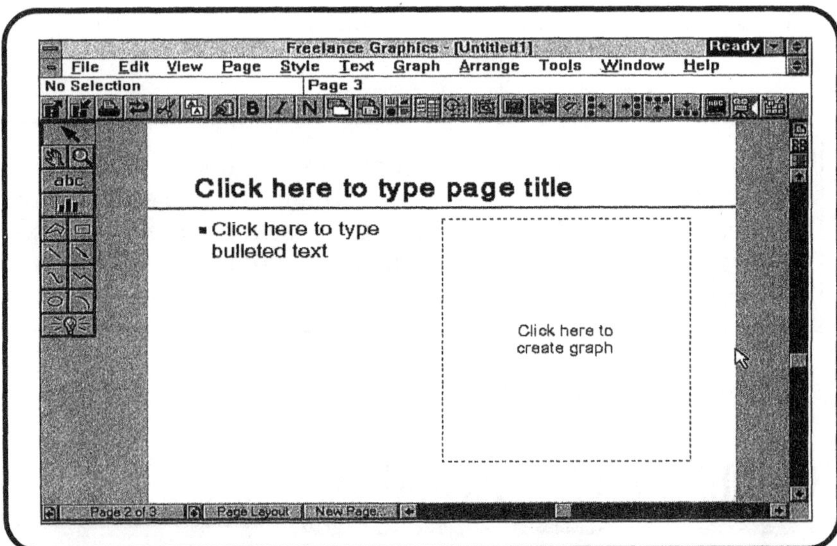

Figure 9.19 Bullet list and graph page layout.

To enter text in the bullet list, just click after the bullet and start typing. When you finish typing the text for the first bullet, press Enter to move to the next bullet. Continue until your bullet list is complete; then click outside the list.

To put a graph in your graph box, create multiple graphs on one page (following Steps 2 through 4 in the preceding Quick Steps) or copy a previously created graph onto the page. Your page will appear like the one in Figure 9.20.

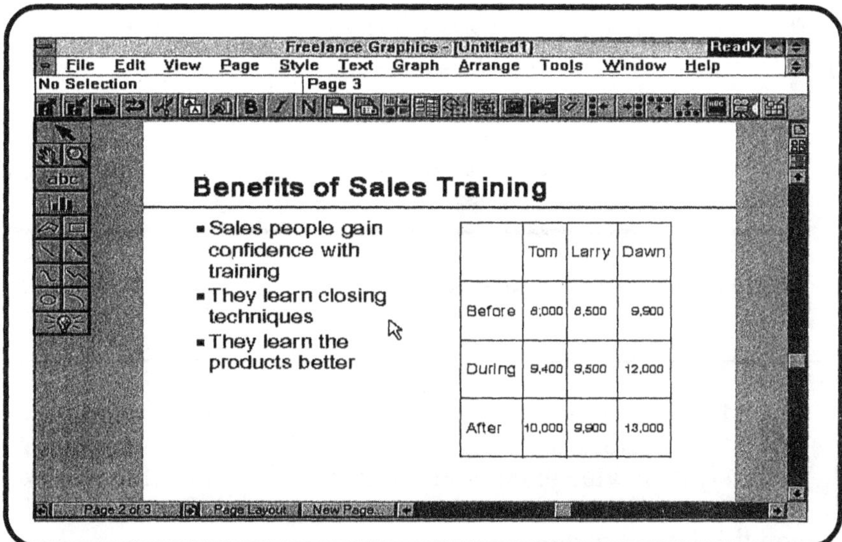

Figure 9.20 Bullet and graph page completed.

The second method of combining a graph with text is to add text labels to the page. To use this method, first create and place your chart on the page. (You can choose any of the Page Layouts—1 Graph, 2 Graphs, Bullets & Graph, Basic Layout, None, or any of the others. Your own additional text can supplement any existing chart.) Next, decide where you want your labels to appear. Click on the Text icon in the Toolbox to enter Text mode. Then click on the part of the page where you want your text to appear and drag the cross hairs to create a box for your text, as you learned in Chapters 4 and 8 on creating text charts. Type the text for your label and then click outside the box. The box disappears, and your text remains on the page. Figure 9.21 shows a chart that has been labelled in this way; text has been added to a page containing a table chart.

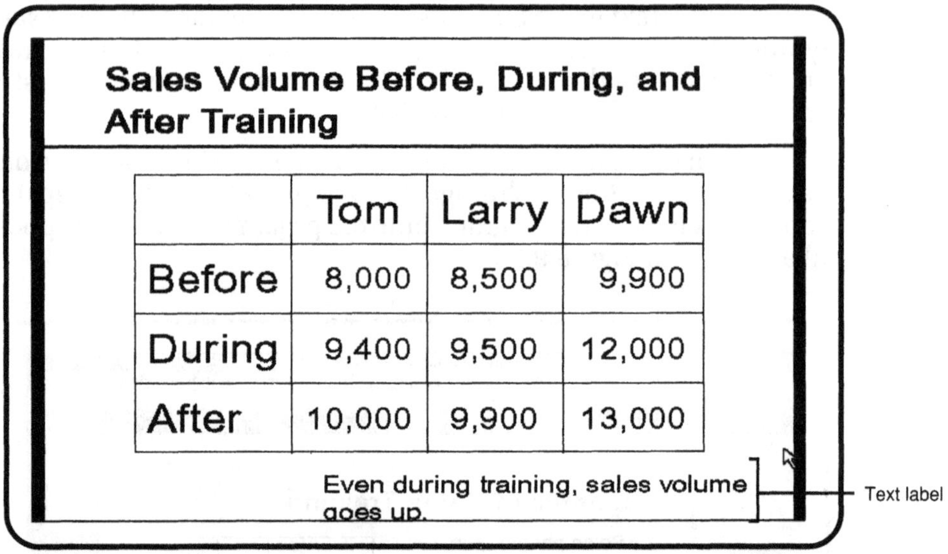

Sales Volume Before, During, and After Training

	Tom	Larry	Dawn
Before	8,000	8,500	9,900
During	9,400	9,500	12,000
After	10,000	9,900	13,000

Even during training, sales volume goes up.

Text label

Figure 9.21 Graph with a text label.

FYIdea: Even though charts summarize information, they do not always highlight key information well enough to satisfy busy viewers in your audience. Do some of the work for them. Add a text box to almost any graph to explain what you think it all means.

Organization Charts

A very different kind of graph is the *organization chart* (also called an *org chart*): a series of boxes connected by lines, customarily used to show who reports to whom within an organization.

FYIdea: You do not have to use an org chart just to show an organization. You can also use it as a flow chart for a process, such as manufacturing, to show the order of tasks needed to complete a larger job.

The graphic components you need to create an organization chart are found in the Toolbox, behind the Symbol icon (the light bulb). Click on the icon to bring up the list of symbols. Scroll down to the `diagram.sym` selection on the list. The collection of symbols in this set will be partially displayed in the six boxes at the bottom of the screen. As you scroll through these boxes, you see there are a number of different *templates* that can be used as organization charts. Figure 9.22 shows some of these symbols.

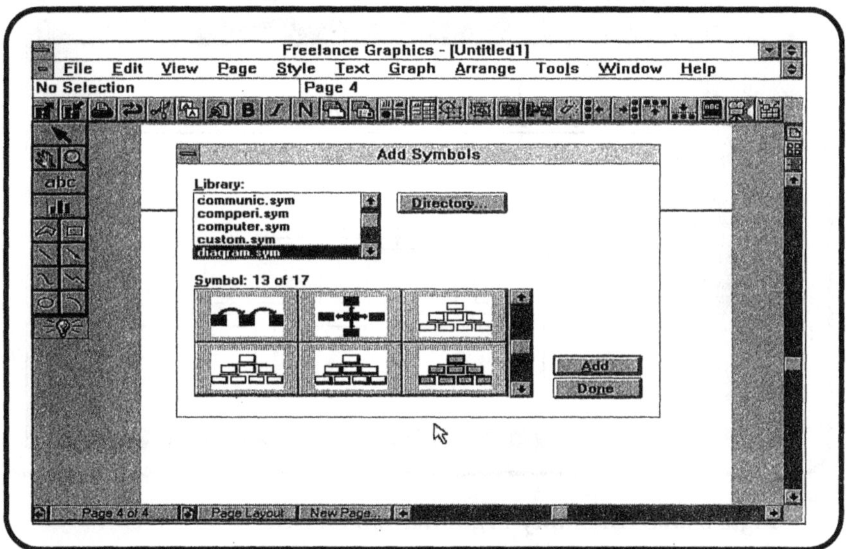

Figure 9.22 Symbols for org charting.

In four of the six sample templates shown, the organization chart has one chart in the top row, three in the second row, and four in the third. That structure may suit your organization just fine. If it does not, you can add and subtract boxes to adapt the model template to your own purposes.

Say, for example, you want to create an organization chart that shows the structure of your small company. To start your chart, bring up a new page if necessary; a basic layout page works well. It has a place for you to add a title, but the rest of the page is blank. You can create your organization chart in that space. Click where it says `Click here to type page title`, and type a title—for the example, **`Company Organization`**. Then click outside the box.

Now you are ready to retrieve a template for your org chart. Click on the Symbol icon in the Toolbox and scroll down to `diagram.sym`. Click twice on any template symbol. Freelance Graphics places this symbol on your page. Click on the symbol to select it and then drag it to the center of the page. Your page should look like the one shown in Figure 9.23.

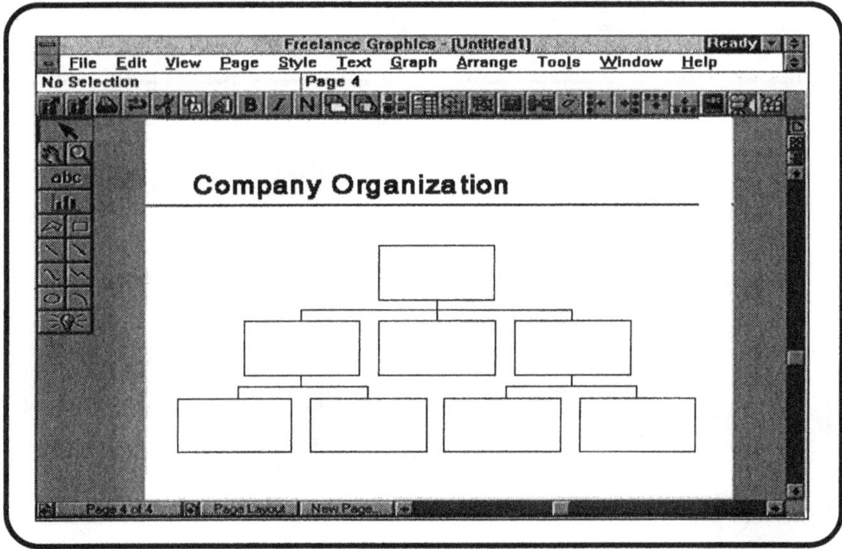

Figure 9.23 An empty organization chart.

Deleting Boxes from a Organization Chart Template

Suppose you don't want to use all the boxes in the org chart. You can delete the ones you don't need. The org chart symbol is already selected when you import it (that is, it has handles on it). If you have deselected it, click on it once to select it.

After it is selected, you can break it up into separate symbols. From the Arrange menu (on the Main menu), choose Ungroup. The org chart breaks up into separate symbols, as shown in Figure 9.24.

Click outside the symbols to deselect all of them. Point to the box you want to select and click once. Freelance selects it. Figure 9.25 shows the middle box selected. After you select it, press Del to delete it.

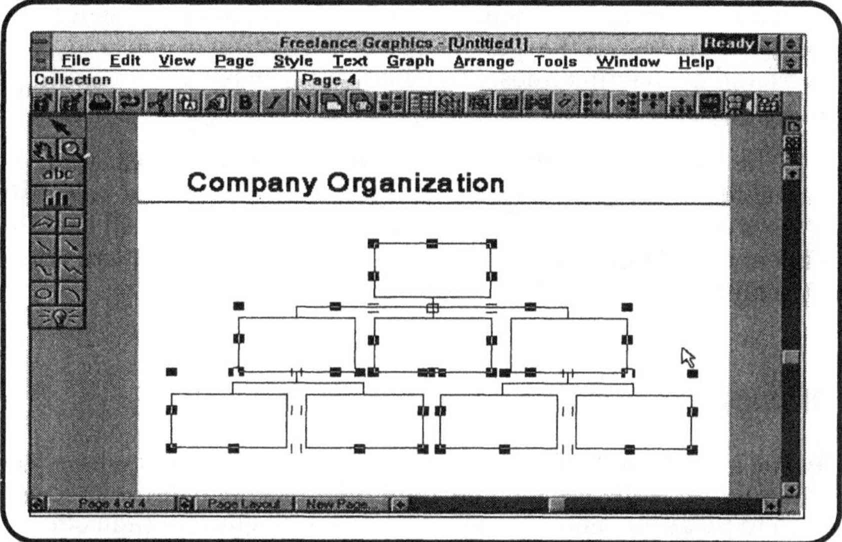

Figure 9.24 You can break up an org chart into separate symbols.

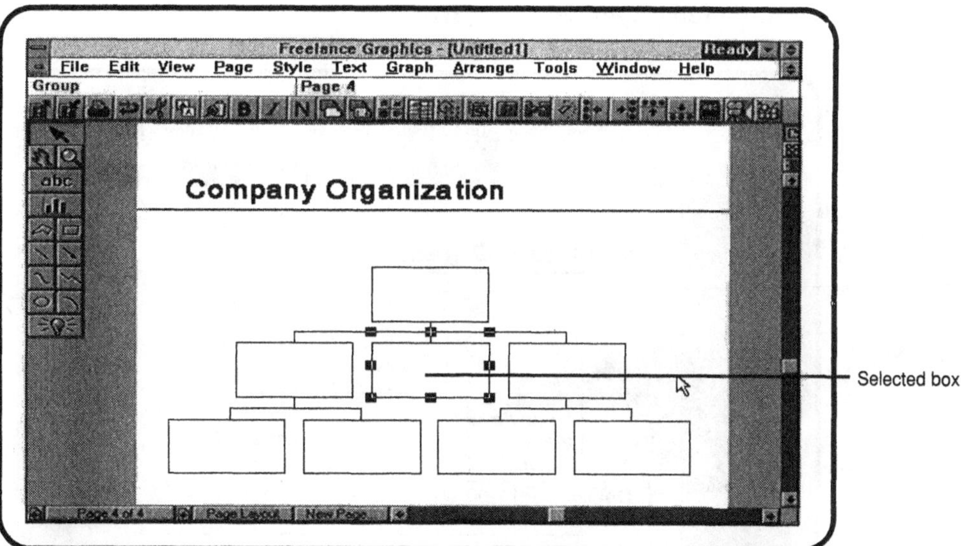

Figure 9.25 You can select a box and delete it.

If you want to add boxes, you can copy existing boxes. First, however, be sure you ungroup the boxes. Then select a box you want to copy, and choose Copy from the Edit menu. Paste the box anywhere on the page. Point to it with the cursor and drag it to the position you want on the page. Copying can be tricky; you copy both a box and connecting lines. See Chapter 12, "Basic Object Editing," for detailed information on selecting and working with objects.

The org chart template that comes with Freelance, then, is adaptable to all your needs. As you find out more about selecting symbols and working with them in later chapters, you will become adept at selecting, deleting, copying, and dragging. You can adapt any template to suit any organization.

Adding Text Labels to an Organization Chart

Adding labels to an org chart is like adding text labels anywhere else in Freelance. Click on abc and then click on the chart where you want to place the label. For instance, click on abc and then click on the top box in the org chart. Type **Robert** and press Enter. Type **Shaw**. Click outside the box. If the text does not look properly centered in the box, click on the text and drag it into position inside the box. Repeat the procedure for each box in the org chart. Figure 9.26 shows a completed organization chart.

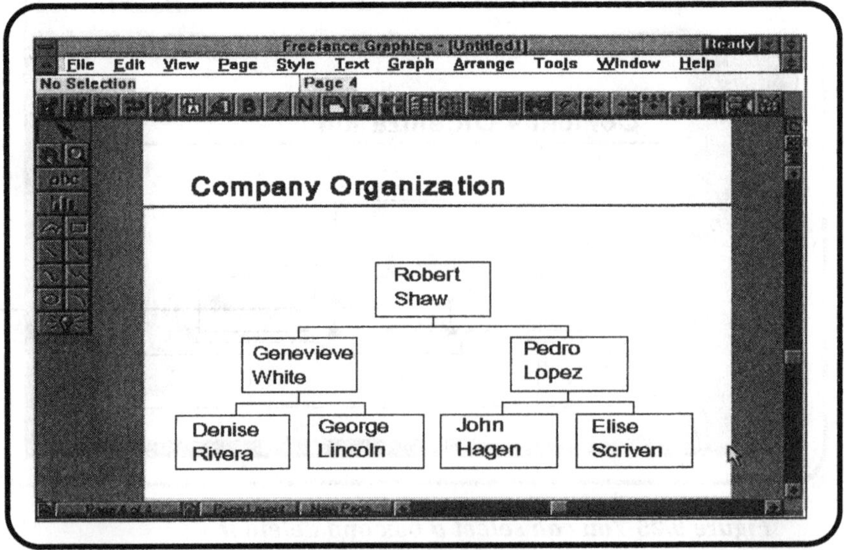

Figure 9.26 Completed organization chart.

> **Tip:** To avoid selecting other chart elements by mistake as you create text, create each text box in a blank area of the screen, click outside the text box to deselect it and then drag the text into the position you want inside a box in the org chart.

The following Quick Steps outline the procedures for creating an organization chart with text.

Creating an Organization Chart

1. On a basic layout page, click on the Symbol icon in the Toolbox, and scroll to the `diagram.sym` symbol set.	You see symbols that can be used for organization charts.
2. Double-click on a symbol you want to use. Drag it to where you want it placed on the page.	Your symbol appears on the page.
3. Choose Ungroup from the Arrange menu.	
4. Select and delete any boxes you do not want.	The boxes disappear from the template.
5. Copy any boxes you want to add.	Additoinal boxes appear on the drawing.
6. Click on the Text icon.	You see an input box.
7. Click outside the org chart.	You see a text box.
8. Type a name. Select and drag the name to the appropriate or chart box.	The name appears inside the box.
9. Repeat Steps 6-8 for each name in the chart.	

□

What You Have Learned

- A stand-alone graph is made without a title page or other accompanying pages. Use the File New to create a presentation with a single page.
- The Graph menu gives you great flexibility for modifying an existing graph. You can change the appearance of the legend, titles, headings, notes, and other elements. Choose your options from the Graph menu.
- Table graphs are a simple and clear way to display numerical data. From the Graph New Gallery dialog box, choose Table.
- You can place one, two, or four graphs on a single Freelance Graphics page. From the Page menu, click on Choose Page Layout and then choose 1 Graph, 2 Graphs, or 4 Graphs.
- You can have a bulleted list next to a graph or put labels on a page with a graph. Choose a Bullets & Graph page layout or use the text tool to add labels.
- You can create organization charts by assembling components from the diagram.sym symbol set behind the Symbol icon. Click on the light bulb symbol in the Toolbox and then choose the symbol from the diagram.sym library.

Chapter 10

Using Color Effectively

In This Chapter

- *How Freelance Graphics uses color palettes*
- *Choosing a different color palette*
- *Editing a color palette*
- *Saving a new palette*
- *Printing to color or black-and-white output devices*

Many experts consider working with color the most complex task in using graphics. In general, to use colors properly you have to have a great deal of knowledge and experience and perhaps a natural tendency to visualize things easily. With Freelance Graphics, however, you can use color in sophisticated ways without being a color expert yourself.

Understanding Color Palettes

Using color effectively used to require an understanding of the color wheel, complementary colors, warm versus cool colors, color families, background versus foreground colors, and so on. Armed with this knowledge, you still had a lot of work to do in selecting and arranging colors.

You no longer need to master this knowledge personally. Artists have designed Freelance Graphics SmartMaster sets for maximum effectiveness in both layout and use of color. Using predesigned color palettes does not mean that you can't make color choices of your own when you use a SmartMaster set. You can still make color changes, but you'll make the changes in the context of a *color palette*—a set of 18 colors selected to work well together. In each palette, there are three background colors, 12 foreground colors, and three colors for text characters.

Freelance Graphics comes with a variety of different palettes. You find them on the Masters subdirectory. They have the .pal extension in their file names. Each SmartMaster set has a specific palette assigned to it, but you can change to another palette while keeping the same SmartMaster. You can also change individual colors within a palette.

Choosing a Palette

To choose a palette, you use the Style Choose Palette dialog box to preview the colors you plan to use. Suppose you are getting ready to make a new presentation. You browsed through the SmartMaster sets and decided that you really like the look of the one labelled Gradate1.mas. When you bring it up on your screen, it looks like Figure 10.1.

You have one concern, however—the color scheme is darker than you'd like it to be. You decide to see if changing palettes will solve the problem. To change the palette, select Style and then Choose Palette. You see the Style Choose Palette dialog box, as shown in Figure 10.2.

The current palette (black.pal) is highlighted. Use the mouse or up and down arrows to browse through the other palettes. For this example, try lblue.pal. To see what the color will look like, select Preview and move the dialog box aside. (To move the dialog box, click on the title bar and drag it to a new location.) If it looks good, click on OK. With the new palette, your SmartMaster page looks lighter, as shown in Figure 10.3.

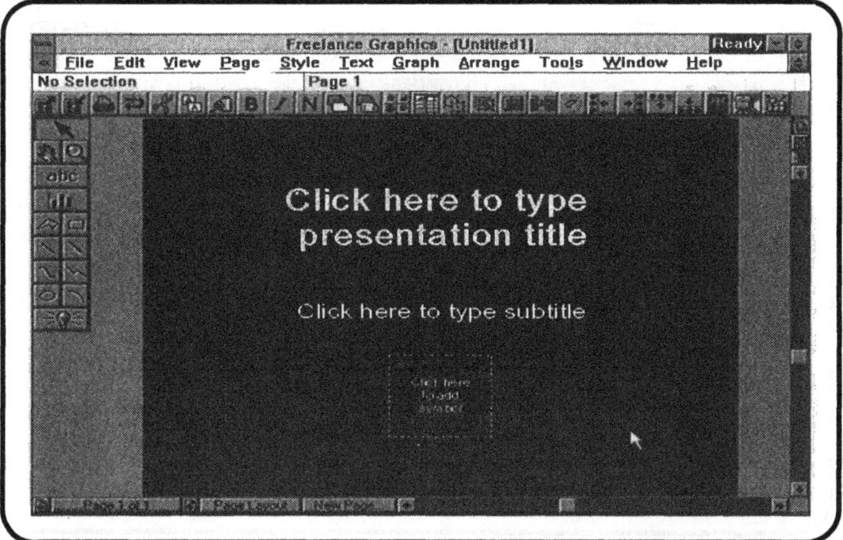

Figure 10.1 The Gradate1.mas SmartMaster set.

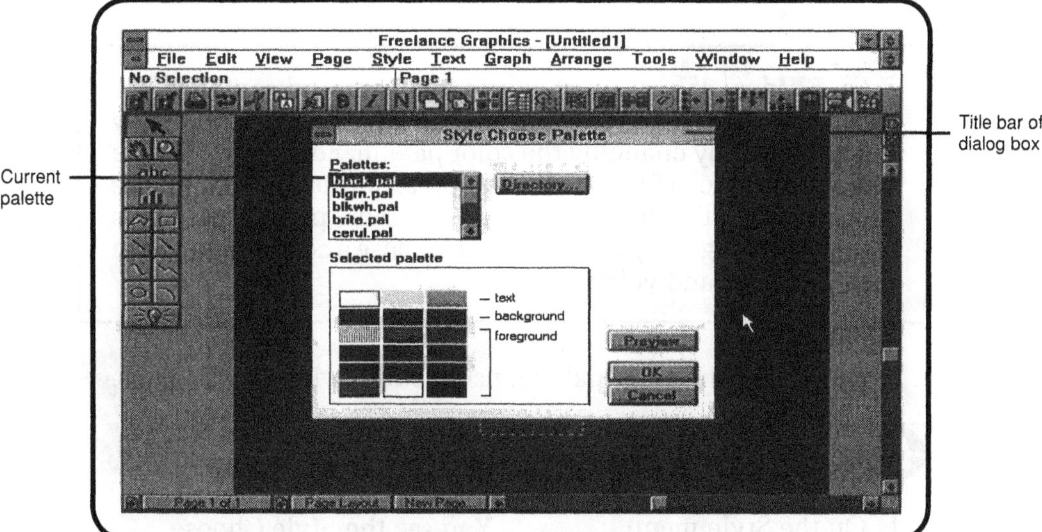

Figure 10.2 The Style Choose Palette dialog box.

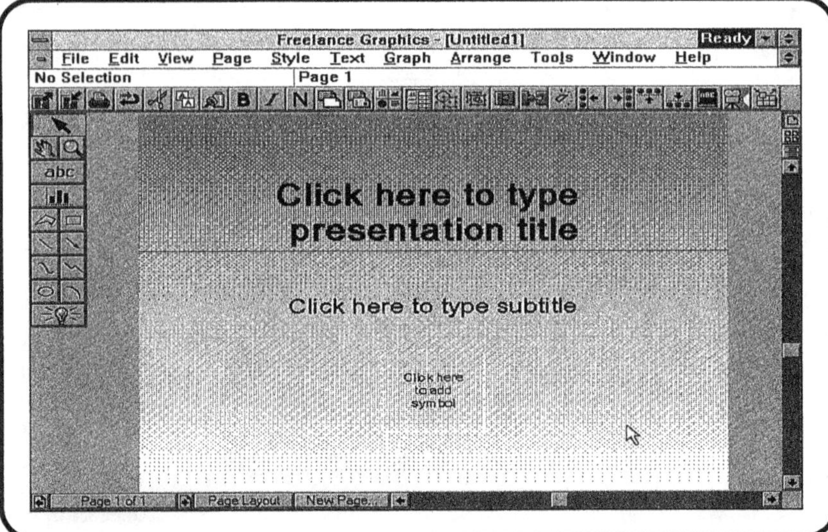

Figure 10.3 The Gradate1.mas SmartMaster with changed palette.

FYIdea: If you want to use the same presentation for different audiences, you may be able to adapt to a new situation just by changing the color palette. For a conservative look, perhaps for a formal business presentation, you might use blues and "cool" colors. For a "warmer" look, perhaps for a less formal showing to a younger crowd, choose a color palette with reds, oranges, and yellows.

To change the color palette, use the following Quick Steps.

Changing Color Palettes for the Same SmartMaster

1. On the Style menu, select Choose Palette. — You see the Style Choose Palette dialog box.
2. Use the mouse or up and down arrows to browse through the palettes. — The palette colors show the selected palette box.

3. Choose Preview to see what the SmartMaster page will look like with the new palette. (Move the dialog box aside.) — You see the presentation page with the new palette.
4. Click on OK when you find the palette you want. — Your palette is changed accordingly. □

Editing a Palette

When you draw objects such as ovals, rectangles, and so on, Freelance Graphics uses colors from the selected palette to fill the objects. It also assigns a color to text, according to the chosen palette. In Chapter 13, "Making Global Presentation Changes," you will learn how to use the Style Attributes dialog boxes to change the color of text or objects.

Occasionally, however, you may need to make the change on a more basic level and change the actual palette colors (useful if you need to make global changes). You could change all blue objects in your presentation to pink, for example. You might also change palette colors if your output device cannot print a certain color very well but can print another.

To change a palette color means you remove a color from the palette and replace it with another from the *color library* of 256 colors. Changing the color in the palette is known as *editing* the palette.

> **Caution:** Edit palette colors only after careful thought. The Freelance Graphics palette colors have been carefully chosen by graphic artists to give the best results and conform to established rules for using colors.

To change a color in your color palette, begin by choosing Style and then Edit Palette. You see the Style Edit Palette dialog box, as shown in Figure 10.4.

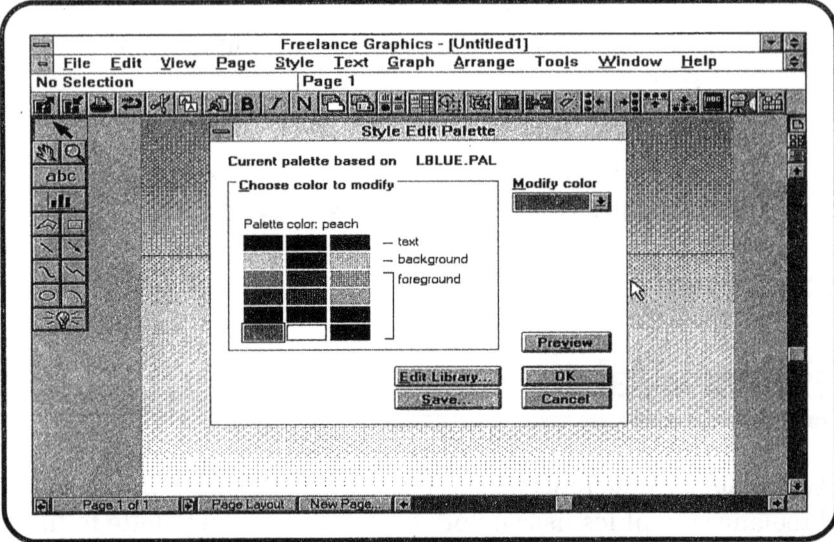

Figure 10.4 The Style Edit Palette dialog box.

If, for example, you believe that the pinks shown in the palette will not print well for you, replace them with red. To do this, click on the first pink box; the name of the color—burgundy—is displayed at the top of the Choose color to modify box. Then click on the Modify color drop-down box. You see the entire color library of 256 colors (from which the color palettes are selected), as shown in Figure 10.5.

You click on a color—red—and it becomes the replacement for burgundy. You return to the Style Edit Palette dialog box, and you can continue to make changes as needed. When you finish editing, click on OK. The following Quick Steps summarize the procedure.

Q Editing the Color Palette

1. Choose Style and then choose Edit Palette.	You see the Style Edit Palette dialog box.
2. Click on the color you want to change.	The color is selected, and its name is displayed.
3. Click on Modify color.	You see the color library in the drop-down box.

4. Click on the replacement color.	You see the Style Edit Palette dialog box with the new color.
5. Click on OK when done editing.	Your presentation uses the new color. ☐

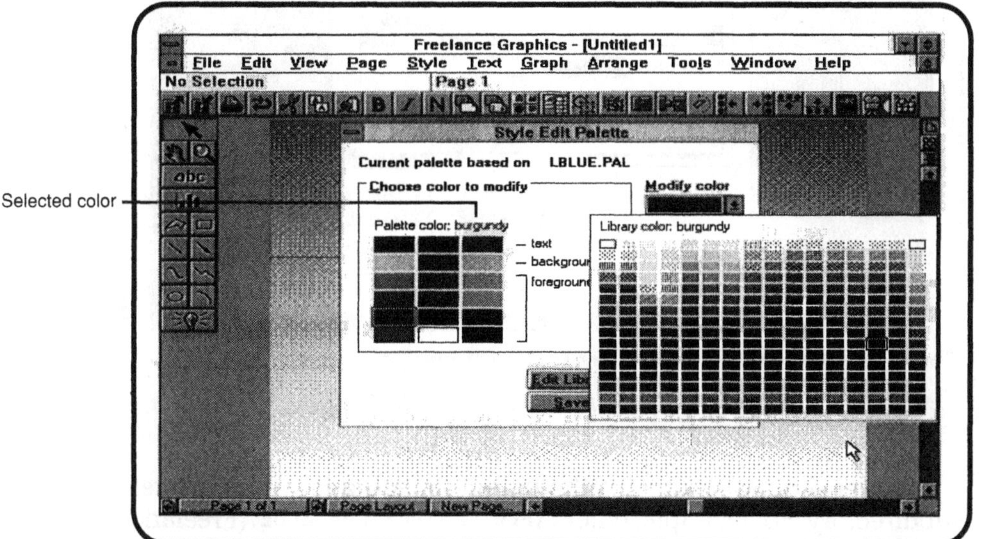

Figure 10.5 The Modify color drop-down box with color library.

Saving the Edited Palette

If you plan to use your edited palette for one presentation only, you do not have to save it separately. Freelance saves it automatically, along with the presentation that uses it. If you create a palette you want to use again, then you must save it under its own name.

To save your palette, choose Style and then choose Edit Palette. In the Style Edit Palette dialog box, click on the Save button. You see the Style Edit Palette Save dialog box, as shown in Figure 10.6.

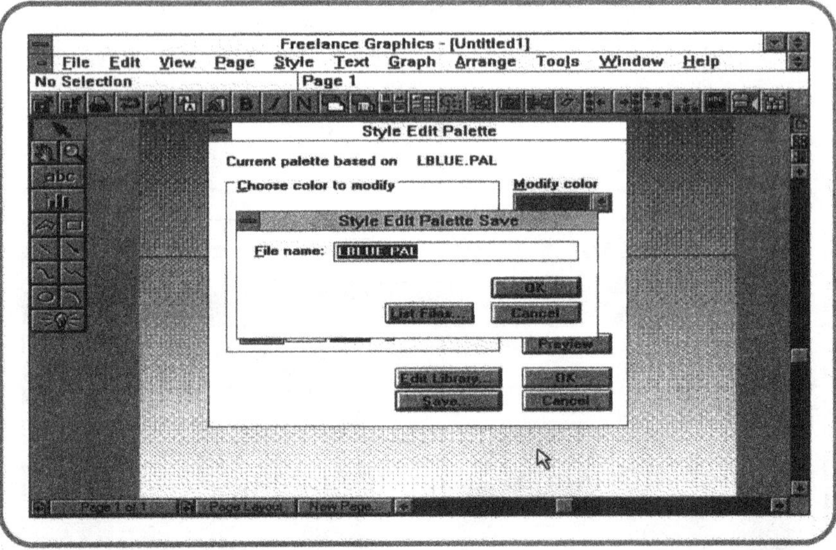

Figure 10.6 The Style Edit Palette Save dialog box.

Enter the new name for the palette, placing it on the Masters subdirectory. For example, type **c:\FLW\MASTERS\NEWLBLUE**. (Freelance Graphics will add the .pal extension.) Then click on OK. When the Style Edit Palette dialog box appears, click on OK again. The next time you need that palette, you will find it on the palette list in the Style Choose Palette dialog box. Use the following Quick Steps to save a palette.

Saving a Palette

1. Choose Style and then choose Edit Palette.	You see the Style Edit Palette dialog box.
2. Click on Save.	You see the Style Edit Palette Save dialog box.
3. Type the drive, directory, and file name for the palette file. Then click on OK.	Your file is saved, and you are returned to the Style Edit Palette dialog box.
4. Click on OK.	Your palette is available, just like other Freelance Graphics palettes. □

Switching Between Color and Black and White

If you give all your presentations as screen shows, then you don't need to be concerned about printing to output devices. If you want to print to color or black-and-white printers, however, there are steps you can take to get the best results.

If you print to a color printer, for instance, the color you see when you print may not be quite the color you see on-screen. You can select a setting to make the output colors better match the screen colors.

Also, if you print from a color display on your screen to a black-and-white printer, you do not have to do anything to control the way the colors print in black and white. Windows does it for you. You can preview what the black-and-white output will look like, though, and take steps to improve it if you are not satisfied.

Printing to a Color Printer

You don't need to take special steps to print to a color printer. But if you find the colors don't match the screen colors well, then you can choose File, then Print, and mark Adjust color library for color printing. Freelance Graphics then uses an alternate color library to attempt to minimize differences in the printed and screen colors.

Letting Windows Translate Color to Black and White

If you print to a black-and-white output device, there are different ways to do it. One way is to let Windows translate your colors to black, white, and shades of gray. This happens automatically, but you may want a screen preview of how this output will look.

Suppose you create a graph in a color palette. To get a screen preview of how Windows will translate your colors, choose Tools and then User Setup. You see the Tools User Setup dialog box, as shown in Figure 10.7.

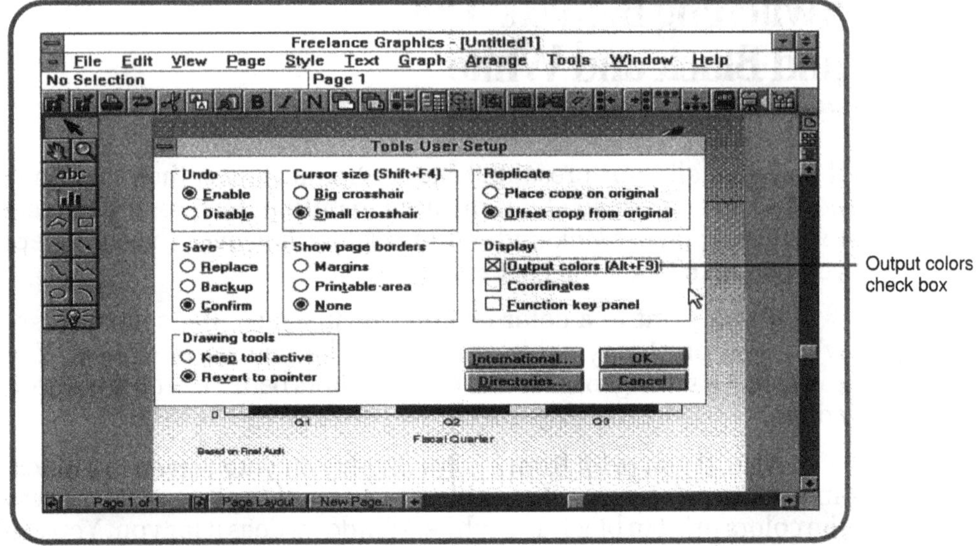

Figure 10.7 Tools User Setup dialog box.

In the Display box you mark the Output colors check box and then click on OK. You see the same screen in shades of gray, and your graph looks like the one shown in Figure 10.8.

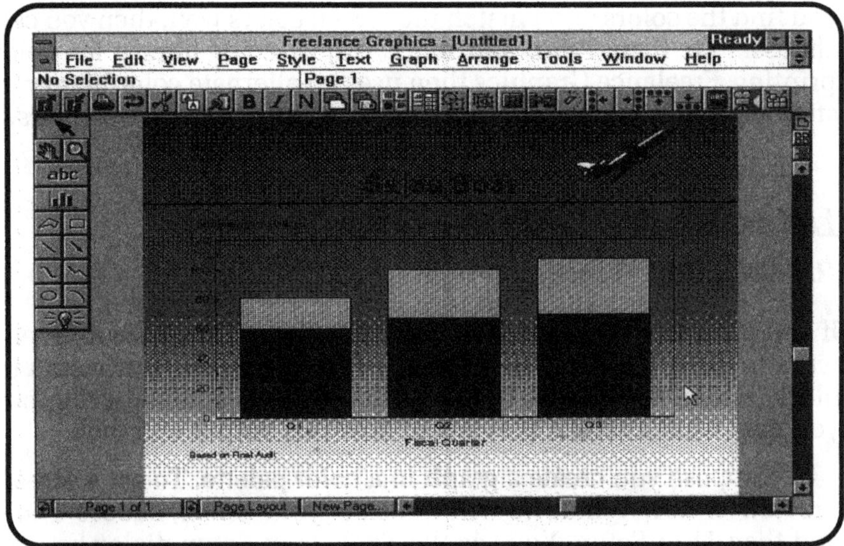

Figure 10.8 Windows translation of screen colors to black-and-white output.

To return to color, choose Tools and then User Setup. Click on the selection box again to remove the mark from the Output colors box and then click on OK.

Choosing a Black-and-white Palette

If you think the bars in your graph do not have enough contrast when you view your screen with colors translated to black and white by Windows, try an alternate method—switching to a black-and-white SmartMaster color palette. To switch to a black-and-white SmartMaster palette, choose Style and then Choose Palette. You see the Style Choose Palette dialog box (see Figure 10.2). Select the blkwh.pal color palette and click on OK. Your presentation appears on-screen in black and white, as shown in Figure 10.9.

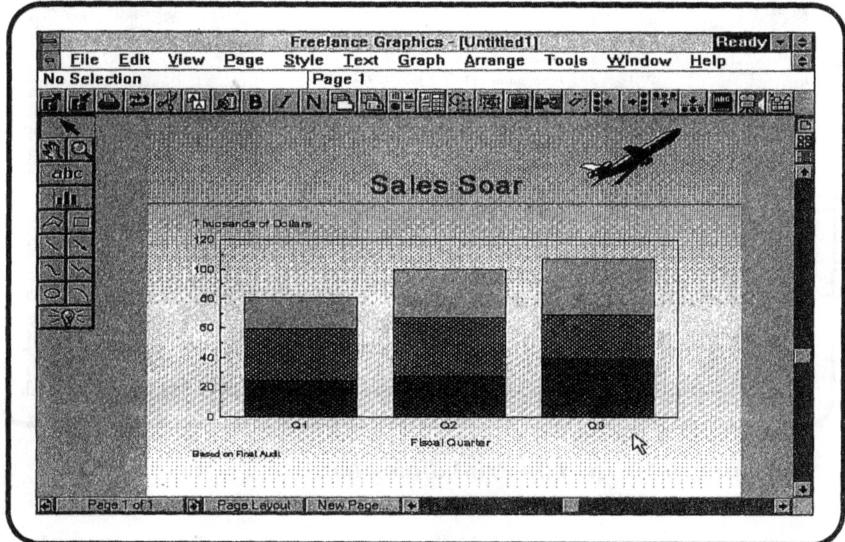

Figure 10.9 Graph done with black-and-white palette.

Switching to Black-and-white Palette for Printing

If you prefer the way your graph looks in Figure 10.9 to the Windows translation of colors in Figure 10.8, you can keep the original color palette for screen shows and use the blkwh.pal palette for printing to a black-and-white printer. To do this, follow these steps:

1. Choose Style and then Choose Palette.
2. Reselect the original lblue.pal color palette and then click on OK.
3. Click on the Tools menu and choose User Setup.
4. Deselect Output colors (under Display) and choose OK. Your original colors return to the screen.
5. Choose File Print, and you see the File Print dialog box, as shown in Figure 10.10.

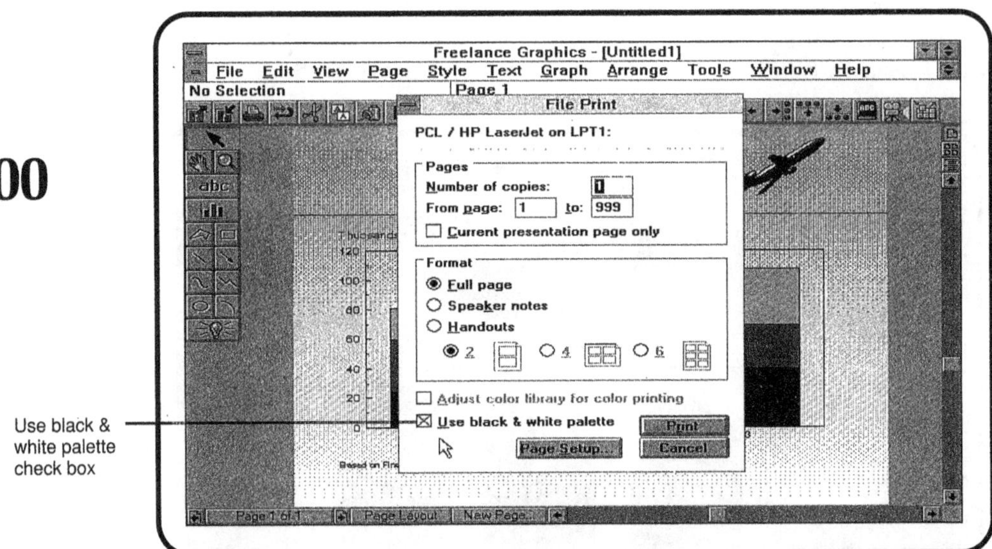

Figure 10.10 The File Print dialog box.

For this example, check the Use black & white palette box. When you print, Freelance Graphics will automatically switch to the black-and-white palette. The rest of the time, when you are working on the screen, you see the colors of whatever palette you use.

What You Have Learned

- To change to a new color palette, use Style Choose Palette.
- In cases where you need to remove a palette color and substitute another, use Style Edit Palette. Highlight the palette you want and then choose OK.
- To reuse an edited palette for other presentations, use the Save option in the Style Edit Palette dialog box. Use the Modify color drop-down box to select a new color and then choose OK.
- Changing to the black-and-white palette named blkwh.pal will give good results for black-and-white output devices. Use the Style Choose Palette.

Chapter 11

Simple Drawing Techniques

In This Chapter

- *Drawing arrows and lines*
- *Adding labels with nonwrapping text blocks*
- *Drawing rectangles and ellipses*
- *Putting drawing tools together to create a concept chart*
- *Customizing the drawing tools*
- *Using symbols to enhance charts*

So far in this book, you have been allowing Freelance to do your artwork for you. If you wanted to use a background or a picture of a truck or house, you used a predrawn one. Freelance does give you the ability, however, to do the drawing yourself and create artwork of your own if you want to. (The artists who created the predrawn symbols, after all, used the drawing capabilities of Freelance to do it.) Drawing gives you the freedom to put almost anything on the page, if you know how to use the drawing tools and—for complex drawings—have the time to create what you need. Here you learn about these basic techniques for creating your own artwork "from scratch."

Getting To Know the Toolbox

The drawing tools are the tools in the Toolbox on the left side of the screen. Figure 11.1 labels each of the drawing tools, and Table 11.1 summarizes each of the tools.

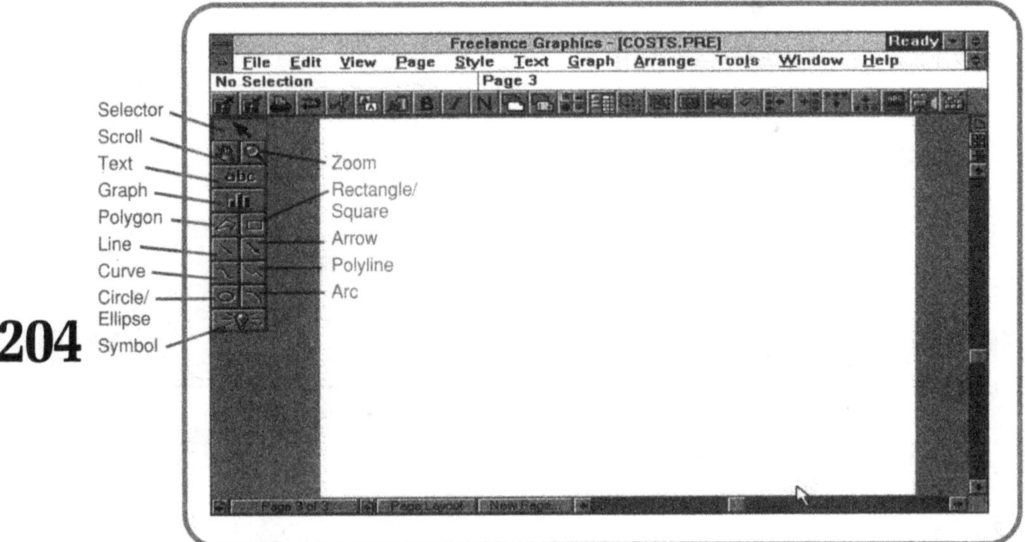

Figure 11.1 The tools in the Toolbox.

Table 11.1 Tools in the Toolbox.

Tool	Use To
Selector	Select objects, choose other tools in the Toolbox, choose commands from the menus, or choose SmartIcons.
Scroll	Scroll the page. When you click on the icon, the pointer becomes a hand. Position the hand on the page and drag in the direction you want the screen to scroll.
Zoom	Enlarge a portion of the page. When you click on the icon, the pointer becomes a magnifying glass. When you click on the page, you zoom in. To zoom out, hold down Shift and click on the page.

Tool	Use To
Text	Add text to the page. When you click on the icon, the pointer becomes a cross hair cursor. Then click on the page. Just type to create a nonwrapping text block. To create a wrapping text block, drag the cross hairs to create a box, click inside the box, and then type.
Graph	Create a graph. If no graph is already selected, this choice takes you to the Graph New Gallery dialog box.
Polygon	Create a multisided object. Click on the tool, click where you want the polygon to start, and then drag to draw each side.
Rectangle	Create a rectangle. After you click on the tool, position the cursor on the page, drag, and release.
Line	Create a straight line with one segment. Click on the icon, position the pointer, and drag.
Arrow	Create a straight line with an arrow on the end. Click on the icon, position the pointer, and drag.
Curve	Create a curve. Click on the icon, position the pointer, and drag.
Polyline	Create a line with multiple segments. Click on the icon, position the pointer, and drag to create a segment. Release and drag again to create another segment. Double-click to end the polyline.
Circle	Create a circle. Click on the icon, position the pointer, drag, and release.
Arc	Create an arc. Click on the icon, position the pointer, drag a line to define the length of the arc, drag a third point to define the size of the curve, and release.
Symbol	Add a symbol to the page. Click the icon and then choose the symbol from the dialog box.

A list of so many tools may seem overwhelming at first. You may wonder, "How can I possibly learn them all?" You do not have to learn them all to accomplish a great deal. In this chapter, you will learn to use the simpler tools, get comfortable with them. Then, if the need arises for using more advanced tools (such as the polyline tool), you can apply your experience with other tools to using new ones.

The steps are basically the same for using any of the drawing tools in the Toolbox. Follow these Quick Steps to get started.

Q Using the Drawing Tools

Step	Result
1. Click on the tool you want to use.	The icon in the Toolbox is selected.
2. Drag the pointer to where you want to draw the object.	The pointer assumes a different shape, most commonly a cross hair cursor.
3. Click on the page.	The object becomes anchored in that place.
4. Drag the pointer.	You see an outline of the shape, drawn with a broken line.
5. Release the pointer.	The shape appears on the page, with selection handles on it.
6. Drag the handles to edit the size of the object, or click and drag the entire object to reposition it.	The object takes on the shape and position you want.

□

Drawing Lines and Arrows

A good place to get started with the drawing tools is with arrows and lines. You can learn to use them easily. Arrows and lines can point to specific features of graphs, such as a peak performance quarter. Arrows, of course, have an arrowhead on one end, but that's the only difference between an arrow and a line. Draw lines and arrows using the following Quick Steps.

Q Drawing a Line

Step	Result
1. Click on the Line icon in the Toolbox.	The pointer changes to become a cross hair cursor.
2. Click where you want the line to start and drag the length of the line. Then release.	The line appears.

□

Tip: Another way to draw a line is to select the Line drawing tool and click at any two points on the page. Freelance will automatically draw a line between the two points.

To draw an arrow, simply follow either procedure for drawing a line but select the Arrow drawing tool instead of the Line drawing tool. When you release the mouse button, an arrowhead will appear at the release point of the line, as shown in Figure 11.2.

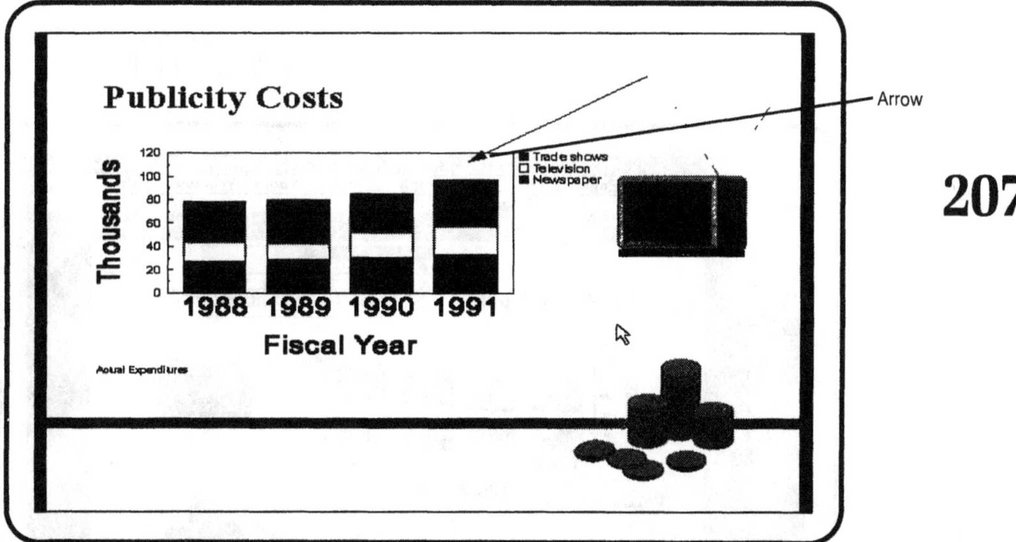

Figure 11.2 Arrows have an arrowhead at the release point.

Tip: If you want the line to keep to 45-degree angles, press Shift while you drag. This technique is useful for drawing multiple arrows, evenly spaced.

FYIdea: Arrows are probably the easiest to use (and safest) of any tools for enhancing your graphics. An arrow indicating what is most important helps make almost any graph better. Use arrows on graphs, charts, diagrams, text charts, or anything you can create with Freelance Graphics.

Adding Nonwrapping Text Blocks

You already know how to add text blocks to your presentation. There's a quicker way to add them if you just want one line of text (a *nonwrapping text block*) for a label or graph description. Such labels are particularly useful when you are adding quick, brief descriptions to elements on an existing page. To add a nonwrapping text block, follow these steps:

1. Select the Text block drawing tool (abc) from the Toolbox.
2. Click once where you want your text to begin. *Do not drag.*
3. Begin typing. Notice that the text block expands as you type, so it fits your text exactly, as shown in Figure 11.3.

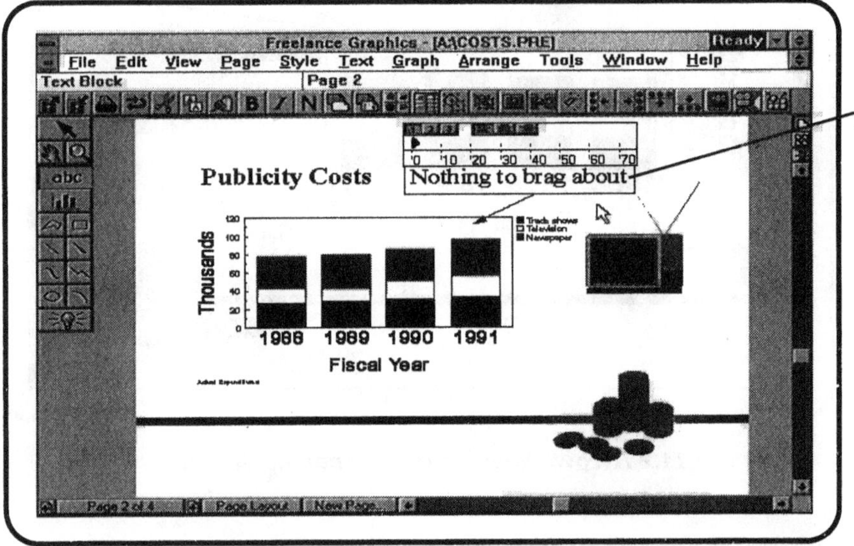

Figure 11.3 Add a graph label quickly with a nonwrapping text block.

Tip: You may have trouble placing the text block where you want it on the page. When you click, you may accidentally select an existing SmartMaster text block. To solve the problem, create the text block in a blank area of the screen, click outside it, and then drag it with the mouse to the position you want.

FYIdea: You can rotate text blocks the same way you rotate other objects. If you want a nonwrapping text block to follow the slope of an arrow or line, select the text block and then choose Rotate from the Arrange menu. Click near the edge of the text block and drag it in the direction you want it to rotate. Figure 11.4 shows a rotated text block.

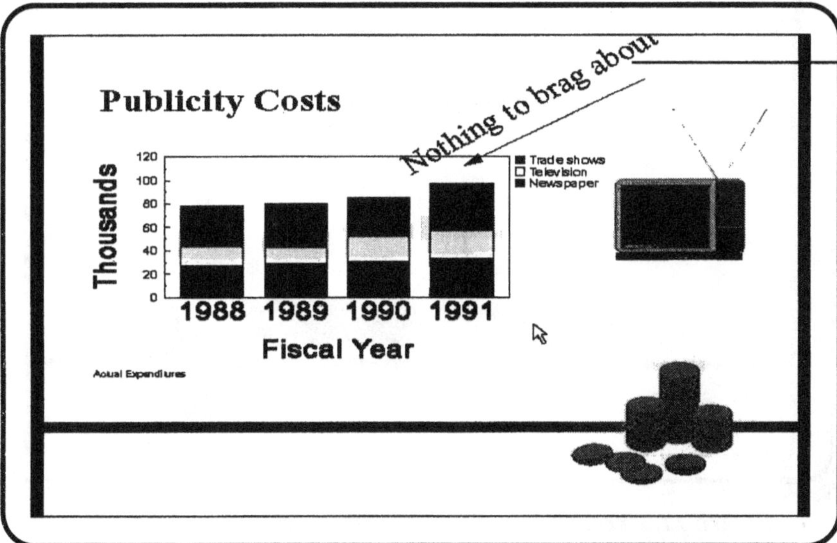

Figure 11.4 You can rotate a text block just as you can rotate objects.

Creating a Concept Chart from Scratch

In Chapter 8, "More About Text," you saw how to create a basic concept chart using text blocks within shapes from the symbols library. You can also create concept charts using the drawing tools. These tools give you greater flexibility in setting up the exact look you want. You draw the rectangles, circles, or other shapes you want to contain the text of the chart, determine their exact size, place them exactly where you want them on the page, add connecting lines and arrows, and modify the look of your drawing in many simple ways.

Suppose, for instance, you wanted to create a drawing like the one in Figure 11.5. First, look at how you can create it by using the default settings for each of the tools and without modifying the environment you are working in. Later in the chapter, you will explore how to enhance your artwork by customizing both the drawing tools and the drawing background.

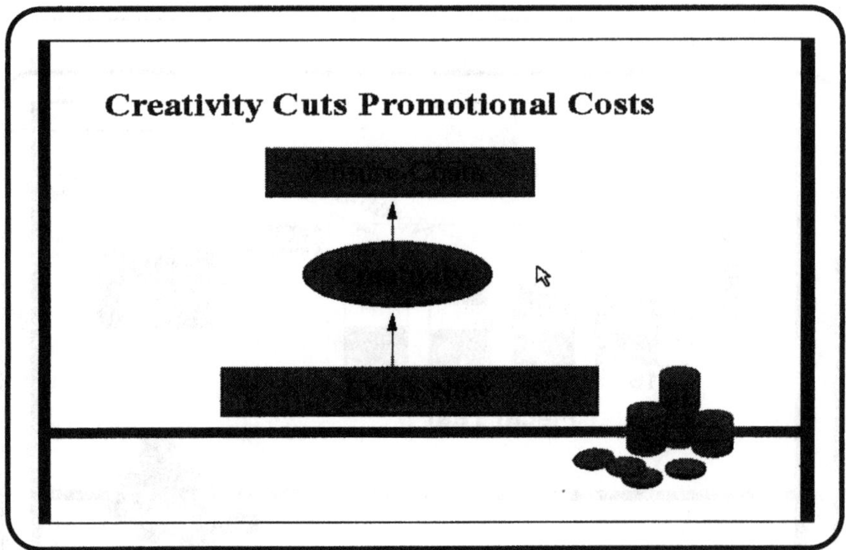
Creativity Cuts Promotional Costs

Figure 11.5 You can create a concept chart using default drawing tools.

Creating Rectangles and Ovals

To create rectangles like those in Figure 11.5, use the Rectangle tool from the Toolbox. When you select this tool, the familiar cross hairs appear on the page. By moving the mouse, you can move the cross hairs to any point on the page. Click and hold down the mouse button, and the cross hairs become the starting point for your rectangle—a corner of the rectangle. The position, size, and shape of the rectangle depends on the direction and distance you drag the cross hairs from their starting point.

For the rectangles in Figure 11.5, position the cross hairs near the bottom of the page. Click, drag up and to the right, and release the mouse button. Because you dragged up and right, the starting point of the cross hairs formed the lower left corner of the rectangle. If you had dragged down and left, the starting point of the cross hairs would have been the upper right corner of the rectangle. To create the second rectangle at the top, follow the same steps, but position the cross hairs at the top of the page.

Creating an oval (an ellipse) is similar to creating a rectangle. When you drag the cross hairs, Freelance forms the oval. The exact shape and size of the oval depends on how far and in what direction you drag the cross hairs. You can create an oval that is almost a circle, you can create a long, narrow oval, or you can create anything in between. For example, to add the oval in the middle of the page as in Figure 11.5, click on the Circle/Ellipse tool and position the cross hairs above and to the left of the center of the page. Click the mouse button and drag the cross hairs across and down to create the oval. Release the mouse button when the oval is the size you want.

Add text labels inside the rectangles and oval using the steps for adding a nonwrapping text block. Then click where it says `Click here to type page title` and type the title for the page.

> **FYIdea:** A simple rectangle often makes an excellent border for a chart. If you create a stand-alone chart or if you simply don't want to use the SmartMaster border for a given page, try adding a rectangle instead for the border around the page.

Drawing Squares and Circles

Squares and circles are simply proportional rectangles and ellipses. The technique for drawing either a square or a circle is almost the same as for drawing a rectangle or an oval, respectively. Select the Rectangle or Circle/Ellipse drawing tool and position the cross hair. Then, hold down the Shift key while dragging the cross hairs to form the circle or square. The following Quick Steps summarize the procedure for drawing a circle.

Drawing a Circle

1. Select the Circle/Ellipse drawing tool from the Toolbox. — Your mouse pointer becomes a cross hair cursor.
2. Hold down the Shift key while you click and drag the cross hairs outward from the starting point. — An outline of the circle appears as you drag.
3. Release the mouse button. — The new circle appears. □

> **FYIdea:** You can combine the basic drawing shapes in many different ways to form useful charts. As in the example, you can connect rectangles and/or ellipses with lines and arrows to form flow charts, organization charts, and interesting transition charts (text charts that lead to the next major point in a presentation).

It may take you some time to get familiar with the drawing tools. Even when you are experienced with drawing tools, you have to take time to position the objects accurately. In Chapter 12, "Basic Object Editing," you will learn how to change the shape and position of objects after you create them.

Customizing a Drawing Tool

The concept chart in Figure 11.5 is usable for many purposes, but it is a quick, rough sketch. You can use it for presentations at quick departmental meetings, but it probably would not be appropriate for an annual meeting. You might want to create a more refined and precise version for that. Freelance provides the tools for being quite precise as you work in drawing mode.

Earlier you learned how to customize graph elements—by changing to a larger typeface for labels, for instance, or by using a legend instead of labels. Similarly, you can customize all the drawing tools. Procedures for doing so are the same, though you have slightly different options for customizing each tool.

To customize the Rectangle tool, for instance, double-click on the icon in the Toolbox. You see the Style Default Attributes Rectangle dialog box, as shown in Figure 11.6.

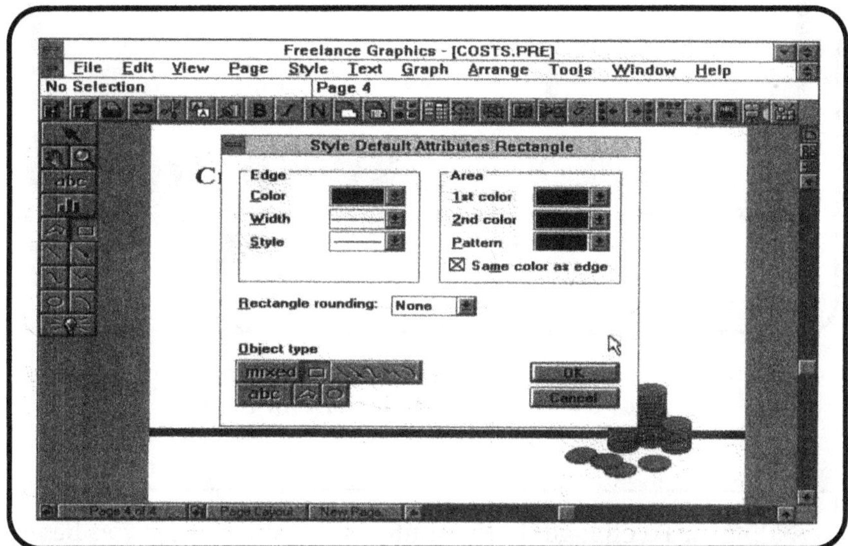

Figure 11.6 Change the appearance of a drawing tool with the Style Default Attributes Rectangle dialog box.

In the Edge box, you can specify the color, width, and style for the line around the edge of the rectangle. In the Area box, you can select the color and pattern to appear inside the rectangle (or inside other closed objects, such as circles and polygons).

In the Rectangle rounding box, you can decide whether to have the corners square or rounded and determine the amount of rounding by selecting Low, Medium, or High (maximum rounding).

The Object type box allows you to set the attributes for other drawing tools without leaving the dialog box for the tool you are currently using. Figure 11.7 shows, for instance, what the rectangles in the sample drawing would look like if you set up the Rectangle tool to have high rounding at the corners and a dotted pattern filling the rectangles.

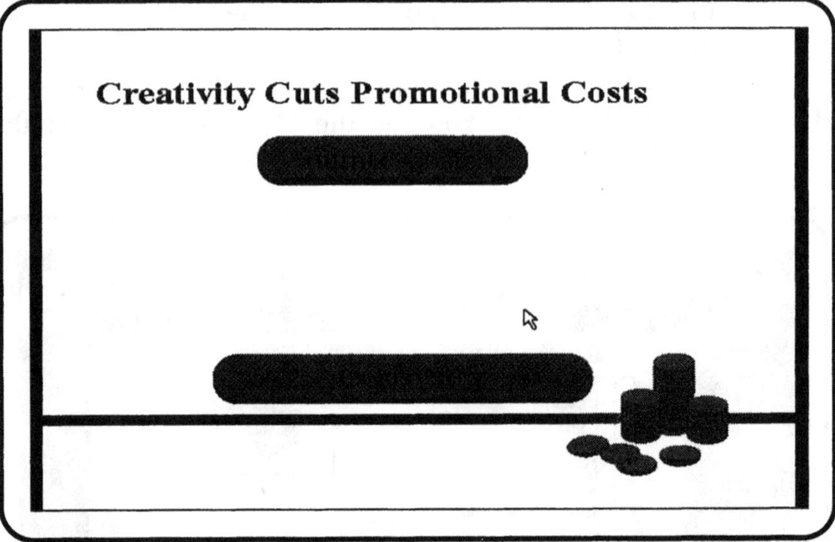
Creativity Cuts Promotional Costs

Figure 11.7 Rectangles drawn with attributes set to high rounding at the corners and a dotted pattern for the fill.

> **Tip:** To change the attributes of an object after you have drawn it, first select the object. Then choose Style from the Main menu and Attributes from the Style menu.

As you become familiar with the program, try out the various attributes for the different tools. For example, the arrows in the sample diagram would be more effective if they were thicker. In the Attributes box, select the Edge option and increase the line width. Figure 11.8 shows the sample drawing with thicker arrows; the boxes are moved slightly further apart to accommodate the larger arrows.

Customizing Your Drawing Environment

You have great flexibility, then, in customizing the shapes you draw. You can change the shapes, colors, and fill patterns for such objects. After you set up attributes such as rounded corners for a rectangle, the attributes remain in effect for all additional rectangles you draw in the current presentation. (For new presentations, the default attributes remain in effect.)

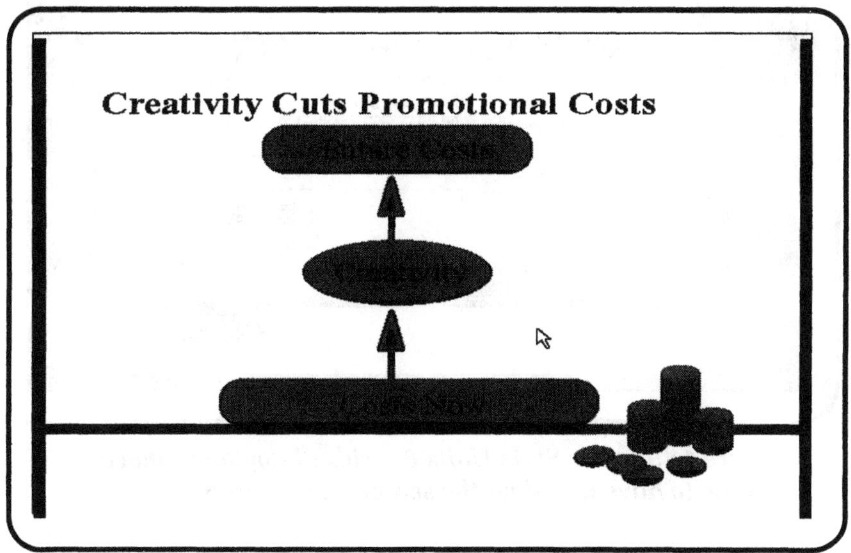
Creativity Cuts Promotional Costs

Figure 11.8 You can change attributes on arrows to have thicker lines.

You can, however, customize more than the individual tools. You can set up the drawing environment itself so that you can be more effective as you work. It can be helpful, for instance, to have a *grid* on the page to help you align objects such as the rectangles, arrows, and the oval in the concept chart. To have a grid on the page as you work, click on the Style menu. Choose Units & Grids. You see the Style Units & Grids dialog box, as shown in Figure 11.9.

Click on Display grid to have the grid appear on the screen. If you wish, you can also select the feature called Snap to grid. When you do, all new objects that you draw align to the nearest line on the grid. They do so whether you have the grid displayed or not. Figure 11.10 shows the same drawing you saw in Figure 11.8, with Display grid and Snap to grid used to align the objects.

> **Caution:** If you forget that Snap to grid is turned on, you may find yourself having difficulty placing objects where you want them. They will keep "snapping back" to some other position. If you have that problem, remember to check the setting on Snap to grid.

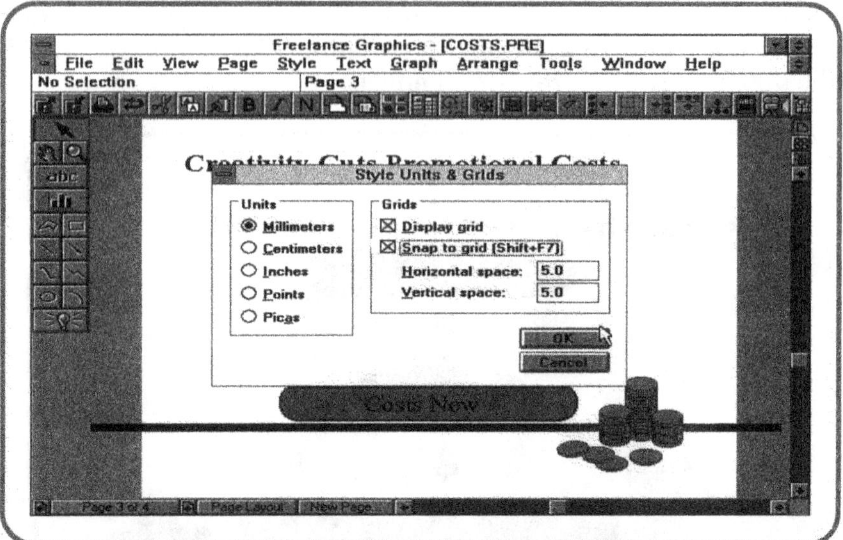

Figure 11.9 In the Style Units & Grids dialog box, you can choose to have a grid on the screen as you draw

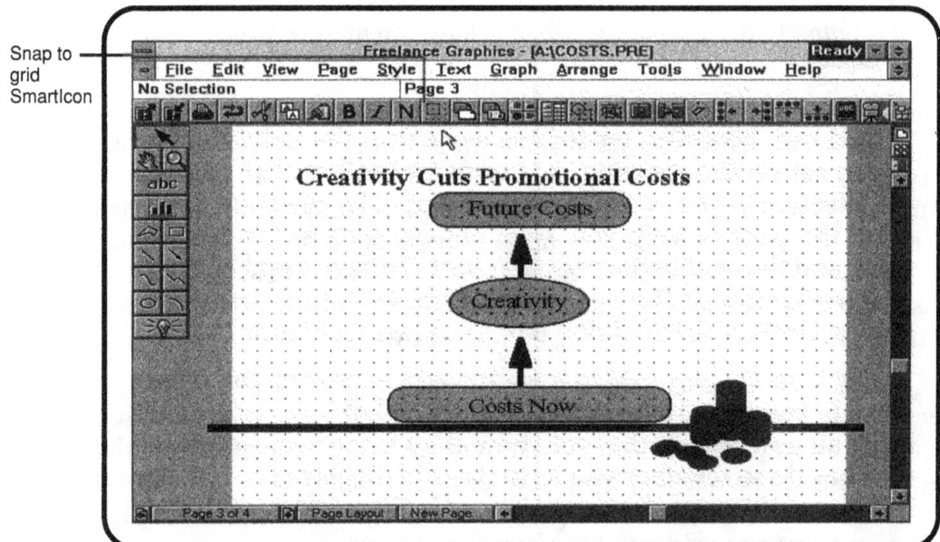

Figure 11.10 You can use Display grid and Snap to grid to align objects precisely.

Tip: To avoid having Snap to grid in effect when you don't want it, it is a good idea to turn on Snap to grid only when you want it and then turn it back off. To do so quickly, you can use the SmartIcon or press Shift+F7.

The Display grid and Snap to grid features are two useful drawing tools. There are others. When aligning objects on the page, you may find working with a large cross hair cursor helpful. In many of the same cases where you are likely to use a grid, you may want a large cursor as well.

To change to a large cross hair, choose Tools from the Main menu and then choose User Setup. In the User Setup dialog box, click on Big cross hair in the Cursor size box. Figure 11.11 shows a big cross hair on the diagram shown in Figure 11.10.

Tip: The shortcut to toggle between large and small cross hairs is Shift+F4.

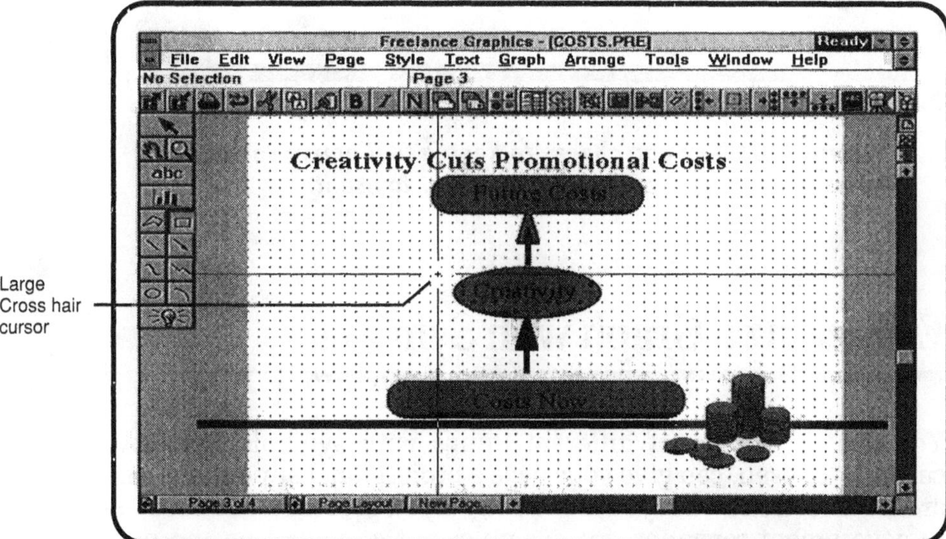

Figure 11.11 You can use a large cross hair to help you position objects.

Freelance's designers have thought of another drawing feature you may want to use, particularly when creating charts that use the same type of object a number of times. In the default setup, you can draw only one object at a time (a rectangle, for instance). To draw another rectangle, you have to click on the Rectangle tool again. If you know you want to draw the same object more than once, you can set up Freelance so that you don't have to click on the tool each time. In the Tools User Setup dialog box, click on the Keep tool active option (see Figure 11.12).

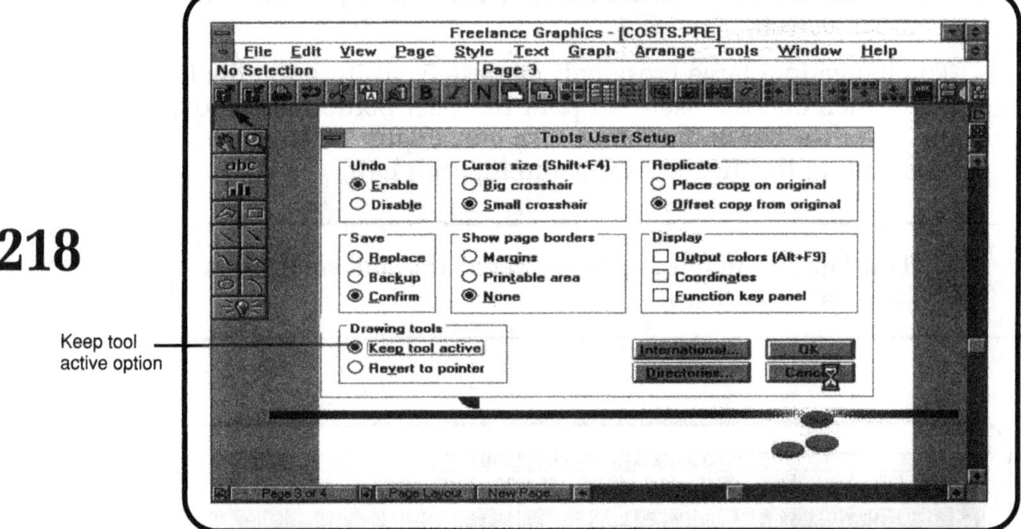

Figure 11.12 You can choose to keep a tool active so you don't have to click on it each time you want to use it.

Enlivening a Graph with Symbols

You can do dozens of different things with symbols. Symbols, carefully chosen, can give your page a professional appearance and arouse interest in what you are saying. If you present a chart related to government revenues, for example, put a symbol on the page showing a government symbol, a flag, or currency (as in Figure 11.13). Use the outline of a symbol as the border of a chart. Figure 11.14 uses a simple rectangle as the border. Figure 11.15 uses a symbol of a truck as the border for a text chart.

***Figure 11.13** If you have a presentation about government, place a governmental symbol on the page. This symbol is from the usa.sym library.*

***Figure 11.14** You can use a rectangle to form the border of a chart.*

To use a rectangle as a border, double-click on the Rectangle tool and, in the Style Default Attributes Rectangle dialog box, set Pattern to None; otherwise, you cannot see through the rectangle.

To use a symbol as a border, click on Arrange from the Main menu while the symbol is selected. Choose Priority and Bottom. That way other elements on the chart, such as text, appear on top of the symbol. You may have to make other adjustments. See Chapter 12 for more information on selecting symbols and working with them.

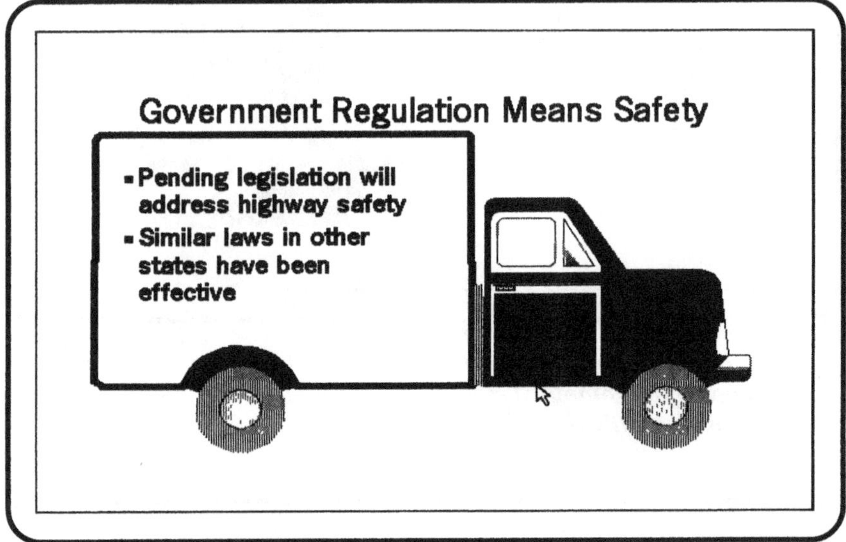

Figure 11.15 Use a symbol for a border.

Use a symbol as a background rather than a border for your chart. Maps work particularly well as backgrounds, as shown in Figure 11.16. On a text chart, place symbols on the page along with text to create a *pictorial text chart*, as in Figure 11.17.

FYIdea: In a bullet chart, replace the bullets with symbols related to the topic you discuss. Talking about milk revenues? Use symbols of milk cartons as the bullets. The audience will enjoy the pictorial effect, even if you are just presenting "dry information."

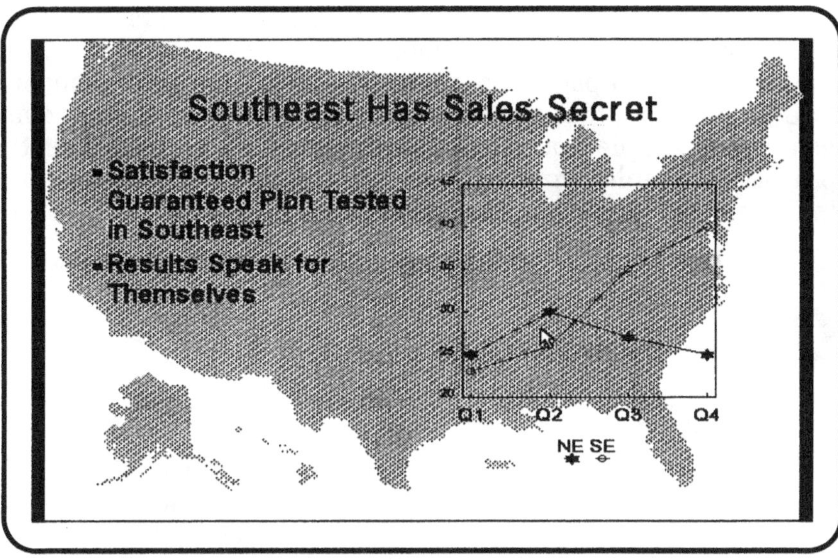

Figure 11.16 Use a symbol as the background for a chart.

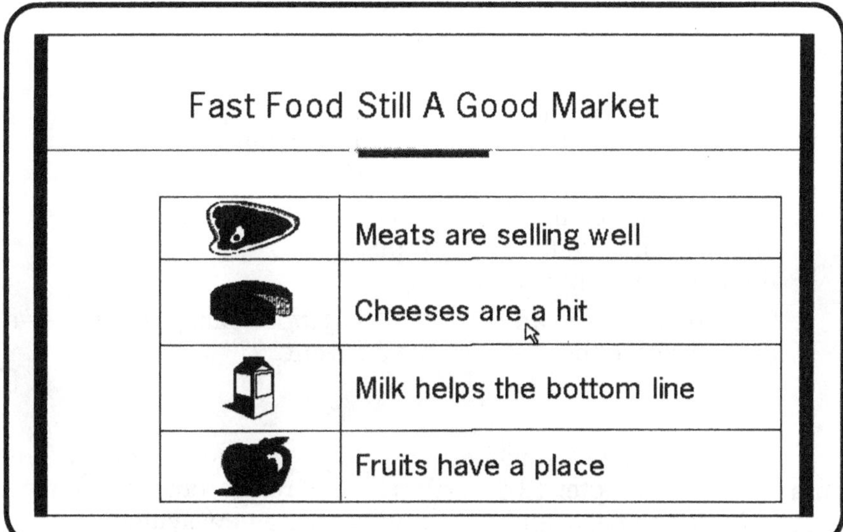

Figure 11.17 Using symbols, you can create a pictorial text chart.

In Chapter 3, "Starting a Simple SmartMaster Presentation," you learned to add a symbol to your title page. In the same way, you can make a graph page more interesting by adding your company logo (or a symbol that represents the subject matter). If your company logo is simple, you can use the drawing tools to create it on the page. If it is complex, you can import it in a graphics file, as explained in Chapter 14, "Importing Data from Other Programs."

To place a symbol on the page, follow these Quick Steps.

Q Adding a Symbol to a Page

1. Click on the light bulb symbol in the Tool box. — You see the Add Symbols dialog box.
2. Browse through symbols in the Library box until you see the one you want. — Each time you highlight a library, you see the first six symbols in the library in the Symbol box.
3. Browse through the symbols using the scroll arrows next to the Symbol box or the keyboard arrow keys. — As each library is highlighted, you see symbols in the Symbol box.
4. Double-click on the symbol you want. — The symbol appears on the page with selection handles on it.
5. Click inside the handles and drag the symbol to the position you want. — The symbol moves to the new position.
6. Click on a handle and drag to resize the symbol. — The symbol changes to the size you want. □

After you have a symbol on the page, you can move it around and change it. Chapter 12 describes how to resize, crop, and change a symbol on the page, and also how to create new symbols.

> **FYIdea:** You can replace the elements of a graph with symbols. Doing a graph showing revenues from trucking? Replace the bars with pictures of trucks.

What You Have Learned

- With the drawing tools in the Toolbox you can draw lines, arrows, ellipses, rectangles, even polylines and polygons. Click on the tool and then drag.
- To draw a line, choose the Line drawing tool from the Toolbox and then click on the beginning and end points.
- To add a nonwrapping text block, select the Text drawing tool, click once, and start typing.
- To draw a rectangle or ellipse, select the correct drawing tool, click at one corner and drag to the far corner. Hold down the Shift key while dragging to draw a square or circle.
- You can customize the drawing tools. For instance, you can give your rectangles rounded corners. Double-click on the tool and then make the change in the dialog box.
- You can customize the drawing environment. For instance, you can have a grid on the page as you work. Choose Style and then Units & Grids.
- You can use a rectangle or a symbol as the border for your chart. Combine symbols with text to create a pictorial text chart.

Chapter 12

Basic Object Editing

In This Chapter

- *Selecting objects*
- *Changing the size of an object*
- *Changing attributes such as color*
- *Ungrouping objects to work with parts of an object*
- *Grouping objects to form a new object*
- *Changing object priority when an object is on top of another*

In Freelance you can edit *objects* just as you can edit text. As with text, you first select an object before editing it. You can edit an object with the mouse or the menus. You can change its size or attributes (which, for an object, are primarily its color and pattern). You can break up objects into parts—a process known as *ungrouping*— and work with the parts. You can also combine parts into a new object, a process known as *grouping*.

Selecting Objects

There are many ways you may want to work with objects. After you place a graphic object on the page, often you will want to move it or change its size, color, or shape. Before you can make any such changes to an object, however, you have to tell Freelance which object you want to work with: you have to *select* the object.

You can select objects in many ways, depending upon your needs or your preferences. Figure 12.1 shows the Select option from the Edit menu. The menu summarizes all the ways you can select objects.

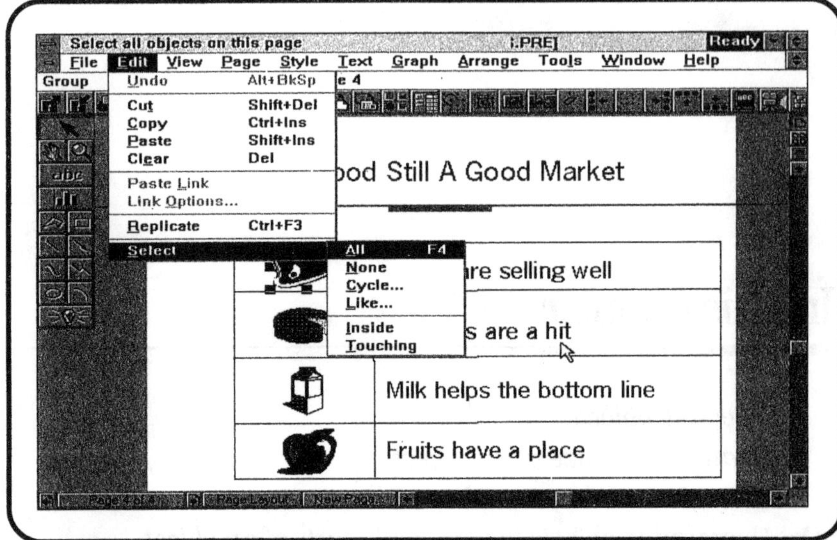

Figure 12.1 The Select option on the Edit menu summarizes the ways you can select objects.

In most cases, it is faster to use the mouse than the menu—as explained in the sections that follow—but some choices (such as Like and Cycle) you can only choose from the menu. Table 12.1 summarizes the ways you can select objects in Freelance using the choices in the Edit menu.

Table 12.1 Edit menu options for selecting objects.

Option	What It Does
All	In Current Page view, selects all objects on the current page. In Page Sorter view, selects all pages.
None	Deselects all objects on the current page.
Cycle	For each object visible on the page, asks if you want to select or deselect it.

Option	What It Does
Like	For selecting objects on the page that have attributes in common with an object that you have already selected.
Inside	For selecting all objects inside the box you drag on the page.
Touching	For selecting all objects within or touching the box you drag on the page.

Selecting with the Selector Tool (Clicking)

The easiest way to select an object is to click on it with the left mouse button. This selects the object you clicked on and deselects all others. Use the right mouse button to select or deselect one object without affecting the others on the page. Be sure the pointer is in the shape of an arrow before you try to select (if it is not, click on the arrow at the top of the Toolbox to begin using the arrow tool). When you select an object, it appears with selection handles on it, as shown in Figure 12.2.

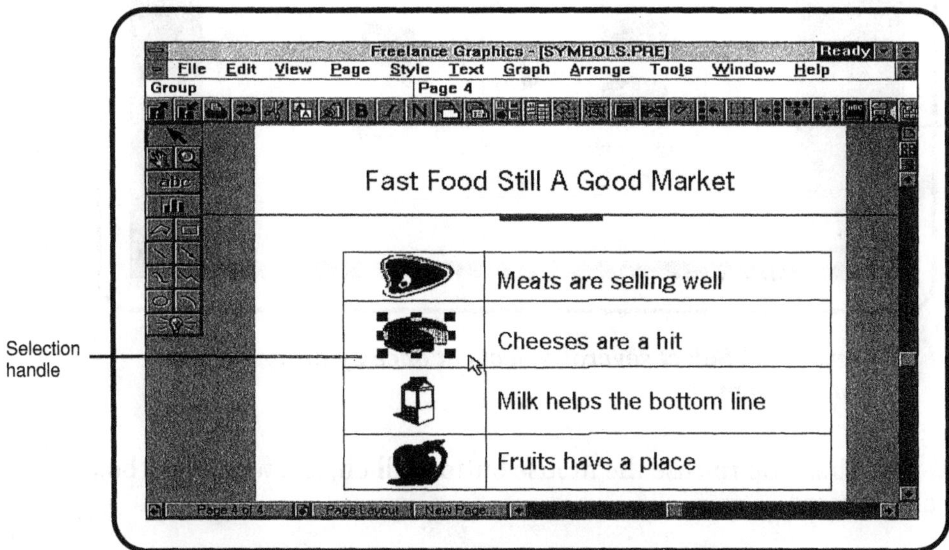

Figure 12.2 Click on an object with the left mouse button to select it.

Note: If your mouse has only one button, hold down the Shift key while clicking to get the effect of using the right mouse button.

Selecting Multiple Objects (Dragging)

You can select several objects at a time by dragging a box around them with the mouse. Use the left mouse button to click and drag a box until it completely surrounds the objects, as shown in Figure 12.3. This action with the mouse is equivalent to choosing Edit, then Select, then Inside from the menu, and then dragging a box around the objects.

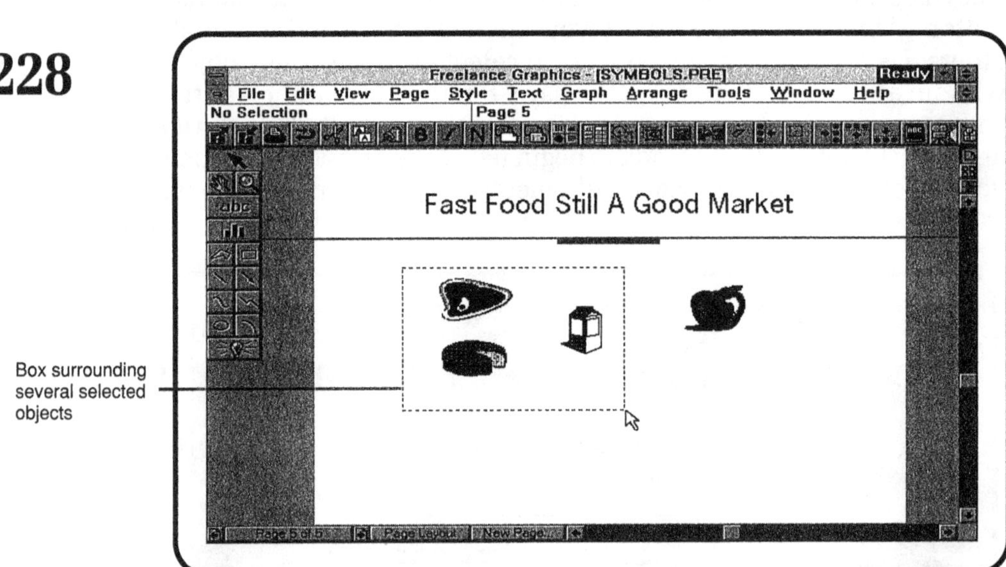

Figure 12.3 Select several objects at once by dragging a box around them.

When you release the mouse button, all objects within the box are selected.

Tip: Use the right mouse button while dragging to deselect the objects within the box.

If you want to select objects that are partially inside the box, choose Select from the Edit menu. Then choose Touching from the submenu.

Cycling

Selecting by *cycling* is useful when the object you want is underneath other objects, or too small to click on easily. Cycling through the objects is a little like looking at mug shots. Freelance Graphics "points" to each object in order of its priority, so you can say, "That's the one, officer!" (Unless you change the objects' priority, Freelance will follow the order in which you drew them on the page.)

To select by cycling, follow these steps:

1. Choose Select from the Edit menu.
2. Choose Cycle from the submenu. The Edit Select Cycle dialog box appears, as shown in Figure 12.4.

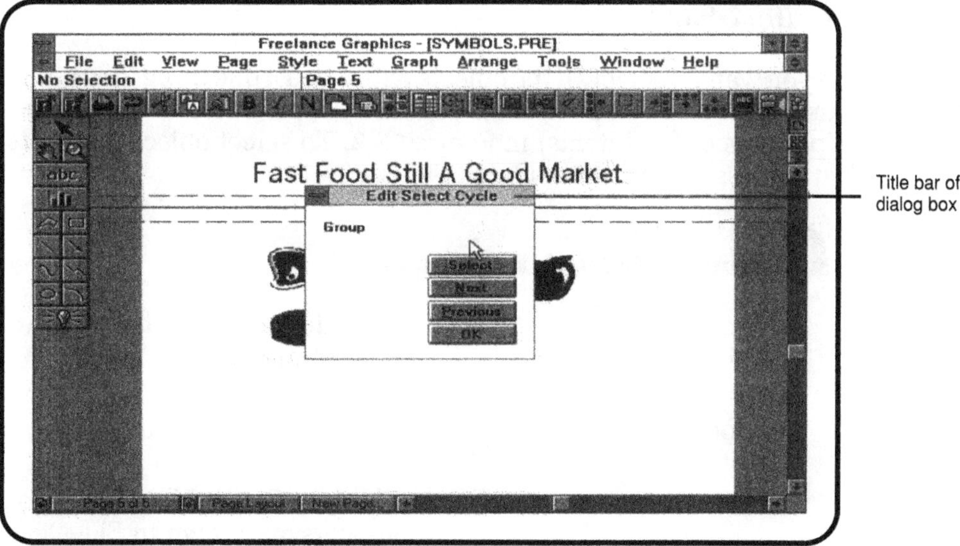

Figure 12.4 The Edit Select Cycle dialog box.

Tip: If the dialog box is blocking your view of the page, click on the title bar of the box and drag it out of your way.

3. To point to an object, click on the Next button. A broken box appears around the first-priority object on your presentation page. Click on the Next button again, and the broken box moves to the next-priority object. (To go in the other direction, click on the Previous button.)
4. When the broken box is around the desired object, click on the Select button.
5. Continue selecting objects by repeating Steps 3 and 4.
6. To close the dialog box, click on OK.

Tip: To select a small object that is surrounded by larger objects, zoom in by choosing In from the View menu and then choose Edit Select Cycle. Freelance Graphics cycles through only those objects currently showing on the screen.

Using Select Like

If you want to select all the objects with at least one thing in common, use the Select Like command. For the example, select all the symbols (pictures of food items) in Figure 12.2. To select objects by shared attributes, follow these Quick Steps.

Using the Select Like Command

1. Click on one of the objects you want to select.	Selection handles show that the object is now selected.
2. Choose Select from the Edit menu.	The Select submenu appears.
3. Choose Like.	The Edit Select Like dialog box appears, as shown in Figure 12.5.

4. Click on the criteria you want to match (for example, object type).

   Selected criteria appear with an X in the selection box.

5. Click on OK.

   All like objects (food symbols in the example) are now selected (see Figure 12.6). □

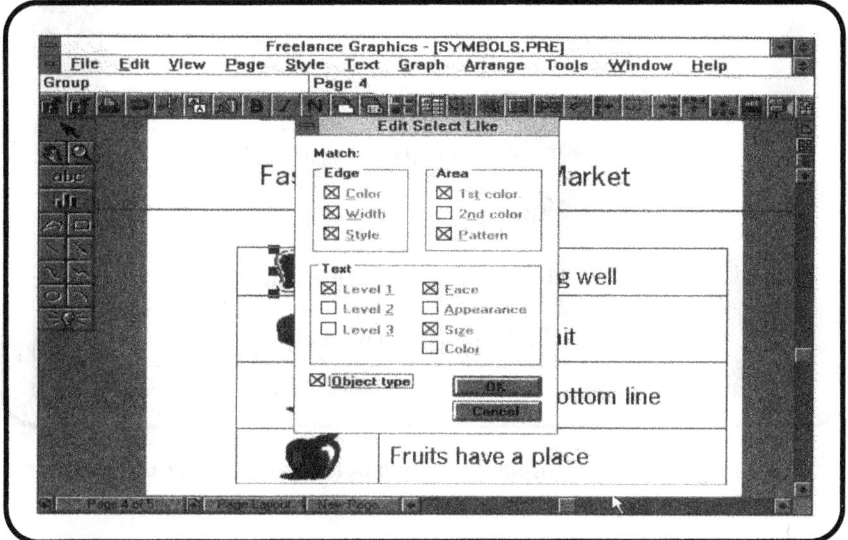

Figure 12.5 The Edit Select Like dialog box.

Deselecting Objects

You can deselect everything by clicking the mouse anywhere on the page *except* on an object. From the menu, choose Edit, then Select, and then None. To deselect only one of your selected objects, click the right mouse button on that object.

Changing the Size of Objects

Like the objects you created in Chapter 11, "Simple Drawing Techniques," (and the graphs you created in Chapter 5 and elsewhere), the predrawn pictures from the symbols library are also objects. You can use the same techniques to resize all the objects on your presentation page.

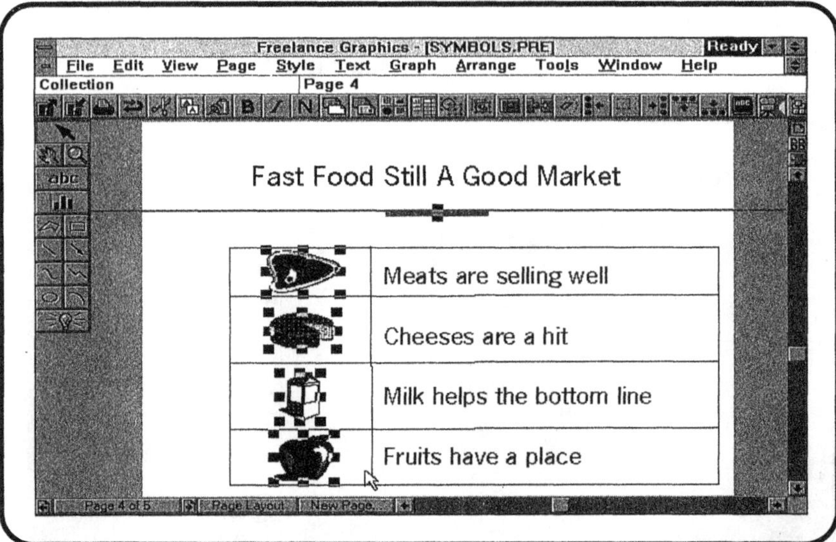

Figure 12.6 With Select Like, you select all similar objects on the page.

For example, click on the light bulb symbol in any presentation page. In the symbol file called finance.sym, double-click on the picture of the dollar bill. (Do *not* drag it into a Click here to add symbol box.) Once you have the picture on the page, you are ready to resize it. Figure 12.7 shows the symbol on the page before you resize it.

To make the symbol bigger, follow these steps:

1. Click on a corner handle.
2. Hold down the Shift key while dragging the mouse away from the center of the object. (Holding down the Shift key maintains the proportions in the object as you change its size.)
3. Release the mouse button. Figure 12.8 shows the result.

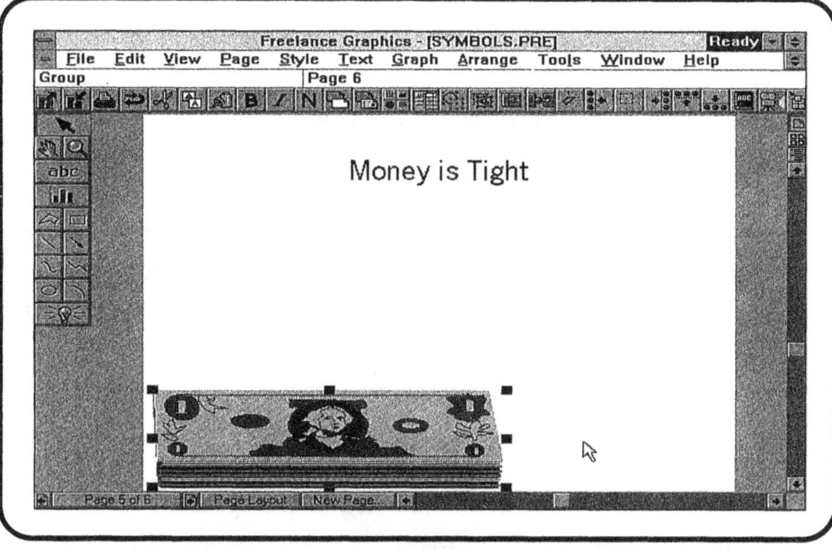

Figure 12.7 Symbol on the page before you resize it.

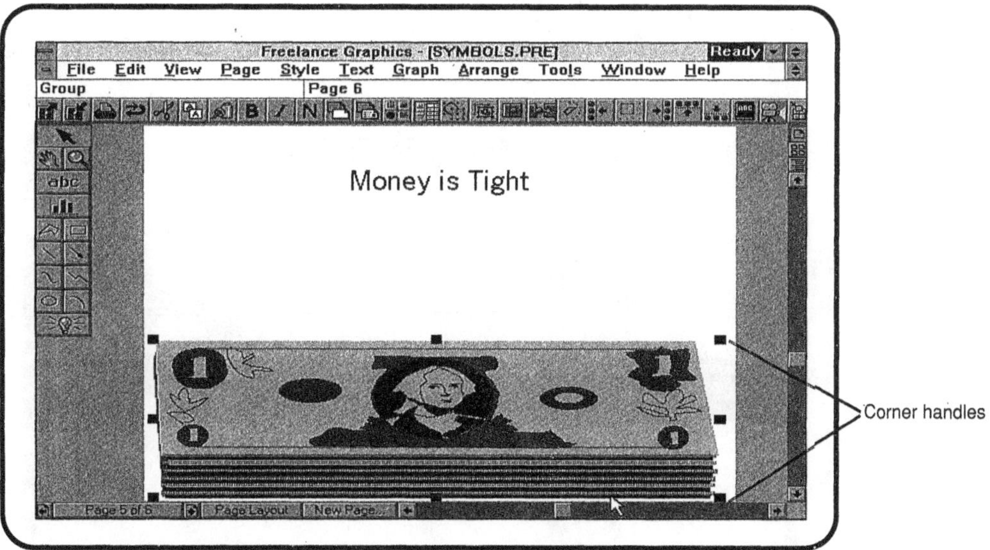

Figure 12.8 Hold down the Shift key and drag a corner handle to resize an object and maintain its proportions.

To make a symbol bigger, then, the basic procedure is to pull out on a corner handle. Next, suppose you want to reduce the symbol's size. Follow these steps:

1. Select a symbol, for example, the dollar bill.
2. Click on a corner handle.
3. While holding down the Shift key, drag the mouse toward the center of the symbol.
4. Release the mouse button.

> **FYIdea:** There are times when you'll want to distort a symbol in order to make a point. For example, you can suggest that money is tight with a long, thin dollar.

To change a symbol's dimensions:

1. Click on a side handle on the end of the symbol.
2. Drag in the direction you want (up for this example).

Figure 12.9 shows a stretched-out dollar. You can change its dimensions by dragging any side handle out or in.

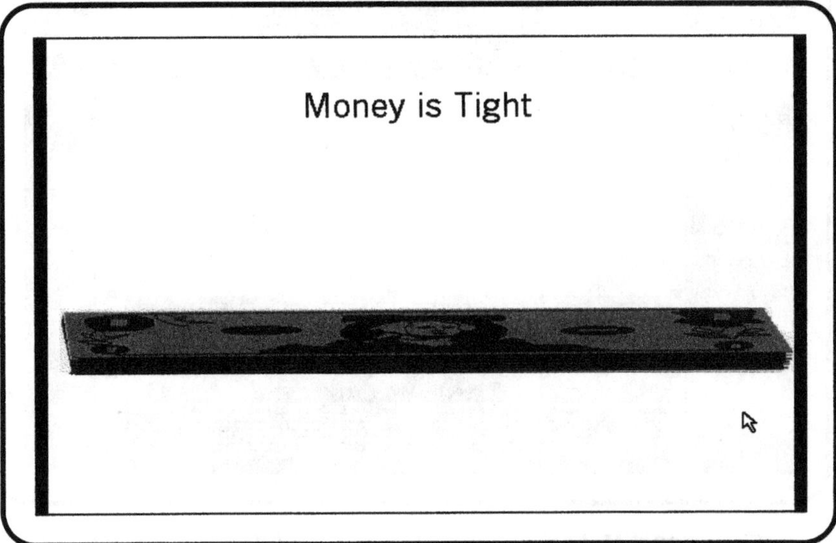

Figure 12.9 Dragging in or out on a side handle changes the symbol's dimensions.

Tip: You can change the size of several objects at once. Just select them all and pull one corner handle.

After you have an object on the page, you can still use it on a predrawn SmartMaster page. Follow these Quick Steps.

Placing an Object on a SmartMaster Page

1. Click on the Page Layout button at the bottom of the screen. — A list of available page layouts pops up.
2. Choose a Page Layout that includes symbols. — The page displays the new layout.
3. Click inside the object and drag it into the box on the page (the graphics box) that says `Click here to add a symbol`. — The object is reduced to fit the box, as shown in Figure 12.10.

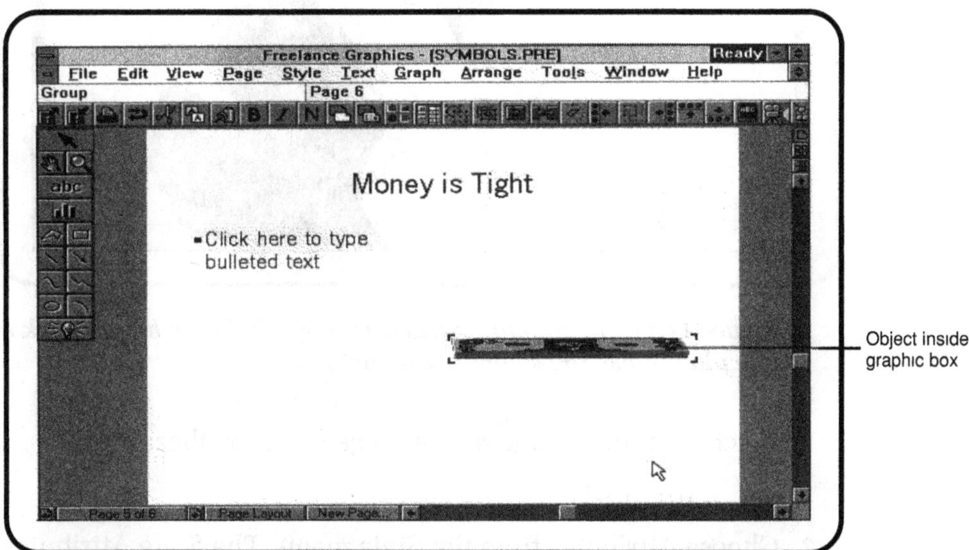

Figure 12.10 Dragging an existing symbol into the graphics box automatically reduces it to fit.

Changing Attributes of an Object

In Freelance you have the freedom to change an object's *attributes*; you can change its color or pattern, or you can change its appearance to accommodate different output devices—black and white for overheads, color for a printer. You may decide that the default colors do not show up as well as you like. You may want to emphasize or de-emphasize one object; you can do either.

For the example, suppose you want to use a map of Michigan as the background for a bullet chart. Eliminating the line on the edge would change the map into a light pattern suitable for a background. Figure 12.11 shows the map before you change its attributes.

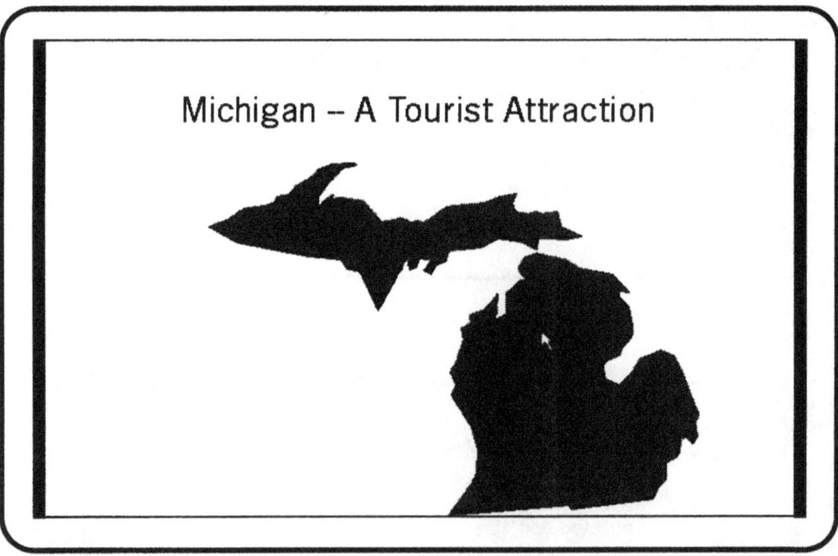

Figure 12.11 The default settings on a symbol may be too dark if you plan to use the symbol as a background.

To change the attributes of an object, follow these steps:

1. Select the object.
2. Choose Attributes from the Style menu. The Style Attributes Polygon & Shape dialog box appears, as shown in Figure 12.12.

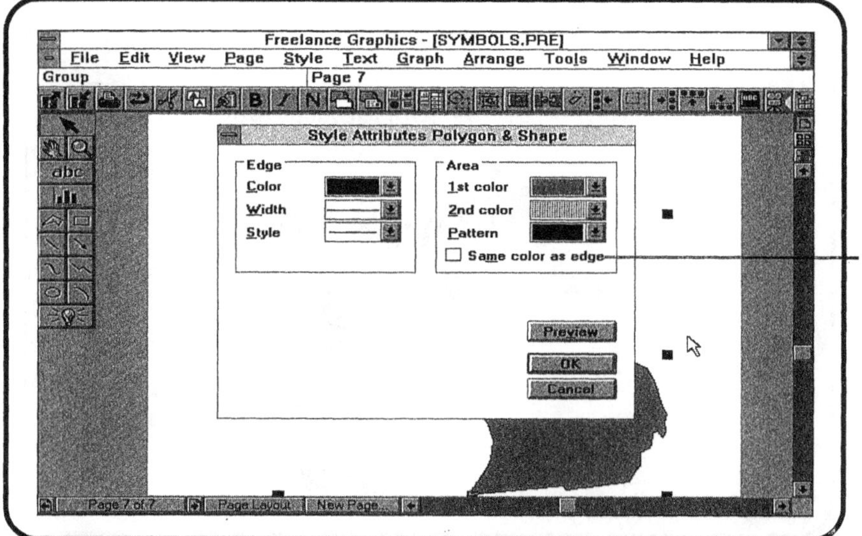

Figure 12.12 The Style Attributes Polygon & Shape dialog box. **237**

3. The attributes for the edge (or outline) of the object are on the left. Click on a Style drop-down menu arrow and then choose None.
4. Set the attributes for the Area (or object middle) on the right. First, if necessary, deselect Same color as edge. Then select 1st color and 2nd color by clicking on them to scroll through the palette.

> **Note:** The second color does not appear if the pattern is solid. Also, keep the object's size in mind when selecting a pattern; bold patterns show up best on large objects. For the sample, select a light, solid color for the first color.

To see how the object looks with the attributes you chose, click on Preview. (If the dialog box is in the way, click on the title bar and drag it somewhere else.) The dialog box remains open to allow for more changes. Click on OK to accept the changes or choose Cancel to keep the previous attributes. Figure 12.13 shows the symbol with the changed attributes.

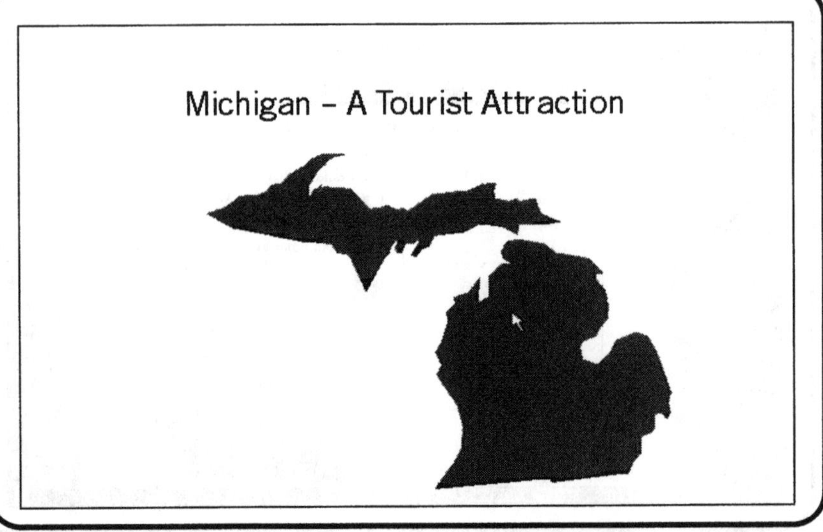

Figure 12.13 With a light pattern, a map is suitable as a background.

Tip: To call up an object's Style Attributes dialog box quickly, click twice in the object.

FYIdea: Even though you usually think of text blocks as being clear, Freelance lets you give them the same colors and patterns available to other objects. Change the attributes of a text block to make it stand out from other text blocks.

Ungrouping Objects

You can break up a predrawn symbol from the symbol library into individual parts by *ungrouping* it. As a result, you can adapt symbols to your needs and even create different symbols from the existing symbols. After you ungroup an object, you can apply other skills for selecting, deleting, rotating, and otherwise working with drawing tools.

Suppose, for example, you want to have a picture of a single bolt with no accompanying nuts for a slide with the message, "Sometimes the simplest hardware is the best." You can use Freelance's predrawn symbol of a bolt with nuts, ungroup the symbol, and delete the part you don't need.

Figure 12.14 shows the symbol as it comes from the commobjt.sym symbol library. (It is symbol 10 of 21.) To ungroup a symbol, follow these Quick Steps.

Ungrouping a Symbol

1. Click on the symbol. — Selection handles show that it is selected.
2. Select the Arrange menu. — You are presented with the Arrange menu's options.
3. Choose Ungroup from the Arrange menu. — Selection handles on the parts of the symbol show that each is now selected, as shown in Figure 12.15. □

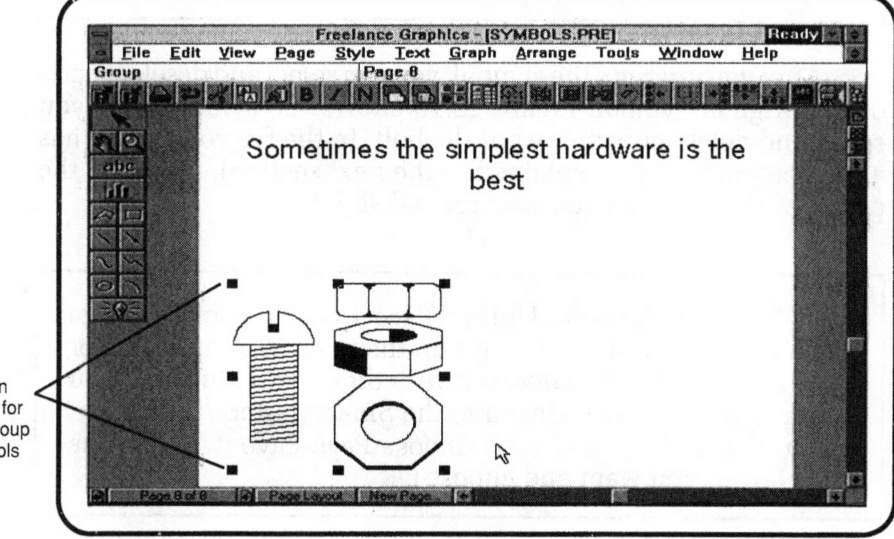

Figure 12.14 The selected symbol from the library before you ungroup it.

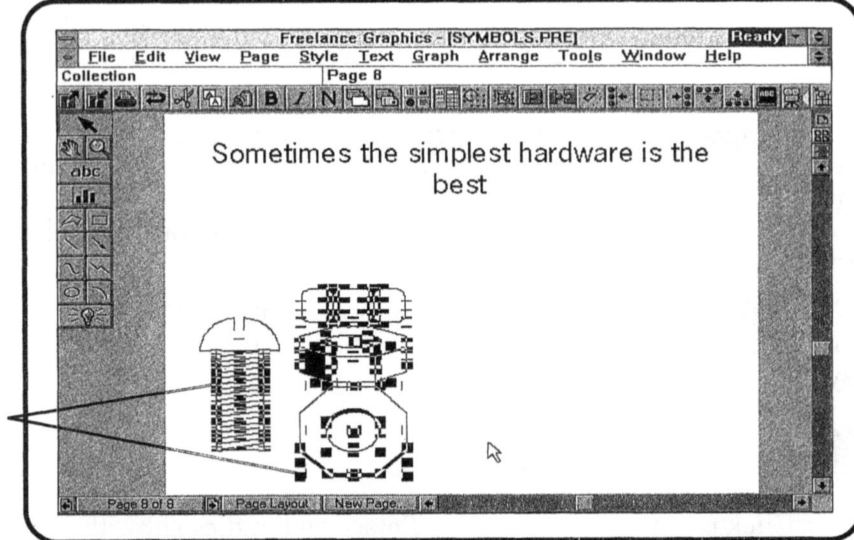

Figure 12.15 The Ungroup command separates a symbol into multiple symbols.

Tip: Sometimes when you ungroup a complicated symbol (such as a flower), it is made up of more groups. Select and ungroup them the same way.

After you ungroup the symbol, you can select and deselect parts of the original symbol. Figure 12.16 shows the symbol after you select and delete everything but the bolt. In the figure, the bolt has also been grouped (as explained in the next section), moved to the center of the page, resized, and rotated slightly.

Tip: By choosing Unlink Page Layout from the Page menu, you can also ungroup the parts of a SmartMaster page in order to select and work with them individually. If you want to have the page linked to the SmartMaster Page Layout again, choose Page and then Choose Page Layout. Select the page layout you want and choose OK.

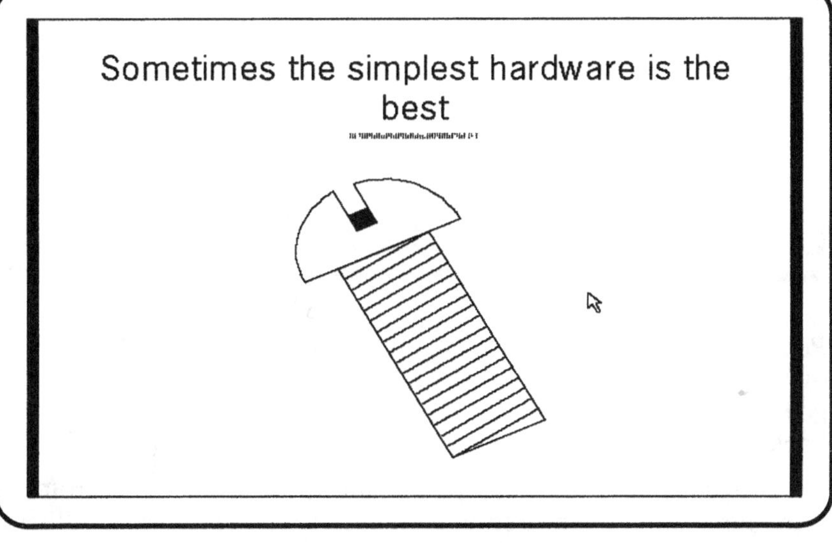
Sometimes the simplest hardware is the best

Figure 12.16 Once you have ungrouped a symbol, you can delete the parts you don't want.

Grouping Objects

Grouping joins several objects so you can move and size them like a single object. When you place a label on a rectangle in a concept chart, for instance, you probably want to keep the label and the symbol together when you move them. To do so, group the label and the rectangle into a single symbol. After you modify a symbol by ungrouping it and deleting some parts, you may want to move or resize the remaining symbol. To work with the symbol as a whole, group the remaining parts into one symbol.

To group two or more objects, follow these Quick Steps.

Q Grouping Objects

1. Drag a box around the objects you want to group. — The objects are individually selected.

2. Select the Arrange menu. — You will be presented with the Arrange menu's options.
3. Select Group from the Arrange menu. — The newly grouped object is now selected. □

Changing Priority of Objects

Priority is the order that objects appear on the page. If your objects overlap, their priority becomes important. The first-priority object goes *behind* all others. If you work with multiple objects, including backgrounds, it's useful to know how to change object priority.

Suppose you want to place the picture of a bolt from the previous section inside a solid rectangle. Click on the Rectangle icon in the Toolbox and drag the rectangle into place. The rectangle covers up the bolt altogether. In Figure 12.17 the rectangle hides part of the bolt, so you can see that both are on the page.

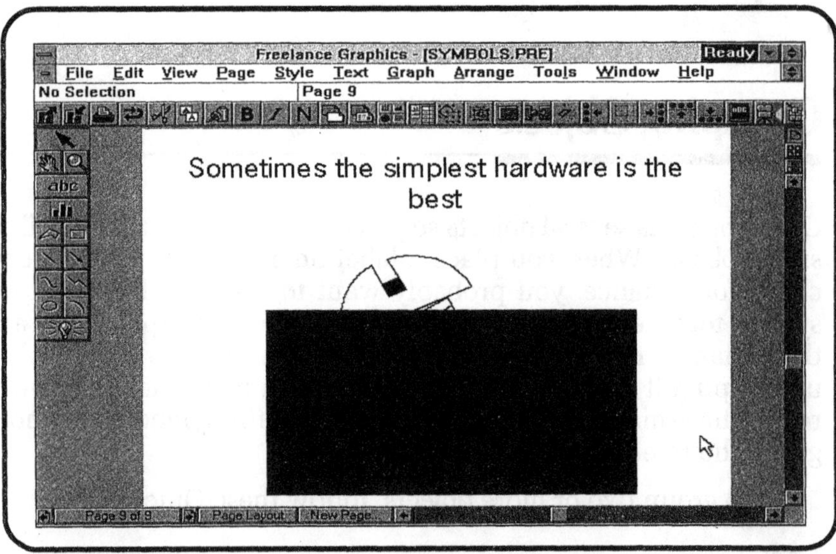

Figure 12.17 A more recent object has a higher priority than an earlier one and appears on top of it.

To place the bolt on top of the rectangle, select the rectangle. From the Arrange menu, choose Priority. Choose either Bottom or

Fall Back One to move the rectangle behind the bolt. Table 12.2 summarizes all the options on the Priority submenu, as shown in Figure 12.18. Figure 12.19 shows the result of changing the priority for the bolt. (The rectangle behind the bolt has also been stretched.)

Table 12.2 Priority submenu options.

Priority	Effect
Top	Selected object moves to the top of the pile of objects.
Bottom	Selected object moves beneath any objects it overlaps.
Send Forward One	Moves the selected object on top of the object immediately above it.
Fall Back One	Moves the selected object beneath the object immediately beneath it.

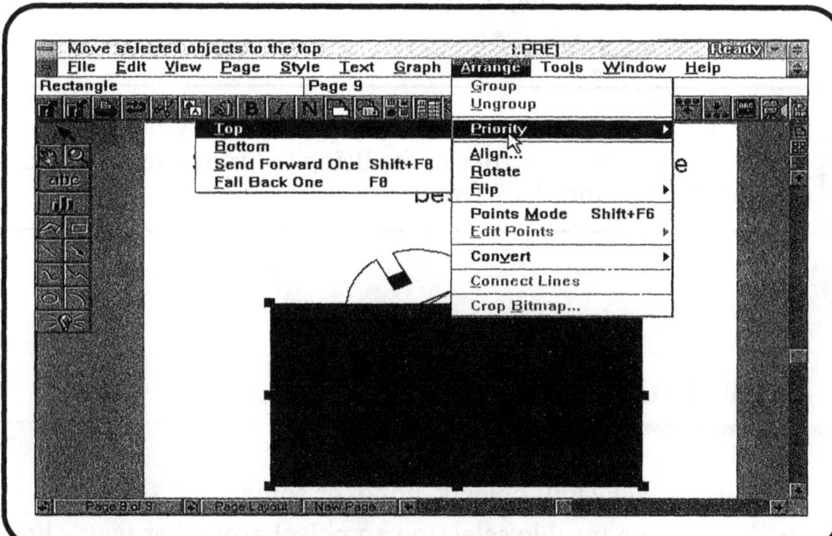

Figure 12.18 The Priority submenu.

FYIdea: If you want to hide part of an object, "crop" the part you want to hide by covering it with a rectangle that matches the background and has a higher priority than what you want to hide.

Sometimes the simplest hardware is the best

***Figure 12.19** After you change the priority, the symbol appears on top of the rectangle used as a background.*

Tip: If you find yourself changing priority often, locate and use the SmartIcons for Bring to Front, Send to Back, Forward One, and Back One.

What You Have Learned

- You can select all objects, none, or some.
- If you have trouble selecting an object any other way, choose Select and then Cycle and go through objects one by one until you can select the one you want.
- Select several objects at once by dragging a box around them with your mouse pointer.
- Deselect all selected objects by clicking anywhere else on the page.

- Text blocks, symbols, graphs, and shapes are all objects. You can edit them in the same ways.
- Change the size of an object by clicking on a corner handle and dragging.
- Hold down the Shift key and drag to keep the proportions the same as you resize an object.
- You can change the attributes of an object, such as the edge, color, and pattern.
- To break apart a symbol so you can edit it, select it and choose Arrange and then Ungroup.
- Create a new object from several objects by selecting them and choosing Arrange and then Group.
- Move an object behind another object by selecting the object and then choosing Arrange then Priority, Bottom, or Fall Back One, or press F8 (Back One).

Chapter 13

Making Global Presentation Changes

In This Chapter

- ► *Changing to another SmartMaster set*
- ► *Changing color schemes*
- ► *Changing text and bullets on multiple pages at once*
- ► *Adding text or a logo to all presentation pages*
- ► *Creating a new SmartMaster set from an existing one*

You have already become familiar with some of the advantages of SmartMasters. In short, they make your design decisions for you. They have another advantage: a SmartMaster is a design for an entire presentation—a group of pages—rather than for a single page.

If you work on the SmartMaster itself rather than on the individual pages, you can make changes that apply to the entire presentation. You can change from one SmartMaster to another, change the color scheme of a SmartMaster, change attributes such as the appearance of the bullets in bulleted lists, and even add something to one SmartMaster page (the Basic Layout page) that then appears on every page in the presentation.

Changing SmartMasters

As you have seen throughout this book, SmartMasters control many things in a presentation. In most cases, they provide a background, which can be anything from a few buttons to a view of Spain or Italy. The SmartMasters determine where elements like graphics, graphs, text, and bullets appear on the presentation pages.

Elements do not appear in the same place for each SmartMaster. A title page for one SmartMaster, for example, is not identical with the title page for another. If you were to switch presentation formats without using SmartMasters, you would face a painstaking process—cutting and pasting elements onto a new background and working to change all the other design features from the previous design into the new design. When you ask Freelance to change SmartMasters, however, the process is much quicker. Freelance fits the old title page content into the new title page format, and all the content from the previous SmartMaster into the format of the new one. What would have been a complex, time-consuming process subject to error becomes a simple one.

For this example, suppose you are the manager of a chain of gift shops called Dawn's Doo Dads. Using Freelance Graphics you have created a graphics presentation for a group of potential financial backers. It's ten pages long, full of facts, figures, and graphs. The day before your presentation something occurs to you. The SmartMaster set you chose—deco.mas—gives your presentation too much of a high-tech look. Figure 13.1 shows the title page of the presentation. You think the look is great, but your gift shops sell country crafts. You decide that a more traditional look would suit the company better.

By simply changing the SmartMaster, you can change the look for the entire presentation. On the Style menu, select Choose SmartMaster Set. You see the Style Choose SmartMaster Set dialog box, as shown in Figure 13.2.

You can use the up and down arrows or the mouse to browse through the different SmartMaster sets. The set you highlight in the SmartMaster Sets list box appears in the Browse SmartMaster Set box at the bottom. Suppose you decide that the mountain.mas SmartMaster has the down-home look you want. Select it and click on OK or just double-click on its name. Your entire presentation takes on the new look. The title page from the old format becomes a title page in the new format. Any graphics pages from the old SmartMaster become the same type of graphics page in the new SmartMaster. Figure 13.3 shows the title page for the new presentation.

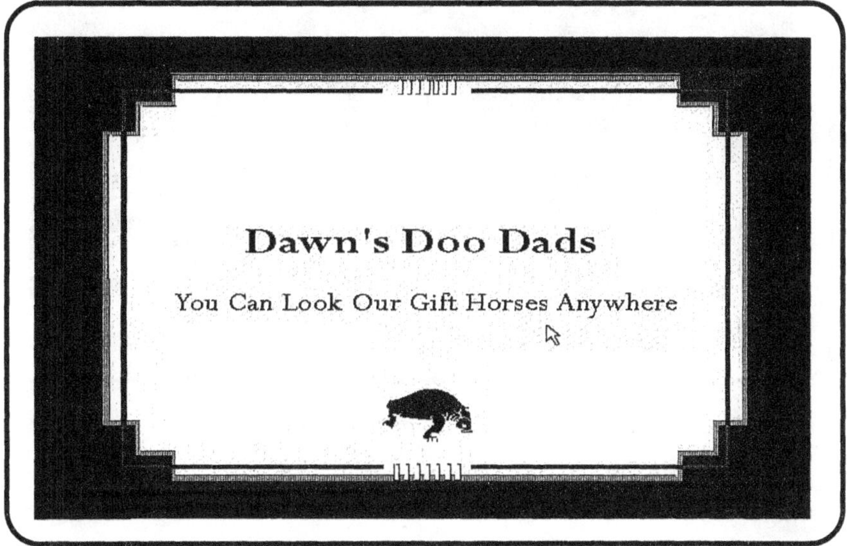

Figure 13.1 Title Page before you change SmartMasters.

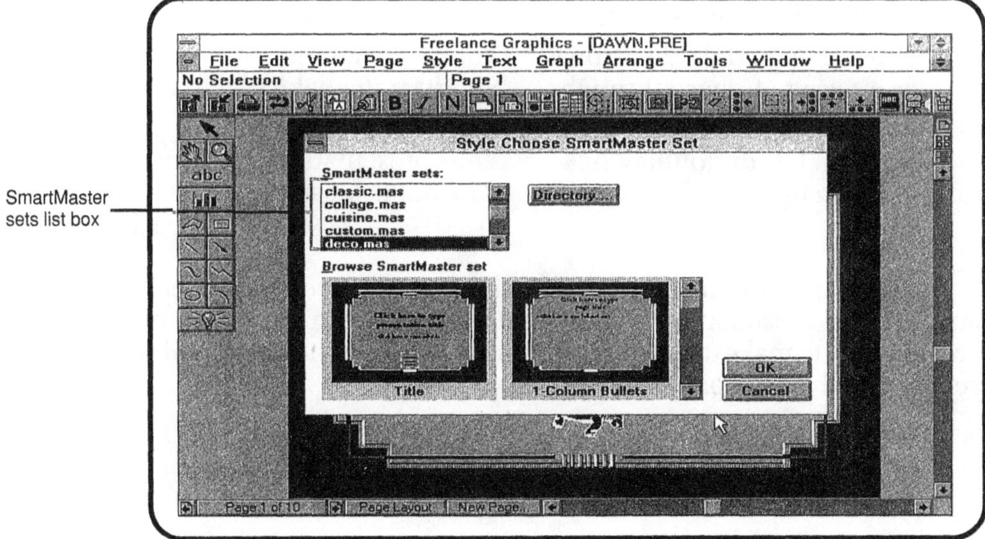

Figure 13.2 Style Choose SmartMaster Set dialog box.

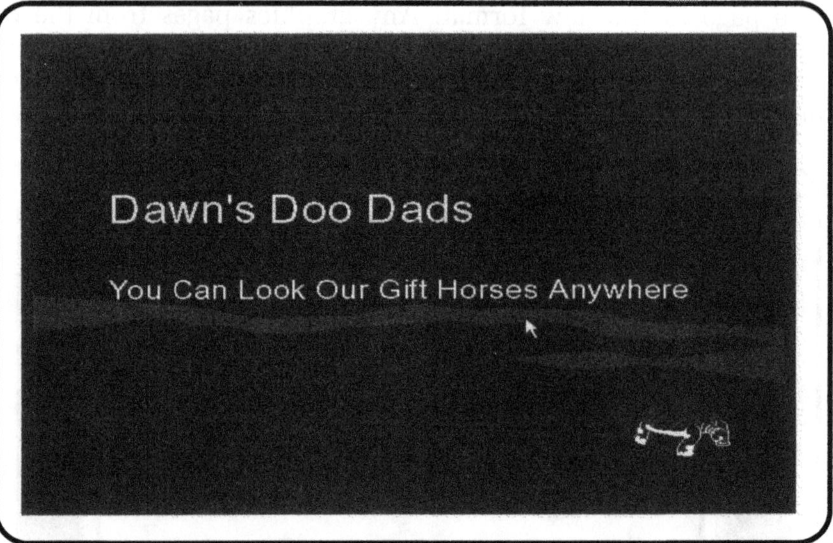

Figure 13.3 Title page for the new presentation.

The following Quick Steps review this process.

Q Changing SmartMasters

1. Choose Style and then Choose SmartMaster Set.	You see the Style Choose SmartMaster Set dialog box.
2. Use the up and down arrows or mouse to browse through the SmartMaster sets.	You see what the SmartMaster set looks like in the sample boxes.
3. Click on OK or double-click on the name of the set you choose.	Your presentation uses this new SmartMaster.

□

Changing the SmartMaster has a dramatic effect on the appearance of the presentation. Yet you do not have to do anything complicated to make the change. Similarly, you can change the color scheme easily, as explained in the next section.

Changing Color Schemes

With Freelance, you can change the color scheme for the entire presentation in the same way you can change the SmartMaster for the entire presentation. The change in color scheme affects only the current presentation. The SmartMaster itself will have the original color scheme the next time you choose it for a presentation.

Suppose, for instance, you want to change to a lighter color scheme for the gift shop presentation. You can go back into the Style menu and select Choose Palette. You see the Style Choose Palette dialog box, as shown in Figure 13.4.

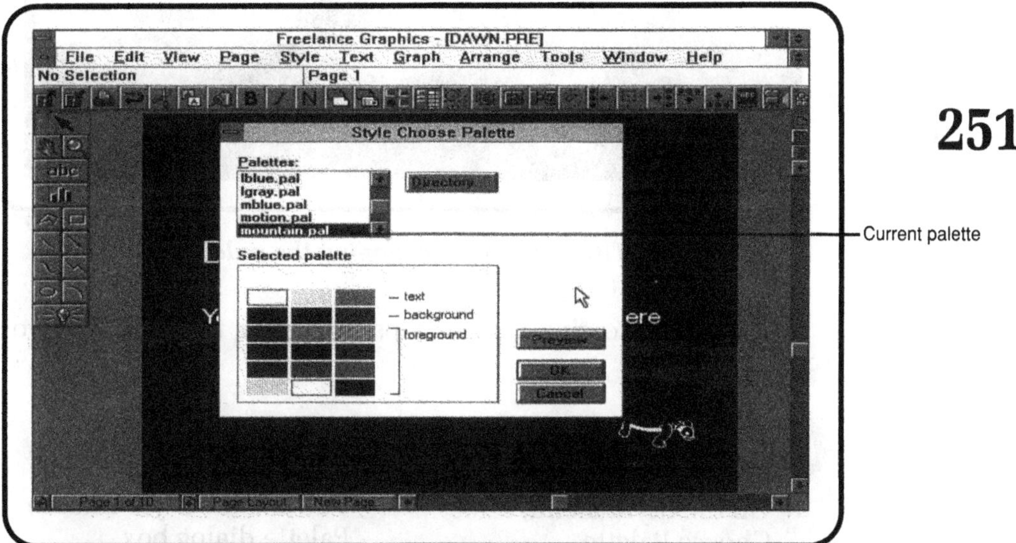

Figure 13.4 Style Choose Palette dialog box.

The current palette, mountain.pal, is highlighted. Use the up and down arrows or mouse to browse through the other palettes.

> **Tip:** After you highlight a palette you want to use, click on Preview to see how the color looks on the slide. It is difficult to appraise the effect of the color just by looking at the palette.

When you see the color you want, choose OK. For the example, choose the brite.pal palette. Figure 13.5 shows the slide with the new palette.

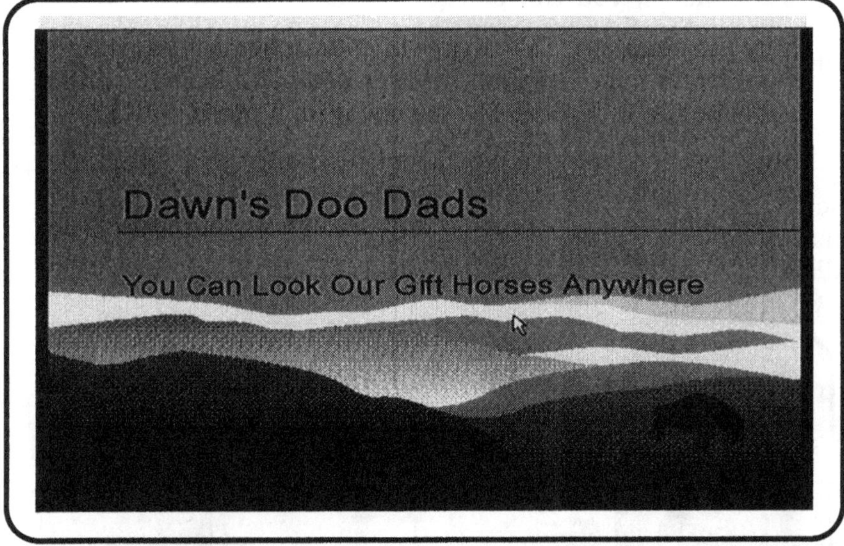

Figure 13.5 Title page after changing the palette.

Use the following Quick Steps to change the palette of your presentation.

Changing Palettes

Step	Result
1. On the Style menu, select Choose Palette.	You see the Style Choose Palette dialog box.
2. Use the up and down arrows or mouse to browse the palettes.	The palette colors show at the bottom of the dialog box.
3. Choose Preview to see what the SmartMaster page will look like with the new palette. (Move the dialog box aside, if necessary.)	You see the presentation page with the new palette.
4. Click on OK when you find the palette you want.	Your palette changes accordingly. □

FYIdea: While exploring the possibilities of color, don't forget the possibilities of black and white. Film makers still sometimes choose to film or photograph in black and white for good reason. The stark contrasts draw people's attention to the message, not the medium.

If you like the new palette but want to rearrange the colors within it, you are free to do so. See Chapter 10, "Using Color Effectively," for information on changing the colors in the color palette.

Changing Text Appearance

If you have ever worked with a word processor, you know that changing the appearance of text once you have it in place can be time-consuming. Usually you have to select whatever text you want to change and then choose the new characteristics from a menu. In a presentation like the sample one in this chapter, to use a similar approach, you would have to go to each slide you want to alter and change the characteristics of the text for that slide.

You can change text appearance by selecting text and choosing attributes from the menus if you want. With SmartMasters, you can make global changes. You can change the text characteristics in one place, and Freelance will then change them for you throughout the presentation.

Suppose, for instance, you want to enhance the appearance of bullets in bullet charts and have the text appear in italic type. To make such changes, you work on the SmartMaster page instead of the current presentation page. From the Main menu, choose View and then select Smartmaster Pages. You see a message telling you that the SmartMaster view allows you to make changes for this presentation and reminding you to return to the current presentation view after you make your global changes (see Figure 13.6). After you choose OK, you return to what looks like the current page view.

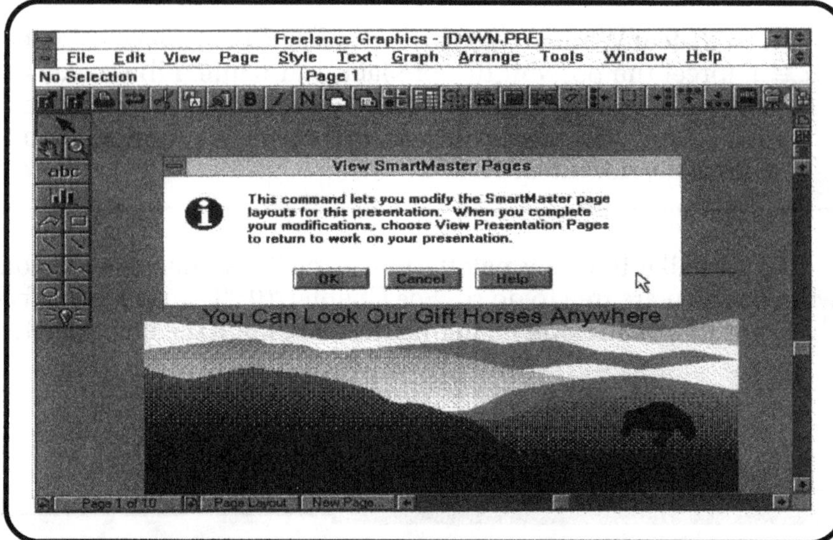

Figure 13.6 When you choose View SmartMaster Pages, a message tells you how to proceed.

The word `SmartMaster` appears in the upper left corner of the screen to remind you that you are now in the SmartMaster view (see Figure 13.7). Notice that the page no longer has any text on it but has the words `Click here to type presentation title` and other prompts. You are no longer on a presentation page; you're on the SmartMaster page.

> **Caution:** Be careful about adding text or graphics to the SmartMaster page itself. In some cases you can. In other cases, Freelance does not allow you to change text. Anything you add, such as a title or graphic, appears on every instance of that page type in the presentation. If you add a graphic to a 1-Column Bullet SmartMaster page, the graphic comes up every time you choose that page type in the current presentation.

For example, to change the bullets and text in one-column bulleted lists, first go to Page 2 of 9 in the SmartMaster pages. You are on the page for 1-Column Bullets.

SmartMaster prompt reminds you that you are in SmartMaster view.

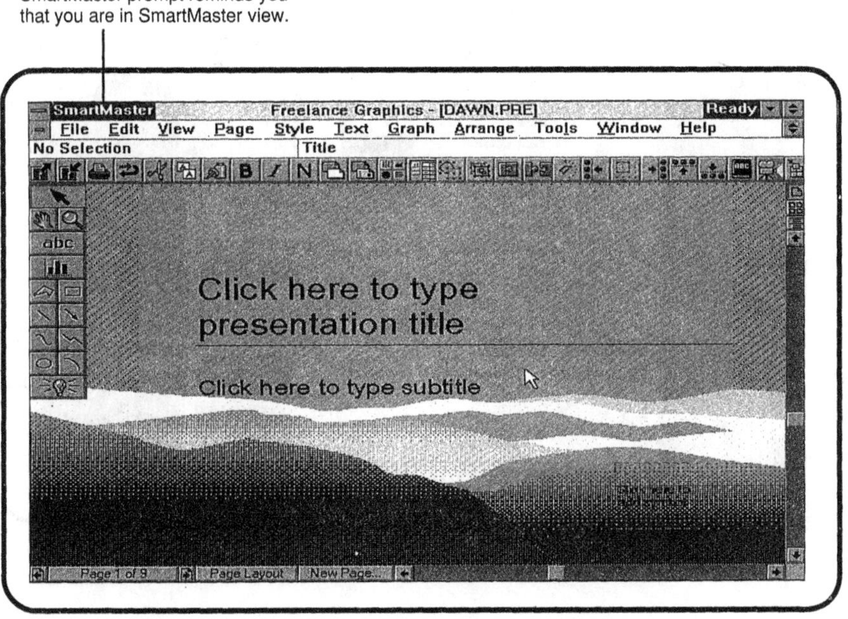

Figure 13.7 Use the SmartMaster page to make global changes.

> **Caution:** When you work on the SmartMaster pages, the page numbers do not refer to the presentation pages. They refer to the nine SmartMaster pages—Title, 1-Column Bullets, etc. Be careful about attempting to change the page type of any of the nine pages. All the pages in a SmartMaster use the Basic Layout page type.

Double-click on the page where it says `Click here to type bulleted text`. You see the Style Attributes Text dialog box, as shown in Figure 13.8. The attributes box is similar to other dialog boxes for working with the presentation page. The main difference is that you change the SmartMaster page, not the presentation page. Changes you make occur on every presentation page in the presentation. There is one additional option—SmartMaster text block. If you want, you can add a text block and define it as a SmartMaster text block. When a presentation page uses the SmartMaster page layout where you have added the SmartMaster text block, that block will behave like other SmartMaster text blocks.

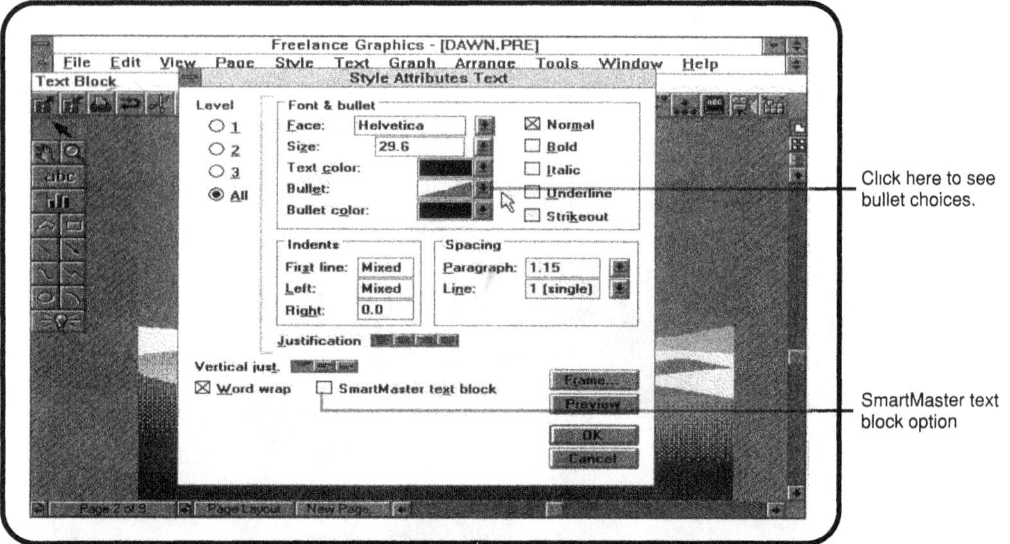

Figure 13.8 Style Attributes Text dialog box.

When you choose Bullet, the drop-down box gives you a large choice of bullet styles. For example, choose a star-shaped bullet. Also, click in the Italic box. When you have made all the changes you want, select Preview and move the dialog box aside. The SmartMaster text block shows the new attributes—in this example, the new bullets and the words `Click here to type bulleted text` in italics. Click on OK to accept the changes.

To see your presentation with the new look, choose View Presentation Pages. In the example, the pages that used the 1-Column Bullet format now have star-shaped bullets with italicized bullet text. Figure 13.9 shows the example page using the 1-Column Bullet page before changing the bullet style and the font in the SmartMaster page. Figure 13.10 shows the same page after making these changes.

To change the text attributes of your presentation, use the following Quick Steps.

Changing Text Attributes

1. Choose View SmartMaster Pages.	`SmartMaster` appears in green at the upper left of the screen.
2. Move to the SmartMaster page number for the type of page you want to modify (such as Page 2 of 9 for 1-Column Bullets).	The type of page appears on your screen.
3. Double-click on the area of the text you want to change.	You see the Style Attributes Text dialog box.
4. Change bullets, text, and other attributes. Then click on OK.	Your changes show in the SmartMaster page.
5. Choose View Presentation Pages.	You see your changes incorporated into your presentation. □

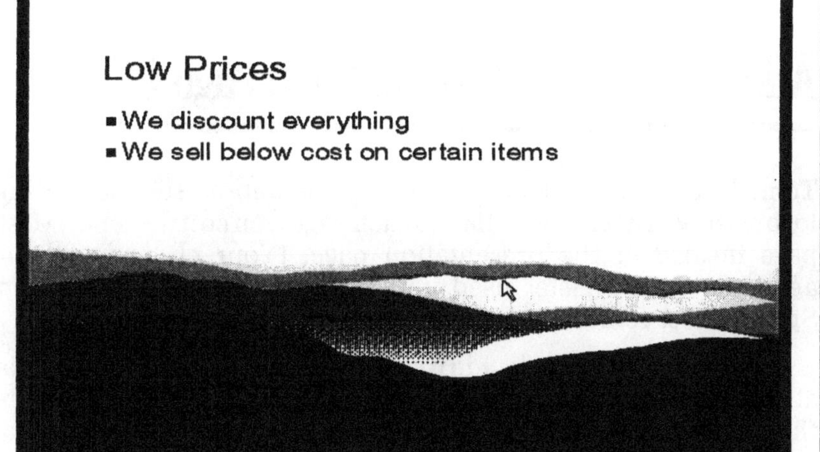

Figure 13.9 A 1-Column bullet page before changing the SmartMaster.

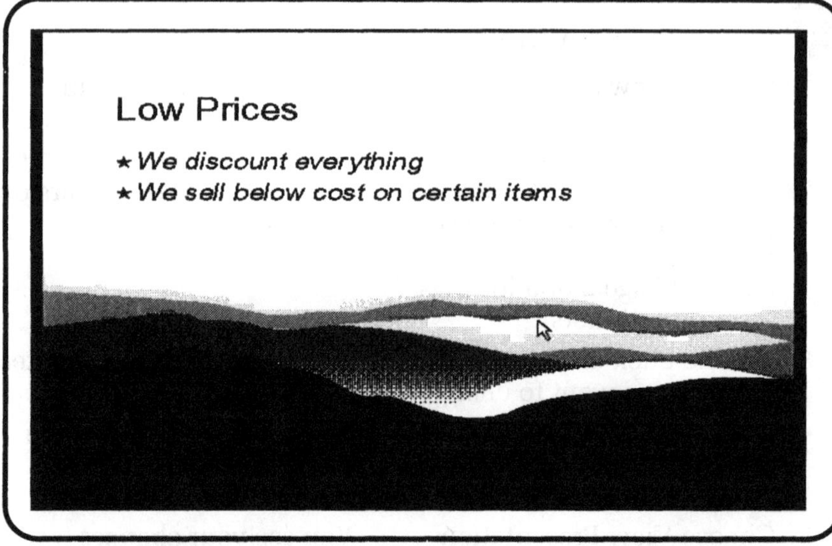

Figure 13.10 A 1-Column bullet page after changing the SmartMaster.

Adding Text or a Logo to Each Page

To make a change to each page of a presentation, such as adding a logo or the word "Confidential" to each page, you edit the SmartMaster page instead of the presentation page. (Your change will only affect the SmartMaster used with this presentation. The original SmartMaster remains unchanged for future use.)

For example, you decide to put "Preliminary and Confidential" at the top of each page of your presentation. First, from any page but the title page, choose View SmartMaster Pages. Next, click on Page Layout at the bottom of the page to be sure that Basic Layout has a checkmark next to it. (In the SmartMaster view, all pages except the Title Page use Basic Layout.) Click on the Text icon in the Toolbox and then click at the top of the page above the title and draw a text box, as shown in Figure 13.11.

In the text box, type `Preliminary and Confidential`. Click outside the box when you finish. Freelance Graphics adds this text to each SmartMaster page except for the title page. Figure 13.12 shows one of the presentation pages with this added text.

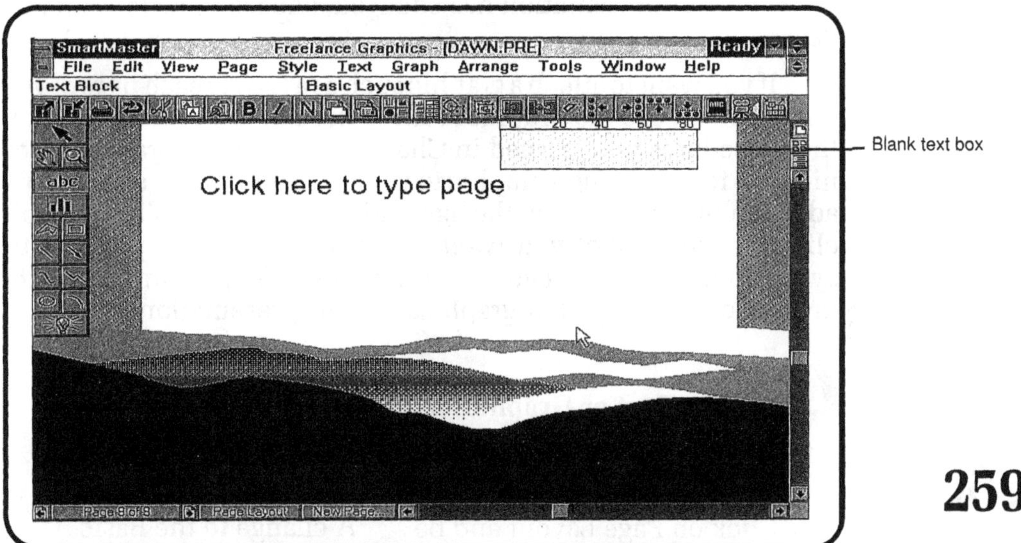

Figure 13.11 You can add a text box to a SmartMaster page.

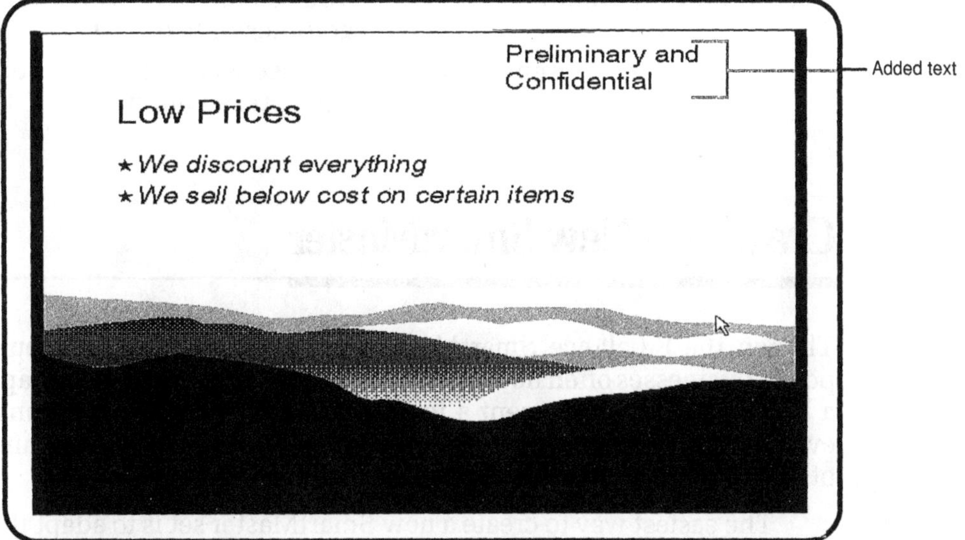

Figure 13.12 Presentation page with added text "Preliminary and Confidential."

To add the text to the title page as well, use Edit Copy to copy the text to the Clipboard. Then click on the Page indicator and choose Title page. Use Edit Paste to attach the text to this screen. To see how your presentation has changed, choose View Presentation Pages.

If you want to attach a graphic such as a logo to each page of your presentation, use the Graphics icon instead of the Text icon. Follow the procedures you learned in Chapter 11, "Simple Drawing Techniques," for attaching a graphic to your presentation. A quick way to add graphics is to click on the light bulb icon in the Toolbox, double-click on the symbol you want, and then resize and position the symbol on the page. The following Quick Steps summarize this process of adding text or graphics to your presentation.

Q Adding Text or Graphics to all Pages

Step	Result
1. Choose View SmartMaster Pages.	`SmartMaster` appears in green at the upper left.
2. Click on Page Layout and be sure Basic Layout is checked.	A change to the Basic Layout SmartMaster page will affect all pages but the title page.
3. Add text or graphics.	You see the page with your graphics or text.
4. Choose View Presentation Pages.	You see your logo or text on your presentation. □

Creating a New SmartMaster

Though the Freelance SmartMasters are sufficient for most purposes, businesses often have specialized needs of their own. Perhaps a business wants to present a look of its own in its presentations, even if it is a simple, black-and-white look. For such reasons and others, you may want to create your own SmartMaster sets.

The easiest way to create a new SmartMaster set is to adapt the set from an existing set. Follow these Quick Steps.

Creating a New SmartMaster Set from an Existing One

1. From the File menu, choose Open or click on the File Open SmartIcon.
   You see the File Open dialog box.
2. From the File types pop-up box, choose SmartMaster set.
   `SmartMaster Set (MAS)` shows in the File types pop-up box.
3. In the Directories list box, navigate to the MASTERS subdirectory. Double-click to move up one directory and then double-click on MASTERS.
   A list of masters appears in the Files list box, as shown in Figure 13.13.
4. Double-click on the file you want to adapt. (You can choose the Custom.mas SmartMaster. It has the standard number of pages and page names for a SmartMaster set, but the pages are otherwise blank. You can fill them with your own designs.)
   Freelance opens the file in Page Sorter view (see Figure 13.14).
5. Double-click on the page layout you want to modify. For example, double-click on 1 Graph.
   You see a SmartMaster view of the page layout you want to work with.
6. Make changes to the SmartMaster page, as explained in the previous sections in this chapter.
   The page takes on the new look you provide.
7. Move to any additional pages you want to modify, such as the 1-Column Bullets or Bullets & Symbol. Then repeat Step 6.
   You again see the SmartMaster view of the page layout.
8. From the File menu, choose Save and then save the SmartMaster under a different name from the one you opened initially.
   The new SmartMaster, with the new name, now appears in the list of files in the MASTERS subdirectory. □

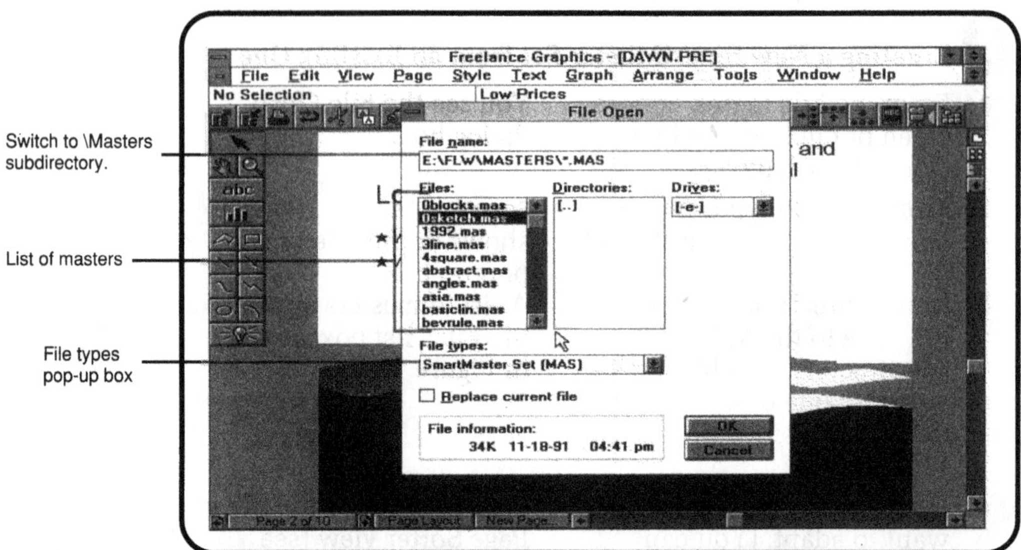

Figure 13.13 The Files list box in the File Open dialog box.

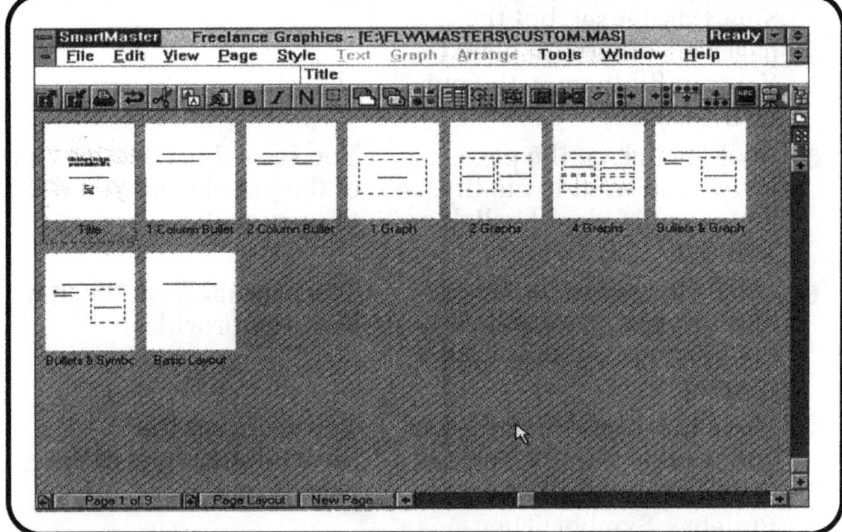

Figure 13.14 Files open in the Page Sorter view.

What You Have Learned

- To give your presentation a new look, you can change the SmartMaster set with the Style Choose SmartMaster dialog box.
- To change the appearance of your presentation, choose a new color palette using the Style Choose Palette dialog box.
- To change the way your presentation text looks, change to View SmartMaster Pages and bring up the Style Attributes text dialog box.
- To add text or a logo to each presentation page, choose View SmartMaster Pages and then make the change on the Basic Layout page.
- To create a SmartMaster of your own, open an existing SmartMaster, adapt it to your purposes and then save it under a new name.

Chapter 14

Importing Data from Other Programs

In This Chapter

- *Using the Clipboard to pass data, graphics, or text from one Windows application to another*
- *Using File Import to read text files*
- *Importing data from a 1-2-3 worksheet to use in graphing*

One of the facts of life for a modern computer user is that the data you want often resides somewhere other than in the program you currently use. If you use a graphics program, it is likely that the data is somewhere other than in the present program. People use spreadsheets, database programs, and even word processing programs to compile their data. When the time comes to present the data using a graphics package, it is often essential to be able to use the data from the original source without having to retype it. In this chapter you learn how to use data from other sources in your Freelance for Windows presentations.

Importing with the Clipboard

The *Windows Clipboard* is no more difficult to use than Cut and Paste (or Copy and Paste). The difference is that instead of doing the procedure within a single program, you perform the cut within one Windows program and the paste within another.

PowerPoint, for instance, has excellent clip art from the artists at Genigraphics Corporation. If you have both Freelance and PowerPoint, you may see something in PowerPoint that you want to use in Freelance. You can use PowerPoint to cut the artwork into the Clipboard, and Freelance to paste it back into your page.

Figure 14.1, for instance, shows some clip art within PowerPoint—a picture of two donkeys. Figure 14.2 shows the same clip art after copying it to the Clipboard and pasting it into Freelance Graphics for Windows.

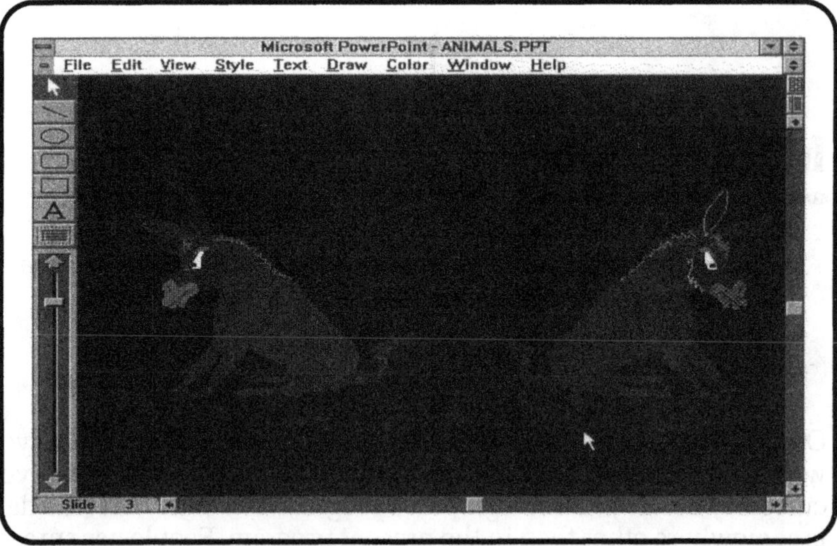

Figure 14.1 Clip art in another Windows program.

The following procedure summarizes the process of using the Clipboard to import text, graphics, and data.

- ► In another Windows application, use the Copy command to place material into the Clipboard. Then go to Freelance Graphics. (If Freelance Graphics is running already, click on the icon—or its window if the window is already open—with the mouse, or use other Windows commands to switch to it.)

Figure 14.2 Clip art from another Windows program copied to Freelance.

- In Freelance, bring up the presentation page on which you want the drawing to appear. Choose Edit Paste.
- After you import your drawing, you can add text to complete your presentation page.

The following Quick Steps summarize this procedure.

Q Importing Text or Graphics Using the Clipboard

1. In another Windows program, select text or graphics to transfer and use Edit Copy.	Your text or graphic moves to the Clipboard.
2. Switch to Freelance Graphics.	You see the presentation you are working on.
3. Choose Edit Paste.	Your text or graph appears on your presentation page. ☐

> **FYIdea:** You might want to collect some of your favorite clip art from other applications. A simple way is to create a separate Freelance application, which you might call something like "mysym.pre" for "My Symbols." Copy the symbols onto the page. When you want them later, you can open MYSYM and copy them to the Clipboard. You don't have to open the other Windows application.

The Clipboard works well for bringing in items from other Windows applications. But what if you are working with a non-Windows application? Then you cannot use the Clipboard. When you use Cut or Copy for a non-Windows application, whatever you cut does not go into the Windows Clipboard. But you can import text and data directly, as explained in the next section.

Importing a Non-Windows Text File

Most programs, including non-Windows programs, allow you to save a document as a type of text file often known as an *ASCII file*. After you save it as an ASCII file, it does not have special formatting you may have added (such as bolding or special fonts) nor does it have page formatting (such as indenting or special page sizes). It does not have graphics. But it does have the text itself.

Suppose, for instance, you want to transfer a text file that contains biographical data about you, a restaurant manager. You wrote the biography on your old word processing software, and you exported it to an ASCII format so that you could access it using other programs. It's in a file called BIOGRAPH.PRN. You decide to use the Freelance Graphics File Import function to read in the BIOGRAPH.PRN file. Here are the steps you follow:

- On the presentation page where you want the text, click on the Text icon in the Toolbox and then click on the page to create a text block. (Your imported text will begin at this point.) Figure 14.3 shows your page with the text block before importing the text.

- Choose File Import. You see the File Import dialog box, as shown in Figure 14.4.
- Use the File types box to select the file type (in this case, ASCII) and then use the directory and file boxes to display and find the file to import. Or you can just type the file name in the box at the top.
- Be sure the drive and subdirectory are current, then type **BIOGRAPH.PRN**, and click on OK. Freelance Graphics reads in your ASCII file and then displays it in the text box, as shown in Figure 14.5.

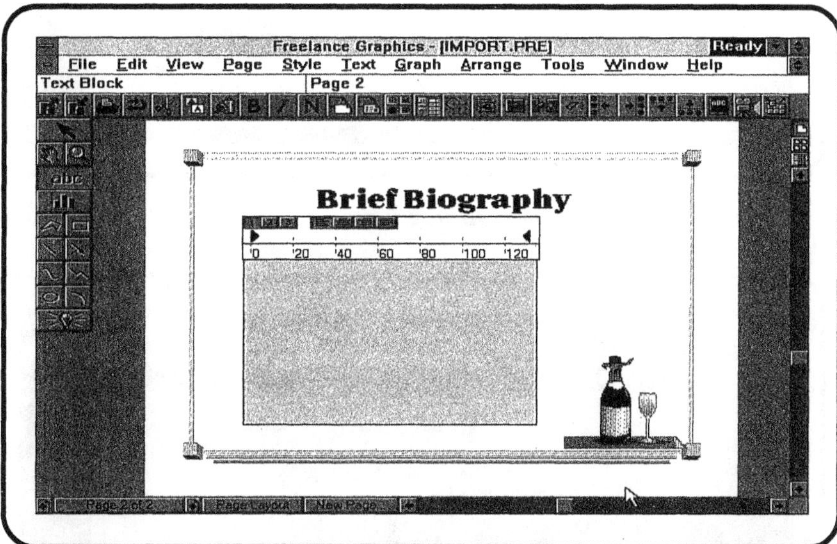

Figure 14.3 Page with text block before importing text.

Once the text is in the box (as in this case), you may have to adjust the text size, change the spacing, and make other changes so that the text will look right on the page. Figure 14.6 shows the text made to fit into the text box.

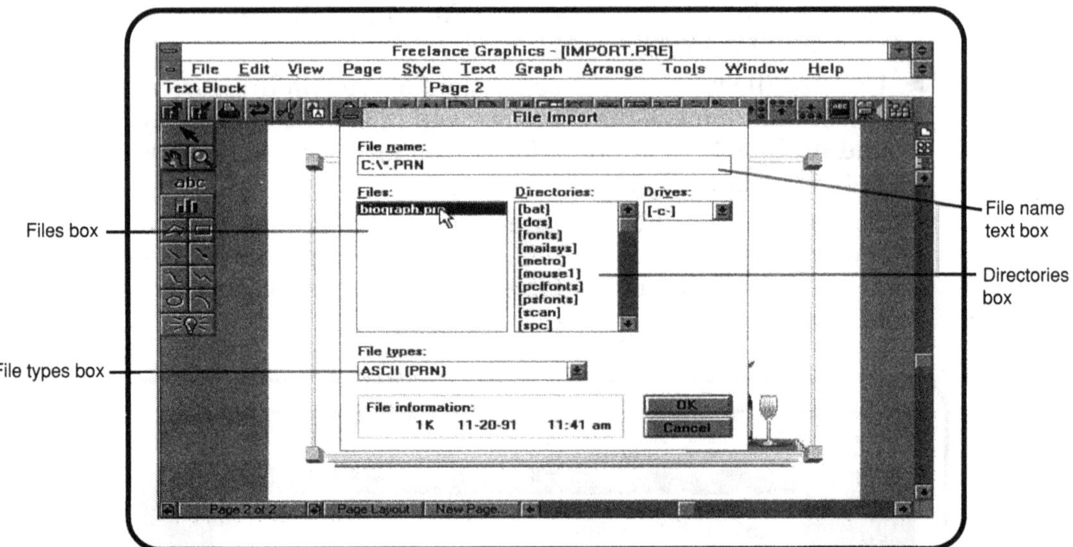

Figure 14.4 File Import dialog box.

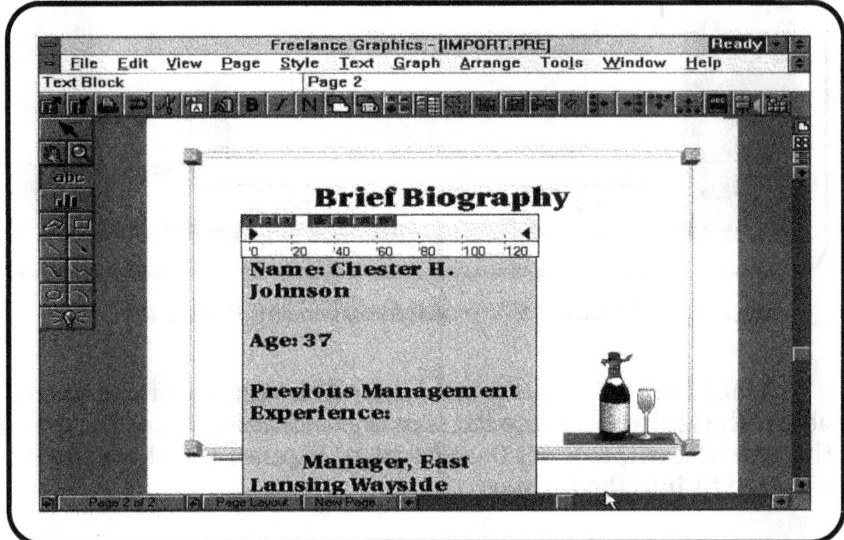

Figure 14.5 Text box with imported text.

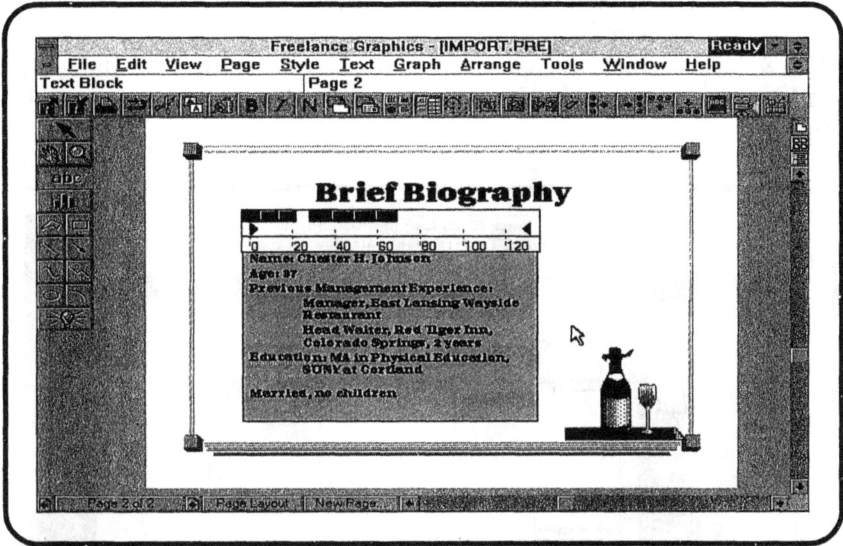

Figure 14.6 Text from preceding figure made to fit on the page.

Text is one thing—data is often something else. You may keep your data in a spreadsheet. Chances are you keep it somewhere other than Freelance, which is not the logical place to keep your books or compile statistics. Often it is not efficient to use either the Clipboard or an ASCII import for data. If the data is in columns and rows, you generally want to keep them; ideally, they should become columns and rows of data in the Freelance Edit Data & Titles window. The next section explains how to do this.

Making a Graph from Imported Data

If you want to make graphs from data you import from other sources, Freelance Graphics can read data from Lotus 1-2-3 worksheet files—or from dBASE, SYLK (Symbolic Link format files with the .SLK extension), or ASCII files. Suppose, for example, you have a Lotus 1-2-3 worksheet from which you want to import data.

First, follow the procedures you learned in Chapter 5, "Adding Graphs to Your Presentation," to make a new graph. That is, open a new presentation page with a one-graph format. Click on the Graph icon in the Toolbox or choose Graph New. In the Graph New Gallery dialog box, choose bar graph. Then click on OK. You see the Graph Data & Titles window. Instead of manually entering your data, click on Import. You see the Import Data File dialog box, as shown in Figure 14.7.

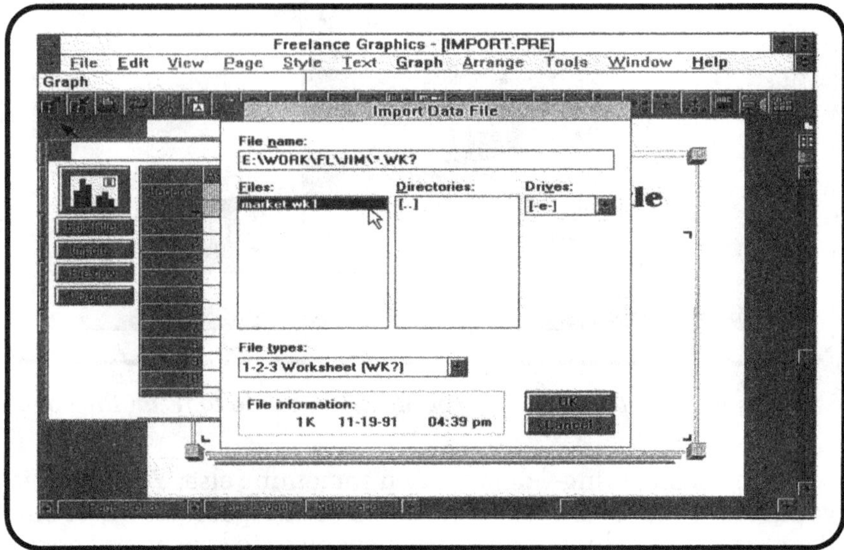

Figure 14.7 Import Data File dialog box.

In this dialog box, you can indicate a file type and search directories, or just type the file name. This example uses a file called MARKET.WK1. After you enter the file name, drive, and directory, click on OK. Freelance displays your file data in the Graph Import Data window, as shown in Figure 14.8.

Here you select the data fields you want to import by highlighting the appropriate cells. For this example, highlight the entire table. When you finish, click on OK. You see the Import Data Destination dialog box, as shown in Figure 14.9. Table 14.1 summarizes the options in the Import Data Destination dialog box.

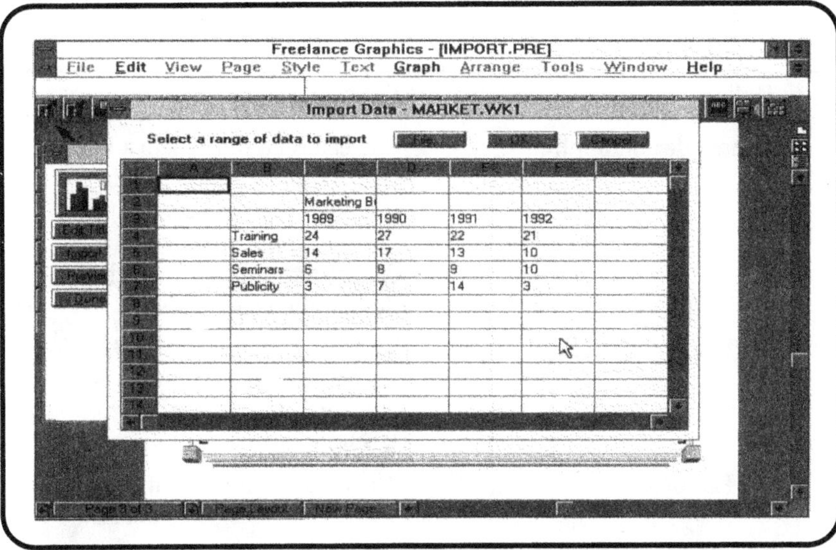

Figure 14.8 The Import Data window.

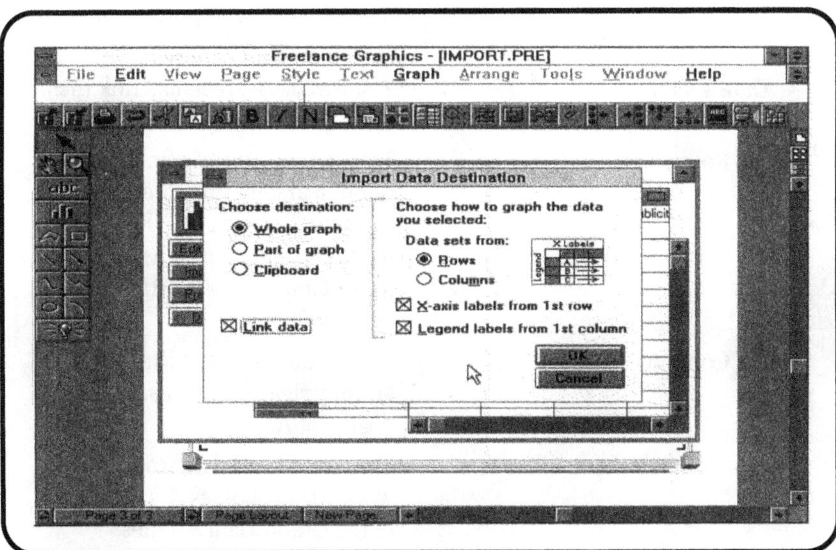

Figure 14.9 The Import Data Destination dialog box.

Table 14.1 Options in the Import Data Destination dialog box.

Option	Description
Choose destination...	You can send the data to a Whole Graph, Part of a graph, or the Clipboard. The choices on the right side of the dialog box change depending on which destination you choose.
Whole graph	The data you select will create the entire graph, including all data sets and (optionally) axis labels or legends.
Part of graph	The data you select will be part of a graph, such as "Data Set A."
Clipboard	This option pastes the data into the Windows Clipboard but not into the Graph Data & Titles window until you position the cursor there and choose Paste.
Data sets from...	You can have Freelance link the data by rows or by columns.
Rows	This option uses the first row of numerical data from the worksheet as "Data Set A." (Rows from the worksheet appear as columns in the Graph Data & Titles window.)
Columns	This option uses the first column of numerical data you selected as "Data Set A."
X-axis labels from 1st row	The first row of data from the worksheet becomes X-axis labels in the Graph Data & Titles window.
Legend labels from 1st column	If you choose Data sets from Rows, select this option to have the first column of data from the spreadsheet become legend labels in the Graph Data & Titles window.

Option	Description
X-axis labels from 1st column	If you choose Data sets from Columns and select this option, the first column of data from the spreadsheet becomes X-axis labels in the Graph Data & Titles window.
Legend labels from 1st row	If you choose Data sets from Columns and select this option, the first row of data from the spreadsheet becomes legend labels in the Graph Data & Titles window.

For the example, specify that the data will go to a Whole graph. Also mark the Link Data box. The Link option is available when you bring in data from Lotus 1-2-3. It means that when you update data in the worksheet file, Freelance automatically updates the Freelance Graphics file the next time you open the Freelance file. Select Data sets from Rows and then select both X-axis labels and Legend labels from the 1st column. Click on OK.

Freelance copies your data onto the Graph Data & Titles window. In the example, it does not copy the title from the top of the worksheet. A message appears saying that Freelance does not copy text into graphic cells. It does copy the X-axis labels, the legend labels, and the numerical data, as shown in Figure 14.10.

FYIdea: By setting up links, you can keep your Freelance graphs current, even for presentations you open infrequently. Perhaps you work frequently in a spreadsheet showing regional sales but only occasionally have to display the data as a Freelance graph. Set up a link. Each time you open the graph, it will have latest data from the spreadsheet automatically.

Once you are back in the window, you use it the same way you always do (refer to Chapter 5). Add data or titles or notes as you wish. When you are satisfied with the data, click on Done. Freelance creates your graph on the page. The finished page looks like the one shown in Figure 14.11.

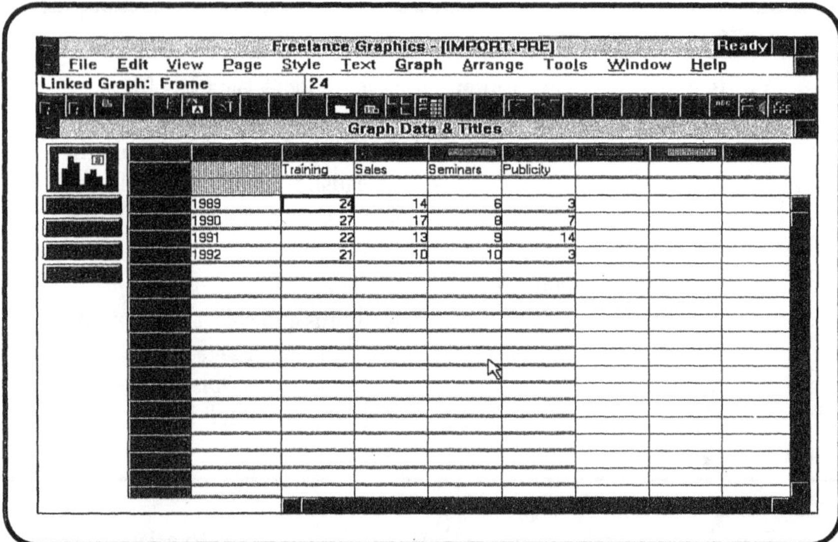

Figure 14.10 Data copied from a worksheet into the Graph Data & Titles window.

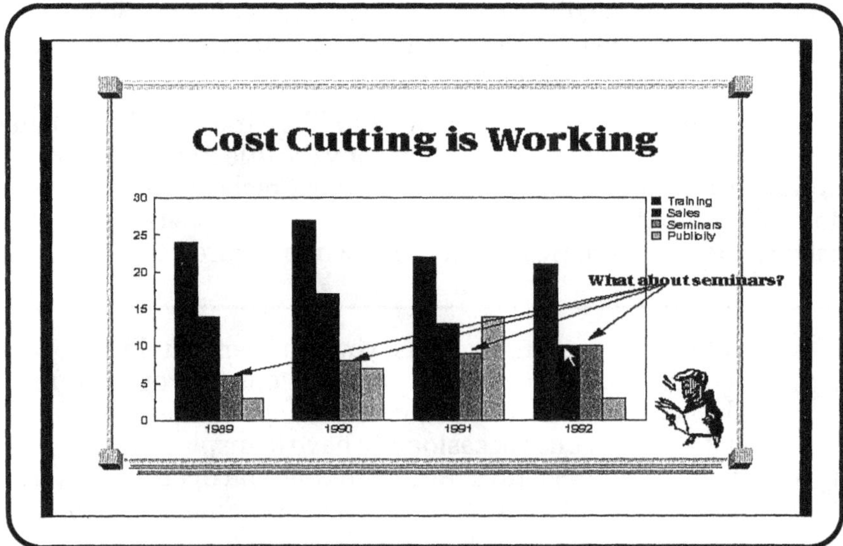

Figure 14.11 Finished graph using imported data.

If you need to return to the Graph Import Data window, press the F6 function key from the Graph Data & Titles window. The Graph Import Data window will appear on your screen, and again you can select which fields to use in your graph. The following Quick Steps summarize this procedure.

Importing Graph Data

1. From the Graph Data & Titles window, click on Import. — You see the Graph Import Data File dialog box.
2. Specify the file to import and then click on OK. — You see the Graph Import Data window.
3. Select the data to graph and then click on OK. — You see the Import Data Destination dialog box.
4. Specify how much data to use and in what format. Then click on OK. — Freelance copies your data to the Graph Data & Titles window.
5. Add titles and headings as needed. Then click on Done. — Freelance creates your graph on your presentation page.

FYIdea: You can link numerous presentation files to the same worksheet. This means you can use the same worksheet to create presentations for multiple purposes—such as external presentations, departmental presentations, and management presentations. When you update the worksheet, you update all the presentations at once.

What You Have Learned

- With the Windows Clipboard, you can import text, data, or graphics from any other Windows application into Freelance.

- Use Edit Paste to move data, graphics, or text from the Clipboard into your Freelance Graphics file.
- When you import a text file, you do not import attributes like bolding. You also do not import the layout. But you do import what may be most important—the words themselves.
- File Import lets you read a file from your disk into a text block on your presentation page.
- After setting up a graph format, use Import to read into the Graph Data & Titles window.

Chapter 15

Customizing Freelance Tools

In This Chapter

- ► *Setting up the Freelance environment*
- ► *Moving the SmartIcon palette*
- ► *Adding or removing SmartIcons from your palette*
- ► *Adding a new SmartMaster layout*
- ► *Customizing SmartMaster text prompts*
- ► *Adding text prompts and placement blocks to a SmartMaster*
- ► *Saving a customized SmartMaster*

In Freelance Graphics for Windows, not only do you have flexibility in how you can use graphic tools, you have freedom in how you design the tools themselves. You can set up your working environment the way you want it and tailor the SmartIcons to suit your purposes. You can set up the SmartMasters the way you want them and change them as your purposes change. You do not have to use just the page layouts and SmartMasters Freelance gives you; you can create your own.

Setting Up Freelance the Way You Want

In Chapter 11, "Simple Drawing Techniques," you saw how to customize the drawing environment. You can use a large cross hair cursor, have a grid appear on the screen as you work, and elect to have your drawings "snap to" the grid. There are many other ways you can set up the Freelance drawing environment. If you want, you can make your preferred settings the ones that are in effect each time you start Freelance.

To change the settings for the tools environment, use the Tools User Setup menu and select the choices you want to have in effect. Follow these Quick Steps.

 **Changing the Settings for the Tools Environment**

1. From the Tools menu, choose User Setup. — You see the Tools User Setup dialog box, as shown in Figure 15.1.
2. Click on the choices you want to have in effect. — An X or a black dot appears in the selection box next to each choice you have in effect.
3. Click on OK. — You exit the dialog box with the new settings in effect. □

Table 15.1 summarizes the choices you can make in the Tools User Setup dialog box.

Table 15.1 Options in the Tools User Setup dialog box.

Option	Description
Undo	You can have Undo either enabled or disabled. If this option is enabled, Freelance stores the last ten operations in memory and allows you to use the Undo command on them.
Cursor size	The cursor can be a large or small cross hair. (See Chapter 11.)

Option	Description
Replicate	You choose where the copy goes when you use Edit Replicate in drawing.
Place copy on original	The replicated copy appears on top of the original.
Offset copy from original	The replicated copy sets slightly to the side, so you can see it.
Save	You specify what you want Freelance to do when you save a copy with the same name as the original.
Replace	The new file takes the place of the old one, which is deleted.
Backup	Freelance saves the current file and saves the previous version of the file to the backup directory. (See "Directories" later in the table.)
Confirm	Freelance asks whether you want to replace the original, use it as a backup, or cancel the Save operation.
Show page borders	You can choose among displaying margins, displaying the border of the printable area, or displaying none. Figure 15.2 shows a page with the border of the printable area displayed. Figure 15.3 shows a page with the margin displayed.
Margins	This option displays the margins of the page using a broken rectangle.
Printable area	This option displays the border of the printable area.
None	This option displays no broken rectangle.
Display	This option offers toggles for three settings—Output colors, Coordinates, and the Function key panel.

(continues)

Table 15.1 (continued)

Option	Description
Output colors	The colors that appear on your display screen (your monitor) match those available on your output device.
Coordinates	If this option is selected, Freelance displays two sets of coordinates in the line below the menu: X and Y coordinates to represent the distance between the pointer and the bottom left corner of the page, and Height and width coordinates to show the height and width of an object as you draw or size it (see Figure 15.4).
Function key panel	This option displays the Function keys at the bottom of the panel (see Figure 15.5). You can click on a function key on the panel to use it. The keys listed are valid for the activity you are doing. If you press Shift, Alt, or Ctrl, the function key panel changes.
Drawing tools	This option allows you to keep the current tool active (as explained in Chapter 11) or revert to a mouse pointer after you use it.
International	Displays the Tools User Setup International dialog box, shown in Figure 15.6, where you can set formats for date, time, number, and currency.
Directories	This option displays the Tools User Setup Directories dialog box (see Figure 15.7), where you can specify the path and name for the working directory, master directory (for SmartMaster sets, palettes, and symbols), and backup directory.

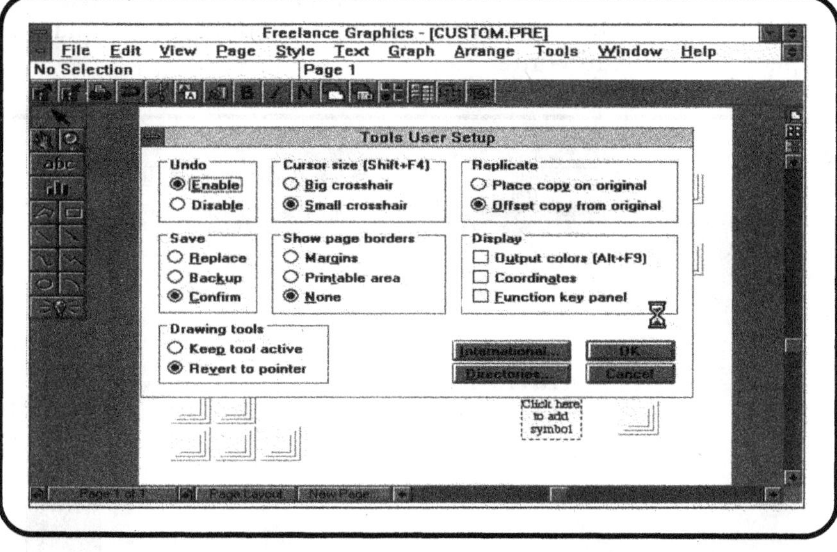

Figure 15.1 Use the Tools User Setup dialog box to customize your working environment.

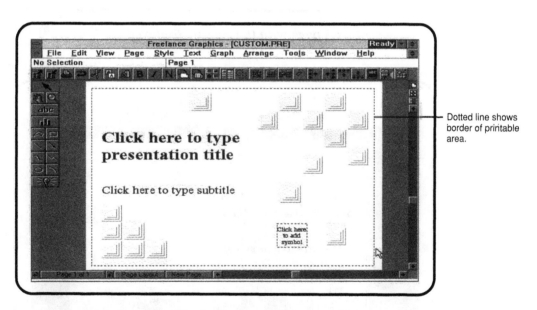

Dotted line shows border of printable area.

Figure 15.2 A page with the border of the printable area displayed.

If you have a color monitor and a black-and-white printer (a common configuration), be careful about selecting Output colors under Display and leaving it on inadvertently. No matter what else you change to try to correct the "problem", your screen display will appear in black and white.

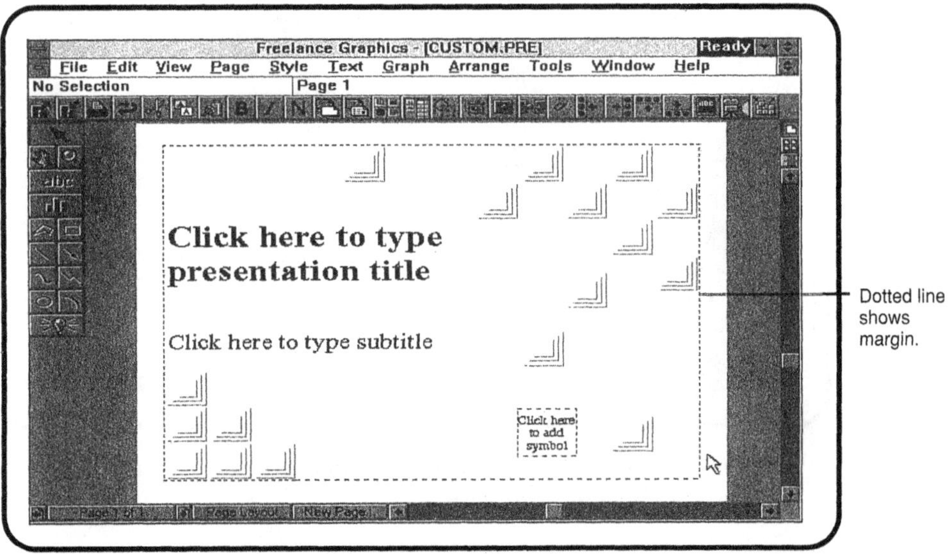

Figure 15.3 A page with the margin displayed.

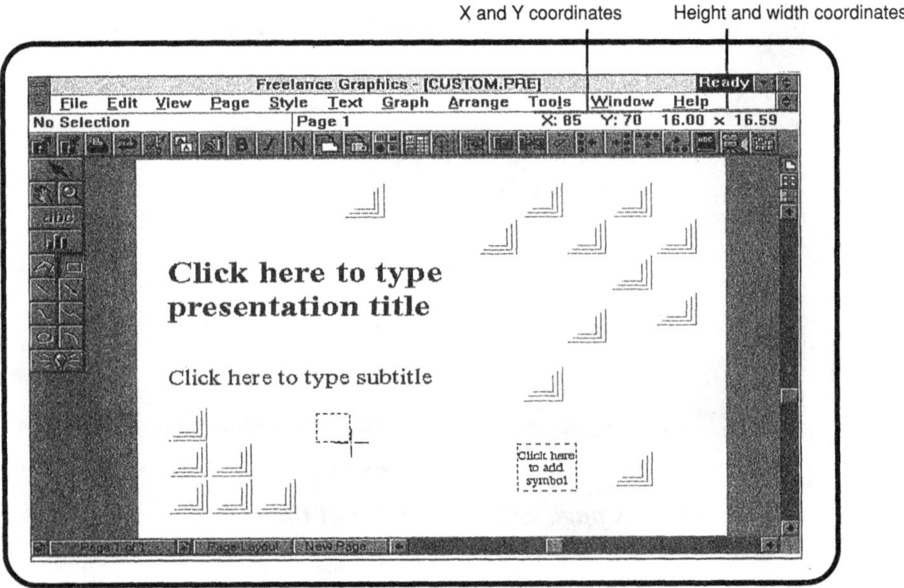

Figure 15.4 Freelance displays two sets of coordinates in the line below the menu.

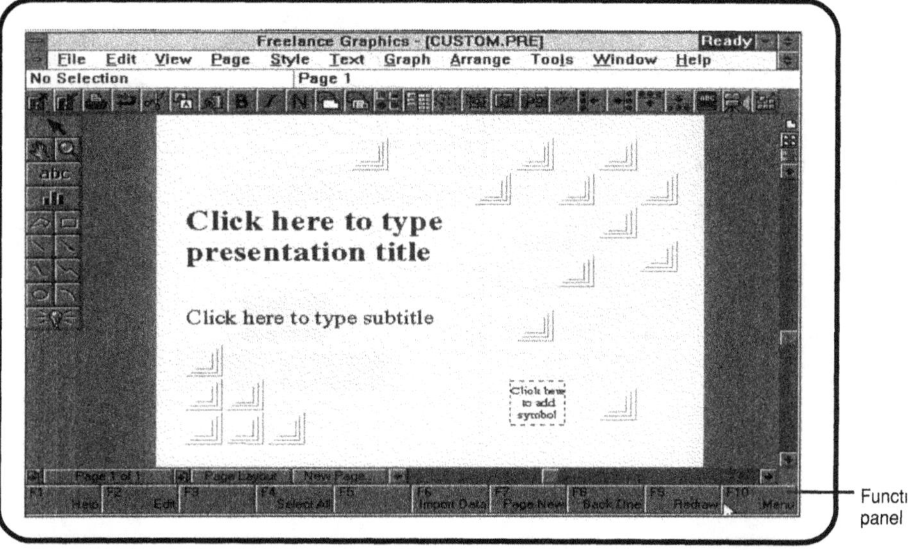

Figure 15.5 If you select Function Key panel, you display a set of function keys at the bottom of the screen.

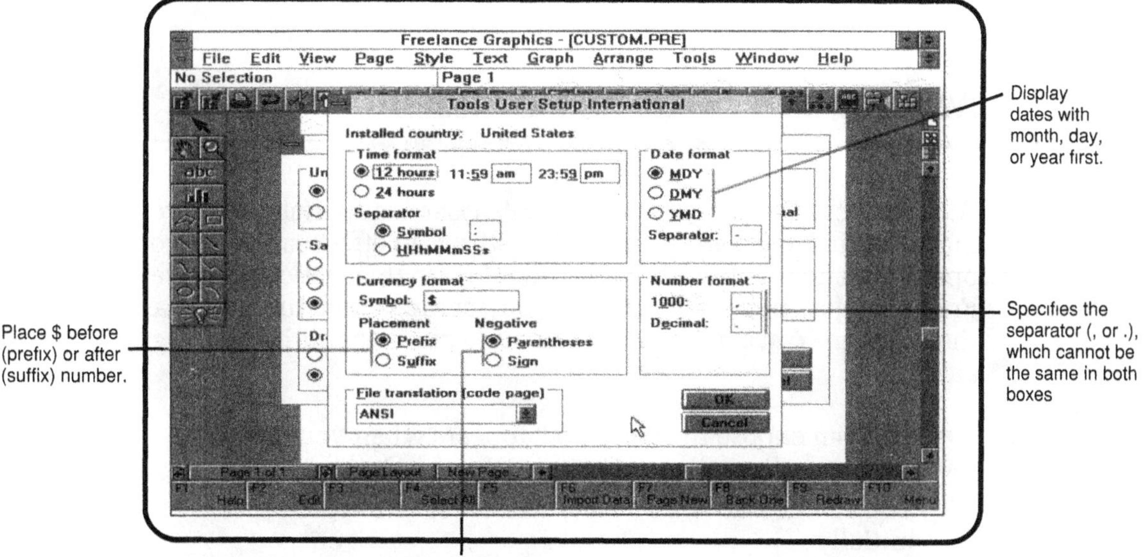

Figure 15.6 With the Tools User Setup International dialog box, you can set up date, time, and other settings to match a country.

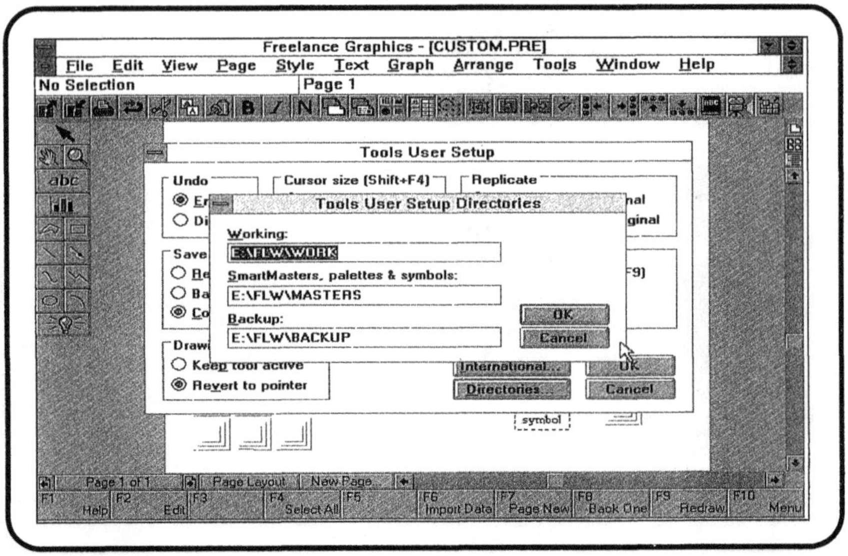

Figure 15.7 In the Tools User Setup Directories dialog box, you can set up paths and names for directories.

Making Your Settings Permanent

After you choose settings in the Tools User Setup dialog box, you may want to have some or all of the settings in effect each time you open Freelance. Unless you follow the steps in this section, however, Freelance goes back to its initial default settings each time you start the program. You can also control a number of other initial settings, such as:

- ▶ You can choose the view that appears when you start the program—Page Sorter, Current Page, or Outline.
- ▶ You can decide which SmartMaster set and palette you see initially.

Freelance reads all such settings from a file called DEFAULT.PRE in the MASTERS subdirectory if the file exists on your system. Until you create it the first time, there is no such file in Freelance. To make your settings permanent, follow these Quick Steps.

Q Setting Permanent Defaults

1. From the File menu, choose New to create a new presentation.	You see the File New dialog box.
2. Choose the Smart-Master that you always want to see when you start the program and then choose OK.	You are on the first page of a new presentation, using the SmartMaster you selected.
3. Set up Tools User Setup the way you want it and go to the view you want to see when you start the program.	The new file has the selected tools active and displays the view you chose.
4. From the Tools menu, choose Save Default Presentation.	Freelance saves the current presentation as DEFAULT.PRE in the MASTERS subdirectory. It uses the settings in DEFAULT.PRE each time you start a session or create a new file. ☐

Tip: To return to the original default settings you had when you installed the program, delete the file called DEFAULT.PRE from the MASTERS subdirectory.

Customizing the SmartIcons

In Chapter 2, "Getting Started with Freelance Graphics," you learned about the SmartIcons in Freelance Graphics. They give you a shortcut in performing a variety of operations. You do not have to work with them the way you first find them, though. Freelance Graphics lets you choose where to display the SmartIcons on your screen and which icons to include in your palette.

Moving or Hiding the SmartIcon Palette

When you first start Freelance Graphics, the SmartIcons display as a bar across the top of the screen. If you want to change the position of the palette, choose Tools SmartIcons. You see the Tools SmartIcons dialog box, as shown in Figure 15.8.

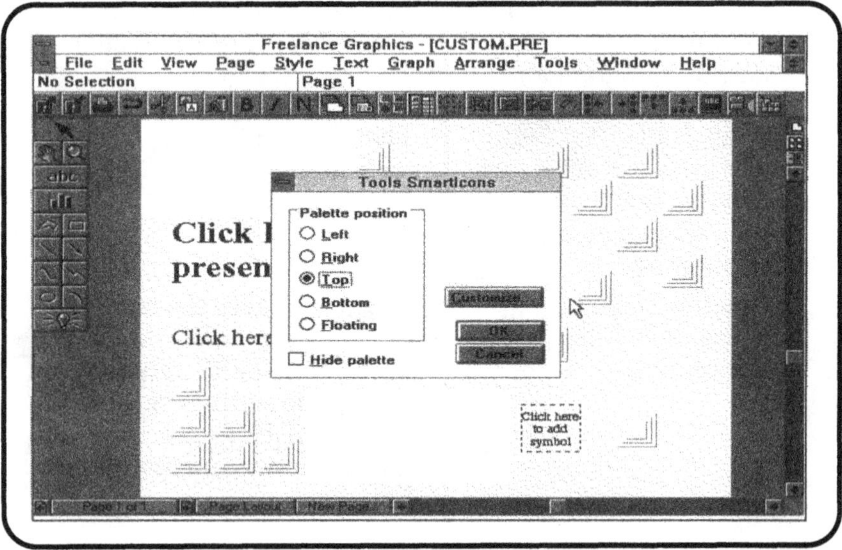

Figure 15.8 The Tools SmartIcons dialog box.

Click on the Left, Right, Top, or Bottom options to display the SmartIcon bar in the indicated area of the screen. Click on the Floating option to drag the SmartIcons wherever you want and resize the window to suit your needs. Figure 15.9 shows a floating SmartIcon palette sized to show all the available SmartIcons.

One advantage of floating SmartIcons is that you can see more SmartIcons than in the other display modes. If you have set up a number of custom SmartIcons (or simply have become a heavy user of SmartIcons), floating SmartIcons may be the only way you can have all your SmartIcons available at once.

Click on the Hide palette option to remove the SmartIcon bar from the screen altogether. Click again to clear the Hide checkbox and display the SmartIcon bar. (For the examples in this chapter, the SmartIcons will appear at the top of the screen.)

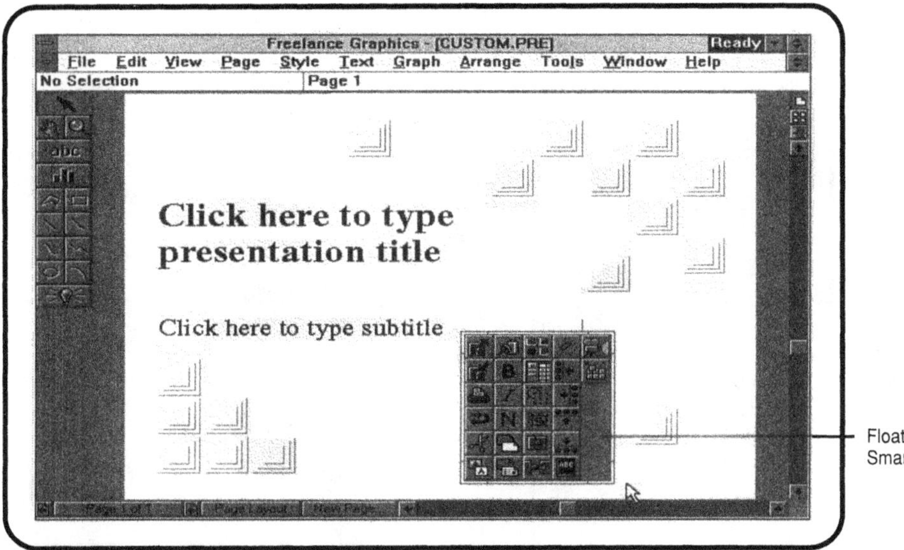

Figure 15.9 Floating SmartIcons with the window sized to show all available SmartIcons.

FYIdea: Particularly when you use the Page view (as opposed to the Outliner), you may find yourself working in just one corner of the screen. Perhaps you want to modify a symbol or create some other graphic. Put your tools right next to your work. Use Floating SmartIcons and drag them next to where you are working.

Adding a SmartIcon to Your Palette

There are more SmartIcons available with Freelance Graphics than just the ones you can see on your screen when you do not have floating SmartIcons. If you make frequent use of an operation that doesn't have a SmartIcon in your palette, you can customize the palette to include that SmartIcon. To customize the SmartIcons, choose Tools SmartIcons Customize. You see the Customize SmartIcons dialog box, as shown in Figure 15.10.

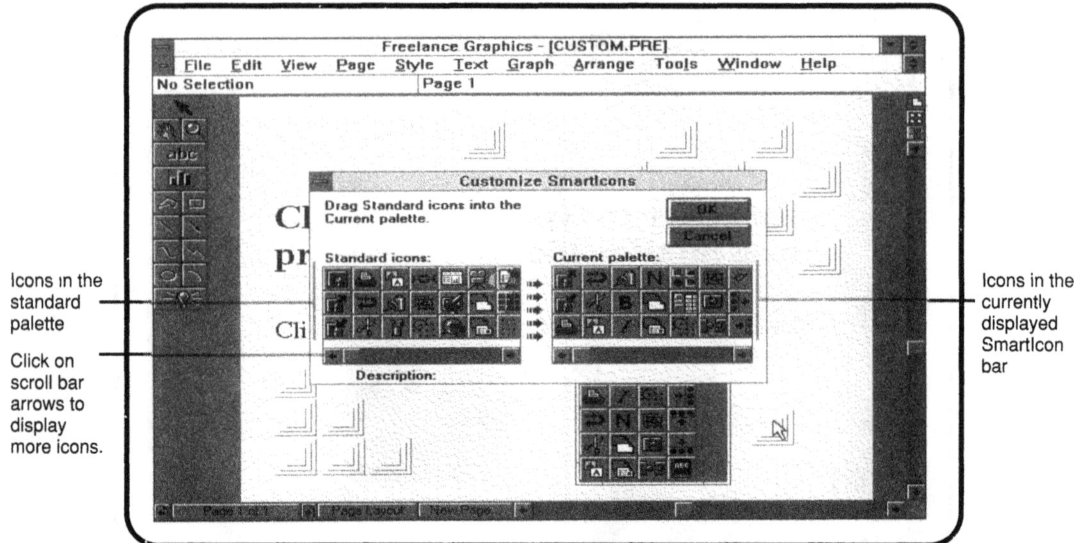

Figure 15.10 Customize SmartIcons dialog box.

The box at the left shows the Standard icons (all the SmartIcons available for you to assign to the Current palette); the one on the right shows the Current palette. You can click on the scroll arrows or drag the box in the scroll bar to see all that's in these boxes. To learn the meaning of a SmartIcon, click on it. A description of its function appears printed at the bottom of the Customize SmartIcons dialog box, as shown in Figure 15.11.

At first, the SmartIcons that come in the initial palette may seem to be all you need. Soon, however, as you begin to discover the power of point-and-click, adding icons becomes quite attractive. Some people experience a kind of "icon mania."

To add an icon to the Current palette, click the mouse on the icon you want in the Standard icons box and then drag the icon to the Current palette box. Release the mouse button, and your new icon appears in the Current palette. If you put one icon on top of another, Freelance moves the other icons to make room for the new one.

Suppose, for example, that you want to add the SmartIcon for Choose Palette to your palette. Scroll to display it in the Standard icons box. The Choose Palette icon shows a series of small boxes, half using one color palette and half another; click on it and drag it to the Current palette box. Figure 15.12 shows your current icons with the new SmartIcon added. The following Quick Steps summarize the procedure for adding icons to the SmartIcon palette.

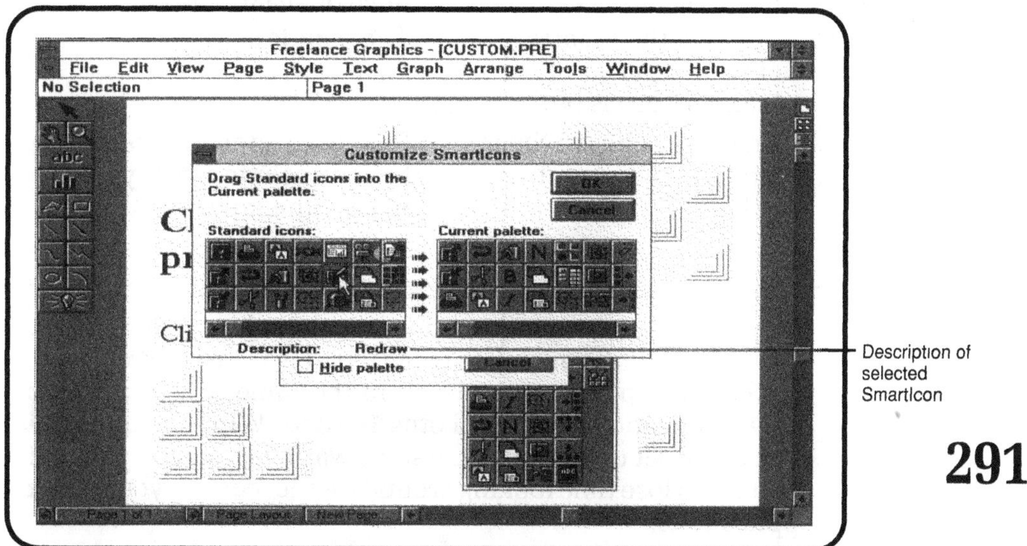

Figure 15.11 Click on a SmartIcon to see a description of it.

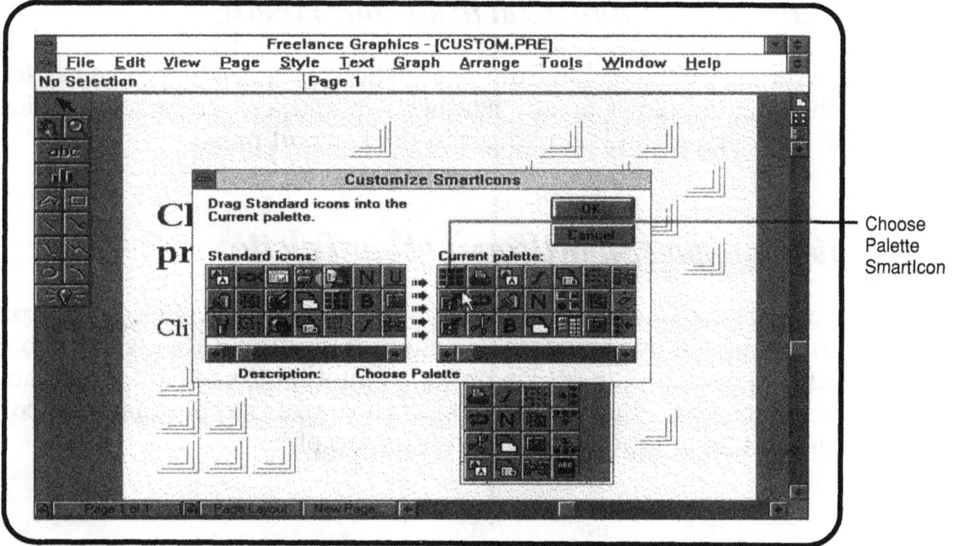

Figure 15.12 Selected SmartIcons with added icon.

Adding a SmartIcon to the Selected Palette

1. Choose Tools SmartIcons Customize. — You see the Customize SmartIcons dialog box.
2. Click on the SmartIcon of your choice in the Standard icons box. — The icon is selected.
3. Drag your chosen SmartIcon to the Current palette. — Freelance adds the SmartIcon to your palette when you release the mouse button. □

FYIdea: After you set up your palette in a way you like, do not limit yourself to using it that way just in Freelance. You can set up your SmartIcons in the same way as in other Lotus applications (such as Lotus 1-2-3 for Windows and Ami Pro). If you set up the icons the same way everywhere, you will not have to lose time looking around for the icons as you switch applications.

Removing a SmartIcon from Your Palette

To remove a SmartIcon from your palette, reverse the process. Click on the icon in the Current palette box and drag it anywhere outside the box. The icon is no longer in the Current palette.

Rearranging SmartIcons in Your Palette

To move the SmartIcons around in your palette, just click on the icon you want to move and drag it to another location. Don't worry about putting the new SmartIcon on top of another SmartIcon. Freelance Graphics shifts the SmartIcons down or over so that the new icon appears before the one you put it on top of.

Customizing SmartMaster Sets

In Chapter 13, "Making Global Presentation Changes," you saw how to use SmartMaster sets to make global changes. By adding an element to the Basic Layout page format in a SmartMaster, you can have the element appear in every presentation page that uses the SmartMaster. You can go one step further. You can also customize the SmartMaster as a tool. That is, you can use the SmartMaster to set up the environment that you or someone else sees on the presentation page. You can create new blocks for adding text and graphics to the page.

Suppose, for example, that your company teaches courses in public speaking. You want your sales managers to use Freelance Graphics to create presentations quickly, according to a formula that you lay out. You decide to customize a SmartMaster set. Begin by choosing View SmartMaster Pages. You see `SmartMaster` in green at the upper left of the screen. Next, select a SmartMaster set to customize. From the Style menu, select Choose SmartMaster Set. For this example, customize dotline1.mas. Select it in the SmartMaster Sets box and then choose OK.

In Chapter 13, you learned how to change the color palette and the text attributes, as well as how to add text or a logo to SmartMaster pages. You can make any of these changes now. But you can also change the actual page layout.

For this example, make changes to the 2-Column Bullet page layout. You want to have a box to put a graph below the bullet columns and a text box below the graph (for typing a statement summing up the benefits). After you open the dotline1.mas SmartMaster file, you need to bring up the 2-Column Bullets page to edit. Click on the Page Selector in the lower left corner and then click on Page 3 of 9 (for 2-Column Bullets). You see the 2-Column Bullets format as it appears in the SmartMaster, as shown in Figure 15.13.

Adding a Text Block

In this example, add a text block at the bottom of the screen where the salespeople can type a few words summing up their message. To add a text block with a prompt, first click on the Text icon in the Toolbox. Then click on the page where you want the text block to begin. Type the prompt, in this case `Type selling point here`. Choose Style Attributes to display the Style Attributes Text dialog box, as shown in Figure 15.14. Select SmartMaster text block. Then click on OK. The following Quick Steps summarize this procedure.

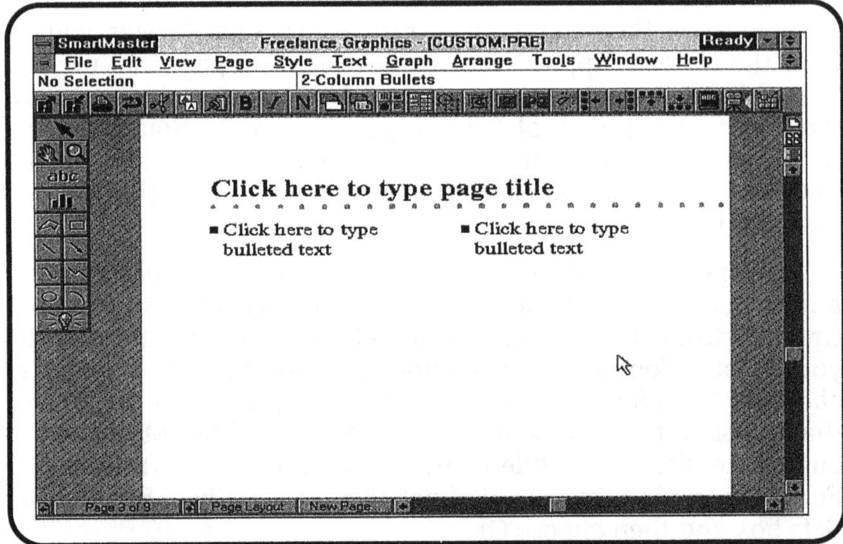

Figure 15.13 2-Column Bullets format before changes.

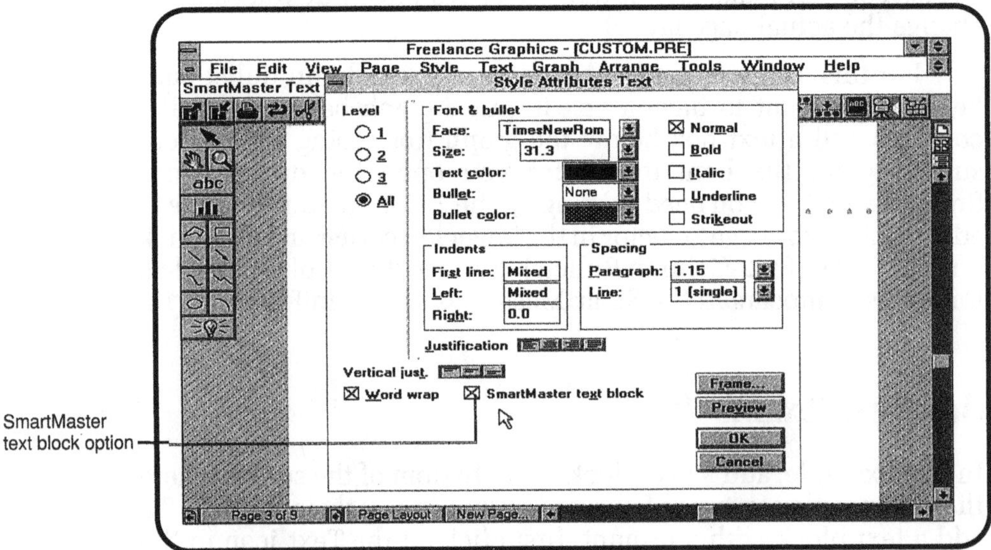

Figure 15.14 Style Attributes Text dialog box, for making a text block into a SmartMaster text block.

Adding a Text Block

1. In SmartMaster Page view, click on the Text icon in the Toolbox. — You get a cross-shaped cursor.
2. Click on the page where you want to add the block. — You see a new text block.
3. Type the prompt for the block and then select Style Attributes. — You see the Syle Attributes Text dialog box.
4. Select SmartMaster text block and choose OK. — The block becomes a Smart-Master text block on the screen. □

Adding a Placement Block

In the example, there's one more thing to add to the custom page: a SmartMaster block for a graph. To create this block, first click on the Rectangle icon in the Toolbox. Next, drag a rectangle where you want your placement box to be. Double-click on this rectangle, and you see the Style Attributes Rectangle dialog box, as shown in Figure 15.15.

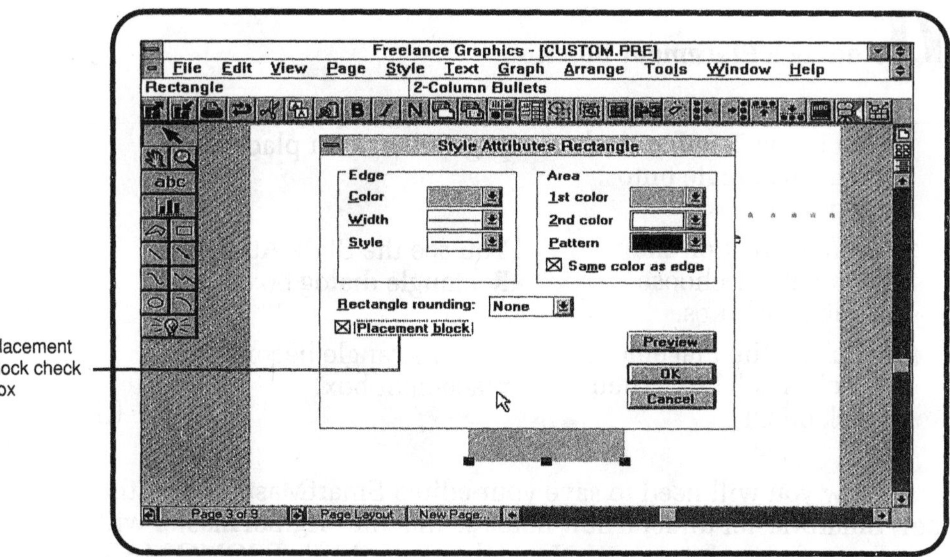

Figure 15.15 Style Attributes Rectangle dialog box.

Click in the Placement block check box to indicate that you have created a placement block and then click on OK. The placement block with a dotted border appears on your screen with the prompt `Place graphic here` inside it, as shown in Figure 15.16. The following Quick Steps summarize the procedure.

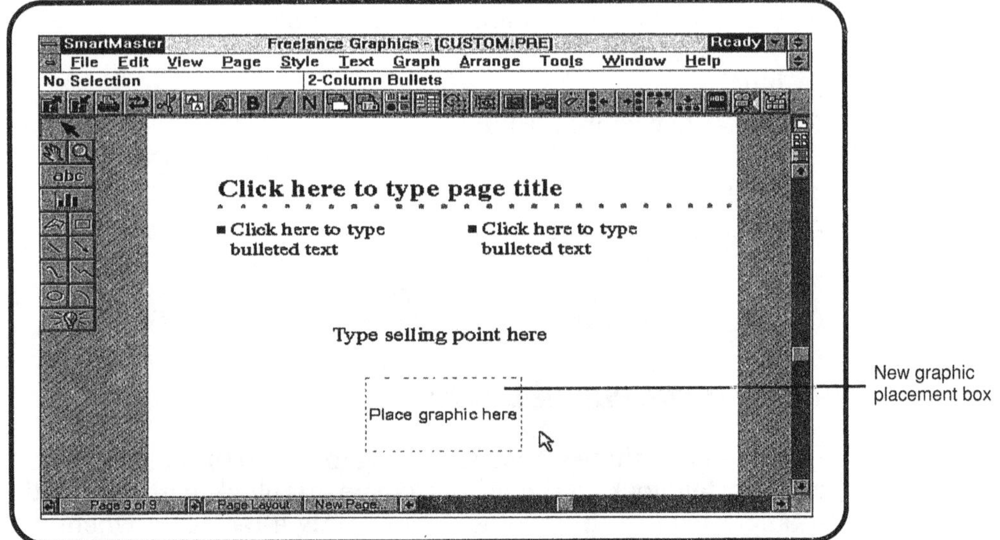

Figure 15.16 Finished page with new graphic placement block.

Adding a Placement Block

1. Click on the Rectangle tool in the Toolbox and drag a rectangle onto your page. — A rectangle appears on the page where you place it.
2. Double-click on the rectangle or choose Style Attributes. — You see the Style Attributes Rectangle dialog box.
3. Click on the Placement Block check box. Then click on OK. — Your rectangle becomes a placement box.

☐

Now you will need to save your edited SmartMaster. Save the new SmartMaster under a new name so that the original master will remain on file for future use. Name the example file PROMO.MAS.

1. Click on File and then Save As.
2. In the File name box, type **C:\FLW\MASTERS\PROMO**.
3. In the Save file as type box, select SmartMaster Set (Mas).
4. Click on OK to save the Customized SmartMaster set.

When you want to use this customized SmartMaster set, you'll find it on the list with all the other SmartMasters. Just select it and create your presentation.

What You Have Learned

- You can change settings in your working environment that determine whether Undo is in effect, where a copy goes when you use Edit Replicate, and other tool settings.
- You can make your preferred settings permanent by storing them in a file called DEFAULT.PRE in the MASTERS subdirectory.
- You use the Tools SmartIcon menu to change the location of the SmartIcons.
- In the Customize SmartIcons dialog box you can view, add, and remove SmartIcons from your palette.
- After adding or modifying a SmartMaster text prompt, you check the text block check box in the Style Attributes Text dialog box to indicate that this is a screen prompt.
- After adding or modifying a Smart Master placement block, you check the Placement block check box in the Style Attributes Rectangle dialog box to indicate that it is a placement block.
- You save a customized SmartMaster under a new name using File Save As.

Appendix A

Windows Primer

Microsoft Windows is a *graphical user interface* (GUI), which runs on top of DOS (your computer's Disk Operating System). With a graphical user interface, you don't type commands. Instead, you use a pointing device, usually a mouse, to select the command from a menu or to select a graphic symbol (icon) from the screen. Although many users consider the Windows screen (interface) easier to use, you need to know how to use it before it will seem easy.

In addition to a graphical interface, Windows offers a *multitasking* environment. This means that you can run two or more programs at the same time—each in a separate "window" (thus the name Windows)—and switch smoothly from one program to another.

The Program Manager

One program in Windows—the *Program Manager*—manages all the other programs. It is your starting point when you begin Windows and your ending point when you leave. You also turn to it during any Windows session when you want to start up a new program. Figure A.1 shows the Program Manager, though your own Program Manager may not be identical to this one.

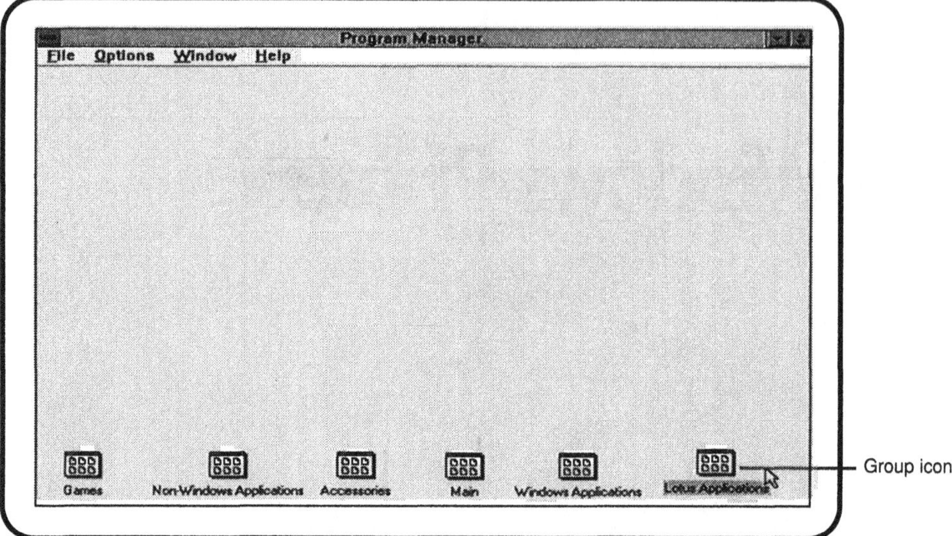

Figure A.1 The Windows Program Manager screen.

In Windows the overall screen space is the *desktop*. As you work on the desktop, you can start applications, rearrange them, or remove them just as you would on any desktop.

Icons

As you work in the Program Manager, you see *icons* (small pictures that represent programs); there are two types—group icons and applications icons.

A *group icon*, as the name suggests, contains a group of application icons. At the bottom of the Program Manager window, you see a number of group icons—Main, Accessories, Games, Non-Windows applications, and so on.

When you double-click on a group icon, it opens to display the application icons within it. Figure A.2 shows the Lotus Applications group after you open it.

The icons labelled `Freelance Graphics`, `Freelance Install`, and so on, are *application icons*. When you double-click on an application icon (such as the Freelance Graphics icon), you start the program running in a window of its own.

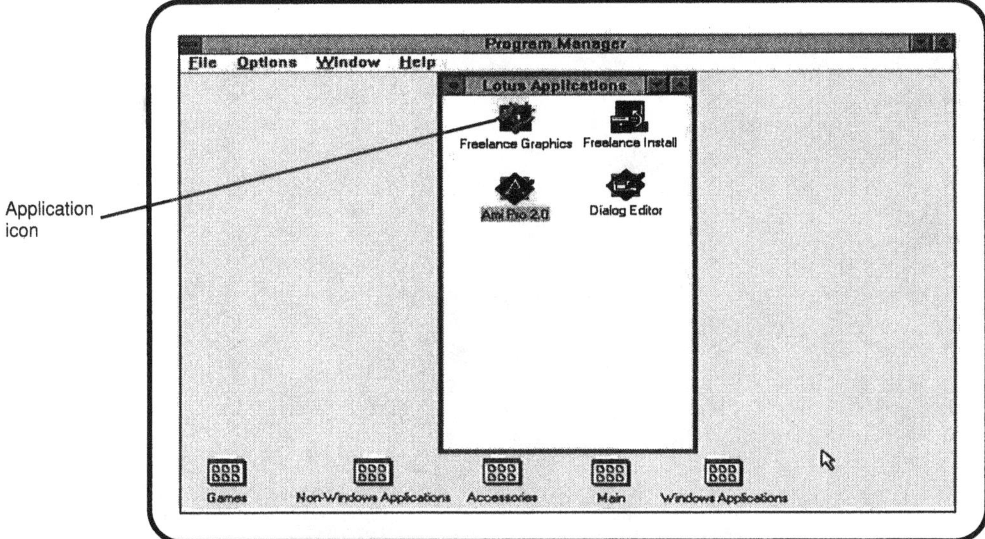

Figure A.2 Lotus Applications group.

When you run a program, you can reduce it to an icon without actually exiting the application. Later, you can double-click on the icon to restore the application to its full size. Figure A.3 shows the Freelance Graphics application reduced to an icon at the bottom of the screen. In the "Maximize and Minimize Buttons" section later in this appendix, you find out how to reduce an application to an icon.

Parts of a Window

Microsoft Windows are much more flexible than the windows in a house. You can manipulate them in many ways, but all windows work the same way—whether they are in the Program Manager or in a program itself. Figure A.4 shows the parts of a Windows 3.0 window.

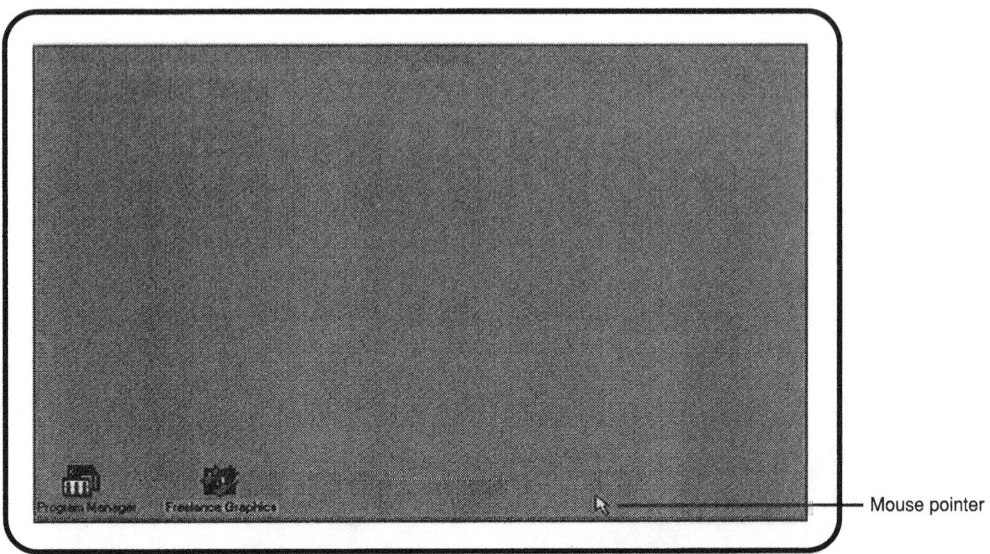

Figure A.3 The Freelance Graphics application reduced to an icon at the bottom of the screen.

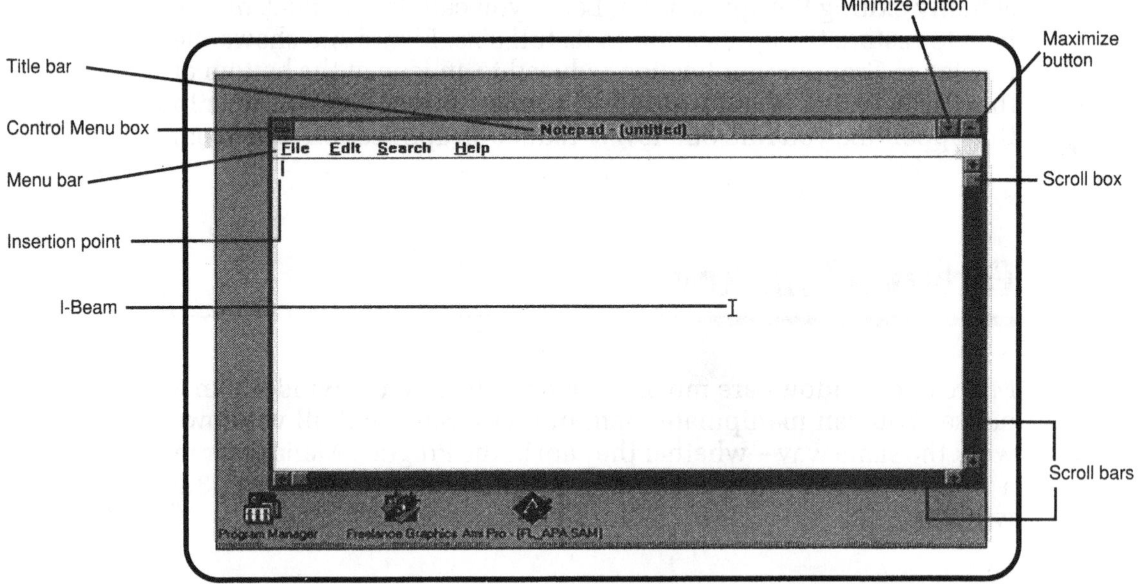

Figure A.4 The parts of any Windows 3.0 window.

Control Menu Box

There are a two basic ways to control the size and location of a window:

- ► Using the Control menu with either the mouse or keyboard.
- ► Using the Maximize, Minimize, and Restore buttons with the mouse.

The Control menu in the top left of any Windows application screen contains the commands for working with a window: Restore, Move, Size, Minimize, Maximize. Figure A.5 shows the Program Manager's Control menu. To display the Control menu, click on the Control menu box in the upper left corner of the screen.

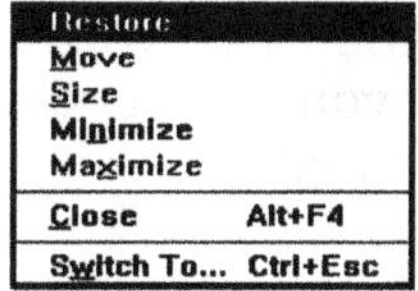

Figure A.5 The Control menu for the Program Manager.

As with other menu commands, you can execute the command by clicking on the command with the mouse. To execute the command using the keyboard, press Alt plus the underlined letter in the command name.

The Control menu includes one command that you can only execute from this menu—Switch To. When you select Switch To, you see a Task List of all the applications you are currently running. From this list, you can switch to another application or exit an application.

The following sections explain how to use the Maximize, Minimize, and Restore buttons to change the size of a window. To perform the same operations with the keyboard, choose the commands from the Control menu.

Maximize and Minimize Buttons

In the upper right corner of any Windows application window are two buttons—the *Minimize button* (an arrow pointing downward) and the *Maximize button* (an arrow pointing upward). Use these buttons to resize a window with one click of the mouse.

When you first open a window, it comes in a preset size that is less than the complete size of the screen. You can tell if your window is less than full size if there is a highlighted border around it. To have the window fill the whole screen, click on the Maximize button.

After you maximize a window, the Maximize button changes to a Restore button—a button with a double arrow pointing up and down. To restore the window to the previous size, click on the Restore button.

To reduce the window to an icon, click on the Minimize button. The icon appears at the bottom of the screen. You have not closed the program; it is still running. However, you can now use the available desktop space to display another program.

To restore an application after you minimize it, double-click on the program icon (or, if you prefer, click once and then choose Restore from the pop-up menu).

Changing the Size of a Window

You can change the size and proportion of a window to fit the desktop in any way you want. Move the mouse pointer to one of the window's corners or sides. The pointer becomes a double-headed arrow. If you drag on a corner, you resize in two dimensions. For instance, if you click on the top right corner and drag toward the middle, the top and right side move in as you drag. If you click and drag one of the sides, you move that side only.

To resize a window using the keyboard, select the Size command from the Control menu and then press the arrow keys to move the pointer to a corner or side of the window. When the pointer changes to a double-headed arrow, press the arrow keys to move the corner or side in the direction you want. When the window is the size you want, press Enter.

After you resize a window, the Maximize command works as it did before; it causes the window to fill the screen. If you choose the Restore button, however, the window returns to the size you set and not to its original size.

The Title Bar

The *title bar* serves several purposes. It displays the name of the application. It appears highlighted when an application is the active window. And it is useful for moving the window. Simply click on the title bar and drag the entire window to the location you want. The Control menu is at the left of the title bar; the Minimize and Maximize buttons are at the right.

> **Tip:** To move a window using the keyboard, select Move from the Control menu commands, press the arrow keys to move the window to the new location, and then press Enter.

Scroll Bars

There are two *scroll bars* on the screen, one along the right side and one along the bottom. (If the bottom scroll bar does not appear, click on the Maximize button.) Use the vertical scroll bar to scroll up and down in an application and the horizontal scroll bar to scroll left and right in an application.

The scroll bar has arrows on each end and a scroll box in the middle. These can help you use the scroll bars smoothly.

- ► To move a line at a time, click on one of the arrows. To scroll continuously, click on one of the arrows and hold down the mouse button.
- ► To move a screen at a time, click just above or just below the scroll box.
- ► To move to a specific point in the application (such as a point two-thirds of the way down), drag the scroll box to the point you want.

> **Note:** When you work in the scroll box, the application cursor remains in place. After you locate the position you want, click in the application to move the cursor to that point.

Multiple Windows

One of the main reasons to use Windows is to work with multiple programs at once, or with multiple documents within any single program. To work with multiple applications, first use these steps to open the applications:

1. From the Program Manager, double-click on the first application you want.
2. From within that application, click on the Control menu and use the Switch To command to return to the Program Manager.
3. Double-click on a second application.

Repeat the process to open as many applications as your computer's memory will allow. If you prefer, instead of using the Control menu, you can minimize an application after you open it. You then return to the Program Manager, where you can open a second program.

Once you have more than one application running at once, you can readily move from one to the other. If you maximized a program (that is, made it take up the entire screen), you can use the Control menu and the Switch To command to move to any other program. Often, however, it is convenient to size the multiple windows so that you can see all of them at once on your desktop.

Click and drag the sides or corners of any individual window to make it a size that suits you. Perhaps you may have one window take up the top half of the screen; click and drag the sides or corners of another to place it where you want it (perhaps along the bottom half of the screen). Figure A.6 shows a screen with multiple applications open in sized windows.

Once you have multiple applications visible on the screen, to make any application active instead of any other, move the pointer into that application and click.

Tip: To move from one application to another without accidentally disturbing anything in the new application, click on the title bar of the application you want to move to rather than somewhere else on the window of the new program.

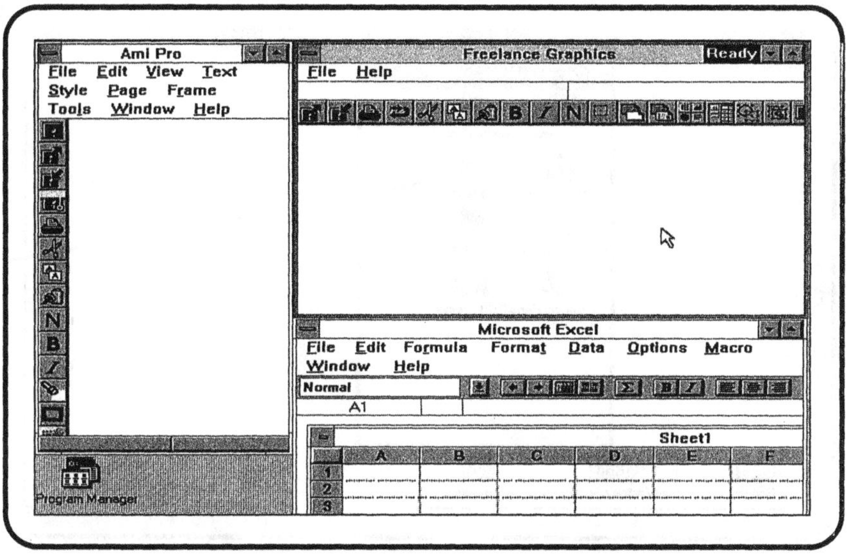

Figure A.6 Change the size and dimensions of windows to fit them on the screen in a way that is useful.

If you find your desktop becoming messy and confusing, you can have Windows rearrange it for you. From the Control menu, choose Switch To. From the Task List, choose Cascade or Tile. If you choose Cascade, Windows arranges your applications one on top of the other, so you can see the title bars of each. If you choose Tile, Windows arranges the applications proportionately so that each is a rectangle on the screen. (You can also select Cascade or Tile from the Window menu.)

The Clipboard

The Windows *Clipboard* is a temporary storage area that serves all Windows applications and non-Windows applications you run from Windows. It is itself a Windows program that is part of the Windows Main group, shown in Figure A.7. When you cut or copy material using the Cut or Copy commands from the Edit menu in an application, the Clipboard serves as a convenient place to keep the material temporarily.

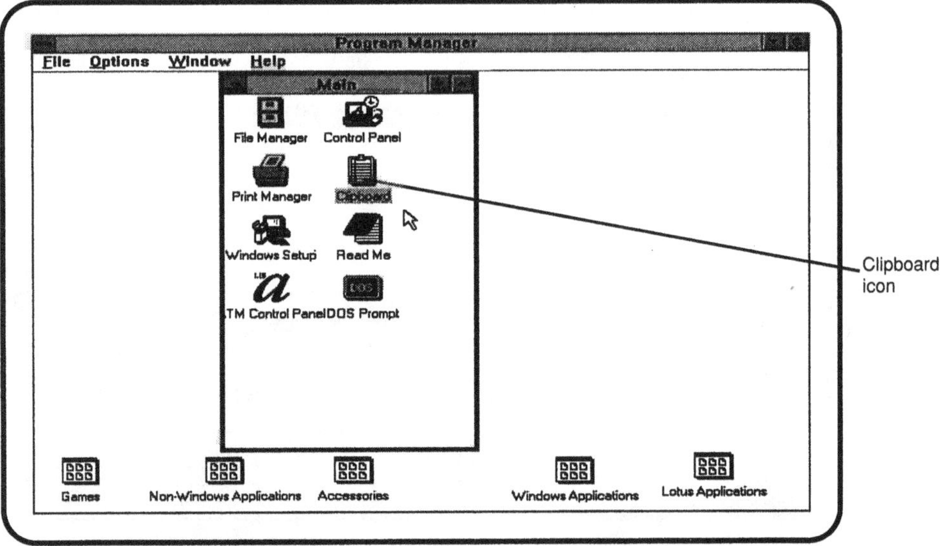

Figure A.7 The Clipboard in the Windows Main group.

To use the Clipboard with multiple applications, cut or copy information from the first application into the Windows Clipboard. Make a second application the active window and use that application's Paste command to place the information in the second program. For instance, you might choose to copy a piece of clip art from some other Windows program such as PowerPoint and then use the Paste command to place it in Freelance Graphics for Windows.

You can also place information in the Clipboard from a non-Windows application running in a window. First, from within the Windows application, select the information to copy. Open the Windows Control menu. Choose Copy. Windows copies the selected information to the Clipboard.

Tip: You can check the contents of the Clipboard at any time. To open the Clipboard program, click on the Control menu and switch to the Program Manager. Double-click on the Main group to open it. Double-click on the Clipboard icon to display its contents. To return to your program, close the Clipboard. If your program is visible, click on it with the mouse. If it is not, open the Control menu in the Program Manager and use the Switch To command to return to your program.

As you use Windows with various programs, you will find many more capabilities than the basics explained here. Refer to Chapter 2, "Getting Started with Freelance," for a discussion of additional Windows basics—particularly dialog boxes and menus.

Appendix B

Installing Freelance Graphics for Windows

Before you explore the features of Freelance Graphics for Windows, you have to install the program on your PC. This appendix details what you need and the steps to take when installing the program.

Hardware and Software Requirements

You need the following hardware and software to install Freelance Graphics for Windows:

- A 286-, 386-, or 486-based computer that will run Microsoft Windows 3.0 or higher.
- A hard disk with at least 10.5M (megabytes) of free space available for the program. After installation, if you want, you can reduce the required disk space (up to 6M) by removing one or more files from the Freelance Graphics directories on your hard disk. To learn how to remove files after installation, refer to the "Deleting Files" section at the end of this appendix.
- At least 2M of Random Access Memory (RAM) after you have installed DOS to operate in Windows Standard or Enhanced mode. For optimum performance, Lotus recommends an additional 2M of extended memory.

- An EGA, VGA, Super VGA, XGA, IBM 8514A graphics adapter (graphics board), or equivalent resolution adapters.

Caution: To run QuickStart, the on-line tutorial, you must have a VGA graphics adapter, a Super VGA or XGA, or an IBM 8514A graphics adapter configured to a VGA mode. (QuickStart does not run on an EGA monitor.)

- A graphics monitor.
- An IBM or Microsoft serial, bus, or InPort mouse.
- An output device: a printer, laser printer, or plotter. You also can use your screen as the output device.
- Microsoft Windows version 3.0 or higher.
- MS-DOS version 3.1 or higher.

Starting the Install Program

As soon as you have the right equipment in place and have Windows running under DOS, you are ready to install Freelance Graphics for Windows. To give you fewer disks to work with as you install, Lotus has compressed the files on the disks. That is, you cannot just copy the files to your hard disk. You need the installation program to "inflate" the files and put them on your hard disk.

1. Start Windows and open the Windows Program Manager.
2. Insert the disk labelled **Install** into drive A (or the drive you choose for installing the program) and close the drive door.
3. From the File menu, choose Run to display the Run dialog box.
4. Type `A:INSTALL` in the text box where you see the insertion point, as shown in Figure B.1. If you want to install Freelance Graphics from a floppy drive other than drive A, type the letter for that drive (for instance, `B:INSTALL`).
5. Click OK or press Enter.

The Installation program displays a message box that tells you it is copying the working files to the hard disk. Then it displays the Welcome to Install dialog box, as shown in Figure B.2.

6. To continue installation, choose OK.

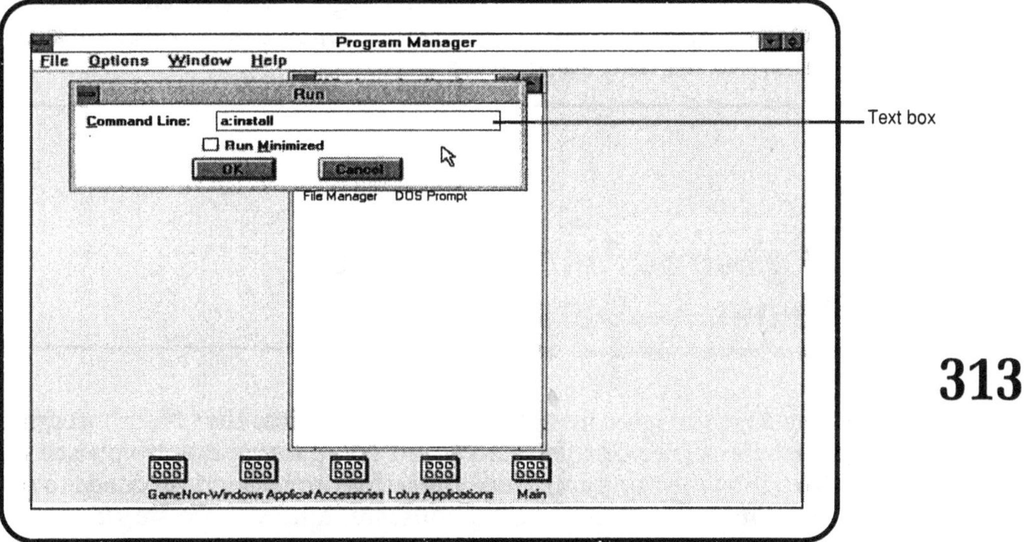

Figure B.1 Type A:INSTALL in the Run dialog box in the Program Manager.

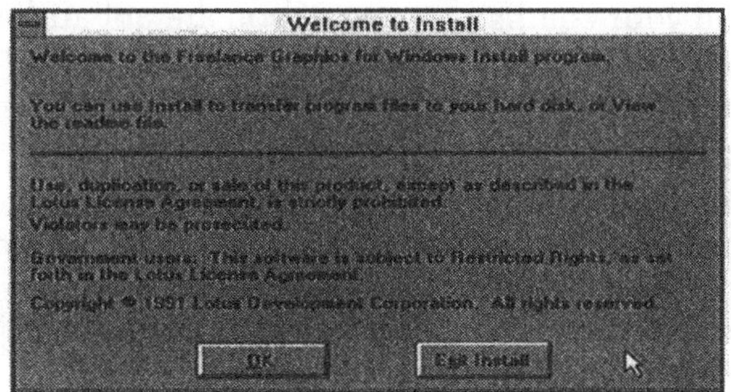

Figure B.2 Welcome to Install dialog box.

> **Note:** Throughout installation, Freelance Install asks you to enter information in text boxes and to choose from different options. To choose an option or text box, you can click on it using the mouse. If you prefer to use the keyboard, press the Tab key until you highlight your choice and then press the space bar to select or deselect an option. Click on OK with the mouse (or press Enter on the keyboard) to accept the screen and move to the next step.

Registering Your Name and Company Name

The first time you install Freelance Graphics, the Install program asks you to register your name and company name. If you are re-installing the program, Install skips this prompt and proceeds to the Main menu. To register your software, follow these steps:

1. Type your name.
2. Click the Company name box or press Tab to move to the company name text box.
3. Type in your company name. If you are not affiliated with a company, just type in your own name again. (The name and company name can be up to 30 characters each.)
4. Choose OK.
5. Now you confirm the accuracy of the information you have just entered. If the information is inaccurate, choose No to return to the registration screen, so you may type the information correctly. If the information is accurate, choose Yes to continue installing the program.

Viewing Product Updates

The Main menu appears and gives you the choice to install Freelance Graphics or to view product updates (see Figure B.3).

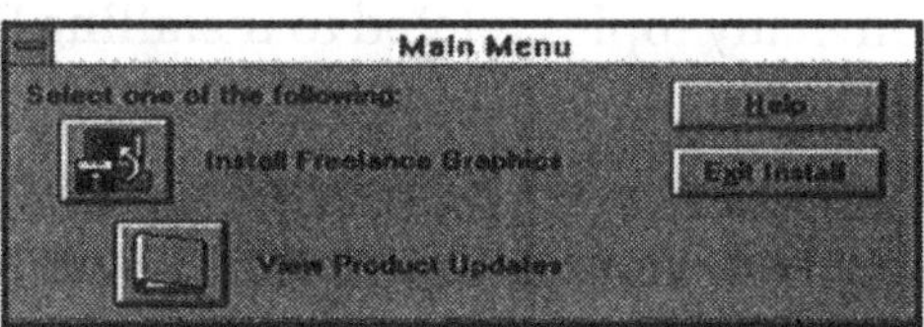

Figure B.3 Main menu for Freelance install program.

You may want to take the time to view the product updates. If you choose View Product Updates, you see a file called READ.ME, which contains information that is often too recent to make its way into the documentation. This file appears on the Windows Notepad. If you click on the View Product Updates button, you see a screen like the one in Figure B.4. After you finish reading the updates, choose File and then Exit from the Notepad menu.

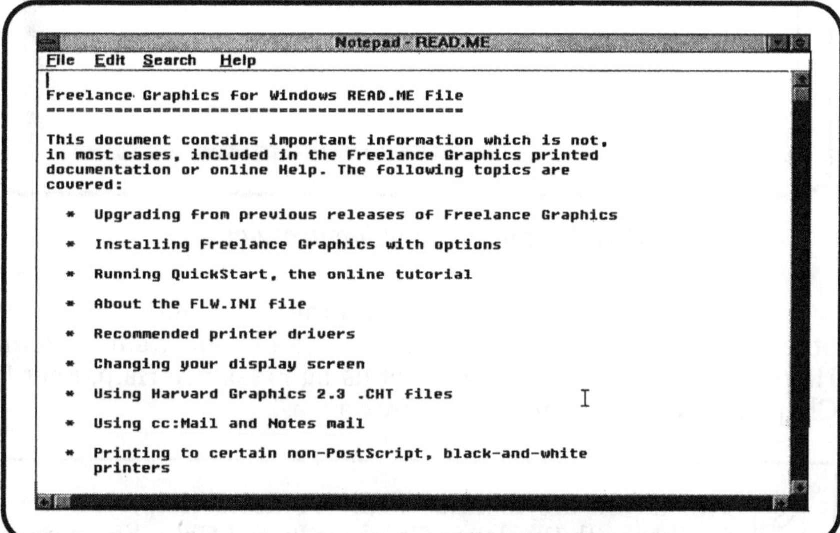

Figure B.4 Sample View Product Updates screen.

Using Install's Help Files

The Install program offers a thorough Help utility. You can get help on the current screen you are using, or you can go to the Index and get help there on many topics related to installing Freelance Graphics for Windows.

To get help, choose the Help button. If you choose Help from the Main Menu dialog box, you see the screen shown in Figure B.5.

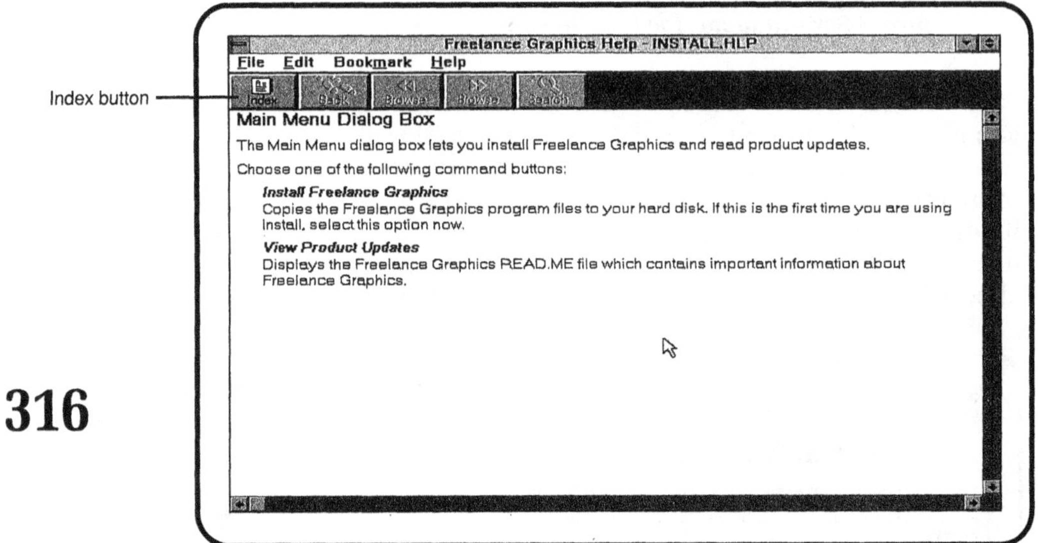

Figure B.5 Help file for the Main Menu dialog box.

To get help on any topic, click on the Index button from any other Help window and then choose the topic you want from the Help Index. For a full discussion of using Freelance Help, refer to Chapter 2, "Getting Started with Freelance."

> **Tip:** If you are familiar with Windows Help, you are familiar with Freelance Graphics Install Help. You navigate, use menus, and click on subtopics the same way you do in Windows Help.

Choosing Install with Defaults or Install with Options

To continue installation from the Install main menu, choose Install Freelance Graphics. The program scans your system to find out how much disk space is available and then displays the Type of Installation dialog box, as shown in Figure B.6.

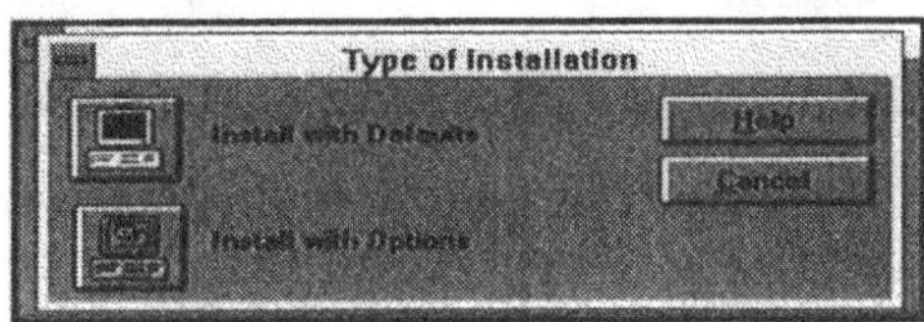

Figure B.6 Type of Installation dialog box.

You can choose two types of installation: Install with Defaults or Install with Options. With either choice, the Install program suggests the disk drive and directory (C:\FLW) where it will install Freelance Graphics. You can either accept the default or type in an alternative of your own.

If you choose Install with Defaults, the program then creates the following subdirectories:

\MASTERS	Will contain the files for your SmartMaster Sets, symbol libraries, and palettes.
\TUTORIAL	Contains the files for Freelance's excellent interactive tutorial.
\WORK	Empty after you complete installation, but it will contain any presentations you create.
\BACKUP	Empty initially, but it will contain backups of presentation files if you choose to make them.

With Install with Defaults, the Install program automatically places icons for Freelance Graphics and Freelance Graphics Install in a group named Lotus Applications in the Program Manager.

If you choose Install with Options, you can specify the names of the subdirectories instead of using the defaults. To choose a different name, type it into the Specifying Files and Directories dialog box, as shown in Figure B.7.

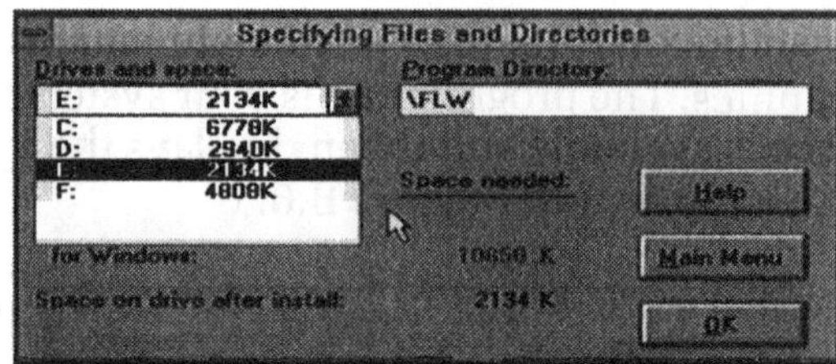

Figure B.7 Specifying Files and Directories dialog box.

If you want to specify a new name for each subdirectory, choose Install with Options. As long as you have enough room on your disk to install the program, the Specifying Program Directory dialog box appears. If you attempt to install to a hard disk that does not contain enough space for the full version of Freelance Graphics, a message box appears, telling you there is not enough room on that disk. Choose OK.

> **Tip:** If you do not have enough space to install Freelance Graphics, you can use the Install program to allow you to review your drives and the space available on each. From the Type of Installation dialog box, choose Install with Options. After scanning your drives, the install program shows a dialog box telling you the amount of space needed and the amount of space available on each drive.

If a drive with enough space for Freelance Graphics does not exist in your system, exit the Install program and either delete files from a hard disk to create enough space or add another disk to your system.

Tip: If you are re-installing Freelance Graphics (previously, for instance, you may have installed an earlier version of the program), the Install program will allow you to write over the program already on the disk. However, it cannot detect the space that the previously installed program takes up as space available. If a message box tells you that your hard disk does not have room, you can exit Install, delete some or all of the previous Freelance Graphics files from your hard disk, and restart Install.

Copying Files to Your Hard Disk

Once you have enough disk space and reach the Specifying the Program Directory dialog box, you see a prompt that asks you either to accept the default disk drive and directory name, or to type in your preference in the text box, as shown in Figure B.8. You can give the program directory a new DOS name (eight characters or less) or type in the name of an existing directory you would like to use. You can also choose to install the program to a different hard disk in your system, as long as the display box shows it has the space available.

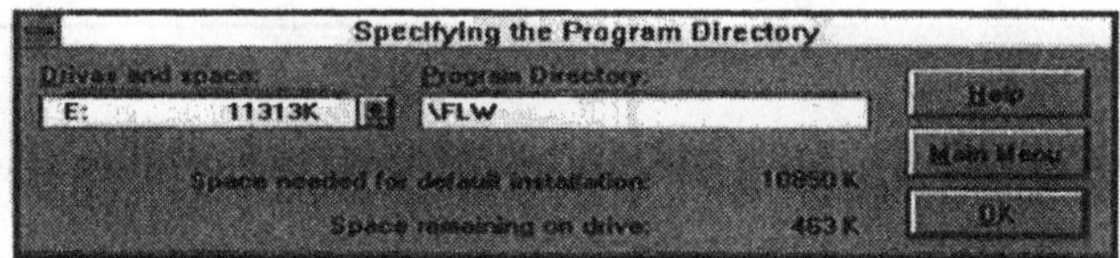

Figure B.8 Specifying the Program Directory dialog box.

The Specifying Program Directory screen also shows the amount of space the full installation of Freelance Graphics will take up on your computer's hard disk. When the disk and directory names are the ones you want, choose OK. The Confirm Directory box displays the disk and directory names you specified. If you did not specify a file already in your system, a message tells you that the directory does not exist and asks if Install should create it for you.

If you want Install to create a directory with that name, choose Yes for that option. If you want to go back to the Specifying Program Directory screen to enter a different directory name, choose Yes for that option. After you confirm the correct directory, Install creates the directory on the disk you indicated.

If you choose to install with options, a message box appears that gives you the option to install icons. With this screen you can choose which icons to install into the Program Manager and which group windows are to receive the icons. To select the icons displayed, press F for the Freelance Graphics for Windows icon, or press I for the Install icon. Then choose OK.

The Default Preferences screens appear. Each screen allows you to change the file name and path for a subdirectory. Choose the appropriate text box(es) and type in any changes you would like to make to each screen. Choose OK.

The Confirm Directory screens appear, asking you if you want the Install program to create the directories you have chosen. For each directory, choose either Yes (to confirm) or No (to return to the previous screen and change your default preferences).

Install displays a screen showing its progress as it transfers files from the Install floppy disk to your hard disk.

Installing the System Disks

A message appears asking you to insert the first system disk.

```
Insert System Disk 1. Close the drive door and choose OK .
```

A dialog box appears that shows the percentage of the floppy disk copied, so you can check the screen to see how far along the program is at any point during installation. The dialog box also displays the percentage copied of all the floppy disks you will use to install the program.

As the Install program finishes copying each installation disk, it tells you which disk to insert into the disk drive next. When the installation is complete, a screen displays instructions to start Freelance Graphics. Choose OK.

Installing ATM Fonts

The Install program gives you the option of installing the Adobe Type Manager program and ATM fonts that will enable you to display and print high-quality text. If you do not want to install ATM fonts, click on No to return to the Installation main menu. (Installation of the ATM fonts requires at least 750K of available space on your disk.)

> **Note:** You can install ATM at any time without having to reinstall the entire Freelance Graphics program. From the Windows Program Manager, insert the ATM program disk into drive A (or the drive you choose to install the program). From the File menu, choose the Run option, type **A:INSTALL** in the text box where you see the cursor, and choose OK. The ATM Installer dialog box appears, as shown in Figure B.9.

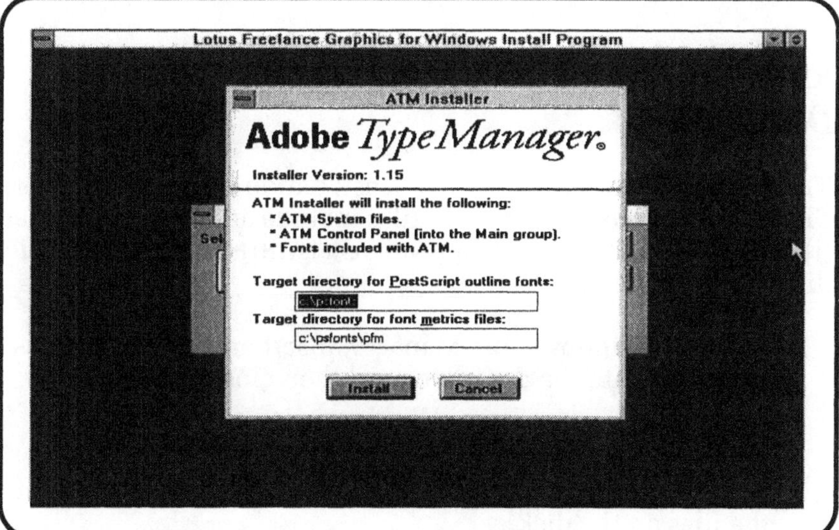

Figure B.9 ATM Installer dialog box.

The box recommends a target directory for the PostScript outline fonts and a target directory for font metrics files.

1. Accept the directories. If you installed Windows on a drive other than drive C, you may want to change the drive letter.
2. Choose Install (or choose Cancel if you do not want to install). The ATM Installer installs the fonts.
3. At the final installation screen, choose OK to return to the main menu.
4. To use ATM fonts with Freelance Graphics, you must exit to DOS and start Windows.

Reinstalling Deleted Files

If, for any reason, you delete any of the SmartMaster files, palette files, symbols files, QuickStart files, or program files from your hard disk, you can easily reinstall them. To reinstall one or more deleted files, there are two steps—identifying the disk that contains the deleted file(s) and then reinstalling the file(s).

Identifying Which Disk Contains the Deleted File(s)

The Freelance Graphics files on the installation disk are compressed files, so the extensions for these files include an exclamation mark (!). For instance, FLW.HLP appears as FLW.H!P on the installation disk.

1. From the Windows File Manager, insert any of the installation disks into the disk drive and then close the door.
2. Choose the A: drive icon. Windows displays the A:\ folder icon.
3. Choose the A:\ folder icon. Windows displays the names of the files on the disk.
4. Check the list of files on the disk for the file(s) you deleted from the hard disk.
5. Close the A:\ folder window.
6. Repeat Steps 1 through 5 until you locate the disk that contains the deleted file(s).
7. Close the File Manager.

Reinstalling the File(s)

After identifying the Freelance Graphics files you want to copy, you can reinstall them. This procedure assumes that you will use drive A and that you installed Freelance Graphics on hard drive C in the default program directory and path. If you installed the program into a different disk drive, a different directory, or a different path, substitute the appropriate information in the following instructions.

1. Insert the Freelance Graphics installation disk that contains the deleted file(s) into disk drive A and close the drive door.
2. To reinstall deleted files, you can go to the Program Manager and choose the Run option from the File menu or begin at the DOS prompt.
3. Type the following command:

```
C:\FLW\INFLATE A:\FILENAME C:\FLW\DESTINATION DIRECTORY
```


Here is a list showing the significance of each part of this command:

C:\FLW represents the drive and directory in which you installed Freelance Graphics.

INFLATE starts reinstallation.

A:*FILENAME* represents the floppy disk drive in which you inserted the installation disk and the name of the file to be reinstalled.

C:\FLW*DESTINATION DIRECTORY* represents the destination drive and destination directories where you will reinstall the deleted file(s), for instance, C:\FLW\MASTERS.

Note: All files with a .SYM extension, .PAL extension, and .MAS extension belong in the \FLW\MASTERS subdirectory.

If you want to reinstall all the files with the same extension you can use an asterisk (*). For example, to reinstall all symbols on one of the SmartMasters, Palettes, and Symbols disks, type the file name `*.SYM`. In this case, you would type the complete command as follows:

```
C:\FLW\INFLATE A:\*.SYM C:\FLW\MASTERS
```

4. Press Enter.

The program reinstalls the file(s) to the specified drive and subdirectory. To reinstall any other files from the floppy disk, repeat Steps 1 through 4.

Deleting Files

Unless you want to remove Freelance from your disk, you should not delete any of the \FLW program files. You can delete files from the subdirectories listed below:

SmartMaster Sets (.MAS extension)
Subdirectory: \FLW\MASTERS

Palettes (.PAL extension)
Subdirectory: \FLW\MASTERS

Symbols (SYM extension)
Subdirectory: \FLW\MASTERS

QuickStart tutorial files
(all files tutorial files included)
Subdirectory: \FLW\TUTORIAL

You may want to look at the files in the MASTERS subdirectory to decide which file(s) to delete. You can see an example of any of these files with the following procedure:

1. Start the Freelance Graphics program.
2. From the File menu, choose New. The File New Screen will appear.
3. Choose OK.
4. From here you can view examples of the symbols, SmartMaster Sets, and palettes by doing one of the following:

   To view examples of the symbols, select the light bulb icon in the Toolbox. Then, from the Library display box, choose the file you want to view. The file appears in the Symbol box below the Library display box.

To see examples of SmartMaster Sets, from the Main menu choose the Style menu and then Choose SmartMaster Set. Then select the file in the SmartMaster Sets box that you want to view from the Browse SmartMaster Set box below it (double-click to see a larger, more readable example).

To see examples of palettes, from the Main menu select the Style menu and then Choose Palette. Then select the file that you want to view from the Selected palette box.

After you decide which file(s) to delete, you can exit to DOS and delete the files using the DEL command. If you want to reinstall any files that you delete, follow the procedures in the "Reinstalling Deleted File(s)" section of this appendix.

Appendix C

SmartMaster Sets

This appendix shows you the title page from each of the available SmartMaster sets. To select a SmartMaster set for a new presentation, select File and then New. In the File New dialog box that appears, select the SmartMaster you want by highlighting its name. Then press Enter or click OK. (For information on customizing a SmartMaster, see Chapter 15, "Customizing Freelance Tools.")

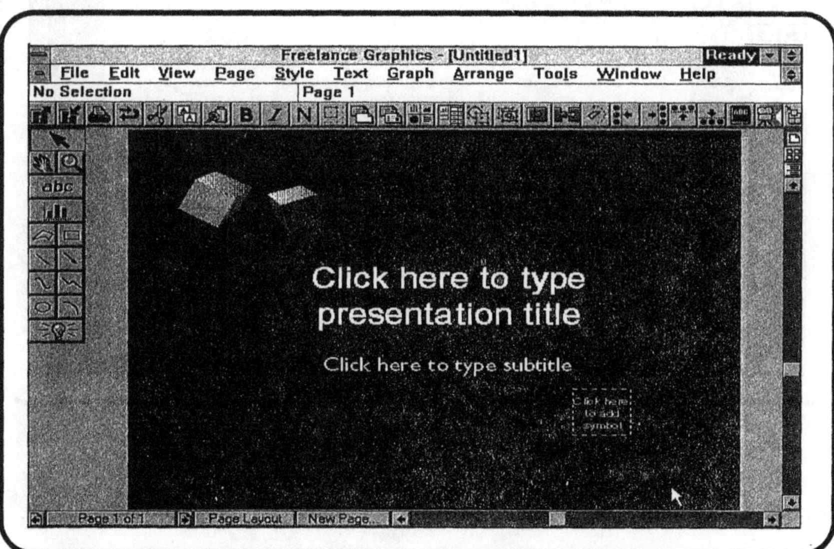

Figure C.1 0blocks.mas

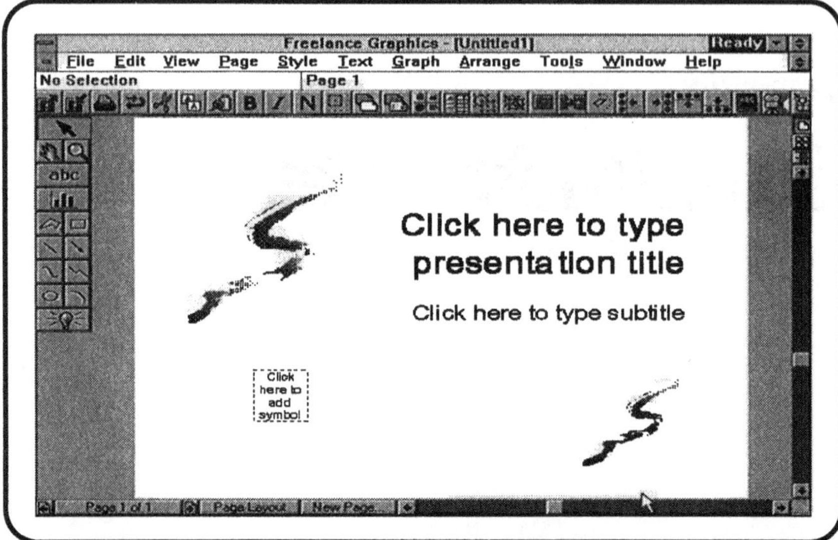

Figure C.2 0sketch.mas

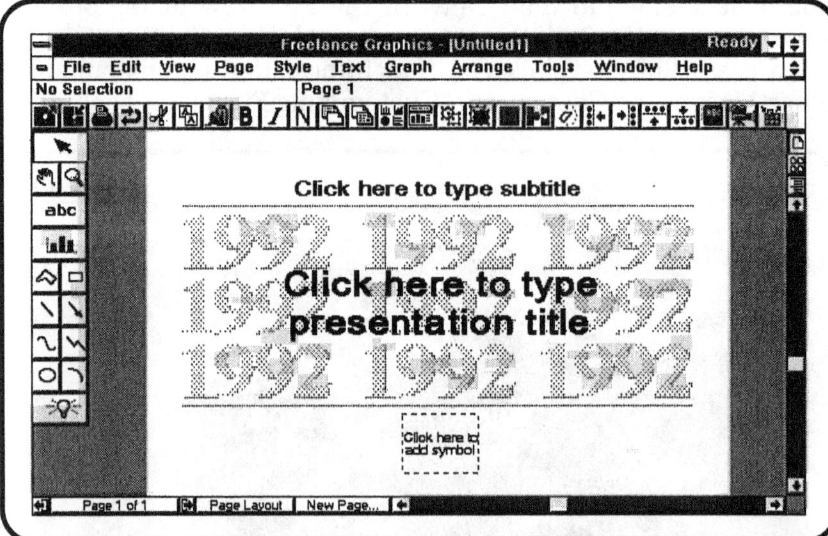

Figure C.3 1992.mas

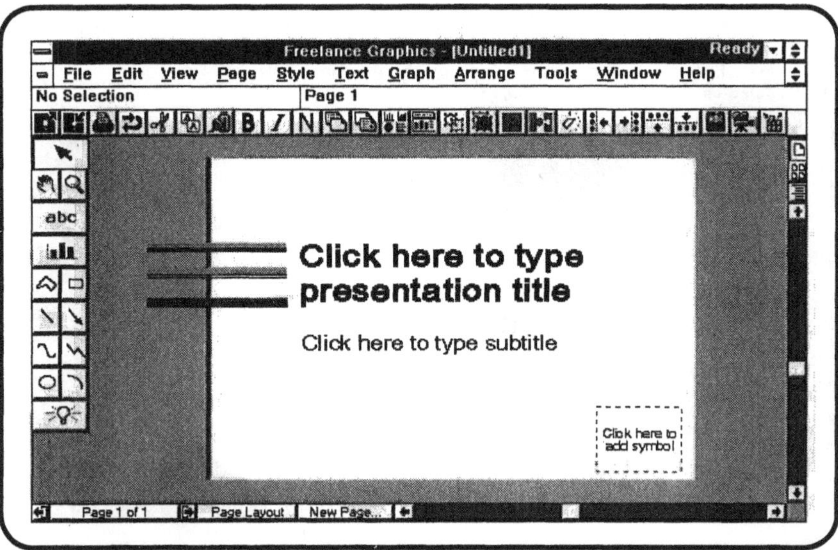

Figure C.4 3line.mas

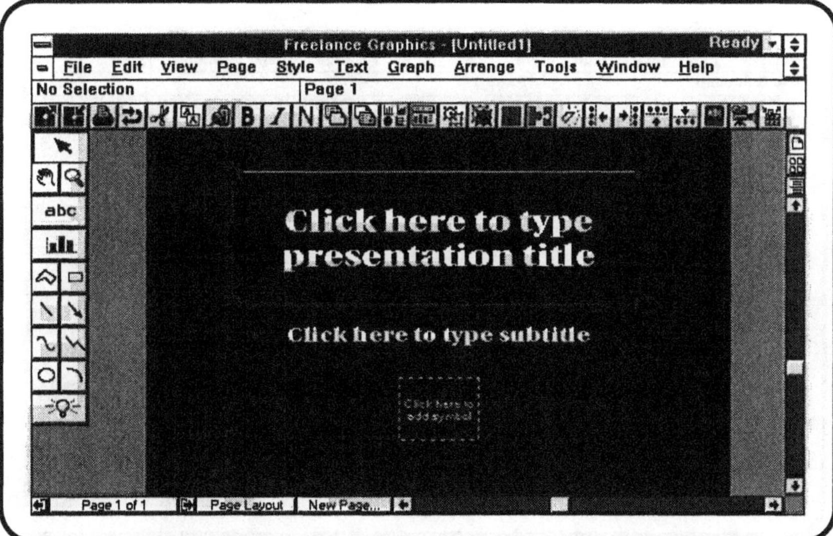

Figure C.5 4square.mas

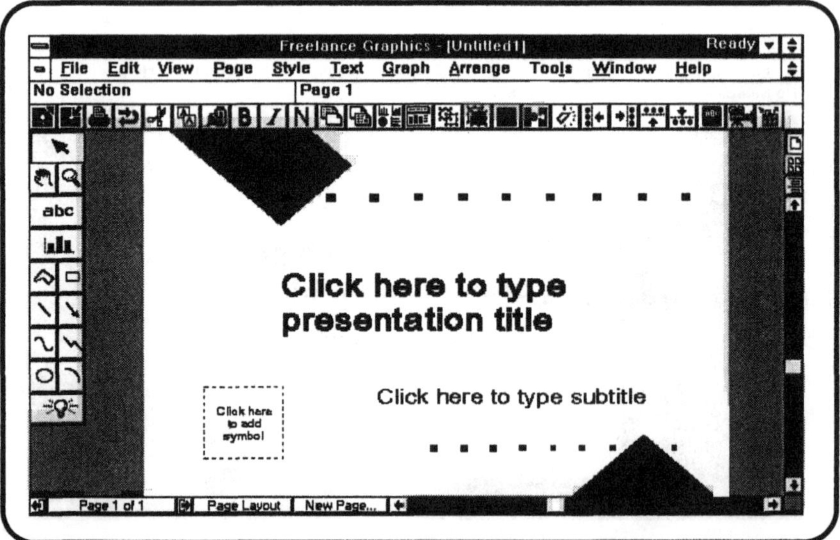

 Figure C.6 abstract.mas

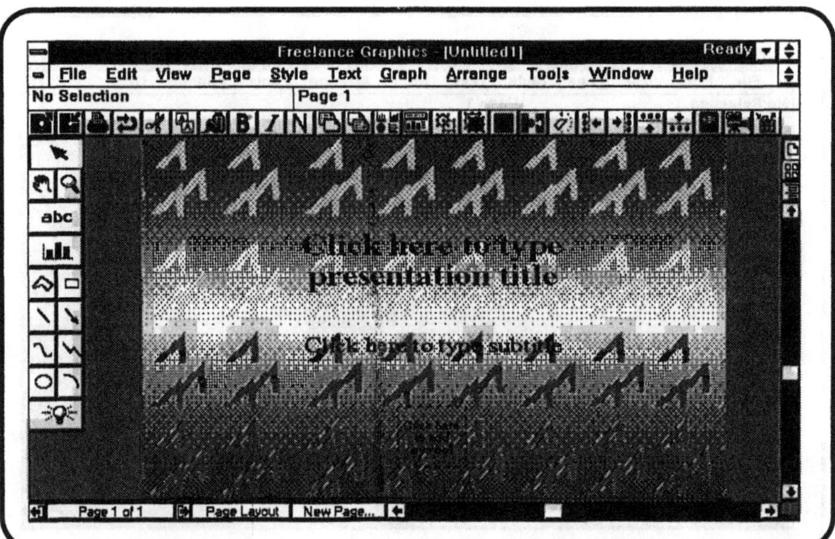

Figure C.7 angles.mas

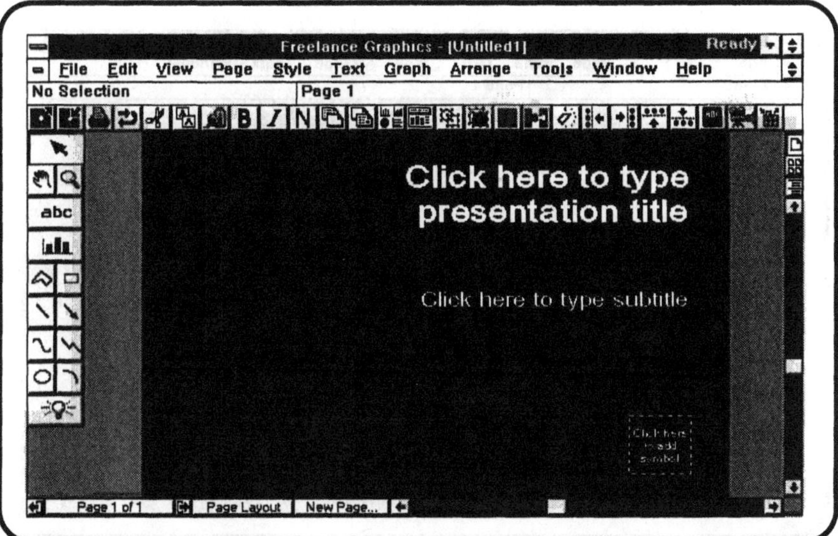

Figure C.8 asia.mas

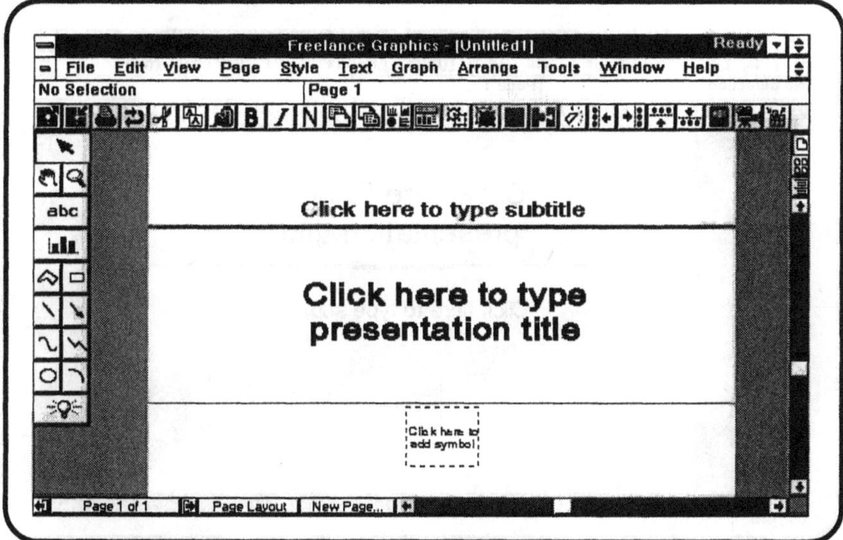

Figure C.9 basiclin.mas

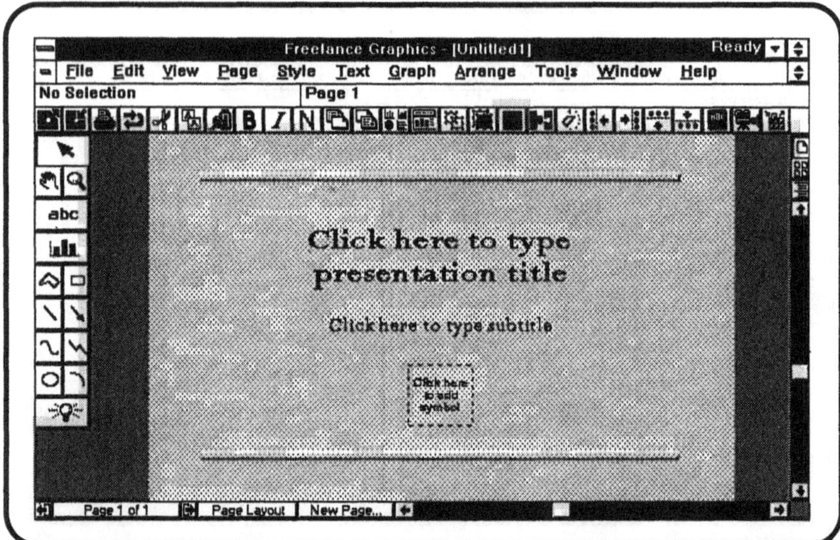

Figure C.10 bevrule.mas

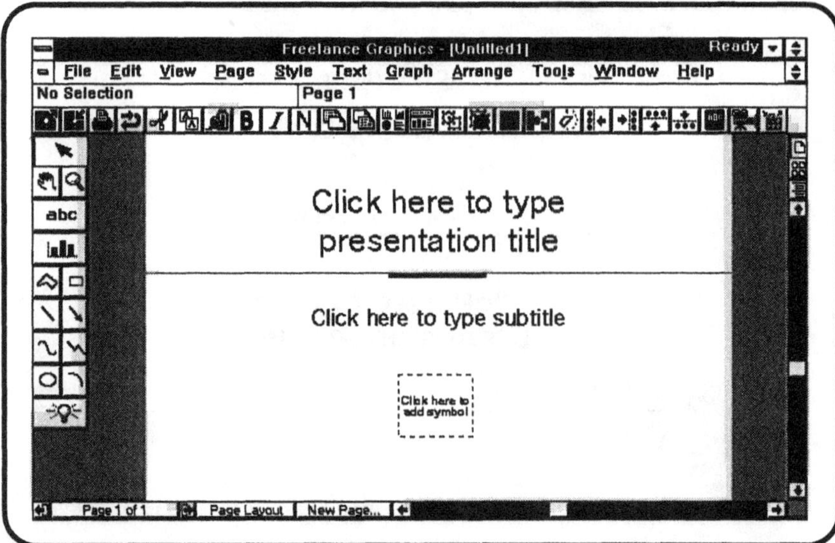

Figure C.11 blocklin.mas

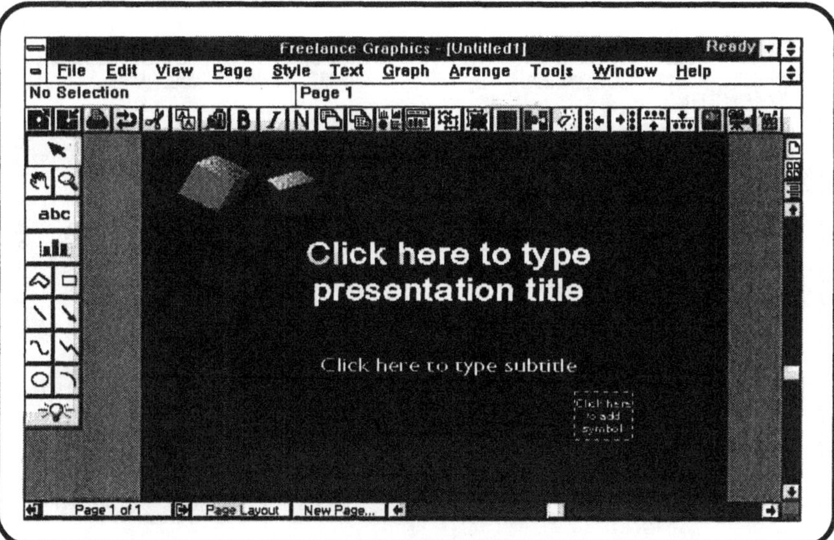

Figure C.12 blocks.mas (0blocks.mas)

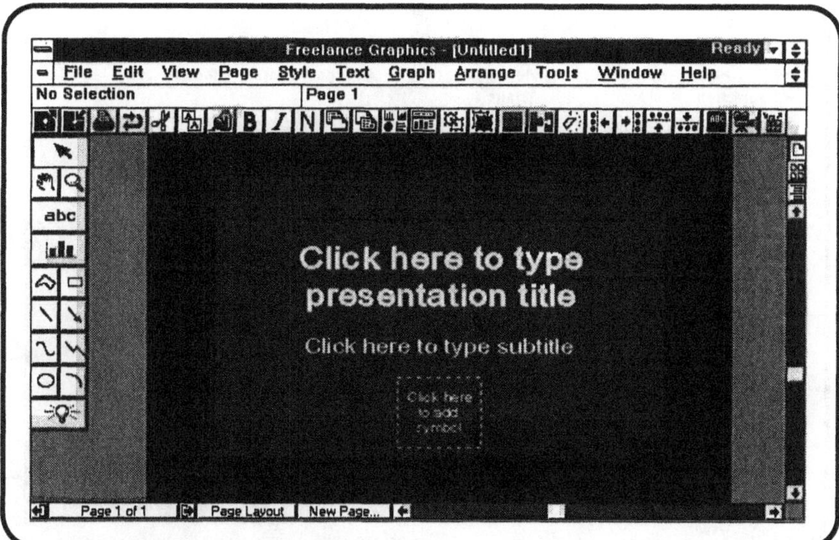

Figure C.13 boxline.mas

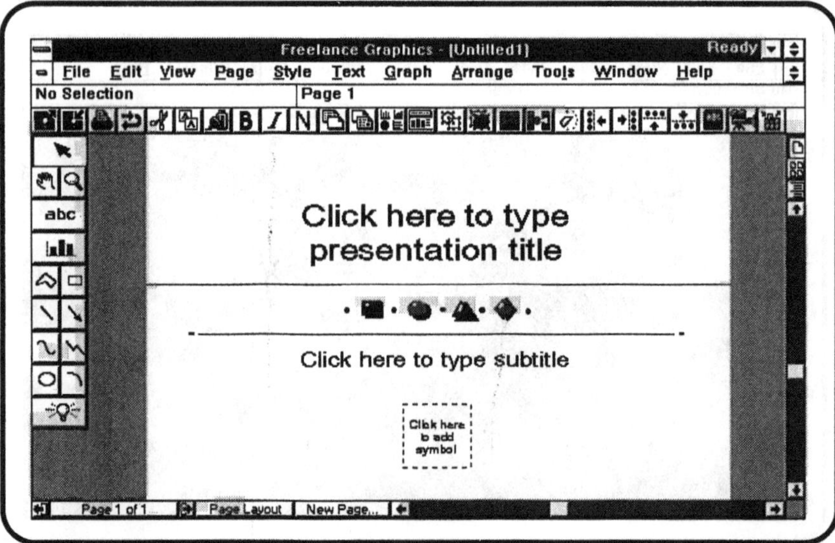

Figure C.14 buttons.mas

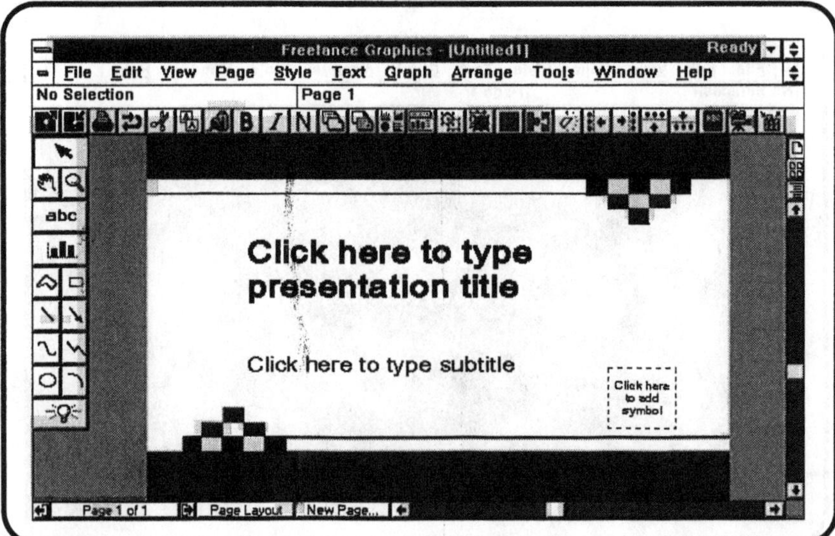

Figure C.15 checker.mas

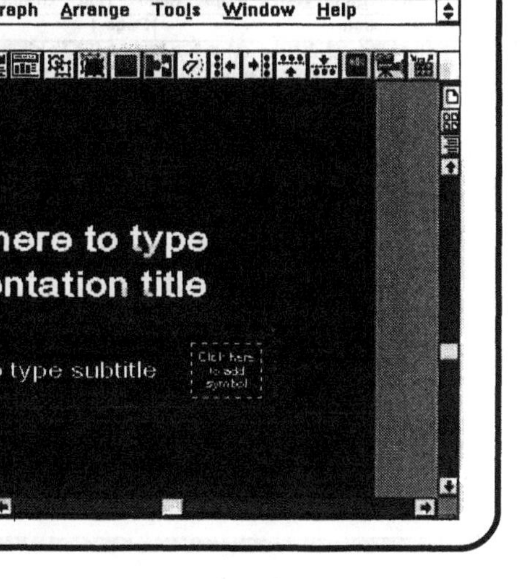

Figure C.16 circle.mas

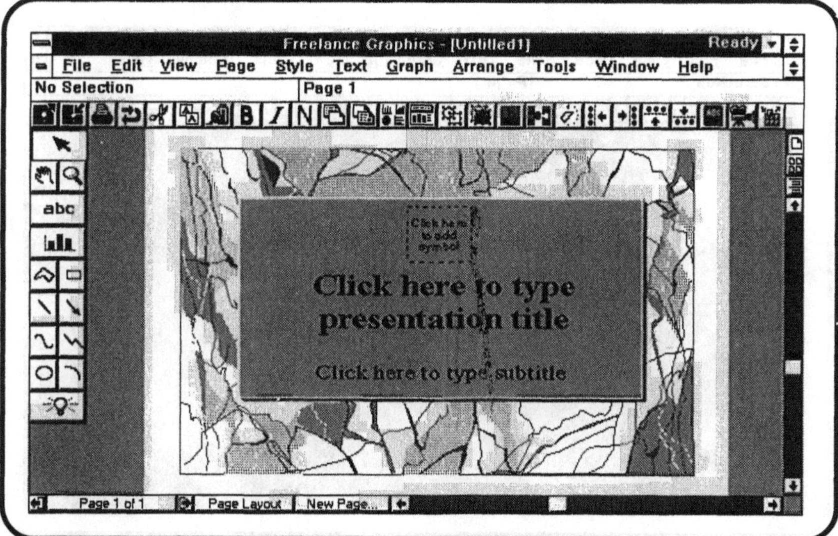

Figure C.17 classic.mas

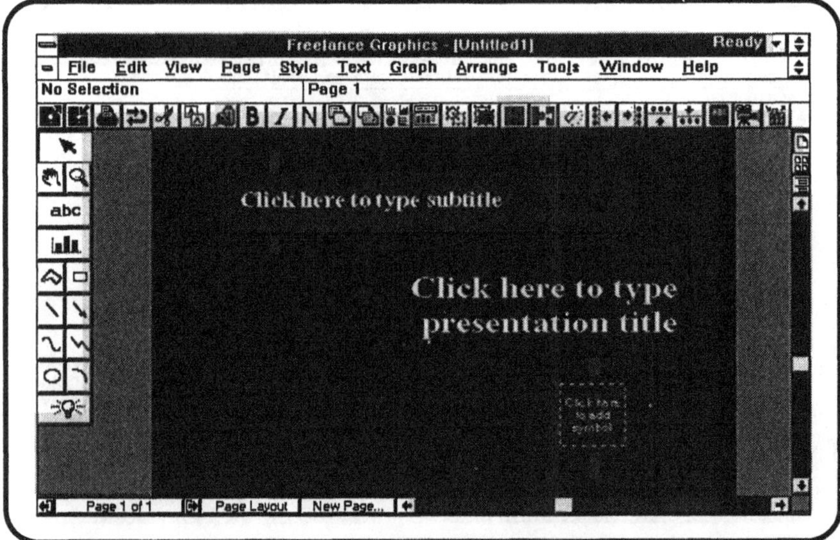

Figure C.18 collage.mas

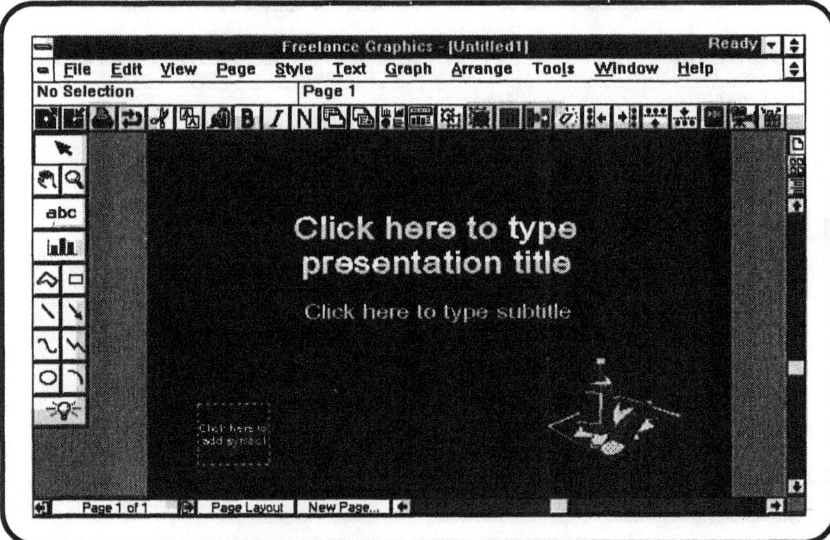

Figure C.19 cuisine.mas

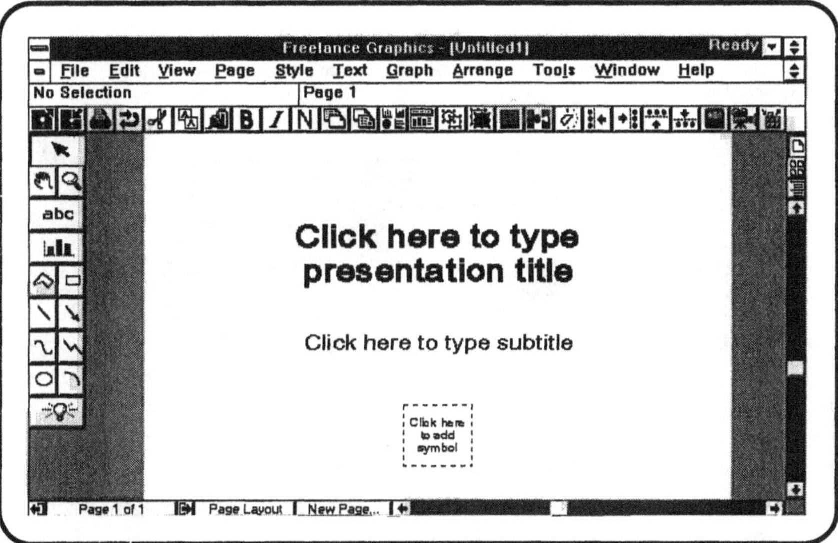

Figure C.20 custom.mas

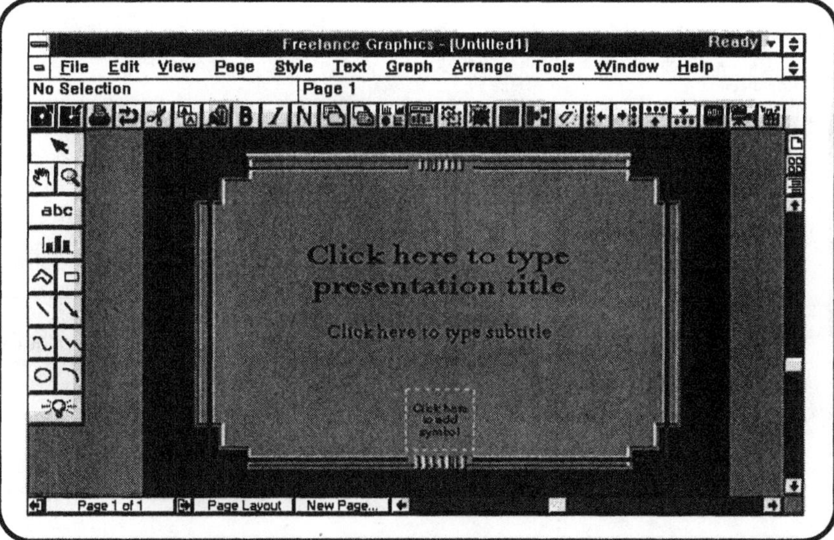

Figure C.21 deco.mas

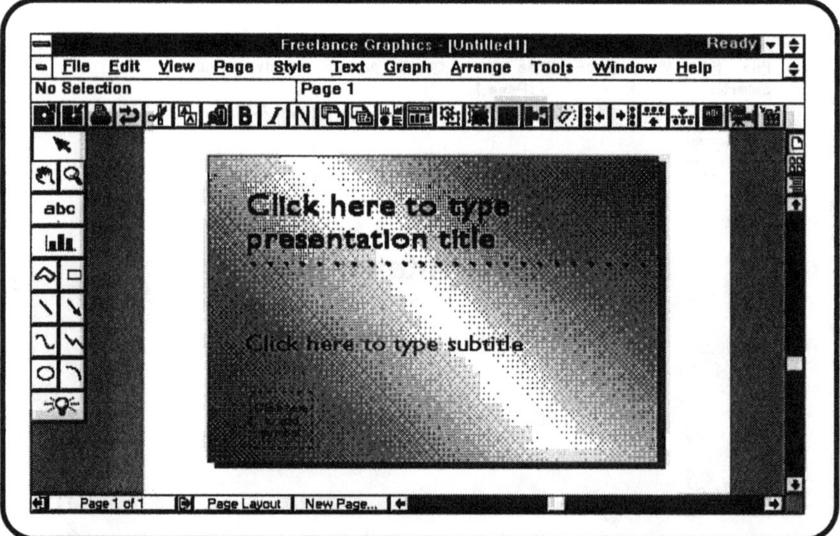

Figure C.22 dotbox.mas

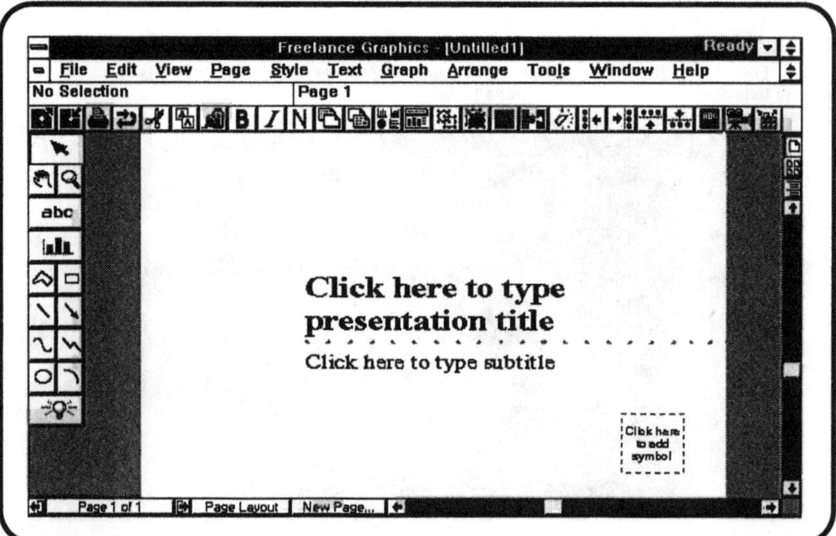

Figure C.23 dotline1.mas

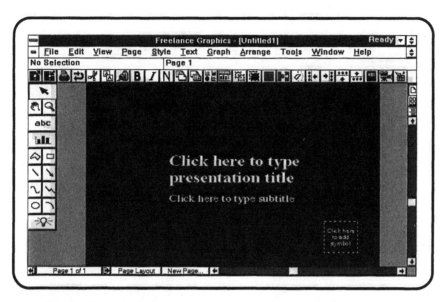

Figure C.24 dotline2.mas

Figure C.25 eec.mas

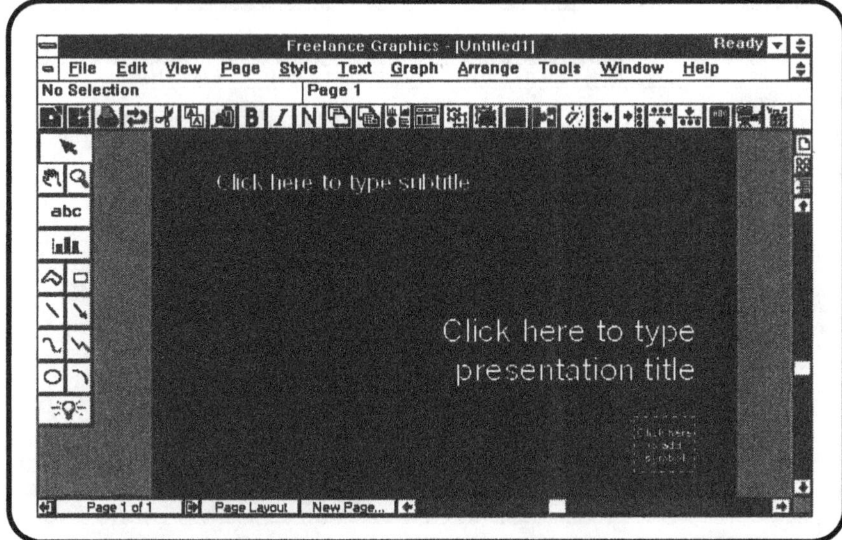

Figure C.26 elegance.mas

Figure C.27 europe.mas

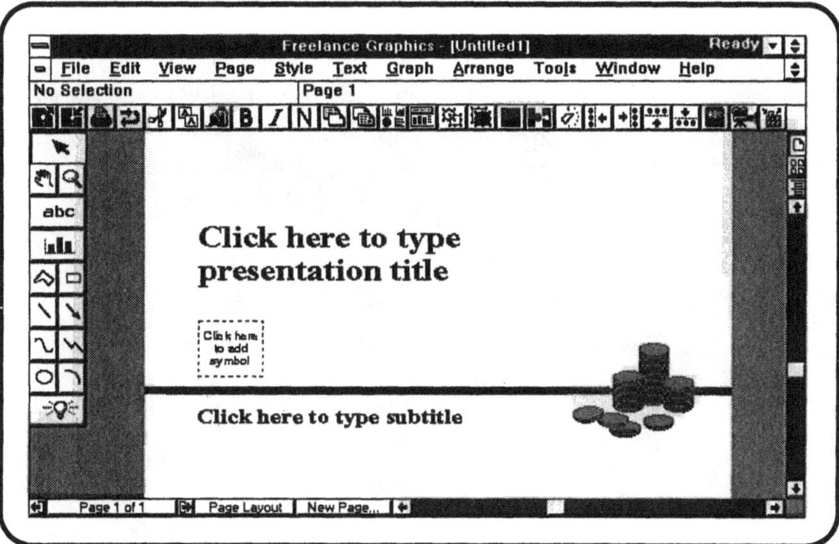

Figure C.28 finance.mas

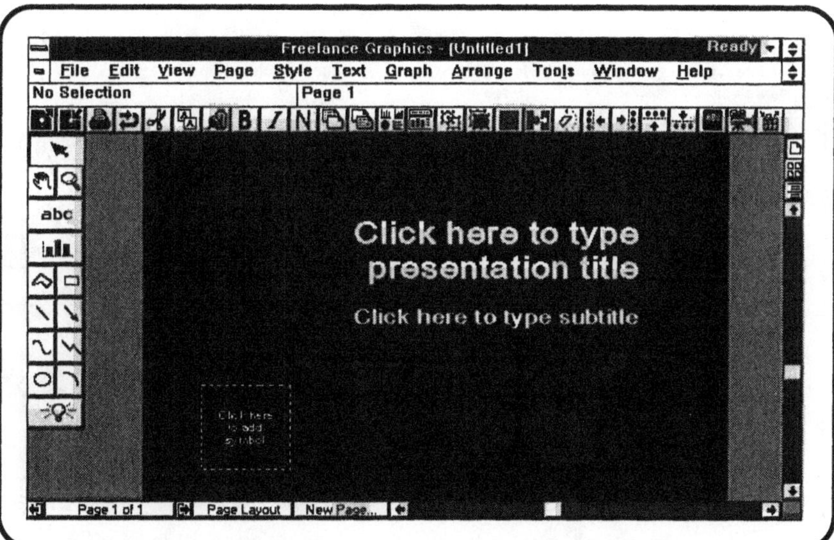

Figure C.29 forest.mas

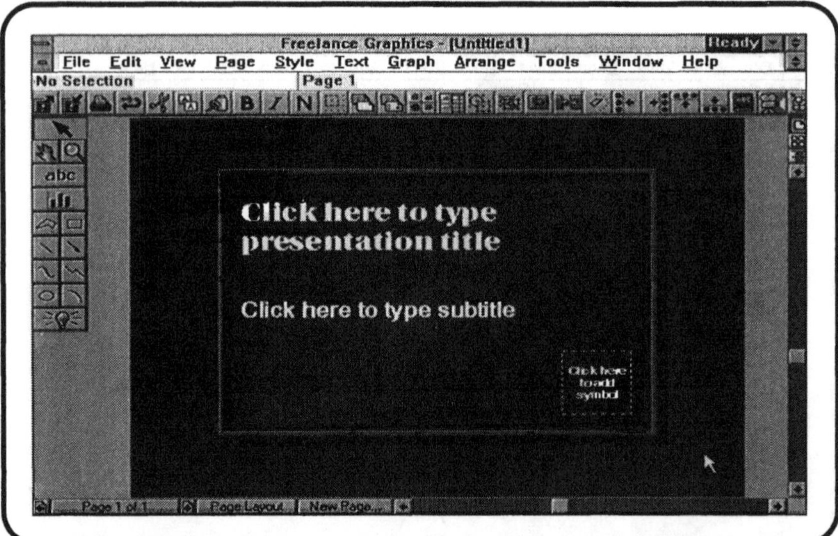

Figure C.30 frame.mas

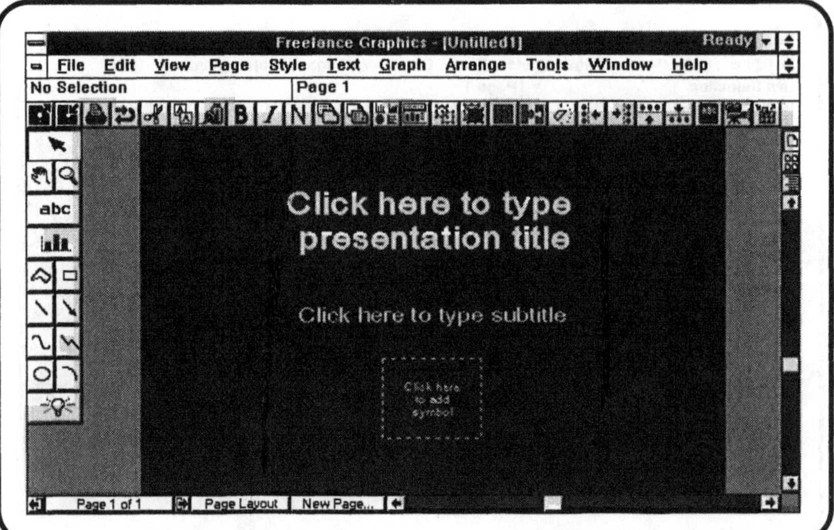

Figure C.31 gradate1.mas

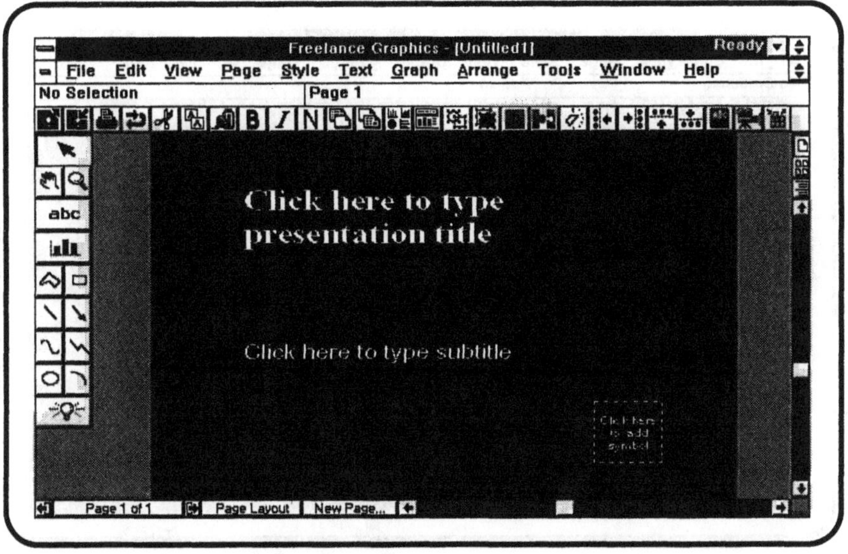

Figure C.32 gradate2.mas

Figure C.33 gradate3.mas

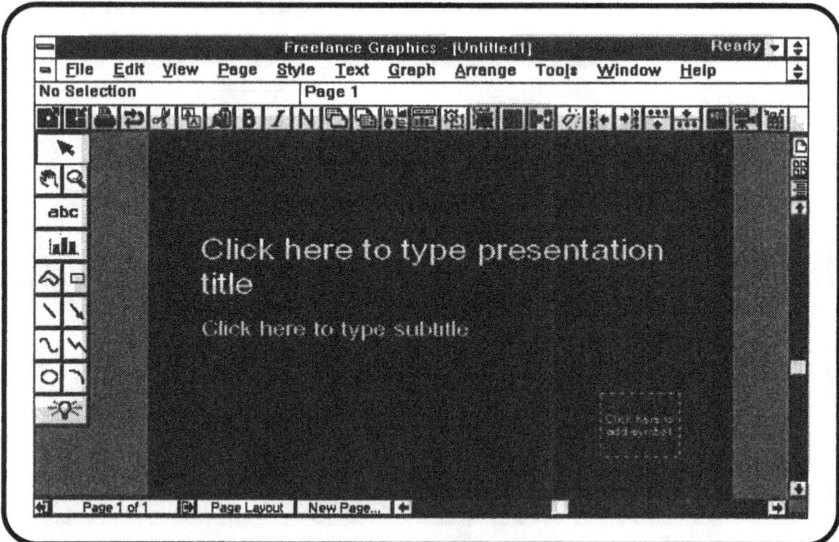

Figure C.34 gradline.mas

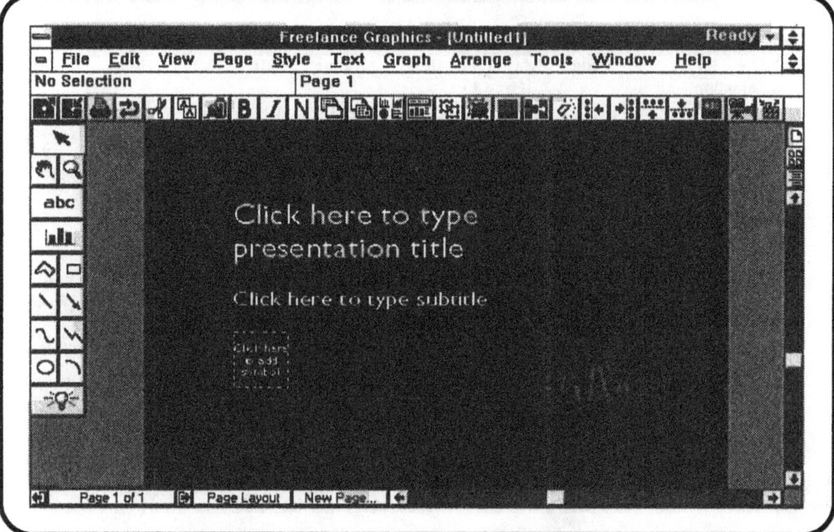

Figure C.35 graphlin.mas

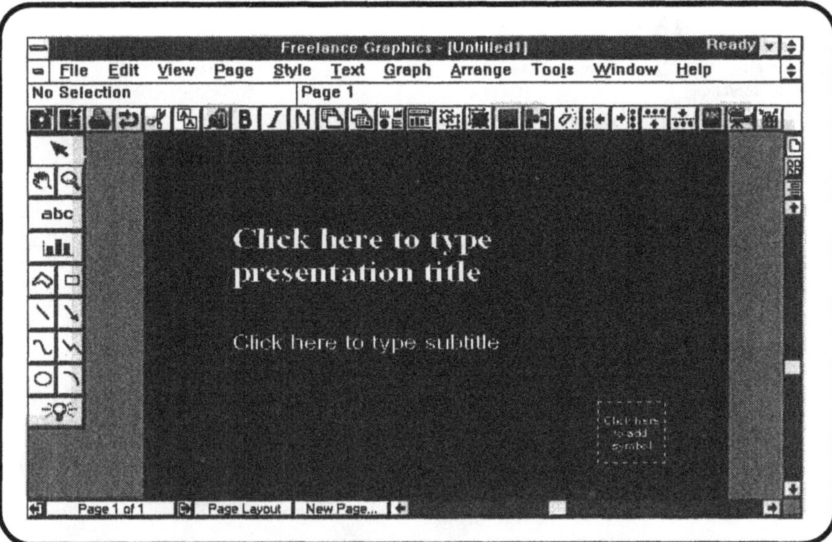

Figure C.36 horizon.mas

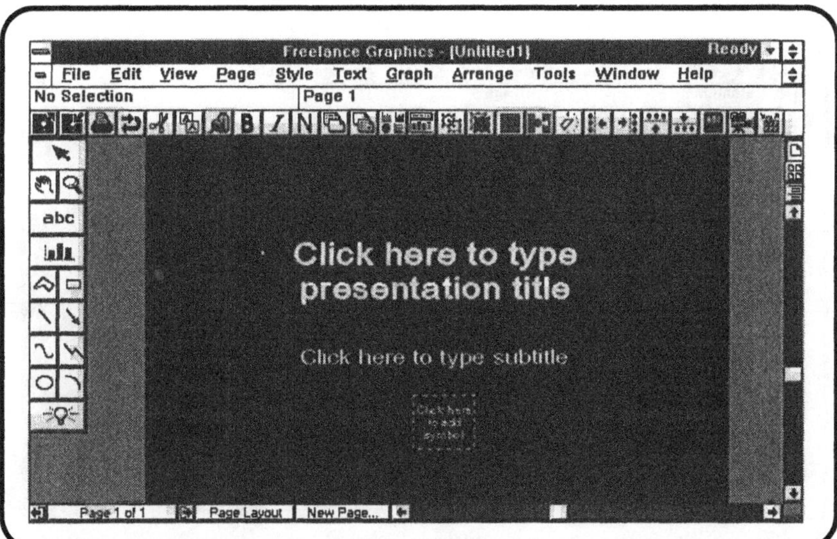

Figure C.37 louver.mas

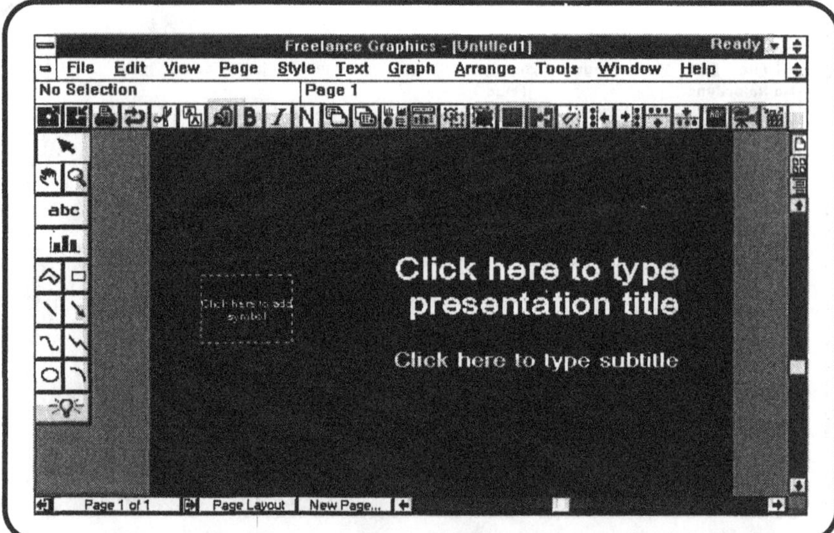

Figure C.38 motion.mas

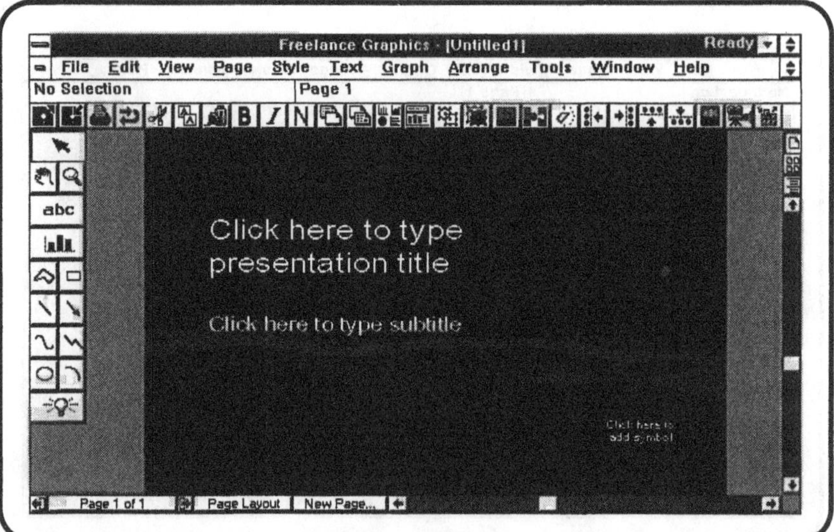

Figure C.39 mountain.mas

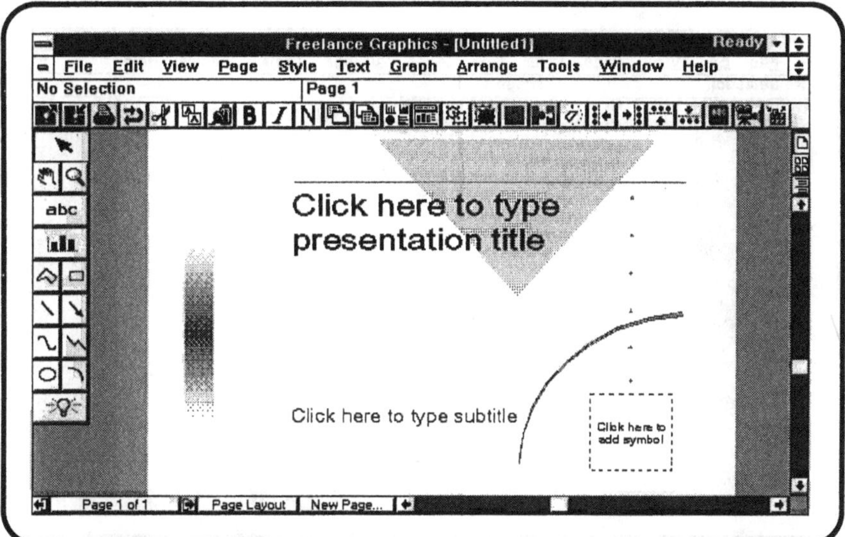

Figure C.40 neo.mas

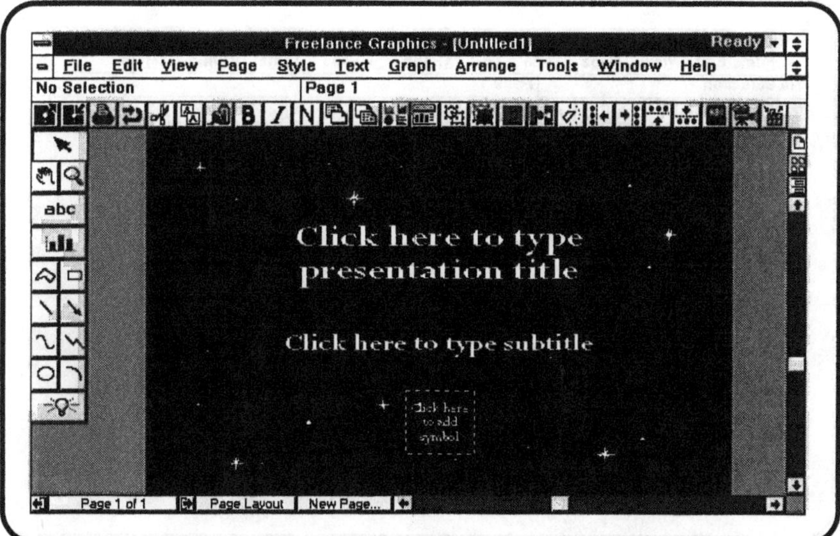

Figure C.41 nightsky.mas

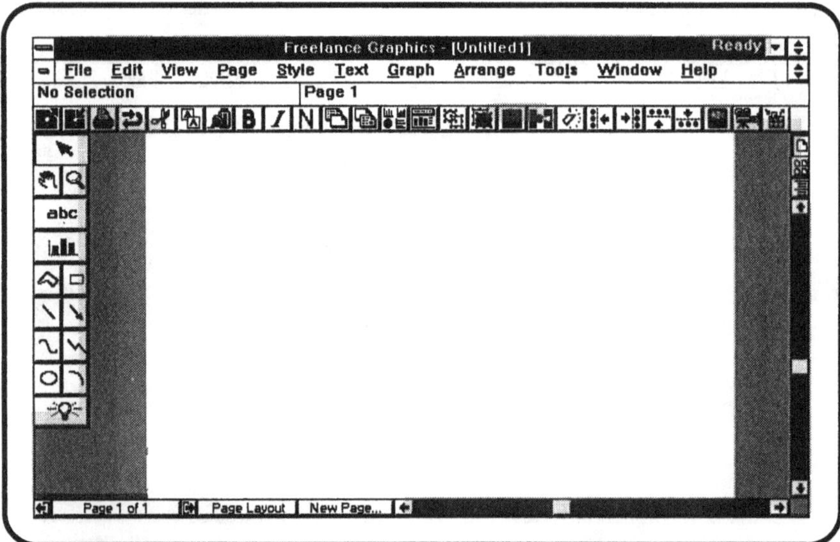

Figure C.42 nomaster.mas

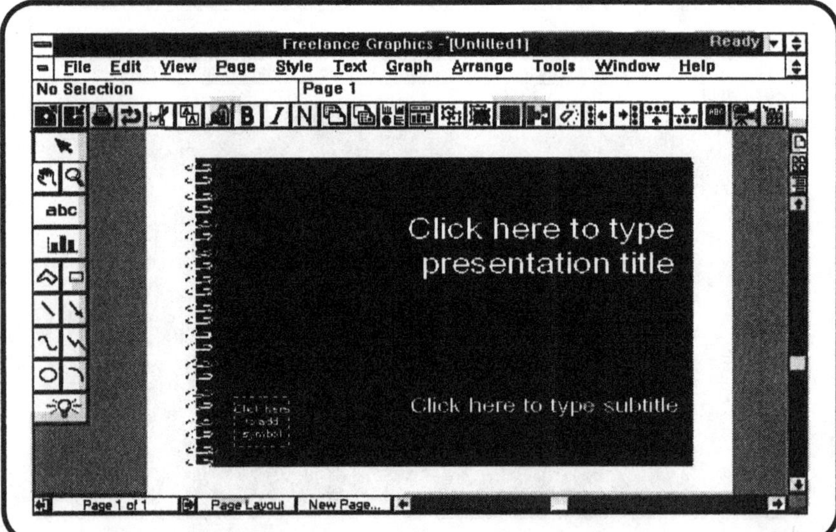

Figure C.43 notebook.mas

Figure C.44 ornate.mas

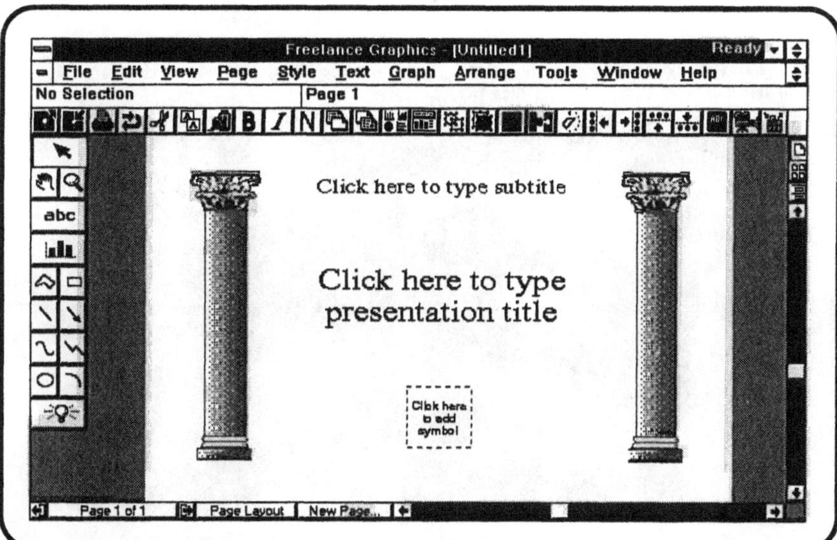

Figure C.45 pillar.mas

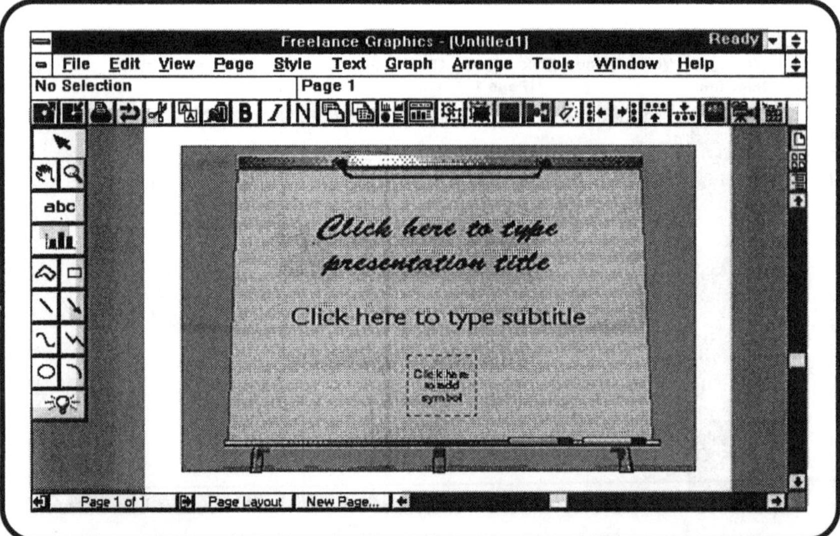

Figure C.46 present.mas

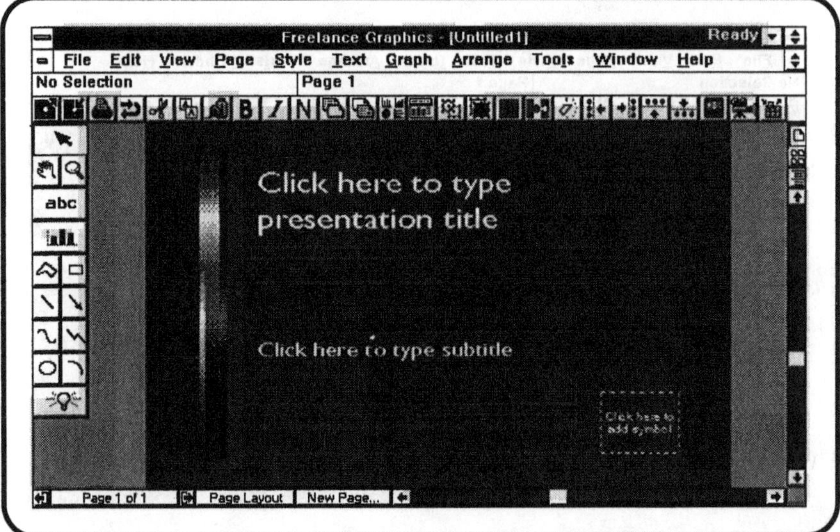

Figure C.47 rainbow.mas

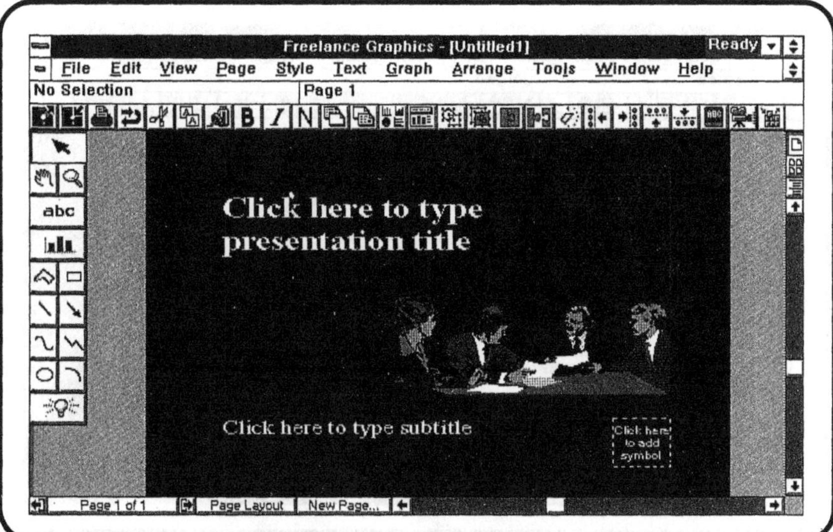

Figure C.48 scrim.mas

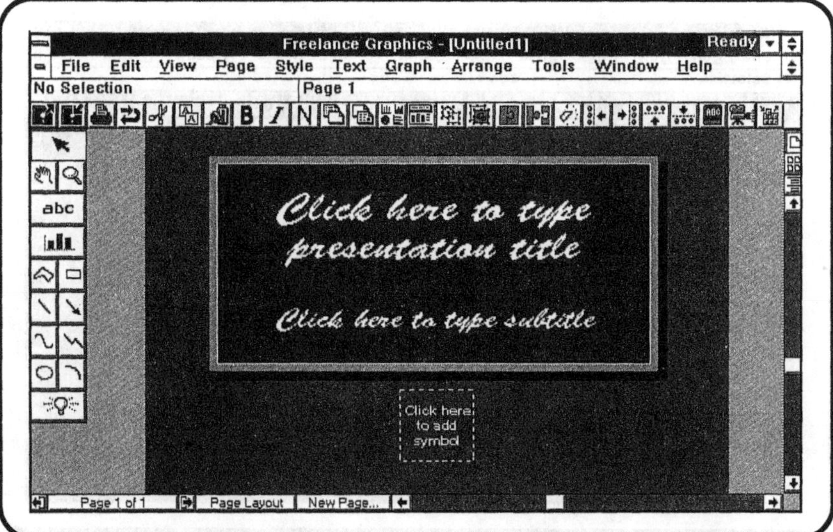

Figure C.49 shadowb1.mas

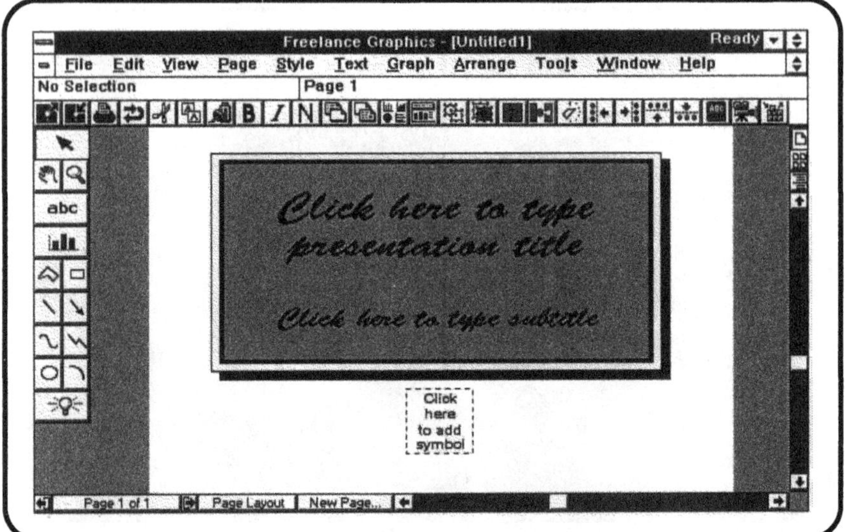

Figure C.50 shadowb2.mas

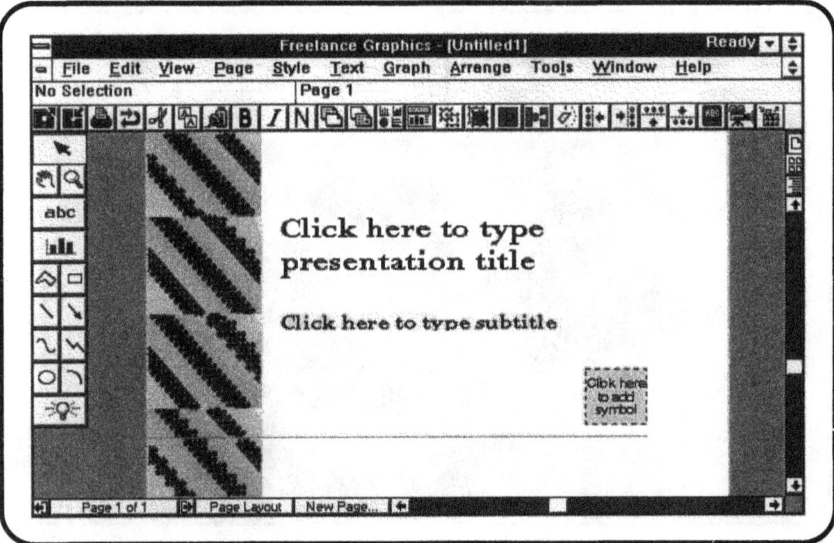

Figure C.51 shimmer.mas

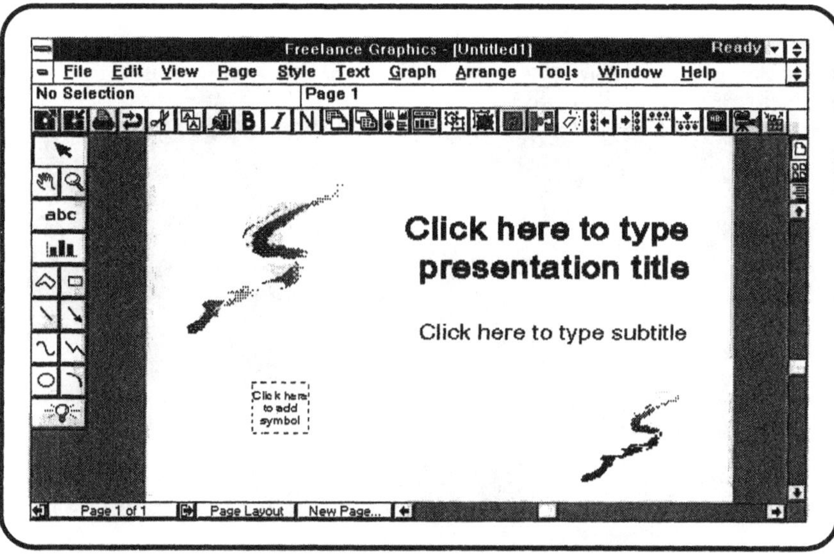

Figure C.52 sketch.mas (0sketch.mas)

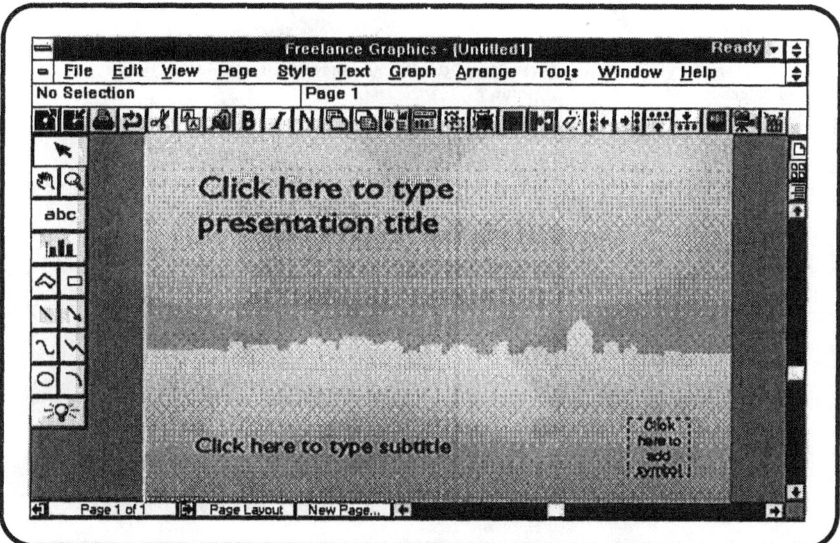

Figure C.53 skyline.mas

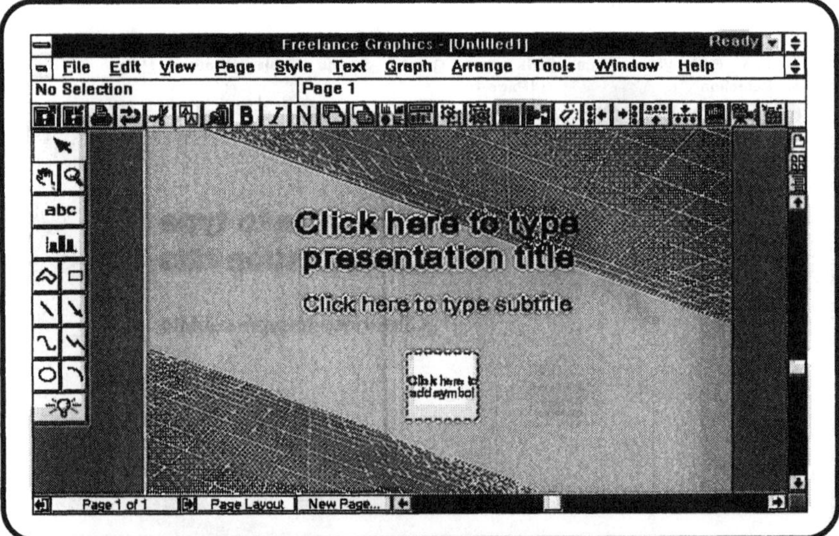

Figure C.54 space.mas

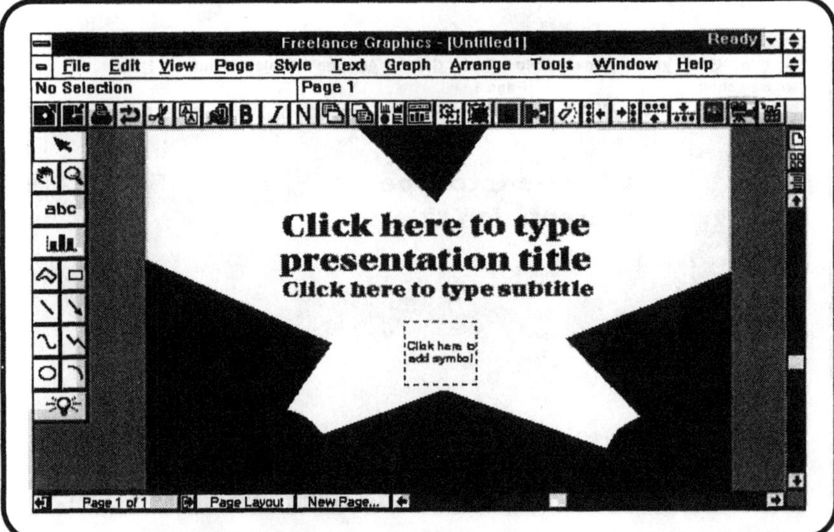

Figure C.55 spotlite.mas

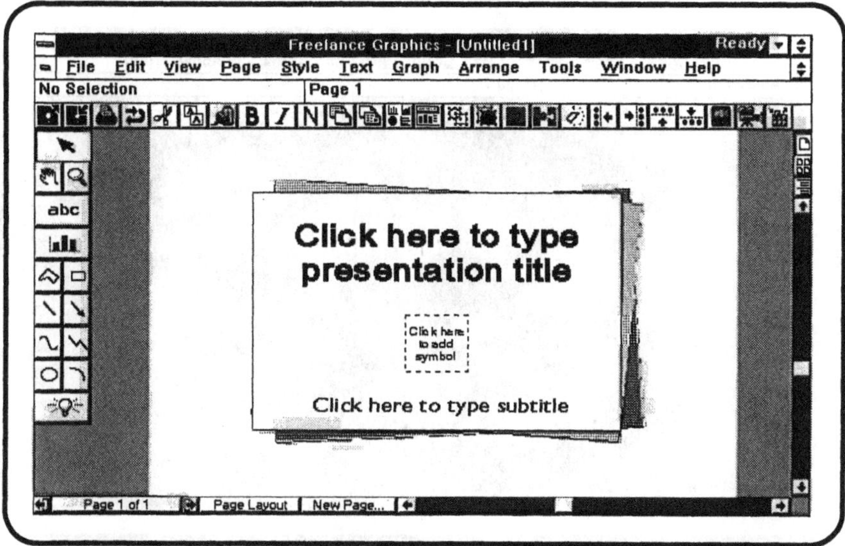

Figure C.56 stack.mas

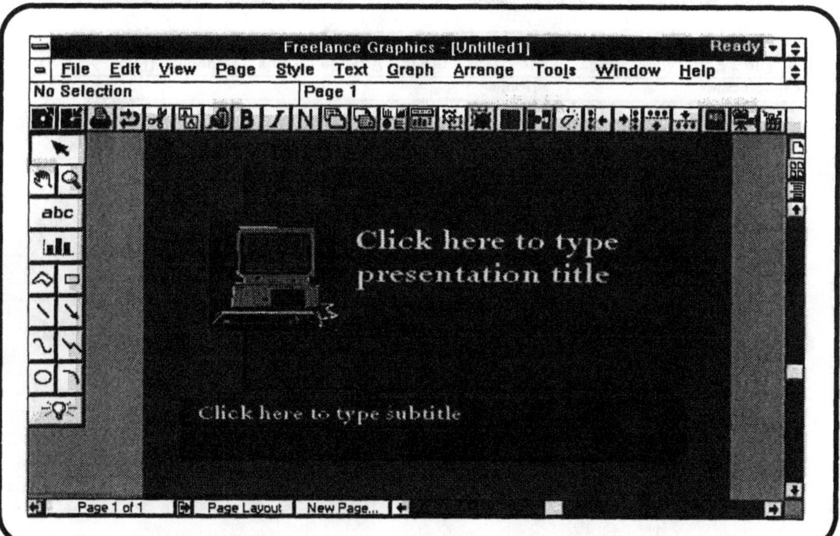

Figure C.57 symbolbx.mas

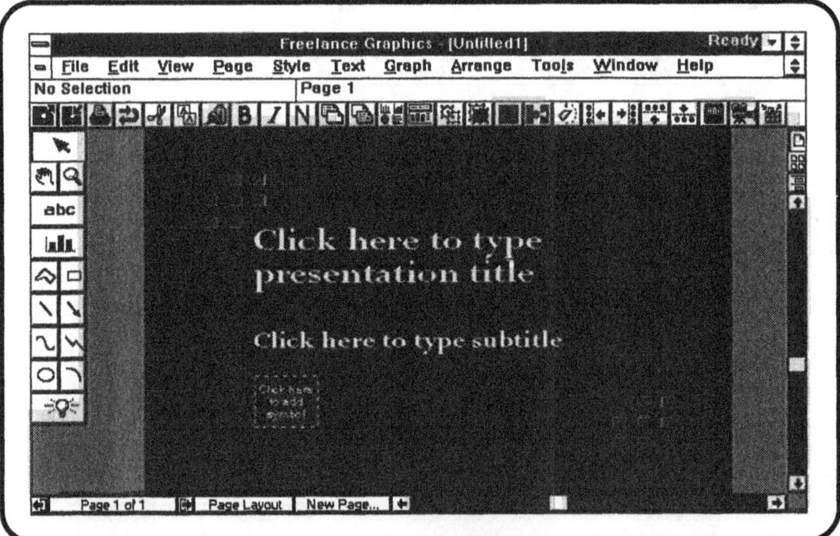

Figure C.58 tiles.mas

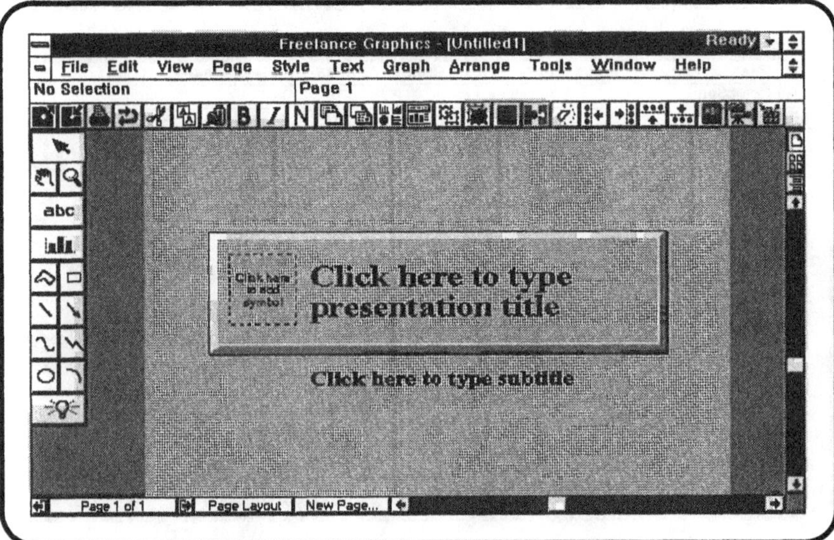

Figure C.59 topbox.mas

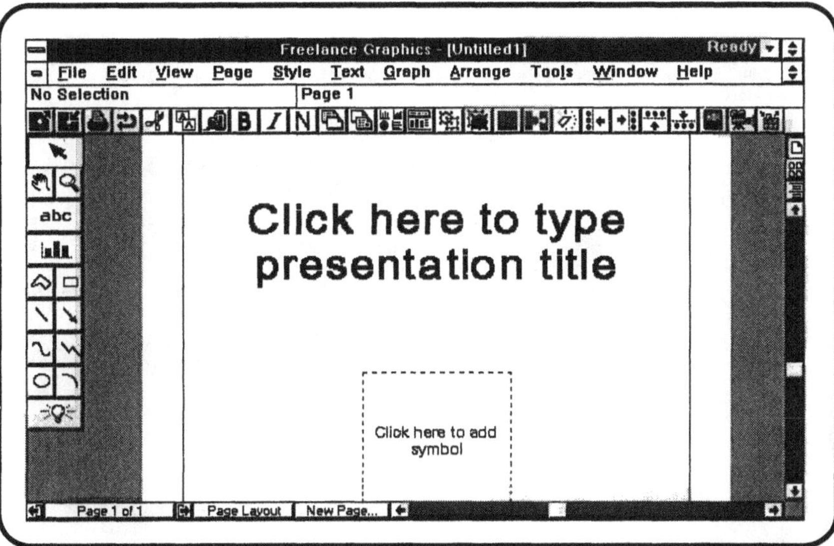

Figure C.60 vtopbar.mas

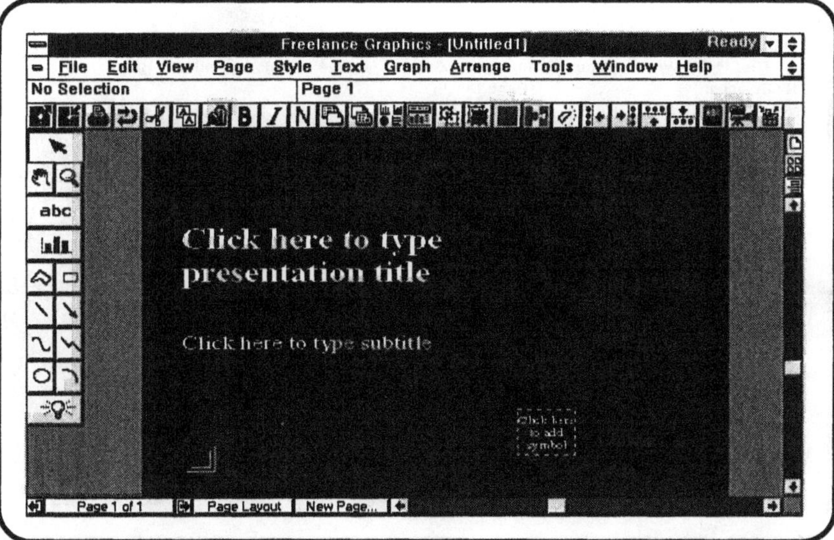

Figure C.61 waffle.mas

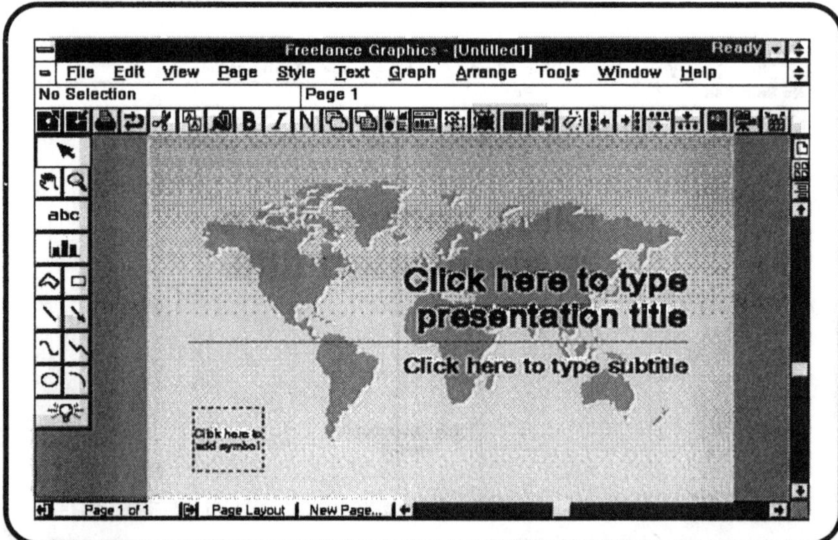

Figure C.62 world1.mas

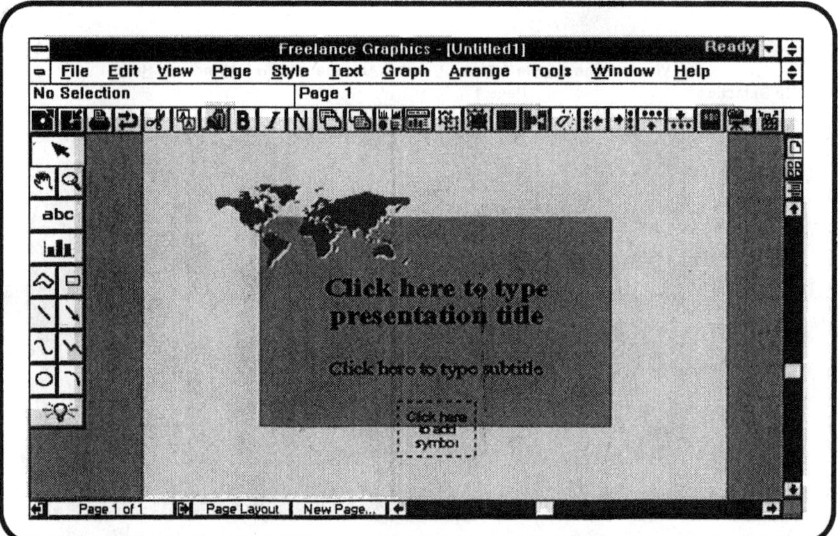

Figure C.63 world2.mas

Appendix D

Creating New Symbols from Existing Symbols

Although Freelance comes with more than 500 predrawn symbols, you need not feel that Freelance provides you with "only" these 500 symbols. With a little imagination and some simple drawing techniques, you can create numerous symbols of your own from the existing symbols. In this appendix, you see examples of two ways to adapt existing symbols:

- *Ungrouping*—breaking up an existing symbol and using only part of it.
- *Grouping*—combining all or part of two different symbols to create a new symbol.

Ungrouping Existing Symbols

Chapters 11 and 12 explained techniques for selecting symbols and for applying various drawing techniques to them. To create a new symbol out of part of an existing symbol:

1. Select the symbol.
2. Choose Ungroup from the Arrange menu.
3. Select the part of the symbol you want for your new symbol.

4. Group it into a new symbol (choose Group from the Arrange menu).
5. Delete the part(s) of the original symbol you do not want.

Figures D.1 to D.10 show samples of new symbols you can create by ungrouping existing symbols.

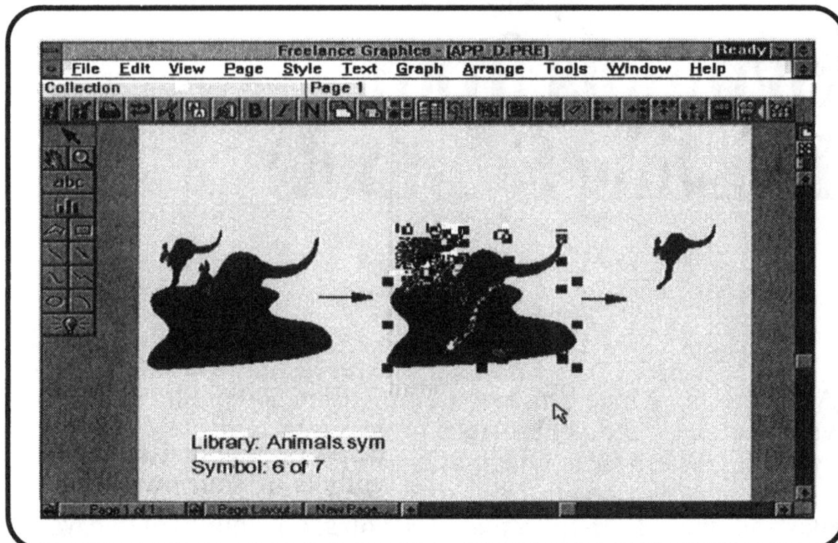

Figure D.1

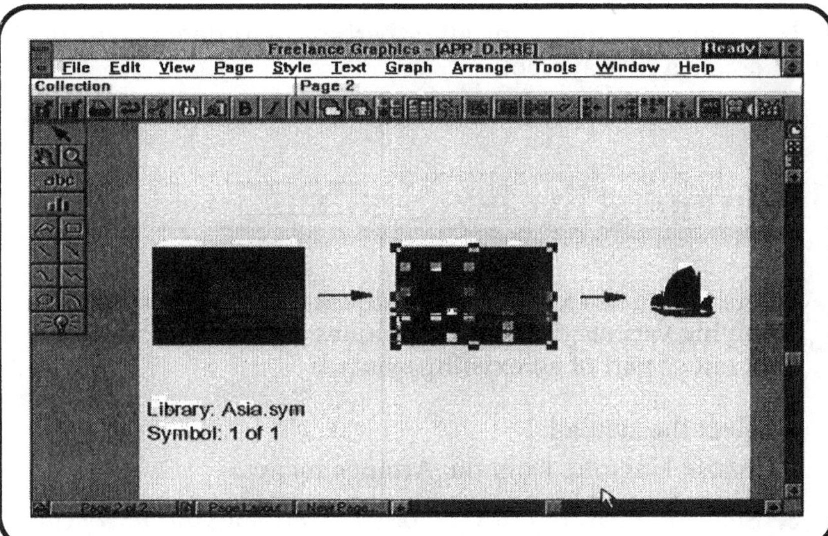

Figure D.2

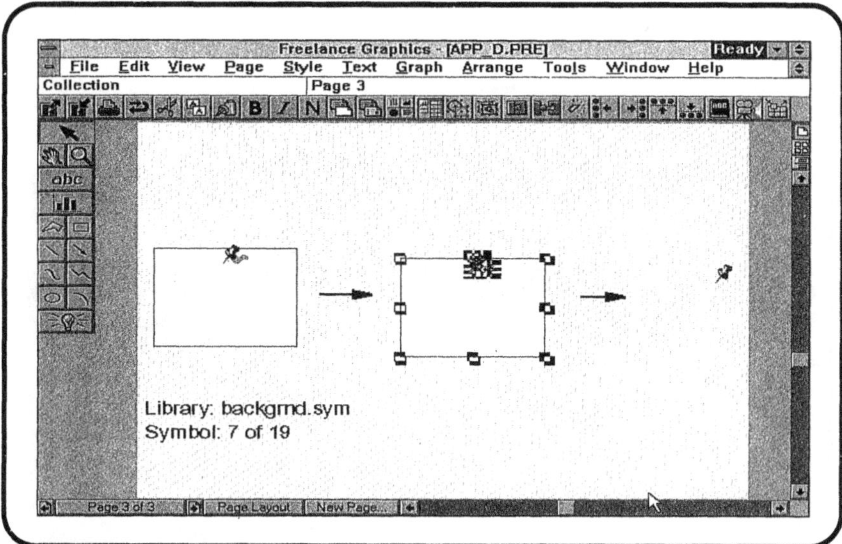

Figure D.3

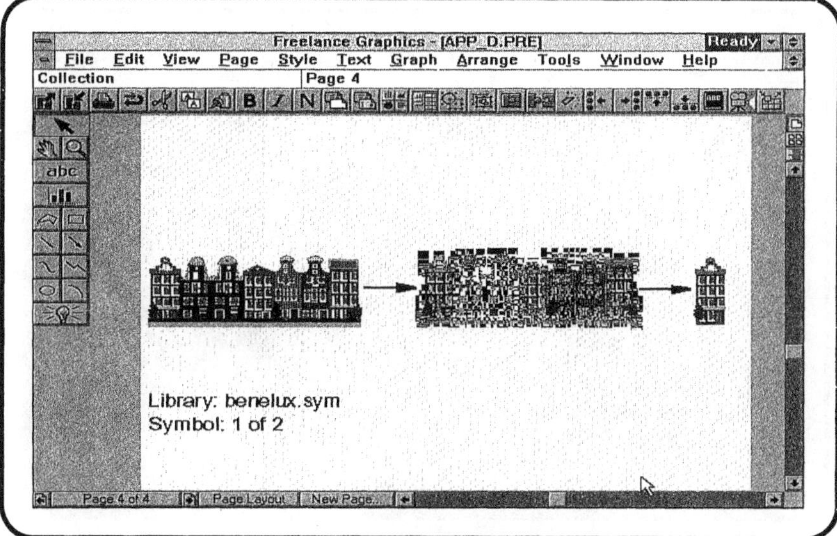

Figure D.4

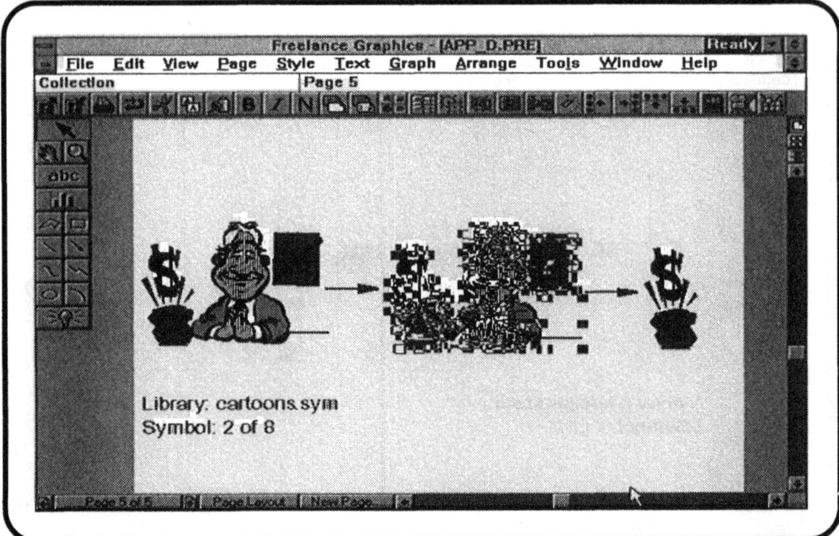

Figure D.5

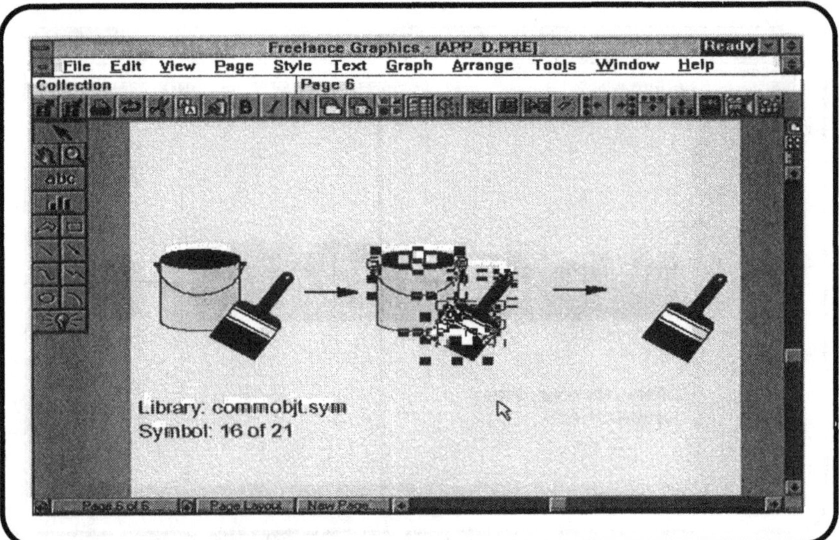

Figure D.6

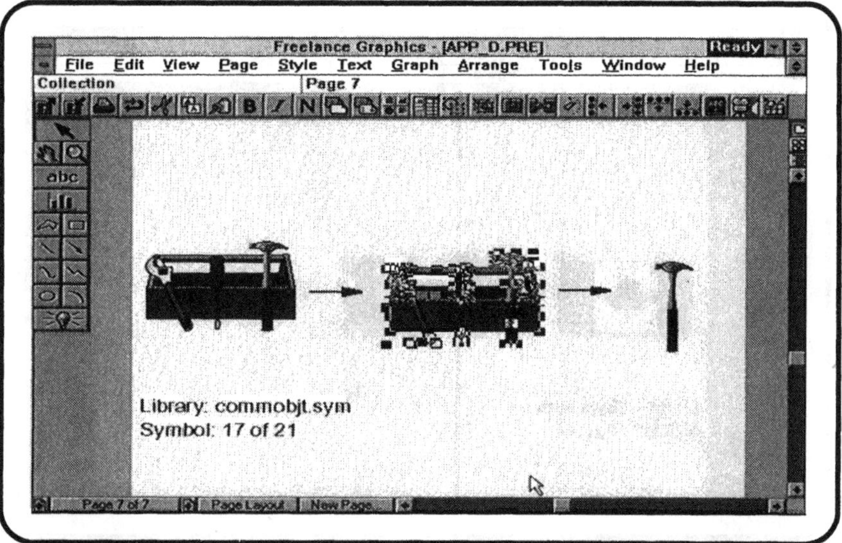

Figure D.7

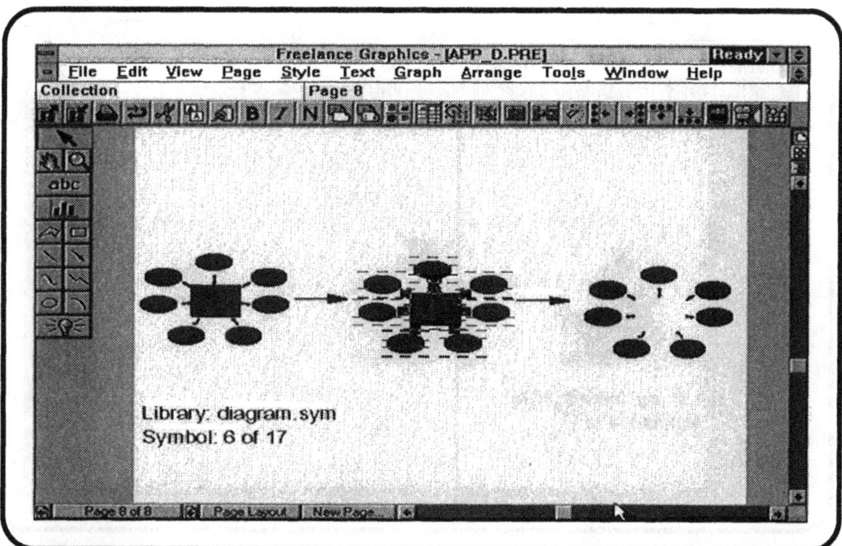

Figure D.8

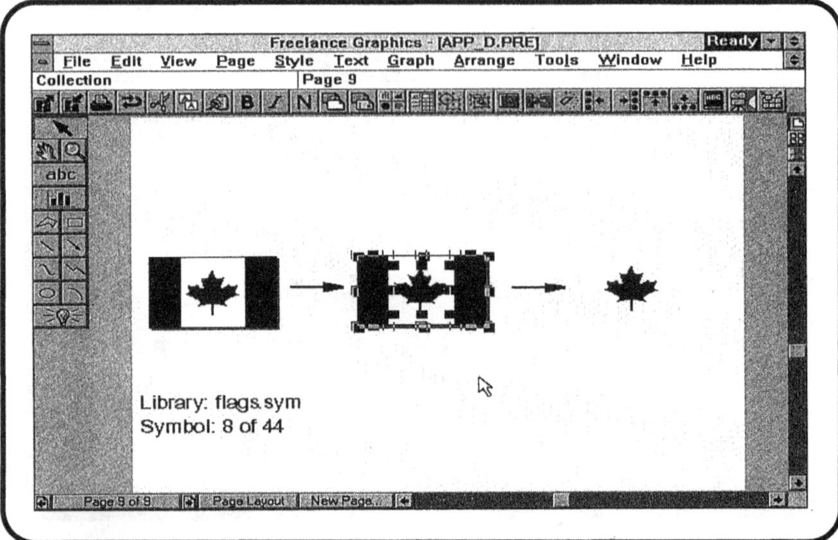

Figure D.9

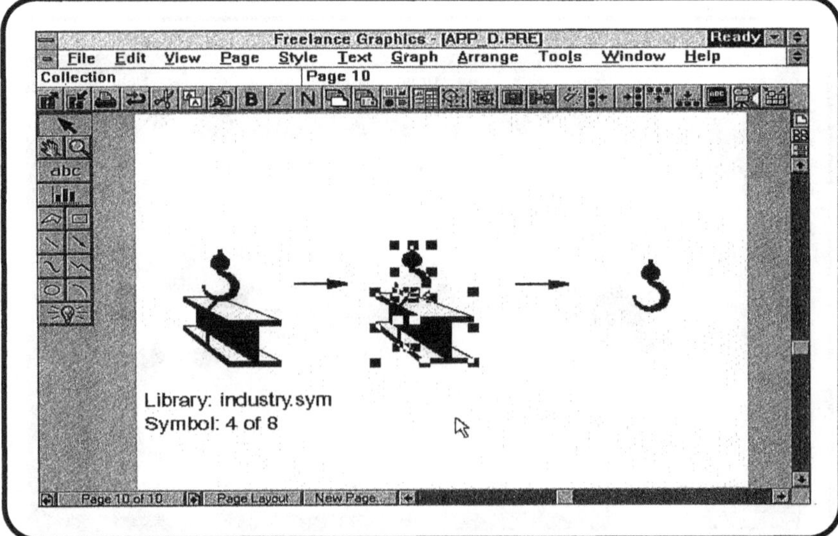

Figure D.10

Combining Existing Symbols

A second way to create new symbols is by combining parts of existing symbols into a new symbol. Follow the same steps as in the preceding section to create parts of existing symbols. To create a single symbol from two or more parts, select all the parts and then choose the Group command from the Arrange menu.

Figures D.11 to D.20 show samples of new symbols you can create by combining existing symbols.

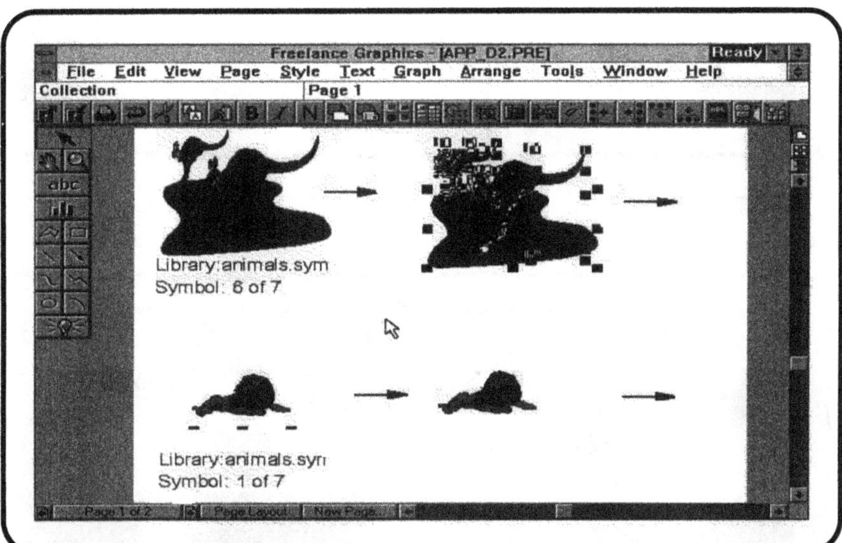

Figure D.11

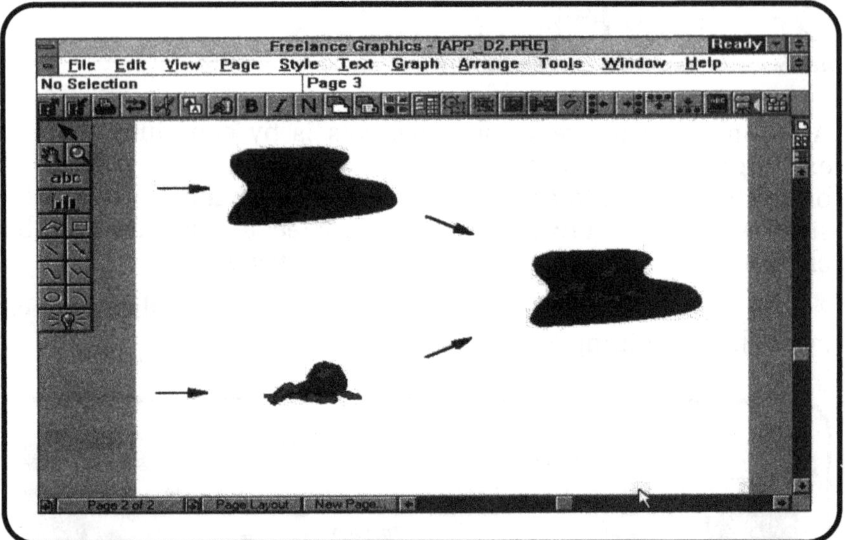

Figure D.12

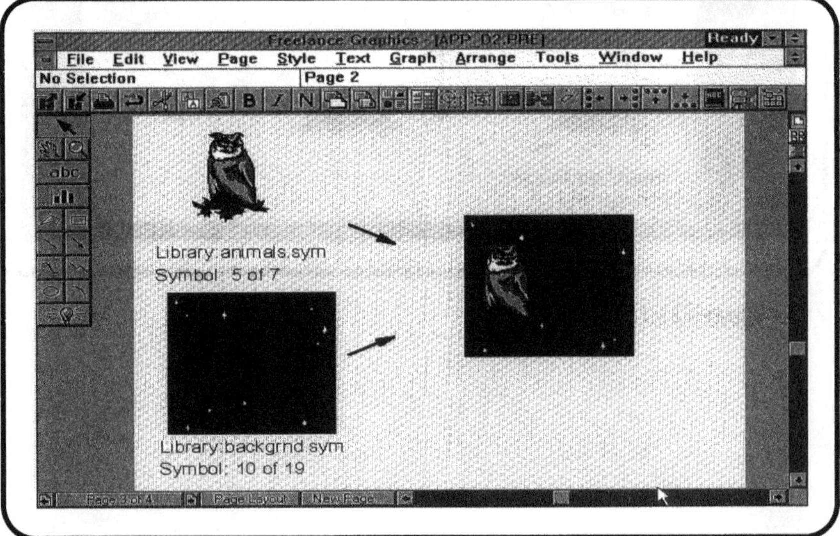

Figure D.13

Freelance Graphics - [APP_D2.PRE]
Ready
File Edit View Page Style Text Graph Arrange Tools Window Help
No Selection
Page 6
abc
Library:women.sym
Symbol: 7 of 12
Library:offobjct.sym
Symbol: 5 of 15
Page 4 of 6
Page Layout
New Page...

Figure D.14

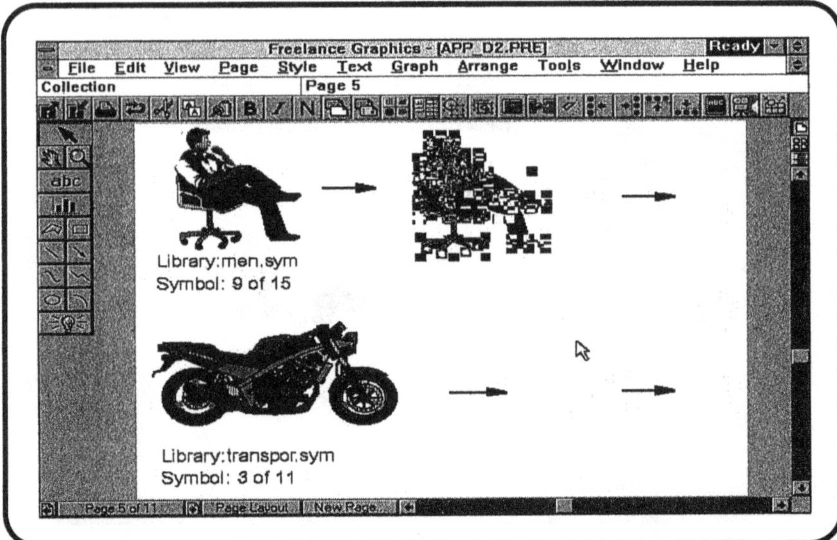

Figure D.15

Figure D.16

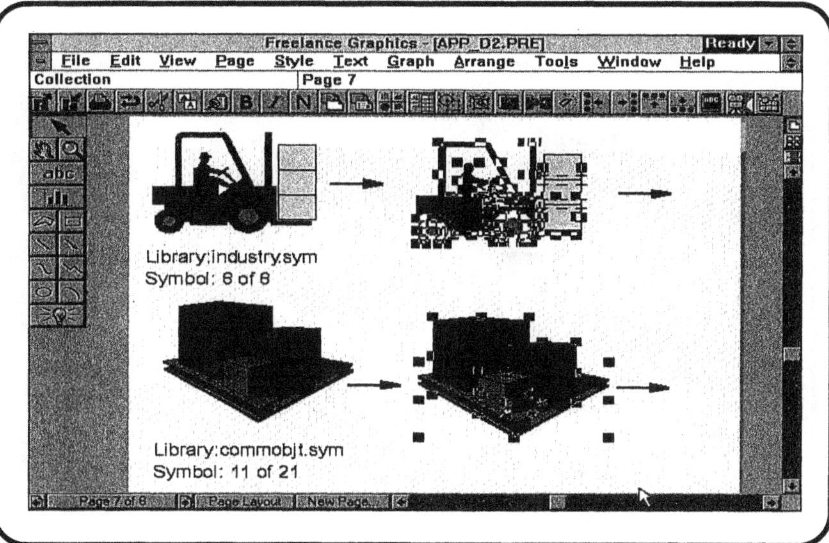

Figure D.17

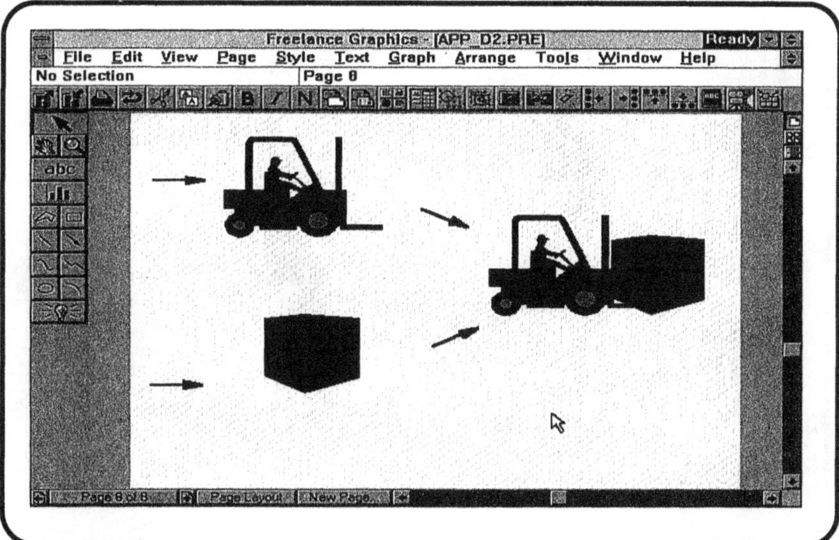

Figure D.18

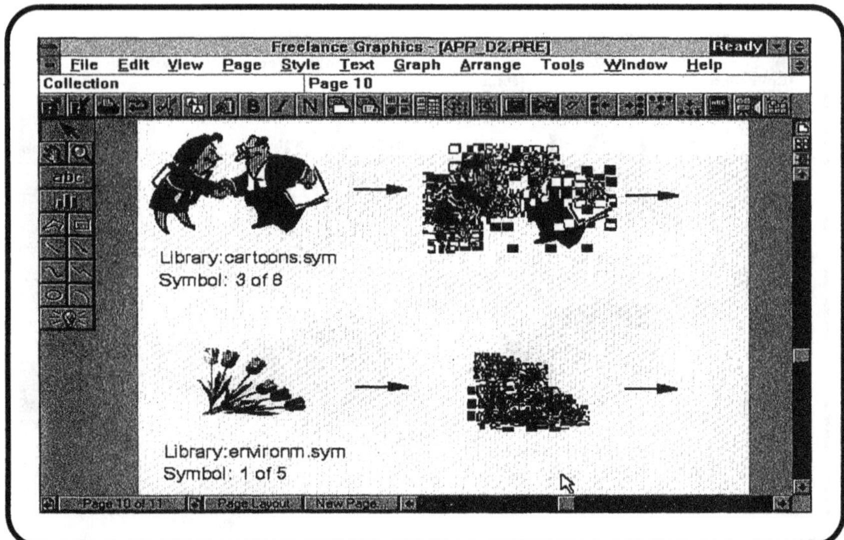

Figure D.19

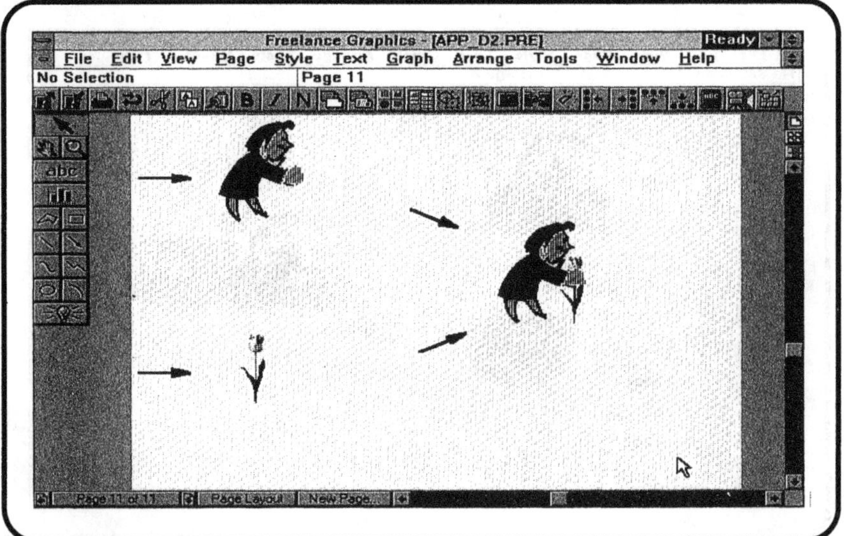

Figure D.20

Adding the Symbols to a Library

After you create new symbols, you can add them to the *symbol library*, which gives you the same access to them that you have to any other symbol. To add a symbol to a symbol library, choose Add to Symbol Library from the Tools menu. You see the Tools Add To Symbol Library dialog box, as shown in Figure D.21.

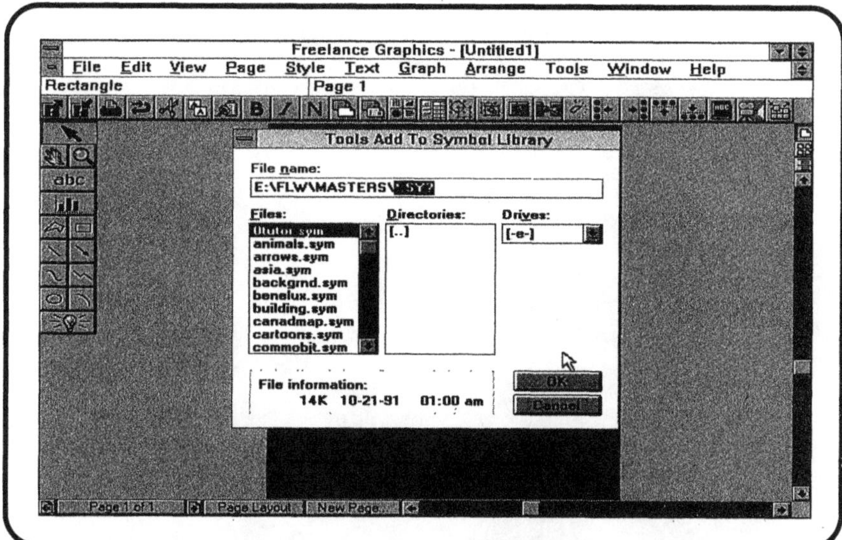

Figure D.21 The Tools Add to Symbol Library dialog box.

Specify the file in which you want to store the symbol. (You may want to use the library named custom.sym, which is designed specifically to hold new symbols you create.) Choose OK.

Index

Symbols

C

E

F

R

S

Freelance Graphics for Windows SmartIcons

File New

File Open

File Save

File Print

Undo Last Operation (Edit\Undo)

Edit\Cut

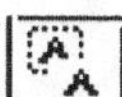
Edit\Copy

Edit\Paste

Edit\Clear (Del)

Edit\Paste Link

Edit\Replicate

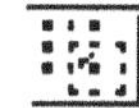
Edit\Select\All

View\Full Page

View\Redraw

View\SmartMaster Pages (toggle with View\Presentation Pages)

View\Screen Show

Page\New

Page\Duplicate

Style\Choose SmartMaster Set

Style\Choose Palette

Style\Units & Grids\ Snap On (toggle with Snap Off)

Text\Appearance\ Normal

Text\Appearance\Bold

Text\Appearance\ Italic

Text\Appearance\Underline

Arrange\Group

Arrange\Ungroup

Arrange\Priority\Top

Arrange\Priority\Bottom

Arrange\Priority\Send Forward One

Arrange\Priority\Fall Back One

Arrange\Align Right

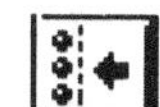
Arrange\Align Left

Arrange\Align Top

Arrange\Align Bottom

Arrange\Rotate

www.ingramcontent.com/pod-product-compliance
Lightning Source LLC
Chambersburg PA
CBHW081504050326
40690CB00015B/2925

* 9 7 8 1 5 8 3 4 8 0 3 3 5 *